AF457862

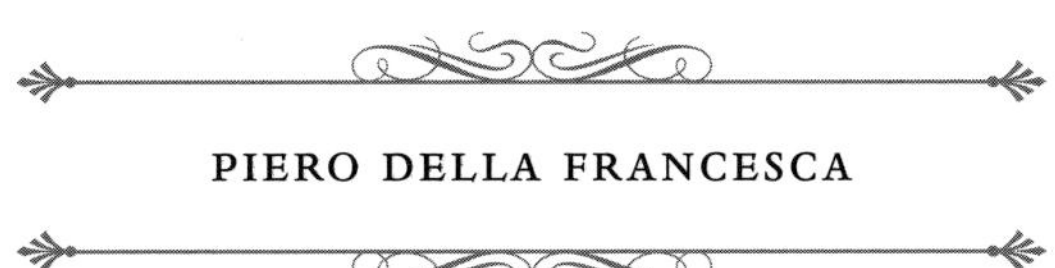

PIERO DELLA FRANCESCA

PIERO DELLA FRANCESCA

Artist & Man

JAMES R. BANKER

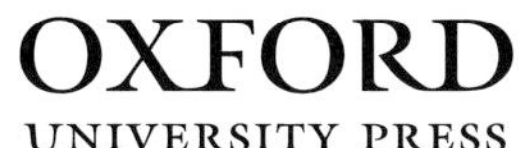

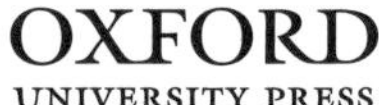

Great Clarendon Street, Oxford, OX2 6DP,
United Kingdom

Oxford University Press is a department of the University of Oxford.
It furthers the University's objective of excellence in research, scholarship,
and education by publishing worldwide. Oxford is a registered trade mark of
Oxford University Press in the UK and in certain other countries.

First Edition published in 2014

Impression: 1

Published in the United States of America by Oxford University Press
198 Madison Avenue, New York, NY 10016, United States of America

British Library Cataloguing in Publication Data
Data available

Library of Congress Control Number: 2013938929

ISBN 978–0–19–960931–4

As printed and bound by
CPI Group (UK) Ltd, Croydon, CR0 4YY

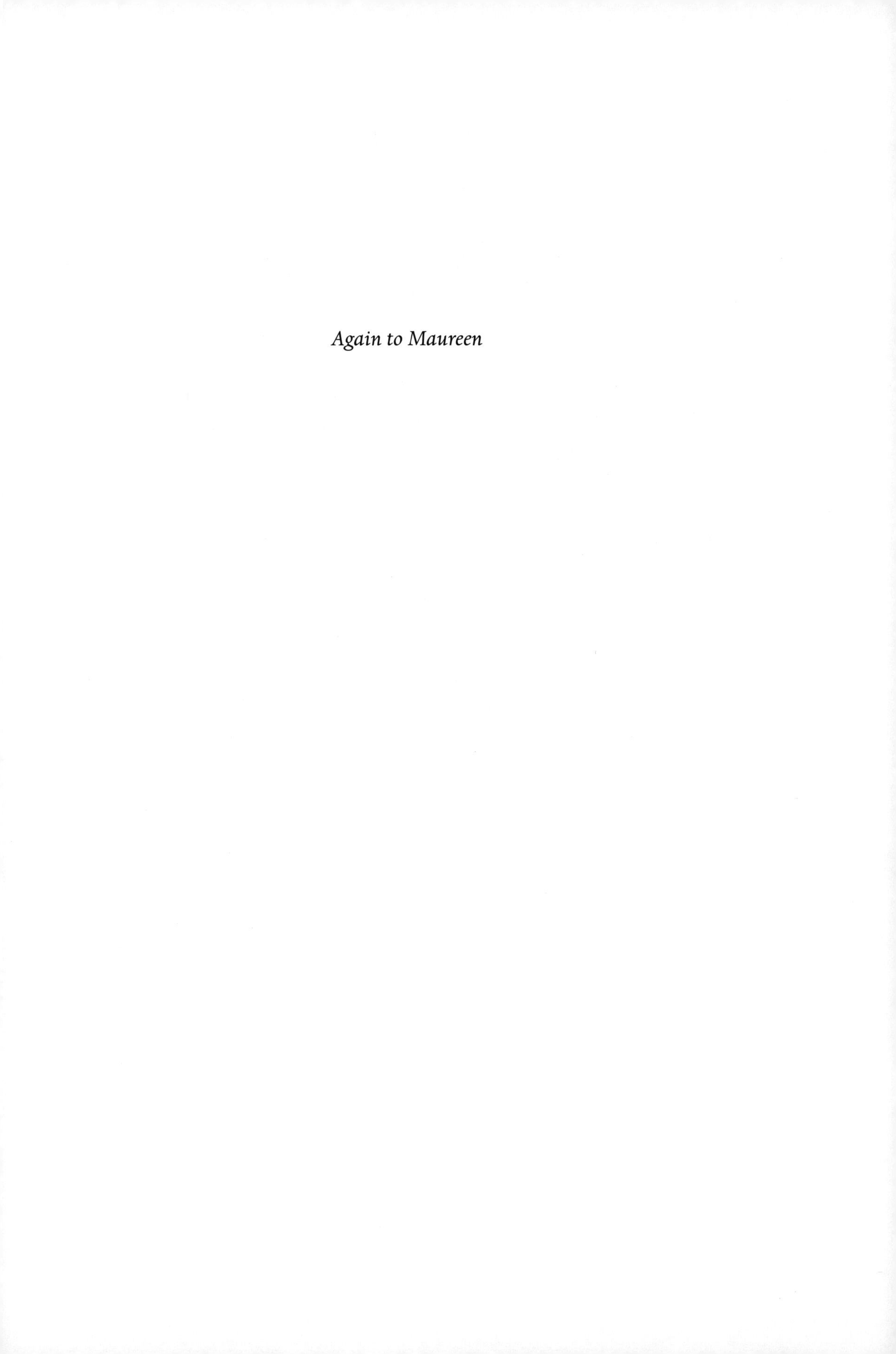

Again to Maureen

ACKNOWLEDGMENTS

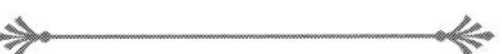

Anyone who carries out research in Italy for ten years will encounter many people who make a project such as this one possible. I wish to express my gratitude to these individuals, who have contributed in a variety of ways to whatever success this book may enjoy. In some cases people provided their assistance before I left my home country, whereas others contributed to my research and writing phases in Italy. This book would not have been possible without the sustenance of the individuals and institutions cited here. I am confident that future students of Italian history will be able to rely on the aid of other interested parties, but I am worried that the financial support of institutions for the benefit of Renaissance studies has already been so compromised that future research will prove to be more difficult.

For financial support I would like to thank the American Philosophical Society for sponsoring my research on watermarks, and the History Department and School of Humanities and Social Sciences at North Carolina State University for their generous program of sabbaticals. Only if these kinds of programs continue will it be possible for scholars from North Carolina State University who study non-American peoples to make contributions to understanding cultures beyond their own. Also in my home institution of North Carolina State University I wish to give a special mention to the Interlibrary and Tripsaver Office of the Library, and especially to Marihelen Stringham for introducing scholarly materials in the humanities to a university that specializes in the study of technology and science.

I owe a special mention to those who have read chapters or this entire book at one of its various stages of preparation. I wish to thank Eve Borsook, Keith Christiansen, Donal Cooper, Andrea Di Lorenzo, Machtelt Israëls, Cecilia Martelli, Matteo Mazzalupi, and Steven Vincent. I especially wish to express my gratitude to Priscilla and Douglas Walter for reading every chapter from the viewpoint of educated and inquisitive non-specialists. I would also send my thanks to the final anonymous reader for his/her many helpful suggestions. I owe more gratitude than I can express to Donald Weinstein, who read and paid sensitive attention to the ideas and presentation of the manuscript. Any grammatical errors or tortuous passages in my writing are the result of ignoring my readers' suggestions.

I have enjoyed the hospitality and generosity of the people and institutions of Sansepolcro. Serena Magnini at the Fondazione Piero della Francesca has always been ready to provide assistance with the Fondazione's resources, particularly by making available its library in the Casa di Piero. Mariangela Betti, Direttore, Istituzione Culturale

Museo Biblioteca Archivio of Sansepolco, and her staff in the Museo Civico and Library-Archives—Roberto Bianconi, Anita Chieli, Marcella Flenghi, and Carla Maccanti—have opened up the library and museum to me with their prompt and enthusiastic provision of books and images. To Daniele Piccini, Presidente of the Istituzione, I express my thanks for encouraging me to study Piero and the history of Sansepolcro. For aid with typographical problems, I wish to thank Patrizio Scartoni of Grafiche Borgo for his generosity and gracious interest. For three decades Luigi and Emanuela Andreini and their family have extended their friendship and hospitality to me and my family. They have answered all my questions on language and history with patience and substantial knowledge of their town. I and this book owe more to them than can be expressed in words.

I wish to thank the directors and staff of Villa I Tatti, Harvard University Center for Renaissance Studies, for providing a hospitable and beautiful site for encountering other researchers and finding obscure but necessary books and journals. The directors and staff of the Archivio di Stato in Florence are owed a special expression of thanks for having provided what they must have considered endless requests for notarial records.

I wish to thank the editors and technical staff at Oxford University Press. I owe a special debt of gratitude to my editor Matthew Cotton for his encouragement and timely aid at every step from consideration of the proposal to delivery of the final draft. To Emma Barber I extend my thanks for her attentive guidance of me and my manuscript through the production phases of publication. For his vigilant copy-editing, I wish to thank Richard Mason. For her careful, expert reading, I express my gratitude to my proofreader, Rosemary Roberts.

The following individuals have extended their assistance and friendship to me at various stages of my research and writing. I wish to extend my gratitude to Hélène de Bellaigne, Roberto Bellucci, Carlo Bertelli, Jane and Robert Black, Luca Boschetti, Gian Luca Braschi, Dario and Fernanda Casini, Luciano Cheles, Argante Ciocci, Don Andrea Czortek, Frank Dabell, Marisa Dalai Emiliani, Paolo D'Alessandro, Andrea De Marchi, J. V. Field, David Franklin, Cecilia Frosinini, Don Alberto Gallonini, Enrico Giusti, Dick Goldthwaite, Gianni and Grazia Gorizi, Cristina Gotti, Tom Henry, Carol Lansing, Marilyn Aronberg Lavin, Giovanna Lazzi, Enrico Londei, Kate Lowe, Carlo Maccagna, Roberto Marcuccio, Matteo Martelli, Matteo Mazzalupi, Pier Daniele Napolitani, Giovanni Pagliarulo, Enzo and Giuliana Papi, Marcella Peruzzi, Armando Petrucci, Franco Polcri, Fabrizio Raffaelli, Paola Refice, John Riddle, Michele Rosi, David Sabean, Valerio Sanzotta, Piero Scapecchi, Gian Paolo Scharf, Koichi Toyama, Giovanni Tricca, Vladimiro Valerio, and Steven Vincent.

My daughters, Peri and Heather, and grandson David have shared my love of Italy and have encouraged me in more ways than they can know. My wife Maureen has participated in all the stages of preparation of this volume, over decades in fact, and has shared with me its pleasures and labors. She is the most creative person I know, and I have learned much about artistic thinking and practice from her. She has also prepared the line drawings in this volume and has read every chapter more than once. I wish fervently to thank her.

CONTENTS

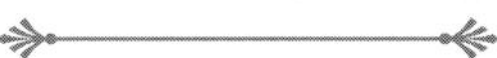

List of Plates xii
List of Illustrations xiii
List of Maps and Figures xv
Abbreviations xvi
Note to the Reader xvii
Short Chronology of the Life and Work of Piero della Francesca xviii
Prologue xx
Maps xxiv

1 Piero's Formation in Sansepolcro 1
Sansepolcro 2
The Della Francesca Family 4
Piero as Apprentice and Assistant 7
The Baptism of Christ 10

2 In Search of Piero, the Persistent Traveler, 1439–50 17
Piero and the Culture of Florence 17
Piero North of Tuscany 20
Piero in Sansepolcro in 1445: The Misericordia Contract 21
Ferrara 23
Piero in Ancona 24

3 Piero at the Court of Sigismondo Malatesta in Rimini 29
Jacopo Anastagi 29
Piero's New Stage: The Court of Sigismondo 31
Saint Jerome and a Penitent 34
The Portrait of Sigismondo Malatesta 38
Sigismondo Malatesta Before His Patron Saint Sigismundus 40

4 Piero in Arezzo: *The Legend of the True Cross* 44
The Bacci Family and the Friars and Church of San Francesco 44
Dating the Painting of the Arezzo Frescoes 46
Looking at the Arezzo Frescoes 46
Choices in the High Altar Chapel 52

Piero's Narration of *The Legend of the True Cross* 55
Technical and Conceptual Accomplishments at Arezzo 60

5 Creating the Sacred: Piero della Francesca's Altarpiece for the Confraternity of the Madonna della Misericordia 64
The Confraternity of Santa Maria della Misericordia 65
The Pichi Family 67
The Misericordia Commission 68
The Misericordia Altarpiece 69
The Pace of Painting and Payments 74

6 Greek Geometry in Rome and Piero's *Trattato d'abaco* 79
Francesco del Borgo and Greek Geometry 83
Piero in Rome, 1458–59 86
Piero's *Treatise on Abaco* 88

7 Piero's Return to Patria and Family 96
Workshops of the Della Francesca Family and Piero's Presence in Sansepolcro 98
Madonna del Parto 101
Saint Louis of Toulouse 102
Saint Julian 105
The Resurrection of Christ 107

8 An Arezzo Interlude 114
Two Lost Processional Banners 114
Saint Mary Magdalene and Other Commissions in Arezzo 117

9 The Practice of Perspective: The Sant'Antonio and Sant'Agostino Altarpieces and *The Flagellation of Christ* 120
The Sant'Antonio Altarpiece of Perugia 120
The Sant'Agostino Altarpiece 128
The Flagellation of Christ 134
Jacopo Anastagi 139

10 Piero in Urbino in the Early 1470s 142
Federico da Montefeltro 142
The Uffizi Diptych of Federico da Montefeltro and Battista Sforza 146

11 Piero in Sansepolcro, 1472–75 152
The Fresco of the Glorious Virgin of the Badia 153
Piero as Builder 156
Hercules 158
Marco, Piero, and their Sister Vera 161

12 Piero in Urbino, 1475–77 163
Madonna and Child with Saints and Angels 163
The Senigallia *Madonna and Child* 167
The Treatise *On Perspective in Painting* 169
The Composition of *On Perspective in Painting* 171
The Contents of *On Perspective in Painting* 172
The Audience for the Treatise 179
The Relationship of the Treatise to Piero's Paintings 180

13 The Persuasiveness of Paternal Authority, 1477–81 181
The Lost Misericordia Fresco 181
The Williamstown *Madonna and Child with Four Angels* 183
Piero's Scriptorium and the Four Copies of *On Perspective in Painting* 185
Piero and Archimedes 188
Piero's Political Activities 193
Family Service 196

14 Piero in the Last Decade of His Life 198
The Little Book on the Five Regular Bodies 199
The Nativity of Christ 205
Piero in his Final Years 208
Piero's Preparation for Death 211

Conclusion 215

Notes 220
Selected Bibliography 240
Picture Acknowledgements 254
Index of Life, Paintings, and Treatises 255
General Index 265

LIST OF PLATES

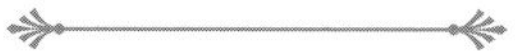

I. Piero della Francesca, *The Baptism of Christ*, 168 × 116 cm. National Gallery, London

II. Piero della Francesca, *Saint Jerome and a Penitent*, 49 × 42 cm. Galleria dell'Accademia di Venezia, Venice

III. Piero della Francesca, *Sigismondo Malatesta Before His Patron Saint Sigismundus*, 2.57 × 3.45 m. Il Tempio (San Francesco), Rimini

IV. Piero della Francesca, *The Legend of the True Cross*, High Altar Chapel, San Francesco, Arezzo

V. Piero della Francesca, *The Misericordia Altarpiece*, 2.73 × 3.3 m. Museo Civico, Sansepolcro

VI. Piero della Francesca, *Madonna del Parto*, Museo della Madonna del Parto, 2.6 × 2.03 m. Monterchi

VII. Piero della Francesca, *The Resurrection of Christ*, 2.25 × 2.2 m. Museo Civico, Sansepolcro

VIII. Piero della Francesca, *The Flagellation of Christ*, 58.4 × 81.5 cm. Galleria Nazionale delle Marche di Urbino, Urbino

IX. Piero della Francesca, Diptych of *Federico da Montefeltro and Battista Sforza*, 47 × 33 cm each. Galleria degli Uffizi, Florence

X. Piero della Francesca, Senigallia *Madonna and Child*, 61 × 53.5 cm. Galleria Nazionale delle Marche di Urbino, Urbino

LIST OF ILLUSTRATIONS

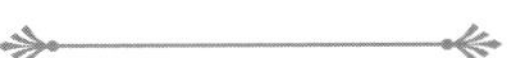

1. Anonymous, *Tavola Votiva*, Votive panel with a view of Sansepolcro, 68 × 57.5 cm. Museo Civico, Sansepolcro 3
2. Matteo di Giovanni, Flanking Saints for Piero della Francesca's *Baptism of Christ*, 3.58 × 3.52 m. Museo Civico, Sansepolcro 11
3. Piero della Francesca, *Saint Jerome in the Desert*, 51 × 38 cm. Gemäldegalerie, Staatliche Museen, Berlin 25
4. Piero della Francesca, *Portrait of Sigismondo Malatesta*, 44 × 34 cm. Musée du Louvre, Paris 38
5. Piero della Francesca, *The Legend of the True Cross*, High Altar Chapel, left wall, Church of San Francesco, Arezzo 48
6. Piero della Francesca, *The Legend of the True Cross*, High Altar Chapel, right wall, Church of San Francesco, Arezzo 49
7. Piero della Francesca, *Death of Adam, The Legend of the True Cross*, 3.9 × 7.47 m. Right Lunette, Church of San Francesco, Arezzo 50
8. Piero della Francesca, *Saint Luke*, Chapel of Cardinal D'Estouteville, Church of Santa Maria Maggiore, Rome 51
9. Piero della Francesca, *Madonna della Misericordia*, detail of the *Misericordia Altarpiece*, 168 × 91 cm. Museo Civico, Sansepolcro 70
10. Piero della Francesca, *Trattato d'abaco*, Ashburnhamiano 280 (359*–291*), fol. 3r, Biblioteca Medicea Laurenziana, Florence 80
11. Piero della Francesca, *Saint Louis of Toulouse*, 123 × 90 cm. Museo Civico, Sansepolcro 104
12. Piero della Francesca, *Saint Julian*, 130 × 105 cm. Museo Civico, Sansepolcro 106
13. Niccolò di Segna, *The Resurrection*, undetermined × 3.745 m. Cathedral, Sansepolcro 110
14. Anonymous, *Volto Santo*, 2.7 × 2.9 m. Cathedral, Sansepolcro 111
15. Piero della Francesca, *Saint Mary Magdalene*, 190 × 80 cm. Cathedral, Arezzo 118
16. Piero della Francesca, *Sant'Antonio Altarpiece*, 3.38 × 2.3 m. Galleria Nazionale dell'Umbria, Perugia 122
17. Piero della Francesca, *Sant'Agostino Altarpiece*, frontal reconstruction, photomontage by Nathaniel Silver, Frick Collection, New York 129
18. Piero della Francesca, *Saint Michael*, panel of the *Sant'Agostino Altarpiece*, 133 × 59 cm. National Gallery, London 132

19. Piero della Francesca, *Triumphs of Federico da Montefeltro and Battista Sforza* (diptych, reverse side), 47 × 33 cm each. Galleria degli Uffizi, Florence 148
20. Casa di Piero, Sansepolcro 157
21. Casa di Piero, Room of *Hercules*, Sansepolcro (facing the eastern wall) 157
22. Piero della Francesca, *Hercules*, 151 × 126 cm. Isabella Stewart Gardner Museum, Boston 159
23. Piero della Francesca, *Madonna and Child with Saints and Angels*, 2.48 × 1.7 m. Pinacoteca di Brera, Milan 164
24. Piero della Francesca, *De prospectiva pingendi*, cod. 1576, fol. 59v, Biblioteca Palatina, Parma 173
25. Piero della Francesca, *De prospectiva pingendi*, Reggio Emilia, Biblioteca A. Panizzi, cod. Reggiano A 41/2, fol. 91v 178
26. Piero della Francesca, Williamstown *Madonna and Child with Four Angels*, 108 × 78 cm. Sterling and Francine Clark Art Institute, Williamstown, Massachusetts 183
27. Archimedes, *Opera*, Lat. 106, fol. 1r, Biblioteca Riccardiana, Florence 190
28. Archimedes, *Opera*, Lat. 106, fols. 27v–28r (formerly 17v–18r), Biblioteca Riccardiana, Florence 192
29. Piero della Francesca, *Libellus de quinque corporibus regularibus*, Urb. Lat. 632, fol. 2r, Biblioteca Apostolica Vaticana, Vatican City 200
30. Piero della Francesca, *The Nativity of Christ*, 124.5 × 123 cm. National Gallery, London 207
31. Piero della Francesca, Preparatory Notes for his Testament, Archivio di Stato, Florence, Serie degli autografi, Box 301, Armadio 6 212

LIST OF MAPS AND FIGURES

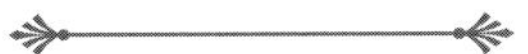

Maps

1. Map of Sansepolcro in the fifteenth century xxiv
2. Map of Central Italy xxvi

Figures

6.1. The Five Regular Bodies (Platonic Solids) 93

12.1. Piero della Francesca, *De prospectiva pingendi*, Book I, Proposition VIII, adapted from Reggio Emilia, Biblioteca A. Panizzi, cod. Reggiano A 41/2, fol. 4v 175

12.2. Piero della Francesca, *De prospectiva pingendi*, Book I, Proposition XII, adapted from Parma, Biblioteca Palatina, cod. 1576, fol. 6r 175

ABBREVIATIONS

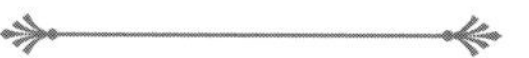

AM	Archivio della Misericordia, Sansepolcro
ASCS	Archivio storico Comunale, Sansepolcro
ASF	Archivio di Stato, Florence
ASR	Archivio di Stato, Rome
ASU	Archivio di Stato, Urbino
ASV	Archivio Secreto Vaticano, Vatican City
BAV	Biblioteca Apostolica Vaticana, Vatican City
Cam. Ap., Intr. et Ex.	Camera Apostolica, Introit et exitus
Collegio Not. Cap.	Archivio del Collegio dei Notai Capitolini
cort.	cortonesi (Italian) or cortonensium (Latin)
CRS	Compagnie Religiose Soppresse da Pietro Leopoldo
den.	denarius, denarii
fol(s).	folio(s)
lib.	libbra, libbre
NA	Notarile Antecosimiano
reg.	register
ser.	series
sol.	soldi

NOTE TO THE READER

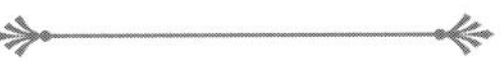

The reader may be aided by consulting the chronology of the life and works of Piero (see pp. xviii–xix). Readers who are interested in the documents of Piero's life and their archival location should consult my *Documenti fondamentali per la conoscenza della vita e dell'arte di Piero della Francesca* (Selci-Lama, 2013). Unless otherwise noted, I have translated Latin and Italian sources myself.

The reader should note that in referring to positions in the paintings and using the terms *right* or *left*, I am indicating the viewer's position, not that of someone in the painting, unless otherwise specified. In the Renaissance, Piero's birthplace was called Borgo San Sepolcro, or simplified to Borgo. The modern Italian state has designated the town as Sansepolcro. I shall use the modern name and occasionally Borgo for variety. Maps of central Italy and Sansepolcro in the fifteenth century are found on pp. xxiv and xxv. In the text and in the Sansepolcro map, street names are cited as they were in the fifteenth century. I have at times used the Italian *Quattrocento* to indicate the fifteenth century. In fifteenth-century Sansepolcro most measurements of length and width were expressed in *braccia* (arm-lengths); one *braccio* equaled 56 centimeters. In footnotes, to indicate where documents are found I have employed the term *folio* (abbreviated to fol. and fols.) to designate the paper number in registers and manuscripts. At times notarial registers of contracts do not have a folio number (written *unfol.*), and here the reader is informed of the contract's position by the date.

Monies are more difficult to explain and require a paragraph. Although in fifteenth-century Sansepolcro most monetary transactions were recorded in *lira cortonese* or *cortonensium* (lira of Cortona, so named but minted at one time in Arezzo), there were no such coins (nor their theoretical components of 20 soldi per lira and 12 denari per soldo) in circulation. The lira of Cortona was a theoretical money of account used only as a means to compute the values of smaller silver coins in circulation, which most commonly in Sansepolcro were from Bologna (*bolognini*), Ancona (*anconetani*), and Florence (*grossi*). For larger transactions, gold florins minted in Florence were used, though occasionally Venetian gold ducats were exchanged. During Piero's lifetime, the florin as well as the ducat were said to be worth 5 *lire* of Cortona, though there were constant fluctuations. Most silver coins lost value against the gold coins over time. In the second half of the Quattrocento, people in Sansepolcro occasionally made transactions in the Florentine coin *fiorini larghi*; these "large florins" were usually valued at around 6 *lire* of Cortona.

An artisan might receive between 25 and 75 florins (125 and 375 lire) a year, depending on his experience and the number of days he was employed or the number of his commissions per year. In Sansepolcro the communal government paid 150 florins yearly to the town doctor and 50 florins (plus use of a house) to the grammar-school teacher.

SHORT CHRONOLOGY OF THE LIFE AND WORK OF PIERO DELLA FRANCESCA

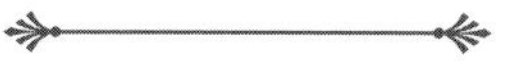

(N.B. If no place is specified, the event occurred in Sansepolcro)

1412? Birth of Piero

c.1426/27–30
Probable apprenticeship, unknown location

1431
Painting of candles for a confraternity

1432
Prepares altarpiece for Antonio d'Anghiari in church of San Francesco

1434–35
Paints with Antonio d'Anghiari in the Badia chapel of San Lorenzo

1435–37
Paints with Antonio d'Anghiari in San Michelangelo, Citerna Sant'Agostino (*Saint Michael*), and Sansepolcro (*Madonna Annunciata*)

1436
Paints flags and insignia for commune of Sansepolcro

1436–39?
Paints *The Baptism of Christ*

1438–39
Probably paints with Domenico Veneziano for the Baglioni family in Perugia

1439
Paints with Domenico Veneziano in Santa Maria Nuova, Florence

1440
Works with the sculptor Michele da Firenze in Modena

1445
Accepts commission from confraternity of the Madonna della Misericordia

1448–49
Probable presence in Ferrara

1450
Paints *Saint Jerome in the Desert* in Ancona

1451
Paints *Saint Jerome and a Penitent*, the portrait of Sigismondo Malatesta, and *Sigismondo Malatesta Before His Patron Saint Sigismundus* in Rimini

1452–53
Begins painting *The Legend of the True Cross* in San Francesco, Arezzo

1453–54
Paints in the Vatican Palace and in Santa Maria Maggiore, Rome

1454
Prepares and perhaps begins painting the Misericordia altarpiece; accepts commission for the Sant'Agostino altarpiece

1454–58
Paints *The Legend of the True Cross* in Arezzo

1454–58
At some point in this period probably paints in the Franciscan Observant church of Santa Maria della Neve

1458–59
Paints in the Vatican Palace, Rome

1459–60
Finishes painting *The Legend of the True Cross*, if not completed in 1458

1459/60–62
Paints *Madonna del Parto*, *Saint Louis of Toulouse*, *Saint Julian*, and *The Resurrection of Christ*, and completes the Misericordia altarpiece

1464–68
Paints flags for two confraternities, *Saint Mary Magdalene* and other paintings (now lost), in Arezzo

Mid-1460s
Completes writing of the *Trattato d'abaco*

1460s (to 1469)
Paints the Sant'Agostino altarpiece

1467–69
Paints the polyptychs of Sant'Antonio in Perugia and Sant'Agostino in Sansepolcro and *The Flagellation of Christ* in Urbino

1470–72
Paints *The Flagellation of Christ* in Urbino, if not painted by 1469

1472–73
Paints the Uffizi diptych of Federico da Montefeltro and Battista sforza

1473–75
Paints a fresco in the Badia, perhaps a *Coronation of the Virgin*; and *Hercules* in the Della Francesca family home (if not painted in the 1460s)

1475–77
Completes the working copy of *De prospectiva pingendi*, begins copying Archimedes' *Opera*, and paints the Brera altarpiece and the Senigallia *Madonna and Child* in Urbino

1477–81
Sets up scriptorium to produce four extant copies of the *De prospectiva pingendi*; finishes copying the *Opera* of Archimedes; paints the Williamstown *Madonna* and the lost Misericordia fresco

1482–83
Resident in Rimini

Early and mid-1480s
Writes and has translated the *Libellus de quinque corporibus regularibus*

1486–92
Resident in Sansepolcro; paints *The Nativity of Christ*

1492 Death of Piero

PROLOGUE

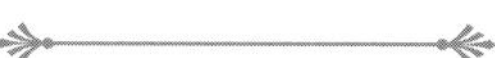

Who was Piero della Francesca, and how did he become the great artist he was? For the four hundred years from his death until the late nineteenth century, Piero's art and person were largely neglected, and few would have asked such questions. Then, as scholars' burgeoning interest in late medieval history converged with the Cubists' fascination with geometrical shapes in the early twentieth century, intellectuals began to recognize Piero for his art, geometrical sophistication, and historical role. Aldous Huxley wrote an admiring essay on Piero's *Resurrection of Christ* (Pl. VII), which he celebrated as the greatest painting in the history of art, and T. S. Eliot referred to his *Baptism of Christ* (Pl. I) in "Mr. Eliot's Sunday Morning Service" ("A painter of the Umbrian [*sic*] school/Designed upon a gesso ground/The nimbus of the Baptized God..."). Painters, among them Philip Guston, demonstrated their admiration by placing reproductions of Piero's images in their studios. More recently, Piero has entered popular awareness in movies and television programs due to the memorable scene in the film *The English Patient* of the actress Juliette Binoche swinging by a rope in the chapel of Piero's *Legend of the True Cross* (Pl. IV), and to John Mortimer's novel and television presentation of *Summer's Lease*, in which the heroine traverses the so-called "Piero Trail" from Arezzo to Sansepolcro to Urbino. Italian Renaissance scholars have come to view Piero's painting and achievements in pictorial theory and geometry as the fullest expression of the early Renaissance fascination with perspective. This has raised his artistic stature to a level with Leonardo da Vinci, Raphael, and Michelangelo.

Given this interest and the resulting research it has stimulated, one might assume that we possess a fully articulated biography of Piero with an account of his life and achievements. But such is not the case. Writers on Piero in Italian or English have often employed the word "enigma" in their titles, highlighting the difficulty of understanding his life and art. There are many admirable studies of the paintings of Piero and a few on his mathematics, but no one has satisfactorily brought together all the materials on his art, mathematics, and his person in a narrative that reconstructs his development. Consequently, no one has yet successfully placed Piero in the many social and artistic contexts that he chose for himself.

The mysteries of Piero's life stem from several factors: he did not often work in the major artistic centers of Renaissance art, Florence, Rome, and Venice; he did not assemble a large workshop with many students who would have preserved his drawings and his memory; and more than other important Renaissance painters, he suffered an almost immediate decline in public and critical interest, despite Giorgio Vasari's appreciative biography. Piero himself is in part responsible for this state of affairs due to his seeming lack of interest in his own reputation. As a consequence of these factors, several of his works were dispersed or destroyed. In attempting to reconstruct the full image of Piero's life and achievements, I must ask the reader to be indulgent in recognizing the elements of mystery while sharing the excitement of discovering the most probable solutions in the reconstruction of Piero's life. Solving some of these mysteries in the painter's life and his art opens up new and yet unanswered ones. This book is intended to introduce the reader to these questions, and to shed light on them as Piero did on the subjects of his paintings.

My approach is to follow Piero's development by placing historical documents in relationship to his paintings and mathematical treatises over his lifetime. Until now, the lack of evidence and the lingering supposition of an unchanging style have impeded such a way of organizing a book on Piero's life. But I have discovered over one hundred previously unknown documents specifically relating to Piero, and in the last two decades others have discovered an additional twenty documents or so. Through them, we are now able to chart the evolution of the man and his thinking. Of course, because we know much about Piero through his paintings, they will remain important as sources of evidence.

This approach obviously requires careful attention to problems of chronology and Piero's travels. My discussions of how to date his activities and where they occurred will, I hope, be one of the more significant contributions of the book. On Piero's chronology the reader should profit from consulting my outline of his life at the end of the preliminary materials (pp. xviii–xix). My solution to the problem of identifying Piero's whereabouts at particular moments is based on a novel treatment of the documents. I have accumulated a substantial number of documents that locate Piero in Sansepolcro in specific years. For example, he frequently served as a witness for his fellow citizens in notarial documents. When Piero appears in Sansepolcro as a witness or in other documents noting or requiring his presence over a few months or years, I calculate that he was there for the period of the chronological run of the documents. And I assume the reverse of this as well: if Piero does not appear in documents from Sansepolcro over an extended period of months or years, I reckon that he was absent from his home town for that entire period. Of course, he may have returned home for a brief visit on occasions when he was absent for extended periods, and one cannot be exact on the beginning and end of these absences.[1]

I am encouraged to follow this approach because it has often confirmed the conclusions of previous researchers based on the then known documents and other forms of evidence. More importantly, it leads to a more precise estimate of Piero's activities. Although I am confident that no great number of additional documents will be discovered for Sansepolcro that would attest to Piero's presence in the town for any extended period of time from 1438 to 1458 (except for 1445 and 1454) and later shorter periods, the findings of this method can be easily readjusted if a formerly unknown document should reveal his presence in Sansepolcro or elsewhere. In fact, such documents are welcomed as they would make our knowledge of Piero's life ever more precise. In the end, I believe my method provides a more secure and detailed base for the chronology of Piero's activities and paintings than any other.

As an aid to understanding Piero's artistic development, I have divided his paintings into three successive phases, with the proviso that he clearly learned and accumulated a number of techniques and stylistic elements that he could choose to employ or not at any one time.[2] The three suggested phases primarily turn on the degree and nature of perspectival organization and painting methods. In the first phase Piero's painting is informed by his powerful sense of proportion and spatial organization, but there is no evidence of orthogonals (drawn lines that converge at a vanishing point in a drawing or painting) or other systematic means to achieve the illusion of the dimension of depth in the depiction of pictorial space. In this phase, where Piero depicts human flesh he uses a *terra verde* (green earth) pigment in the undercoating, a traditional method thought to enliven the complexion of figures. In the second phase, Piero abandons the *terra verde* underpaint and achieves lifelike flesh through other pigments, at times also with an oil medium, in addition to the medium of egg tempera he had used before. More importantly, Piero now employs a thorough-going organization of pictorial space by perspective, achieved by the use of cartoons (preparatory life-size drawings that provide designs or outlines when transferred to the painting surface) and etched perspective lines that converge on the horizon. In the third phase, Piero appears less interested in a rigorously constructed perspective in his paintings. The objects in his paintings still diminish in size the deeper they are in the picture space, but they exhibit less evidence of the means to achieve the perspective, such as cartoons or orthogonals constructed as guidelines on the picture surface. By this phase of development, Piero apparently could achieve a three-dimensional illusion through a freer gauging with the eye.

Despite these changes over his lifetime, three qualities appear to be permanent in Piero's thinking and basic to his accomplishments. First, from his earliest painting and writings Piero demonstrates a fascination with proportion. Proportion underlies his theory and practice of perspective. We cannot say whether his fascination was an innate disposition or whether he learned it through the Greek mathematician Euclid's similar fascination with the subject. Second, and doubtless related to his focus on proportion, was Piero's powerful capacity for compositional organization. Third, Piero possessed an extraordinary ability to think visually, or perhaps better said, he possessed an ability to conceive and represent vast areas of a visual space, most evident in his construction of the mural paintings in the church of San Francesco in Arezzo. Also, in his mathematical treatises he moved beyond the Greek practice of using verbal propositions to represent geometric thinking, instead constructing complex geometric drawings, which acted as far more eloquent proofs than verbal statements ever could.

We begin our investigation of Piero's life with the formation of his interests and early education, which laid the foundation for his achievements. Although only one of his letters and just a few comments of contemporaries have come down to us, we do possess ample documentation relating to his family and his social, political, and economic activities. So we shall explore the settings of Piero's life, especially his family and the culture of the cities where he resided, and mine these revealing sources for clues and answers about Piero himself. It would be a mistake to expect that this would yield an image of the personality similar to those in twenty-first-century biographies. Indeed, the very concept of personality has changed radically since the fifteenth century, when individuals were more highly integrated into social and family institutions. In the end, the best I can hope is to have sketched a persuasive account of Piero's relationship to these institutions—and thereby a convincing outline of the man himself.

If this book had more space, there would be much more discussion of the scholarly contributions of others. I have restricted my endnotes and bibliographic citations to my essential sources of information, doubtless at times only schematically acknowledging important historical research and reflection. I have had to eliminate or summarize many scholarly debates over aspects of Piero's life and art. These are available in more specialized journals and books. A proper study of Piero requires the combined expertise of a historian of painting and perspectival drawings, a historian of mathematics, a philologist, a conservator of paintings, and a scholar highly adept at fathoming the intricate cultures of Renaissance Italy. One life is too short to master all these disciplines, so I rely on the research of the many scholars who have specialized in them. I am especially indebted to the scholarship of Carlo Bertelli, Frank Dabell, J. V. Field, Martin Kemp, Marilyn Aronberg Lavin, Ronald Lightbown, and Pier Daniele Napolitani. Doubtless they will recognize their ideas alluded to in the pages of this book. For a sophisticated analysis of Piero's mathematics, the reader can consult the research of J. V. Field. For the most part, I have based my arguments on published and previously unpublished documents, all of which I have brought together and recently published.[3]

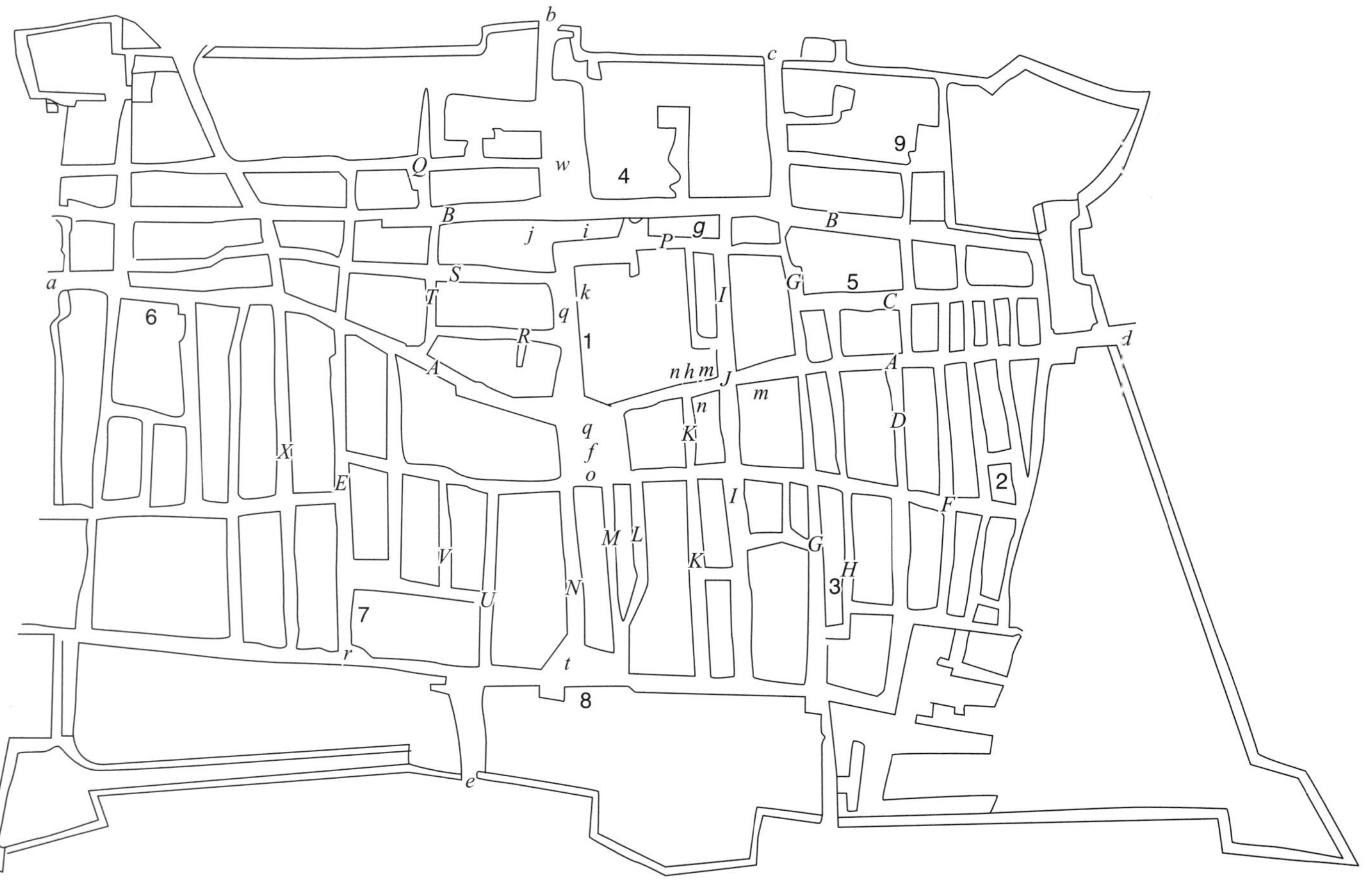

Map 1 Map of Sansepolcro in the fifteenth century

Streets

A. Via Maestra
B. Via delle Giunte
C. Via San Niccolò
D. Via dei Cipolli
E. Via Abbarbagliati
F. Via Sant'Antonio
G. Via San Giovanni Battista (Via del Rio)
H. Via del Buon Umore
I. Via Borgo Nuovo
J. Cantone dei Graziani (Graziani Crossing)
K. Via Agio Vecchio
L. Via Agio Torto (Via Rossi Domina Maria)
M. Via dei Servi
N. Via della Fraternita (Via del Ghiacciari)
O. Via Marcelli
P. Via della Fonte
Q. Via Santa Caterina
R. Via Castelnouvo (Via della Castellana)
S. Via Firenzuola
T. Via Pettorotondo
U. Via San Gregorio
V. Via della Stufa
X. Via del Panico

Gates, Buildings, and Piazze

a. Porta Fiorentina
b. Porta del Castello
c. Porta Libera
d. Porta Romana
(Porta San Niccolò)
e. Porta del Ponte
f. Torre di Berta
g. Casa di Piero
h. Della Francesca Workshop
i. Residenza del Capitano
j. Residenza dei Conservatori
k. Palazzo delle Laudi
m. Palazzo Graziani (two)
n. Palazzo Pichi (two)
q. Piazza Comunale
r. Piazza Santa Croce
t. Piazza Dotti
w. Piazza San Francesco

Churches

1. Badia di San Giovanni Evangelista
2. Chiesa di Sant'Antonio
3. Chiesa di San Giovanni Battista (San Giovanni d'Afra)
4. Chiesa di San Francesco
5. Chiesa di San Niccolò
6. Chiesa della Pieve di Santa Maria
7. Chiesa di Sant'Agostino
8. Chiesa di Santa Maria dei Servi
9. Chiesa di Santa Maria della Misericordia

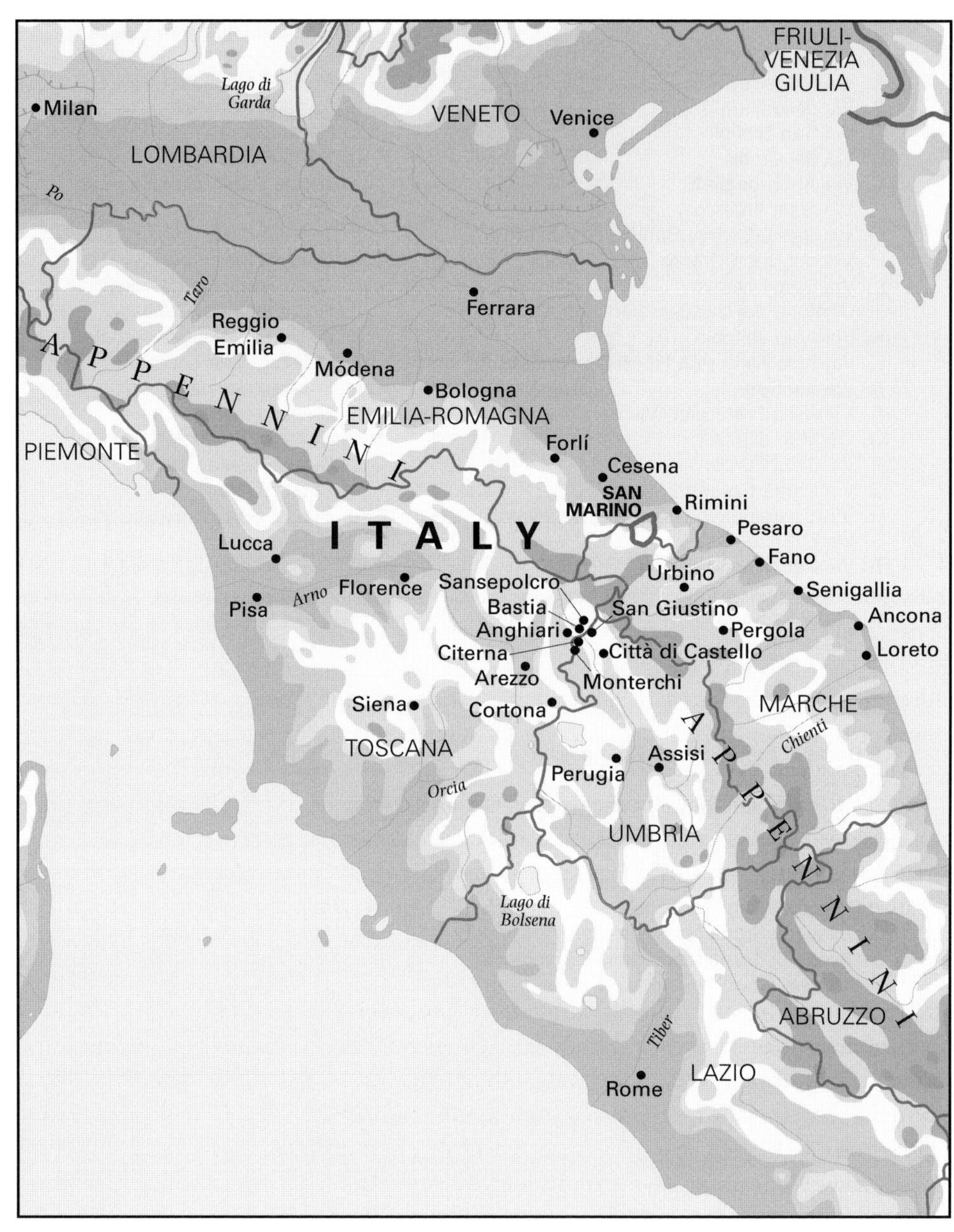

Map 2 Map of Central Italy

CHAPTER I

Piero's Formation in Sansepolcro

Piero della Francesca was born in or around 1412 in Sansepolcro, a small Tuscan town with a population of approximately 4,500 people. Piero undoubtedly attended the town's grammar school, but he never even started studies in a university, nor was he capable of writing Latin treatises—two customary requirements for inclusion in the intellectual elite. How, then, did this young man from a provincial town 79 miles from Florence and 169 miles from Rome and without an extensive formal education become, along with Leonardo da Vinci, both an outstanding geometrician and the most intellectual painter of the Quattrocento?

Piero's forefathers had been modest artisans and merchants of hides and leather, although his father Benedetto sought various means to elevate himself and his family into the town elite. He probably attempted to dissuade his son from becoming a painter because of its meager compensation and lowly status as manual labor. By the end of the Renaissance, painters had achieved a higher social status and most well-known painters were adequately paid, but in Piero's youth painters in the provinces usually had to content themselves with repair work and receiving an occasional commission for an altarpiece or a fresco of a traditional subject. Piero was apprenticed to an anonymous local Umbrian or Tuscan painter in the late 1420s. In the following decade he labored as an assistant for the undistinguished local painter called Antonio d'Anghiari.

Piero would have been approximately twenty-six years of age when in 1438 he completed his work as an assistant to this local master. After that, he most likely became an assistant to the painter Domenico Veneziano. During the decade that Piero had served Antonio d'Anghiari, he had been deeply involved in the artisan culture of Sansepolcro, where carpenters, blacksmiths, masons, cloth makers, and leather workers created objects with their hands using knowledge derived from their masters. In an age of minimal literacy among artisans, written instructions had little or no importance. Hence, oral instructions, observation of the workshop practices of their masters, and examination of the masterpieces of their predecessors constituted the workshop education of young artisans. Piero would have been familiar with the artisanal craft of endowing leather with beauty in order to sell it in the competitive local market, as he observed his father supervising the Della Francesca workshop. He was probably also close to his great-uncle Benedetto d'Antonio Cereo (alternately del Cera), who was a painter's son, an active carpenter in Sansepolcro, and later the maker of the wooden structure for Piero's *Baptism of Christ* (Pl. I). Throughout his life Piero demonstrated his intimacy with the materials employed in the various stages of the production of a painting. For example, he experimented with various preparations in order to achieve a stable and smooth surface for his paintings. Later he tried almost every paint medium and was one of the first Italian painters to introduce oil to his pigments. Piero's education continued throughout his life, but this first phase occurred in the artisans' workshops; here, from non-formal and practical sources, he gained many of his skills and much of his knowledge.

Sansepolcro

Piero was shaped as well by the broader socio-political and religious character of the town of Sansepolcro (Illus. 1). The town was located on the eastern border of Tuscany, in the upper Tiber valley (Map 1). During the early Roman Empire, Pliny the Younger had possessed a villa in this area; he wrote a letter to a friend describing the valley as an "amphitheater" with surrounding mountains, clear air, a broad fertile plain, and engaging people. With Umbria to its south and the Marches to its east, the town enjoyed a strategic military and commercial position. Goods and people moved north through the Tiber valley to Romagna and south to Umbria and Rome, as well as through the Apennine passes to the Adriatic ports to the east and Tuscany to the west. Sansepolcro was the primary location in the upper Tiber valley for the exchange of agricultural products in return for the objects and services of artisans and professional groups. It was also a regional market for the larger area bordered by Arezzo, Perugia, Cesena, and Ancona. In addition, the merchants of Sansepolcro traveled to the larger cities of Florence, Pisa, and Venice with their most profitable exports: the dark blue vegetable dye *guado* (woad) and veils. In exchange, they returned with coarse and fine cloth, sugar, iron, and salt.[1]

During Piero's childhood the town was ruled by the Malatesta family from Rimini. The popes claimed political authority over central Italy, with the exception of Tuscany, and appointed minor noble families to exercise political power over portions of central Italy, with the Malatesta receiving the commission to rule Rimini and its surrounding territory by around 1300. When the Malatesta line failed to produce a direct male heir in 1429, Pope Martin V sought to gain closer control over parts of Malatesta territory, but his agents were unable to withstand the invasions of nearby noblemen and mercenaries. Thus during the 1430s and Piero's young adulthood the town was subject to constant warfare and changes in lordships. This state of affairs ended in 1441 when Pope

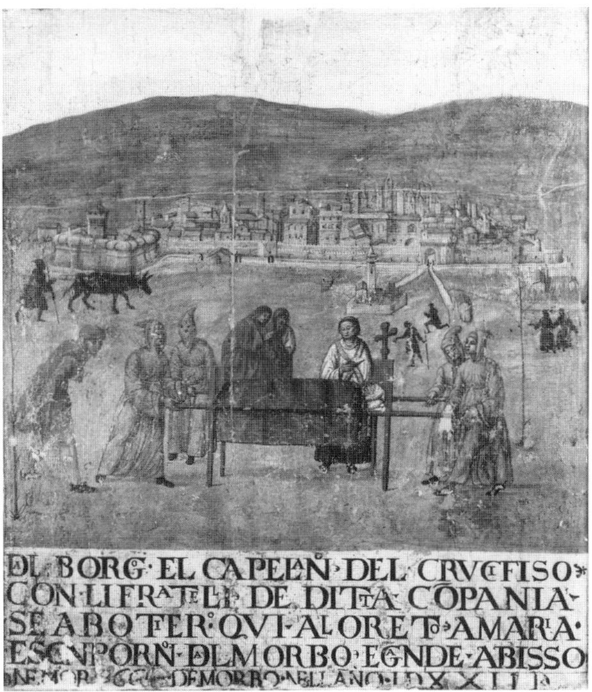

ILLUS. 1 Anonymous, *Tavola Votiva*, Votive panel with a view of Sansepolcro, 68 × 57.5 cm. Museo Civico, Sansepolcro

Eugenius IV granted Sansepolcro to Florence. Integrated into the Florentine territorial state and its Tuscan market, the town entered a long period of peace. Florence assigned a "captain" every six months to represent its interests in Sansepolcro, while daily executive authority was lodged in the hands of four local conservators, with legislative power located in two councils, the twelve and the sixty. All the offices were for limited terms and selection to office was made by placing names in electoral bags and drawing out the requisite number. To be "bagged" and thereby eligible for these offices, one had to be a member of the council of the people (Consiglio del Popolo), a body of 300 men that seldom, if ever, convened and effectively served as a marker of membership in the political class. Under the overall authority of Florence, which could be definitive when the Florentines so decided, the men of Sansepolcro governed through a polity that involved approximately 25 percent of male adults in its offices.

The majority of the people of Sansepolcro were practicing Christians (there were two or three families of Jews, who provided small loans based on pawns to Christians). The ecclesiastical hierarchy of the town, however, was contentiously divided, with religious authority shared between the Camaldolese abbot of the monastery of St John the Evangelist (hereafter the Badia) in the center of the town and the bishop of the nearby town of Città di Castello. The competition for dominance between the abbot and the bishop opened spaces in the religious life of the town that were filled by the three mendicant orders, the Franciscans, the Servites, and the Augustinians, each with its own large church and chapter of friars. Also seizing the opportunity created by the ecclesiastical conflict were the confraternities, laymen organized for religious and charitable purposes. The confraternities worshiped God in their churches through song, flagellation, and sacraments. They viewed their charitable activities of dispensing food to the hungry, providing dowries for impoverished young women, building hospitals for the sick and the dying, and generally assisting the weak and the poor as a means of gaining favor with God. Among the approximately fourteen confraternities in Borgo, the Fraternity of San Bartolomeo was the most important, in part because the town government granted its leaders authority over many social activities, from recording deaths to supervising the tutorship of orphans. In earlier centuries many of the functions performed by these laymen had been exclusively the preserve of the clerics: for example, supervising hospitals, singing praises to Mary and Christ, preaching, and flagellating. One consequence of such social functions and religious observations being entrusted to the laymen of these confraternities was that religious life in Sansepolcro possessed a less ecclesiastical or clerical character than in many other towns. Of course, the clergy maintained exclusive rights to perform the sacraments, but the lay usurpation of roles formerly exercised by clergymen expanded lay access to the sacred. This is most easily seen in the construction of churches by lay confraternities, whose leaders appointed and paid priests for their services, commissioned altarpieces for their altars, and followed Christ's injunction to aid the poor and needy of their society.

The Della Francesca Family

Piero's family was prosperous though not wealthy, respected though not among the elite. From at least the mid-1300s until well after Piero's death, the family occupied a residence on the corner of via delle Giunte and via Borgo Nuovo (Map 2), today called the Casa di Piero (see Illus. 20, 21). Until the fourteenth century only nobles and wealthy merchants possessed family names, but in a development that paralleled increased participation in communal politics and growing wealth, families of artisans, members of professions, merchants, and shopkeepers came to be recognized as deriving from specific ancestors and possessing surnames. The family name "Della Francesca" derived from Piero's grandmother Francesca, who after the early death of her husband Pietro in 1390 served as the family elder until at least 1415. This Pietro was a member of the guild of *calzolai* (leather workers), as were his ancestors and his son Benedetto. For the century prior to Piero's adulthood the Della Francesca bought animal hides and transformed them into leather goods, which were sold in the local market. This occupation could be profitable, but contact with animal skins limited the social esteem of the leather-making guildsmen. Benedetto, Piero's father, sought to elevate himself and his family by supplementing his leather work with various other endeavors—tax collecting, holding the pawns that the town government accepted for taxes, trading in woad, and insisting that his sons adopt more prestigious occupations than leather making.

The exact year of Piero's birth has until recently been subject to debate.[2] Giorgio Vasari, the mid-sixteenth-century biographer of Renaissance painters, sculptors, and architects, wrote that Piero died at the age of eighty-six. His death is recorded in 1492, so Vasari's statement would indicate 1406 as Piero's date of birth. Several historians have placed the date much later—at 1416 and even 1422—based on misinterpretations of documents and perhaps a desire to claim that Piero was a teenager or a very young adult when he painted in Florence in 1439, and was therefore prompt to absorb Florentine culture. As we shall find for events throughout Piero's life, it is often difficult to obtain definitive proof of their date, but we can be reasonably sure that he was born in 1412, give or take a year. This date is based on several arguments. First, the erudite and usually accurate Anton Maria Graziani, whose family purchased the Della Francesca house, wrote around 1600 that Piero was born in 1412. Second, Piero's parents, Benedetto and Romana, are recorded as married in 1411. More likely their wedding occurred earlier; Benedetto was thirty-six years of age in 1411, well beyond the Tuscan average age for beginning a family, and he would have wanted a male heir without delay. Finally the Della Francesca family, in accordance with Tuscan practice, had given its first son the name of the baby's grandfather for the two previous generations, making it near certain that Piero was named after his grandfather Pietro and thus was the firstborn.

Piero's mother Romana gave birth to at least five more children. One son, Francesco, became a monk in the Camaldolese Badia of San Giovanni Evangelista in the center of Sansepolcro. Piero's other two brothers, Marco and Antonio, became merchants and important men of affairs. In the last two decades of Piero's life they would both occupy the Della Francesca house. Piero's two sisters, Vera and Angelica, married husbands of middling importance in Sansepolcro. In Europe in these centuries a bride would bring money, clothing, and at times land to her husband as a dowry that was conceived as a way to support her and the newly formed family as well as a means to pass on her share of her family's patrimony to the children of the union. As head of the Della Francesca family, Benedetto played his part, although the dowries he provided for his daughters were relatively modest.[3]

The story of how Piero broke this familial pattern of mundane vocation to become an extraordinary painter and expert mathematician begins with his education, both formal and informal. Given his later ability to read Latin and to write rudimentary Latin phrases, we may assume that he attended the local grammar school in the years before and after 1420 and that he was accompanied by his brother Francesco. Francesco's chosen career as a monk required a knowledge of Latin. The town hired a teacher to convey the fundamental elements of Latin grammar to boys like Francesco and Piero. Instruction stretched over several years, with fewer students in the upper stages. The boys began by learning letters and sounds, often in group recitations. Then they memorized the rules of Latin grammar and subsequently began to read and analyze classical authors with the master's guidance. From Roman texts the boys often picked out pithy or sonorous phrases that they made into copybooks; these phrases were then available when as adults they wrote their own letters or treatises.[4]

Five boys who attended this grammar school in these years with Piero would later play important roles in his life. The group included his brother Francesco, Malatesta Cattani, Francesco di Benedetto d'Antonio Cereo (known as Francesco del Borgo; his father married Piero's cousin), Jacopo di ser Jacopo Anastagi, and Michelangelo Palamidessi. Excepting Francesca del Borgo and the Della Francesca brothers, the boys lived with their families on the Cantone dei Graziani (Graziani Crossing), where the grammar school in this period was located (see Map 2). The sons of the town's leading families gained an appreciation of Roman culture in the school as well as the ability to read and write in the local Italian vernacular.

We do not know how many years Piero attended grammar school, although it was certainly not long enough to learn to compose sustained narratives in Latin, a skill he never demonstrated. Later Piero wrote three treatises on mathematics and the art of painting. He composed these in an expository vernacular that lacked the elevated quality of classical texts and the pithy classical phrases from a copybook. It was customary during the Renaissance for merchant and aspiring artisan families like that of the Della Francesca for the first son to attend grammar school for a few years until he was thirteen or fourteen and then to prepare him for a career as a merchant, assign him to another merchant as an apprentice, or enroll him in a school of commercial mathematics (*scuola d'abaco*). However, unlike in Florence and north-west Tuscany, there were no schools or teachers of *abaco* in Sansepolcro or the surrounding area in the fifteenth century.

Because we know Piero eventually wrote a treatise on *abaco* and became an expert in Greek geometry, his mathematical background is of great interest, but also of considerable uncertainty. Vasari stated that "Piero applied himself in his youth to mathematics, and although it was settled when he was fifteen years of age that he was to be a painter, he never abandoned this study; nay, he made marvelous progress therein, as well as in painting." We cannot be secure that Vasari had a reliable source for this information, although we know his assistant Cristofano Gherardi (Il Doceno) was born in Sansepolcro and often lived there when he received contracts to execute paintings. Vasari's statement suggests that Piero was apprenticed to a merchant where, as was customary for apprentices, he learned to keep the account books and "applied" himself in mathematics by recording and totaling all expenses and income. Then in 1427 or 1428, at about fifteen years of age, we believe that he persuaded his father to permit him to change his proposed future occupation from commerce to painting. I say "persuaded" because painting, especially in small towns like Sansepolcro, was—as noted above—neither profitable nor prestigious. It appears that Piero and his father had a strained relationship, and that the tension began here when Piero abandoned his father's ambition for him, that of being a successful merchant.

Piero as Apprentice and Assistant

In the fifteenth century painting was an artisan craft. It required an apprenticeship of several years to introduce an aspiring boy to the skills of drawing, grinding paints, preparing brushes and surfaces for painting, making paper for drawings, and a variety of other tasks. In the years from 1427 to 1430 we have no indication of Piero's activities. The sequence suggested by Vasari, as well as Piero's documented activities, which begin in 1431, point to these years of the late 1420s as a period of apprenticeship. With whom Piero began his painting education or whether it occurred in Sansepolcro we do not know. He could have been apprenticed to Simone di Domenico from Arezzo, called Zoppo, a run-of-the-mill painter active for two decades in Sansepolcro. It is more plausible that Piero sought work under the accomplished painter Ottaviano Nelli from Gubbio in Umbria; Nelli received a commission (a contract to paint) in Sansepolcro in 1428 and in fact worked with Piero on a small project in the town in 1436. Or the young Piero may have been apprenticed to master Antonio from nearby Anghiari, with whom he painted as an assistant in the 1430s. Finally, Piero may have chosen, or perhaps his father made the choice, to work with a painter from Siena; patrons of Sansepolcro had commissioned painters from that city in the fourteenth century as well as in the 1430s and 1440s.[5]

Piero enters the historical record in June 1431 when he received a small payment from the confraternity of Santa Maria della Notte, so named because they sang evening hymns (*laude*) honoring Mary and Christ. Its priors probably paid Piero for painting the candles they carried in the procession for the religious holiday of Corpus Christi. The document simply states "To the son of Benedetto di Pietro for painting the shafts of the candles, one lira, 7 soldi, 5 denari." This payment establishes that Piero was no longer an apprentice but had begun to work as an independent painter. His labor was no longer owned by his master.

Later that year Piero's father Benedetto received a small sum to prepare a flag (*palio*) for the winner of a horse race on 1 September and another smaller cloth for a banner. The papal treasurer of Sansepolcro paid Benedetto just over 5 lire for making the two, which were presented to the winner of the competition. It seems improbable that Benedetto himself, at the age of fifty-six and busy in the town government collecting taxes, took the time to do the painstaking job of sewing leather to a lance. Benedetto probably assigned this menial artisan task to his son Piero.[6]

From 1432 to 1437 Piero assisted Antonio d'Anghiari. In five documents during this period the young Piero is recorded as a painter. This again signifies the end of his apprenticeship, which is also demonstrated by the fact that he is paid for specific labor on altarpieces. Piero has become an independent laborer and for a decade will work as an assistant to more experienced painting masters. In 1430 the brothers of the church of San Francesco in Sansepolcro commissioned master Antonio to paint the altarpiece of the high altar for the substantial sum of 140 florins. This was a major project that kept

Antonio in the town for most of the decade. To support his large family, Antonio accepted several additional smaller painting contracts in and around Sansepolcro, and he hired Piero to assist him.

For several months in 1432 Piero worked on the wooden structure of the San Francesco altarpiece. His work probably consisted of applying several coats of gesso (gypsum and dissolved animal skins) to the wooden surfaces that were to be painted. He would have prepared the gesso and then spread several coats of it, buffing each layer to a smooth surface before applying another. The record shows that Antonio agreed he owed Benedetto, Piero's father:

> for the salary and debt of Pietro [Piero], painter, son of said Benedetto, and the wages of said Pietro [Piero] for the labor lent to the said Antonio from the first of the most recent month of June, also from the loan to him by the said Benedetto made on several occasions and down to today [29 December 1432] for the exigencies of said master Antonio for the furnishings of the pictures of the altarpiece of the church of San Francesco.[7]

For Piero's labor and for loans or supplies provided by Piero's father, Antonio agreed that he owed Benedetto 56 florins, a substantial sum that took Antonio six years to repay. Indeed it was finally repaid only by his relinquishing ownership of a house that had been part of his payment for the San Francesco commission.

In the years 1434 to 1437 Piero assisted master Antonio in three separate churches, two in Sansepolcro and another in Citerna, a village located across the Tiber valley. Nothing of these paintings survives. The first of these was in the chapel of San Lorenzo in the Badia of Borgo in 1434–35, though we know little about the subject matter. The testament proposing the chapel and providing for its financing specified an altar and paintings; this suggests both an altarpiece and frescoes, but we do not know whether Piero's work was preparatory or included painting. The same is true of the commission to master Antonio in Citerna, where we find him and Piero painting the chapel of Michelangelo in the church of the same name, probably in 1435 or 1436. And in the last of the three commissions Antonio worked in the church of Sant'Agostino in Sansepolcro, where he and Piero produced an image of the Madonna after the Annunciation (*Annunciata*). Whether this was a fresco or painted on a wooden altarpiece we do not know. For Piero's labor on these three projects master Antonio paid him 60 lire. The modest size of the payment suggests that Piero was not fully employed by Antonio and was probably free to carry on mathematical study or other independent projects.

During this period Piero also embarked on a project on his own behalf: painting the insignia of Pope Eugenius IV. In 1436 the Pope's forces had re-established control of Sansepolcro, and a papal official wished to proclaim his possession. The project was sufficiently large that the town officials employed three men: Piero, Antonio d'Anghiari, and Ottaviano Nelli. The painters labored independently, each being paid separately. Thus we know that Piero functioned here as an autonomous artisan and not as an assistant to Antonio or the better-known Nelli. The three men painted displays of the papal insignia on the towers of the town walls and gates, and painted flags that were mounted on the towers. For providing lime and pigments, and for painting, Piero received the sum of 25 lire, though here as on several later projects his father or brothers actually collected the payments.[8]

From these modest projects over seven or eight years in his native town, Piero gained a wealth of experience. Attaching cloth banners to a lance, using leather to prepare flags, placing layers of gesso on a wooden altarpiece, assisting his employer in preparing or painting modest altarpieces or frescoes, and painting papal insignia on walls and towers, all these plus his proximity to the leather-making processes in his father's *bottega* (workshop) place Piero with men who worked with their hands and produced objects for sale in local and regional markets. In his later depictions of cloth, leather, valuable stones, and furniture, Piero always reproduced the artisanal work with heightened and respectful attention. His artisan preparation and experience in the workshops of artisans remained with him throughout his life. On the other hand, after the 1430s he rejected the practice of his sometime employer Antonio d'Anghiari in accepting small projects and the resulting modest payments. For the rest of his life Piero refused to accept small commissions (with one exception), thereby preserving his time and creative energy for more challenging projects. Antonio apparently believed that as the father of a family of five or six, he required a constant stream of income to overcome the poverty that on at least one occasion he claimed burdened him. Perhaps witnessing the plight of his employer contributed to Piero's choice never to marry and have a family.

In 1438 Antonio d'Anghiari agreed to compensate the Della Francesca family for Piero's assistance in the 1430s. Although Antonio continued to work on occasion in Borgo, from this point forward it would be without Piero's assistance. Apprentices and young painters customarily followed the style of their masters and employers, in part because an apprentice copied the master's drawings and, when permitted to take brush in his hand, would paint within the designs of his master and employer. In developing his own style, Piero would have been influenced to some degree both by his unknown master when he was an apprentice and by Antonio. The greatest Italian art historian of the twentieth century, Roberto Longhi, denied any lasting influence on Piero from his early experience in Sansepolcro. He dismissed Antonio d'Anghiari, saying he was a mediocre Gothic painter.[9] But today we are witnessing a reassessment of Antonio. A *Madonna and Child*, recently rediscovered in a small outdoor building (*tabernacolo*) along a rural road in the Tiber valley near the village of Falcigiano, has been dated to the mid-1430s and attributed to Antonio because he painted in that general area in that period. The art historian Andrea De Marchi judges that Antonio's painting reveals echoes of Florentine painting and suggests that Piero would thus have had at least a familiarity with Florentine stylistic practices prior to 1439.[10]

Other researchers have emphasized the influence on Piero of painters from Siena, based on their predominance in important commissions in Sansepolcro. Altarpieces of Niccolò di Segna from Siena dominated the Badia and the church of Sant'Agostino in

Sansepolcro. Piero could have seen the *Madonna and Child* of the fourteenth-century Sienese sculptor Tino da Camaino in nearby Anghiari. This preference for Sienese representations continued through the middle of the fifteenth century, as is evident in the Franciscans' decision to replace Antonio d'Anghiari with the leading Sienese painter Sassetta (Giovanni de Stefano) for the double-sided altarpiece of the high altar of the church of San Francesco in 1437. Sassetta did not begin painting before 1439 and did not finish his masterpiece until 1444, so it had no influence on Piero's early career, but his commission does show that Siena remained a major source of influence. Thus a case can be made for both Sienese and Florentine contributions to Piero's development. Recent research suggests that *The Baptism of Christ* in the National Gallery in London is Piero's earliest extant painting and in this painting one sees the influence of artists of both cities.[11]

We have been assessing the sources of Piero's painting style, but we should also address the analogous problem of the sources of Piero's knowledge of mathematics. Since he seems not to have had intimate contact with the esteemed mathematicians of Florence, why and how did mathematics become so important to him? Though the documentation is meager, there were some probable sources for Piero's early knowledge of geometry in the 1430s in Sansepolcro. As conjectured above, before turning to painting Piero was apprenticed to a merchant and learned elementary mathematics by keeping account books of incomes and expenses. In the early 1430s his father Benedetto may have had Piero assist him with the account books when he collected taxes for Borgo. As an agent for town governors, Benedetto imported salt from Rimini and Cesena near the Adriatic coast and sold it in Borgo—with a portion of the sales price going to the town government. Since every household was obligated to buy salt, these accounts involved lengthy computations. But this would not have contributed to Piero's knowledge of geometry. If he gained an introduction to this subject in Sansepolcro, he probably acquired it through conversations with the *agrimensores* (surveyors), whom the town hired to measure two- and three-dimensional structures, or during conversations with Niccolò Tignosi from Foligno, whom the commune hired as its doctor in 1437–39. In fifteenth-century universities only prospective medical students studied mathematics; for them it was necessary for their use of astrology in medical diagnostics. The curriculum called for the candidates to read the first four books of the *Elements of Geometry* by Euclid. Tignosi later lectured on Aristotle at the University of Florence and was the first teacher of Marsilio Ficino, the Platonic philosopher. But, more importantly, Tignosi could have shared with Piero the knowledge of Euclid that he had received at university.[12]

The Baptism of Christ

Between 1436 and 1439, prior to leaving Sansepolcro for two decades, Piero began and perhaps completed one of his masterpieces, *The Baptism of Christ*, which today hangs in the National Gallery, London (Pl. 1). An earlier debate on the original location of the painting has concluded with near certainty that it was prepared for the church of San Giovanni Battista (St John the Baptist, also named San Giovanni d'Afra).[13] The width of the *Baptism* panel (116 cm, or 45⅝ in), which equals the width of the central panels of the high altars of Borgo's other large churches, establishes that it was intended for a high altar. An image of St John baptizing Christ would be the appropriate image for the high altar of a church dedicated to John the Baptist—and no other church in Borgo was dedicated to him. Our understanding of this image is complicated by the fact that Piero completed only the central panel, whereas at least a decade later the remainder was completed by Matteo di Giovanni, a painter born in Sansepolcro but who lived as an adult in Siena and whose style was Sienese (Illus. 2). This Matteo painted the two lateral saints of the main tier or register (the portion of the altarpiece with the largest panels, usually a Madonna flanked by two or four saints), as well as the predella (the series of smaller narrative paintings located below the main register) and other smaller saints on the sidepiers (sometimes called columns).

This period, 1436–39, for the painting of *The Baptism of Christ* is earlier than most previous writers have supposed, but they were working under the assumption that Piero was born in 1415 or 1422 and therefore would have been too young and inexperienced to

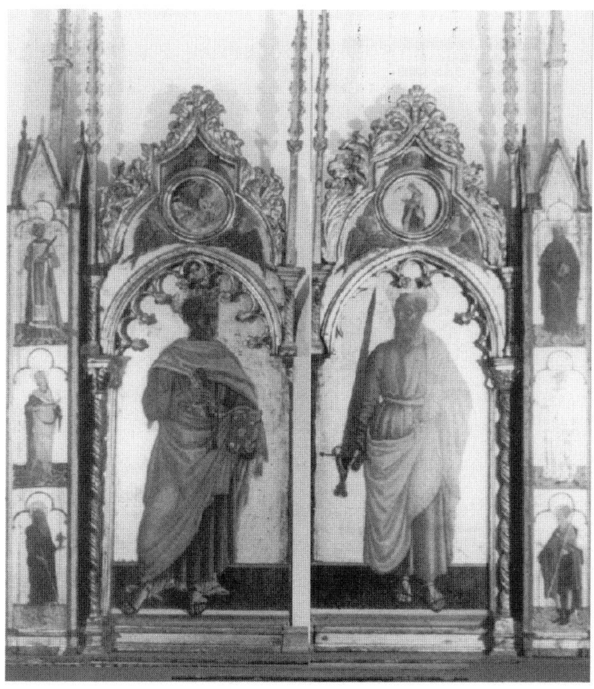

ILLUS. 2 Matteo di Giovanni, Flanking Saints for Piero della Francesca's *Baptism of Christ*, 3.58 × 3.52 m. Museo Civico, Sansepolcro

start painting such a sophisticated work as early as 1436. But, as we have seen, Piero was in fact approximately twenty-five years of age and had had a decade of experience by this time, so he was most certainly not too young and inexperienced to have painted this work in that period. In fact, as we shall now see, it seems probable that *The Baptism of Christ* was Piero's first major commission.

Although Piero's home in Sansepolcro was a couple of modern city blocks from the church of San Giovanni Battista, he can only be documented in the area of the church in the years 1436–38.[14] Moreover, in no other period in the fifteenth century do we find any artistic activity in that church, other than Matteo di Giovanni's completion of the *Baptism*. The altarpiece had been proposed and resources provided for a polyptych for the high altar of San Giovanni Battista in 1419, but nothing happened until 1433, when Don Nicoluccio Graziani, a member of Borgo's leading noble family, became the parish priest. That he played an instrumental role in hiring Piero to paint the *Baptism* for the high altar is indicated by the coat of arms of the Graziani family displayed on the bottom of the columns of the altarpiece. In that same year (1433) Piero's great-uncle Benedetto Cereo received a commission to construct the wooden structure of the altarpiece for the church of San Giovanni Battista, but nothing further happened until several years later, when Piero's name appears in several documents related to the church.[15]

Contracts in Quattrocento Italy required the presence of between two and seven witnesses to be fully legal. The two individuals making the contract or the notary called witnesses to hear the reading of every contract so as to attest later (if necessary) to the contract's contents. At times a notary might collar a nearby person, but usually the witnesses served a friend or colleague by their presence. These documents with their witnesses reveal the social networks of the Renaissance.

In 1436 Piero witnessed a testament of a member of the family of the abbot of Marzano, who possessed patronage rights over the church of San Giovanni Battista. The testament was recorded in the house of the abbot next to the church and one of the other witnesses was a Graziani. In 1437 Piero witnessed, again with a Graziani, three contracts culminating in the marriage of a couple just outside the parish of San Giovanni Battista. Piero's father, Benedetto, also appeared as a witness to a contract in 1437 in this parish, this one "in the doorway of the church" of San Giovanni Battista. Most importantly, in June 1437 Don Nicoluccio Graziani called Piero to his house to serve as a witness to his last will and testament.[16] These documents inform us that the Graziani and Piero were on familiar terms and probably were in discussions regarding the altarpiece for the church of San Giovanni Battista. Despite the many acts witnessed by Piero in his lifetime, he never appears again as a witness in the area of the church, suggesting that his painting of the *Baptism* occurred in the late 1430s and not later in his career.

We know that the wooden structure of the altarpiece had been delivered to the church of San Giovanni Battista by September 1437, because one of the church's lay supervisors acknowledged receiving payment for a house bequeathed to fund the carpentry and painting. The 1437 document states that the payment had been "converted and is in the altarpiece of the church of San Giovanni."[17] By late 1437 the altarpiece must have been at least prepared for painting and, as we have seen, this was the period in which Piero was engaged with the church and its parish priest. He remained in Borgo at least until May 1438, after which he cannot be located there for certain until 1445.

Placing this painting at the beginning of Piero's career eliminates several problems that become apparent if we assume Piero painted it later in his career. In understanding the evolution of his style and practices, we are assisted by the Italian art historian Luciano Bellosi. He argues that the *Baptism* is difficult to place in the sequence of Piero's paintings unless it is seen as the earliest commission. For Bellosi, the *Baptism* lacks several elements typical of Piero's later works and contains other elements that are absent in his subsequent works. "In the *Baptism* the forms are not typical of Piero's most distinctive art; [the forms are] less geometrical and voluminous than in other paintings; the countenances are not similar since they are less spherical."[18] Moreover, Bellosi finds that Piero's treatment of light and colors in the *Baptism* reveals his early proximity and debt to Domenico Veneziano.

There is a general agreement that Piero's visit to Florence in 1439 profoundly informed his development as an artist. The painter Masaccio and the sculptor Donatello were the most important influences, and we find some evidence of their style in Piero's *Misericordia* altarpiece painted in the 1450s and early 1460s (though traditionally dated just after 1445). But, as Bellosi asserts, the *Baptism* lacks any evidence of the influence of these two artists. For Bellosi, Piero stood before Masaccio's *Trinity* in Santa Maria Novella in Florence in "mute admiration" and its influence appears in Piero's *Crucifixion* in the *Misericordia* altarpiece (Pl. V), but not in the *Baptism*. Likewise Piero's later *Resurrection* (Pl. VII) in Sansepolcro is more Masaccio-like than the youthful *Baptism*. Thus Masaccio became important for Piero only after the completion of the *Baptism*. The influence of Donatello is seen particularly in his treatment of drapery. But Bellosi does not find evidence of that treatment of the cloth in Piero's work in *The Baptism of Christ*. Bellosi describes Piero's angular (*angoloso*) style of drapery, derived from Donatello, that becomes apparent in the clothing of the *Misericordia* figures and thereafter, but this is not found in Piero's *Baptism*. The *Baptism* cannot therefore be placed in Piero's later development, when he had successfully integrated Masaccio's monumental figures and Donatello's treatment of drapery into his art. These qualities only become fully apparent in the *Misericordia* altarpiece and thereafter. If we hold with received wisdom that the *Misericordia* was painted first, we must address the question of why Piero abandoned so many of the practices evident in the work when he painted the *Baptism*. Phrased differently, if Masaccio had a profound effect on Piero's painting style (as eventually he did) and the *Misericordia* altarpiece was painted prior to the *Baptism*, why did Piero abandon the Masaccioesque elements already present in the *Misericordia* but not in the *Baptism* and then reintegrate them in his later painting?

Here we find ourselves at the center of chronological and stylistic problems relating to the early development of Piero and his art. Bellosi's insightful treatment of Piero's early style was, it should be emphasized, articulated before the discovery of previously unpublished documents that date Piero's early activity near the church of San Giovanni Battista. His reconstruction of Piero's stylistic development is analogous to the development suggested by the documents mentioning Piero in the years 1436–38. Combining the documentary record with Bellosi's account of Piero's early work suggests the following chronology and reconstruction.

Piero began painting *The Baptism of Christ c.*1436, and not later than 1438. Since it clearly reveals the influence of Domenico Veneziano but neither Masaccio nor Donatello, Piero must have started it before being documented in Florence in 1439 but after some contact with Veneziano. As many have suggested, their association began in 1438 in Perugia, where Veneziano is documented as painting for the dominant Baglioni family. The association of the two painters in Perugia is assumed because Piero is documented with Veneziano in Florence in 1439 and the two painters were more likely to have met in Perugia first, rather than in the more distant Florence. In fact, in that period the Piccinino family, who ruled both Perugia and Sansepolcro, may have facilitated Piero's move down the Tiber to Perugia. In between Piero's association with Veneziano in Perugia and his stay in Florence in 1439, I would suggest that Piero continued painting *The Baptism of Christ*. As we shall see in our discussion of the contract of the commission for the *Misericordia* altarpiece, several of its provisions only make sense if Piero had had an important earlier commission and had encountered delays or problems in completing the painting.

Another piece of evidence for the early dating of the *Baptism* is Piero's use of the traditional method of applying a green undercoat before adding the whites and pinks to represent the areas of exposed human flesh (see Pl. I). Where the top layer of paint has worn away, especially on the stomach and shoulders of Christ, we see this green underpaint. Piero continued to use this green foundation for enlivening the visible human body until his completion of the Berlin *St Jerome* of 1450.[19]

Part of our admiration for the *Baptism* derives from the beauty of the image of Christ as the central figure. Piero showed this essential event in the history and theology of salvation as occurring in the upper Tiber valley. He represented the River Jordan as the Tiber itself with the walls and towers of the town of Sansepolcro located under the mountain of Montevicchi in the background. This part of the Tiber valley was known as the Valley of Walnuts, which Piero acknowledges by featuring a walnut tree in the foreground on the same picture plane as Christ and John.

Another fascinating aspect of the image derives from its depiction of the river. In earlier examples of this subject, Christ was generally depicted knee deep in the Jordan and distanced from the viewer. Piero has instead depicted the two figures close to the foreground, with the water just below their ankles. The water of this part of the river is transparent and nearly invisible, while the water behind Jesus is painted as a slippery reflection of sky, human figures, and the hills depicted in the background. This is a visual representation of refraction and reflection, phenomena discussed in medieval scientific treatises on optics. Either Piero was already familiar with this university-based knowledge or through his visual acuity he observed water's ability to refract and to reflect light rays.[20] This seemingly incidental visual feature of the *Baptism* has important ramifications for our understanding of Piero's development. Could it be that the relatively short course of Latin in the communal grammar school together with study on his own had progressed to the stage that Piero could read Euclid's technical treatise on optics in Latin by 1436–38? And could he have found a copy of a treatise on optics in Sansepolcro? Since the many inventories of the town's libraries fail to show such a work, it is improbable that Piero's sophisticated depiction derived from his reading. I would suggest that his acute power of observation, a power that we shall encounter in many of his paintings both of natural phenomena and man-made objects, made him aware that sunlight behaved differently on water depending on one's angle of vision. It is also possible that someone in Sansepolcro with a university background, the communal doctor Tignosi or Piero's childhood companion Michelangelo Palamidessi, introduced him to the phenomenon.

An essential aspect of Piero's procedure at this early point in his career was his excellent sense of organization or composition, with all components subordinated to his purposes. Such organization is based on his characteristic sense of proportion and his balancing of the formal elements of the painting. Indeed, proportion is the most important element in Piero's painting and in his writings. Of course, proportion is related to perspective; one might say that perspective is applied proportion. Some scholars have projected lines onto Piero's painting of the *Baptism* in unsuccessful attempts to discover a system of perspective, but Piero did not employ his careful mathematical calculations of perspective here, unlike in many of his later paintings. In the *Baptism* he organized space systematically but not with mathematically determined perspective. As J. V. Field, a historian of mathematics, says, Piero's sense of proportion in the painting derived from "natural optics," rather than a perspective system.[21] Piero possessed a "natural" perception of the way objects diminish in size as they recede in pictorial space. Historians of mathematics will note that proportion, though not a system of perspective, was central to Euclid's *Elements*, a work that Piero eventually came to know well and cited explicitly. As with the *Optics*, the tantalizing but unanswerable question is whether Piero at this early stage had the Euclidian text in hand—and the time and language skills to comprehend it.

Light is an essential component of the *Baptism*; it floods all the surfaces and bathes all persons and objects. To many observers today, the presence of such luminescence is a given, but this fascination with the play of light in a painting was, in the mid-fifteenth century, a new phenomenon. Piero and his generation of painters have been called "painters of light" because they were the first to study and represent systematically the myriad manifestations of light on surfaces. This required great attention to shading and thus was linked to the related concern with representing volumes, especially those of the human body and the cloth that covered it. Piero studied the effects of natural light on all surfaces and calculated these effects according to the nature of the surfaces as well as the angles and intensity of the light source.

Because *The Baptism of Christ* is Piero's earliest masterpiece, it is important to summarize its most significant features. At this stage Piero's painting shows his interests in employing light as a means to illuminate individuals and their environment and to articulate the corporeality of the human body. He employs proportion and compositional synthesis of all areas, forms, and colors to create a grand space in which humans can act. He also begins his practice of placing visible markers of the topographical features of Sansepolcro in his paintings.

***

We now leave the story of Piero's youth and young adulthood in Sansepolcro behind us. In spite of the skills he had acquired in these early years, Piero still had a lot to learn. And the vibrant culture of Florence, especially the new mathematical means of representing space that were being developed there, was the place to learn it.

CHAPTER 2

In Search of Piero, the Persistent Traveler, 1439–50

Following his apprenticeship and early experience in his home town until 1438–39, Piero, from his late twenties and for much of his thirties, practiced his craft in Florence, Modena, and Ferrara, without leaving any extant paintings and, with two exceptions, any documents in these cities. These peregrinations no doubt provided a second set of formative experiences for him. In the 1440s either he did not seek commissions or failed to secure them, or time has destroyed the documents and the paintings. The dearth of documentary and physical evidence makes much of the following account of Piero's activities in this decade conjectural; it is the least documented period of Piero's life after his childhood.

Piero and the Culture of Florence

I suggested in Chapter 1 that Piero had assisted Domenico Veneziano in Perugia in 1438. The relationship continued in Florence in 1439. This is seen in the more important of the two documents of this period, which records Piero painting frescoes with Veneziano in the high altar chapel of Sant'Egidio in the hospital of Santa Maria Nuova. The document recounts that on 12 September of that year the patrons of the chapel conveyed "two florins, 15 soldi to the said [maestro Domenicho di Bartolomeo da Vinegia] taken by Pietro di Benedetto dal Borgo a San Sepolchro, who is with him."[1] Although Piero picked up a small sum of money (or perhaps pigments worth that small sum), this does not mean that he was performing the minor functions of a shop boy (*fante*); Veneziano himself accepted an even smaller sum in the same manner in May 1439. Given Piero's earlier extensive experience, it is certain he painted as Veneziano's assistant and not as an apprentice or a day laborer, which were lower in the workshop hierarchy. Except for fragments of a border, the frescoes that Veneziano and Piero painted in the chapel have been completely destroyed. From the document of 1439 little else can be said about the painting there or of their relationship. No one knows the moment or circumstances of the termination of the painters' association or even how long Piero remained in Florence. In 1441 Veneziano hired the painter Bicci di Lorenzo as an assistant and therefore would no longer have needed Piero.

When Piero came to Florence, its governing and intellectual elites were in the process of making fundamental innovations in their culture that would influence Europe through to the modern age. Although the Medici family had established itself as dominant in political life, Florentine writers and citizens were asserting the superiority of republicanism and the active life of the citizen in a Europe that had for centuries prized monarchy and the ascetic life of the monk as the highest ideals. To assist the Florentines in understanding and evaluating their lives of commercial activity and office holding in an urban setting, new models of behavior were sought in the histories and literature of the earlier urban civilizations of Greece and Rome. This movement of humanism taught the superiority of the probable arguments of rhetoric and the exemplars of literature and history over the certainties of the theology, philosophy, and logic of the Middle Ages. Without rejecting Christianity, the humanists attempted to instruct citizens in the daily world of city, family, and friends from examples of life in ancient Greece and Rome. A school to teach the Greek language was set up in Florence, the first in western Europe in over a thousand years. Humanists learned the language and ransacked the libraries of religious institutions for Greek books, and they also sought out previously lost Latin works from the Roman world. As part of their revival of classical culture, the humanists sought to imitate the histories, letters, dialogues, orations, and other literary genres of the Greeks and Romans.

The part of this revolution in Florence that most affected Piero was the profound innovations in visual culture.[2] The architect Filippo Brunelleschi (*d.* 1446) had experimented with methods that fixed the eye's relationship to the image to be drawn and focused what was to be seen by passing the light rays from the image to be drawn using a pinhole or a screen. The purpose was to draw or paint the illusion of three dimensions on a two-dimensional surface. Brunelleschi used geometry to show that the painter could determine the size of objects in his designs by diminishing the objects proportionally to their distance from the painter's eye. This permitted the painter to represent more accurately what the eye saw and to encourage him to paint the space that humans and objects occupied, thereby yielding a more naturalistic rendering of the world.

By 1439 this revolutionary change in the visual culture had become especially manifest in the paintings of Masaccio and the sculpture of Donatello, both of whom we met in Chapter 1. Piero combined what he had earlier learned in Sansepolcro with his new experiences in Florence. As a painter in his late twenties with evolving theoretical interests and an established style, Piero observed and absorbed Florence's revolution of fully rounded human figures, the allure of the play of light on surfaces, and Brunelleschi's scientific perspective that had emerged in the years before his arrival.[3] Piero would have noticed a profound difference between the paintings of Masaccio and most or all of the paintings that he had viewed in Sansepolcro, including what he had learned from Antonio d'Anghiari. In Masaccio's paintings Piero would have noted the modeling of the human body in particular but also his careful organization of all the objects in the pictorial field. He would have seen how Masaccio aspired to represent muscular and corporeal figures in a compositional three-dimensional space. The space itself was constructed to enable the full integration of the human figure into the natural or material world. The representation of humans in this new space and the necessary emphasis on what the eye saw tended to accentuate the material or corporeal aspect and thereby yielded a fuller view of the carnal in the human figure. The spiritual had to be inferred by the viewers from their knowledge of iconography. Painters represented humans as possessing a dignity in the historical world and a free will within a field of choices available in an environment uninfluenced by magical or intrusive supernatural forces.

From the sculpture of Donatello, Piero would have noted the possibilities of shaping cloth to give a sense of fully developed, monumental figures. Though Piero ultimately moderated Masaccio's and Donatello's more emotional and rugged view of the human in his own art, these two masters were fundamental in Piero's second formative phase. Part of the power of the representation of cloth to suggest an underlying human form derived from the depiction of the play of light on the folds and fabric of the cloth. From his employer Domenico Veneziano and the works of Fra Angelico, Piero could have learned the capacity of light to illuminate every part of the pictorial field and every object within it. The light of the sun, its reflection and absorption, fascinated the generation of painters working in Florence in 1439, but Piero's proximity to Domenico Veneziano must have been fundamental in his learning to appreciate the representation of light and its ability to focus the viewer's attention on specific objects without losing any of the total pictorial environment.[4]

Piero eventually wrote three treatises on mathematics and perspective in painting. It has been suggested that besides Florentine influences in painting, Piero also absorbed Florentine mathematical and geometrical knowledge, but no one has succeeded in demonstrating his contact with the mathematician Paolo Toscanelli, the architect Filippo Brunelleschi, the theorist Leon Battista Alberti, or any other mathematician. We assume Piero's mathematical knowledge increased in this period, though no one has succeeded in revealing what he learned.

Having said this, the most likely contact between the provincial painter and the elite circle of Florentine mathematicians would have been Leon Battista Alberti (*d.* 1472), who was said to have visited the workshops of painters in the mid-1430s.[5] But because Alberti was employed in hosting the Greek Church dignitaries for the Council of Florence in 1439, it is doubtful that he continued these contacts, at the time when Piero was working with Domenico Veneziano. Already in 1435 Alberti had written a vernacular treatise entitled *On Painting*, in which he lays out the means of constructing a perspective drawing. This book provided a theoretical basis for Brunelleschi's experiments concerning the eye's relationship to representations and for the achievements of the Florentine artists. Alberti constructed a mathematical depiction of space, mathematical because space was conceptualized as regular, measurable, and subject to geometrical laws. Piero may have encountered him in Florence or have read his treatise and may have taken the idea of writing on perspective from Alberti's book. But there are substantial differences between Piero's treatise and Alberti's.[6] As an alternative, I would suggest that Piero's *De prospectiva pingendi* (*On Perspective in Painting*) derived rather from his long experience (approximately thirty years) of drawing and painting in perspective, coupled with his belief that proportion was an essential element in painting.

Piero North of Tuscany

One year after conveying the small payment to Veneziano, Piero was probably in Modena and Ferrara. A notary in Modena recorded a "magistro Petro Benediti de Burgo" as a witness on 6 September 1440.[7] It is likely that the document refers to Piero della Francesca for a number of reasons: the linking of Piero's name (despite the different spelling) with that of his father; the use of "Burgo" as a means to identify his place of origin; and his identification as a "magistro." Their combination obviously enhances the likelihood that it is Piero della Francesca still further. Moreover, the contract specifies a terracotta or stone altarpiece to be constructed by master Michele da Firenze intended for the Cathedral of San Geminiano in Modena. So it is not any old agreement that "Petro" is witnessing: it is, intriguingly, the commissioning of a work of art for the high altar. The sculpture was to be painted, which may explain why "magistro Petro Benediti de Burgo" was present for the contract signing, as he would presumably have assisted master Michele by painting the sculpture. Michele da Firenze received other contracts from the Este ruling family in Ferrara, and the document of commission raises the possibility that the altarpiece would be constructed there and moved to Modena. Michele had earlier been active in Arezzo in the 1420s and 1430s. Piero may have encountered him there, and then in the early 1440s joined him in Modena and Ferrara.[8]

We can surmise that Piero was absent from Sansepolcro from 1439 to 1444 and 1446 to 1453 because he did not, as he had in the 1430s and would later in his life, serve as a witness there for contracts for his fellow townspeople. Nor does he appear in any other capacity in the documents of Sansepolcro relating to these years. Also suggestive of his absence is the fact that there were two commissions for paintings in Sansepolcro during these periods, which might have been expected to have been given to Piero had he been present. The first came in the spring of 1444 when Piero's father and the three other conservators of the town granted Antonio d'Anghiari a commission. The town executives agreed that "master Antonio d'Anghiari painter was to be paid 28 lire for pictures in the auditorium of the councils next to the recently constructed tower..."[9] This raises the question of why Benedetto did not use his influence as one of the four conservators of the town to gain the commission for his son. Though the salary was not especially large, the location of the painting in the communal palace was prestigious. Surely if Piero had been in Borgo, then Benedetto would have tried to secure the commission for his son.

Had Piero been in Borgo in June 1444, the men of the confraternity of Santa Caterina without doubt would have asked him to paint a double-sided processional flag. Instead, the Sienese painter Pietro di Giovanni d'Ambrogio received the substantial sum of 55 florins for completing the flag.[10] Thus, in the first half of the 1440s, when there were opportunities for Piero's father and brothers to use their positions of power on Piero's behalf (as was both accepted and expected in Quattrocento Italy), they apparently did not seek—or failed to gain—either of these commissions for Piero. Taken together with the absence of Piero's name from any notarial or other official documents during those years, there seems to be no other explanation for these missed opportunities: he must have been absent from Sansepolcro and the commissions were not sufficiently alluring to merit his return from his activities elsewhere.

Piero's name appears in one document of July 1442 in Sansepolcro, when the town's chancellor listed the 300 members of the council of the people. As we have noted in Chapter 1, the list functioned to record the men of the town who were eligible for other offices. "Petrus Benedicti Petri" is found as a member of the tenth of fifteen groups (*cedule*), each with twenty names.[11] The most senior and influential men were placed at the top of each *cedula*; Piero's relative inexperience is reflected in his placement as the seventeenth of the twenty men in his group. His name on the list does not indicate, as many have assumed, his presence in the town, because the council seldom if ever convened. Absent citizens were not expected to return and may not have been aware of the list. However, Piero's inclusion made him eligible for Borgo's numerous political offices.

Piero in Sansepolcro in 1445: The Misericordia Contract

If, as seems certain, Piero was away for most of the 1440s, we can be sure that he returned to Sansepolcro in 1445, when two documents attest to his presence there. The later of the two is the well-known commission of 11 June to paint the polyptych of the confraternity of Santa Maria della Misericordia in Borgo (which will be discussed more fully in Chapter 5). In an earlier document of 12 April 1445, Piero had served as a witness in a land sale (no relationship has been found between Piero or his family and the men in the contract).[12] This establishes Piero's presence in Sansepolcro in April 1445, a couple of months prior to the Misericordia commission. Piero's group had been chosen to sit on the council of sixty in February 1445 for the period of March to June.[13] Piero may have seized this opportunity to participate in the council, which served as the chief legislative body of Borgo. Alternatively, he may have returned to Borgo to finish or mount the central panel of his *Baptism of Christ* in the church of San Giovanni Battista, if he had not finished it earlier. A provision of the Misericordia contract indicates that the confraternity's officials were concerned that Piero had often been absent from Sansepolcro or had taken years to complete the commission to paint *The Baptism of Christ*. The Misericordia officials as patrons wanted Piero to deliver their altarpiece promptly, so they included a provision in the contract of commission in which Piero agreed to finish the altarpiece within three years.[14]

Other provisions of the contract point to the awareness of both parties of Piero's accomplishments. His salary of 150 florins was a substantial amount, fitting for an established painter. The confraternal officials gave Piero the privilege of constructing the wooden carpentry of the altarpiece, despite the fact that the church of the Misericordia already had an altarpiece that was prepared for painting. The Sienese painter Sassetta had, in a similar agreement, contracted to construct the wooden structure for the polyptych of the church of San Francesco, despite the fact there was already one prepared for painting. The analogous grant to Piero suggests that he was held in comparable esteem by the confraternity officials, no doubt for previous work and probably for the *Baptism*.

Many have assumed that Piero began painting immediately after having received the Misericordia commission in June 1445. There is no evidence for this. And other documents suggest that he left Borgo soon after accepting the commission. For a start, he did not receive the initial payment (here 50 florins) that painters customarily insisted on receiving immediately (for buying gold and painting materials, and to pay for the construction of the wooden structure of the altarpiece). The commission document did call for an immediate payment; the confraternal leaders promised "to give [fifty florins] now on his petition and the remainder when the altarpiece is completed." This formula of an expected payment "now on his petition" is a formula seen in many Borgo contracts and often no money changed hands at this point, so that the phrase "on his petition" becomes pertinent. If the 50 florins had been paid to Piero on this occasion, the next document in the notarial register would have been a *quietatio* (a quittance or receipt) that recorded the payment. There is no such document here or elsewhere among the notary's contracts. Apparently Piero did not immediately petition the confraternity for the 50 florins. It was not until 10 January 1446 that confraternal officials conveyed 100 lire (approximately 20 florins) to Piero's father, who received the payment of part of the initial sum of 50 florins for his son.[15] The confraternity was obligated to pay Piero more than the 50 florins only on the completion of the altarpiece; if the 50 florins had been paid earlier, there would have been no reason for this payment of 100 lire. Therefore, the 100 lire must have been part of the initial deposit. Because Piero had to provide the wooden structure and considerable gold for the background of the altarpiece, he would only have begun work or commissioned a carpenter to construct the wooden framework after he had the 50 florins in hand. From later payment records (see Chapter 5) we know this did not occur until the 1450s.

All the records indicate that Piero departed from Borgo after receiving the Misericordia commission. The document of 10 January 1446 confirming that Piero's father received part of the 50 florins for his son suggests Piero's absence. Moreover, Piero vanishes from the documentary record in Sansepolcro until 1454.[16] Vasari also recounts that Piero was occupied elsewhere soon after the Misericordia commission. He stated that Piero "painted in Santa Maria in Loreto, in the company of Domenico Veneziano, beginning a work in the vault of the sacristy; but because, fearing the plague, they left it unfinished; it was finished by Luca da Cortona." Loreto suffered from plague in the years 1447–52 and most commentators accept the earlier date for the putative departure of Piero and Domenico from Loreto. Vasari could not have seen this attributed work because the old church of Santa Maria in Loreto was destroyed in the years 1469–71 to make space for a new structure. However, this Luca da Cortona, better known as Luca Signorelli, did paint in Loreto in the late 1470s in one of the four sacristies (Sacristy of San Giovanni) of the new sanctuary.[17] Inasmuch as Vasari regarded Signorelli as a student of Piero, he or his informant may have attributed to Piero a painting of Luca Signorelli. In any event nothing of Piero's hand survives in Loreto, and we shall leave his possible presence there as yet another unanswered question.

Ferrara

Most investigators of Piero's life hypothesize a stay in Ferrara in the 1440s, usually placed later than 1440 when he assisted with the sculpture by Michele da Firenze in Modena. The problem is that there are no surviving documents or paintings situating Piero in Ferrara. The supposition of his presence in the town derives from the comments of Vasari and the mathematician Luca Pacioli, and from copies by other artists of Piero's presumed paintings and drawings. Vasari asserted that the lord of Ferrara, Borso d'Este, summoned Piero there, but since Borso did not come to power until 1450, when Piero is known to have been elsewhere, Vasari was in error and should have named Borso's brother Leonello d'Este (Ferrara's ruler from 1441 to 1450) instead. According to Vasari, Piero painted "many rooms in the [Este] palace which were then ruined" by the later Ferrara ruler Ercole d'Este (*r.* 1471–1505), and he also frescoed a chapel in the church of Sant'Agostino. Pacioli gave no details but was content to list Ferrara as one of the cities in which Piero had painted.[18]

Leonello d'Este assembled a learned court in Ferrara commemorated by the Milanese humanist Angelo Decembrio in his dialogue *On Literary Polish* (1447–62). Leonello's father, Niccolò III, had already contributed to the creation of this court, especially by drawing to Ferrara in 1429 the great humanist educator Guarino da Verona as Leonello's mentor. Guarino either brought with him or attracted other humanists to the Este court. Decembrio depicts Leonello as interested in a wide variety of topics, from literary criticism to the iconography of Flemish tapestries, and as having an appreciation of gems, ancient sculpture, coins, and painting. In the dialogue Decembrio recounts the sophistication of Leonello's court and describes the prince leading discussions on a variety of topics, in one of which Leonello asserts the superiority of the poet to the painter because the former has the tools to represent nature more accurately and more fully. According to Decembrio, Leonello accepted as axiomatic the idea that the task of both poet and painter was to represent nature realistically. Many of Leonello's opinions on literature derived from his master Guarino da Verona, while his opinions on painting are traceable to Alberti.[19]

Leonello's humanistic interests included an intense interest in Roman history; in *On Literary Polish*, Decembrio has him debating how the painter ought to represent battle scenes. According to Vasari, Leonello probably commissioned Piero to paint "many rooms" in his palace, with famous battles from antiquity, especially those between the Roman general Scipio and Hannibal, the Carthaginian general. The Italian art historian Carlo Bertelli has argued most persuasively that artists from Ferrara and its region imitated the style of Piero in the century after his presence there. Bertelli finds echoes of Piero's style most fully in two extant battle scenes (now in Baltimore and London) from the early sixteenth century and believes that the anonymous painter of Ferrara had access to Piero's images once in the Este palace, even though the rooms had been destroyed by Ercole d'Este.[20]

Leonello brought into his court at this time Cristoforo and Lorenzo Canozi da Lendinara. The brothers, who were experts in the art of intarsia (designs in inlaid wood), worked for Leonello in his palace of Belfiore in 1449. Luca Pacioli commented that this Lorenzo Canozi was "dear to him [Piero] as a brother."[21] Their friendship developed in this period, when Piero was painting frescoes and the Lendinara brothers were in Leonello's nearby palace.

The Este court had contacts with European culture north of the Alps, and its courtiers were especially fascinated with chivalric romances. Leonello also hosted painters from Flanders, and Piero may have had conversations with them or viewed their paintings. The question of what he appropriated from Flemish contacts has been debated for almost every one of Piero's paintings. There is such uncertainty on this question that I shall not generalize but only make comments later on specific works.

Piero in Ancona

For some unknown reason Piero left Ferrara and is next found in Ancona in 1450. It is now almost certain that, as has long been suggested, Piero completed his *Saint Jerome in the Desert* during his stay in this Adriatic port town. The work in question is a relatively small wooden panel (Illus. 3). His presence in Ancona at this time is confirmed by a contract that Piero witnessed in March 1450 in which Simona, the widow of Conte Giovanni di messer Francesco Ferretti, made her last will.[22] The witnesses included "magistro Petro Benedicti de Burgo Sancti Sepulcri." This is undoubtedly Piero; the only question derives from an additional portion of the clause, which notes the witnesses were "citizens and inhabitants of Ancona." It is not plausible that Piero had been made a citizen of Ancona, because customarily Renaissance towns granted citizenship

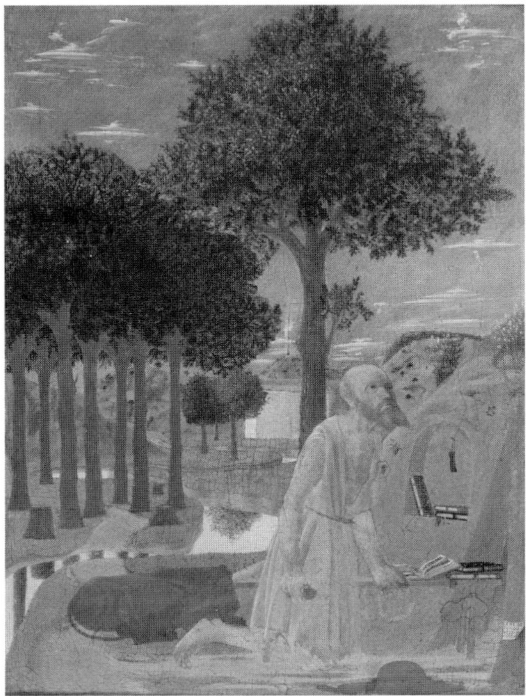

ILLUS. 3 Piero della Francesca, *Saint Jerome in the Desert*, 51 × 38 cm. Gemäldegalerie, Staatliche Museen, Berlin

to an immigrant only after several years of paying taxes. The notary no doubt intended to indicate that some of the witnesses were citizens and other inhabitants. But that Piero was recorded as an inhabitant in March 1450 suggests that he had been resident there at least for several months.

The document places Piero in the Ferretti family home, where the widow Simona elected to remain after her husband's death, rather than choosing to return to her natal family. The Ferretti had been the leading family of Ancona since at least the thirteenth century and held the highest political and ecclesiastical positions. In 1401 the Florentines had honored Simona's husband, Conte Giovanni Ferretti (his father had been made a count by Pope Boniface IX), by choosing him as their *podestà*, thereby assigning him ultimate judicial authority over the courts of Florence. Part of the Ferretti family prestige in Ancona derived from their office holding, part from the noble status of one branch, and part from the commercial activities of another branch. In 1411 Simona's father-in-law—along with his descendants in perpetuity—had been granted Venetian citizenship, probably because of his commercial activities in Venice. Thus the Ferretti enjoyed a set of social and material advantages that endowed them with wealth and authority. As in Ferrara, where Piero had received commissions from the ruling Este family, so here in Ancona he had by now gained sufficient status to be associated with the elite. Whether he lived in one of the houses of the Ferretti cannot be known, but it is apparent that he associated with the wealthiest and most esteemed individuals of Ancona.

Piero signed and dated his *Saint Jerome in the Desert* to 1450 by placing a small piece of painted paper on the bottom of a partially visible tree trunk in the panel's lower right corner with the words: "PETRI DE BURGO OPUS MCCCCL."[23] He rendered the capital letters in a humanistic style by making them square and eliminating any unnecessary flourishes, though they are not perfectly formed or spaced, in part because Piero chose to demonstrate his virtuosity by gently curving the end of the bottom right corner of the paper. As a result this corner extends out toward the viewer, an excellent example of foreshortening.[24]

Piero represents Saint Jerome on his knees with his arms to his side, though the left hand and arm are badly preserved. The saint holds a circle of beads in this hand while in the right hand he clutches a stone and prepares to beat his chest. As in many earlier representations of Jerome in the desert, Piero depicts him as a cardinal (an office he never attained) by displaying a cardinal's hat in the foreground. Jerome's scholarly vocation of translating the Bible from Greek to Latin is conveyed by the presence of six books, one of which is opened on a bench to his left. These elements had been found in earlier examples of Jerome in the desert, but Piero has transformed them. The head of the saint is balding but possesses a slightly forked beard that intensifies Jerome's tilted gaze as he looks up to a crucifixion along the right side of the image, aptly placed according to the rules of perspective. The painting is flooded with light, a light that descends from directly overhead so that there are no shadows.[25] This is especially evident after the most recent cleaning, as are the powerful rays of sunlight in the brook with reflected images of one tree and several trunks. The blue sky overhead and to the horizon is broken only by circular clouds that appear as oval saucers. The bench and the prominent rectangular building in the background add a geometrical quality to the image. Carlo Bertelli has commented on the "geometric banks" of Piero's river that draw the viewer's eyes from the foreground to the quadratic house and hills in the distance.[26] Piero has also painted an arched niche in the rock with three books in it. All the books in the painting are beautifully presented in colorful bindings and at least one has a marbled leather cover. The small plants and trees in the background and even on the rocks attest marvelously to Piero's attention to detail. Overall Jerome inhabits a believable environment, organized for the saint's purposes of penitence and scholarship. Again, as in Piero's representation of the River Jordan in the *Baptism*, the Holy Land is depicted as resembling the upper Tiber valley around Sansepolcro.

The argument that Piero's *Saint Jerome* was painted in Ancona is strengthened by the presence there in the fifteenth century of a copy of his painting. The copyist would necessarily have had Piero's painting in front of him to make such a faithful rendition. Now in the Galleria Sabauda in Turin, this *Saint Jerome in the Desert*, despite its half-circle shape (since it was intended for a lunette), only deviates slightly from Piero's painting. The copy retains many of his details: the spacing of the trees, the distant horizon with two nearly identical hills, the strongly rectangular building in the background, the lion behind Saint Jerome, the placement of the saint, and many other particulars. Certainly there are some changes in details in the Sabauda painting, for example the placement of the arms, the shape of the trees and forms of the rocks, and the elimination of water and reflections in the riverbed. Perhaps the most important pictorial difference is that Jerome's concentrated gaze on the faint crucifixion was changed by the Sabauda painter into the saint's adoration of a slender but prominent crucifix, mounted on a small tree trunk and tilted toward him. Despite these differences, the copyist does not hide his imitation or diverge markedly from his model. The overall impression is that he sought to replicate Piero's painting in its principal features and to add small changes to intensify the penitential elements.

The painter of the Sabauda *Saint Jerome* was Nicola di maestro Antonio from Ancona.[27] His only signed painting is a *Madonna and Child* (Carnegie Museum of Art, Pittsburgh), for which, it has been suggested, his Sabauda *Saint Jerome* once served as the lunette. The two paintings would have been together in the church of San Francesco delle Scale in Ancona and associated with the altar or chapel of Saint Jerome. The Pittsburgh *Madonna* has saints, including Saint Jerome. This is all important because a member of the Ferretti family, Girolamo d'Antonio, commissioned the construction of this chapel in 1469, and the chapel is recorded as completed in the early 1470s. Although this Girolamo was of a different branch of the Ferretti family than the Simona for whom Piero acted as a witness, the two branches were reunited in a marriage of the brother of Girolamo and the niece of Conte Giovanni (Simona's husband) around 1450.

A combination of factors, taken together, makes it sustainable that this Girolamo d'Antonio Ferretti had commissioned Piero to paint the Berlin *Saint Jerome*. These factors include Girolamo d'Antonio's very name (Girolamo is the Italian for "Jerome"), which meant that Jerome was his patron saint; Girolamo's commission of a chapel dedicated to Saint Jerome; Jerome's presence in the Berlin panel; and Piero's witnessing in the house of the Ferretti clan.

Piero's *Baptism* from the late 1430s and his *Saint Jerome* from 1450 are stylistically similar, although in the latter there is a toning down of colors to more muted golds, greens, and browns. The painting from Ancona illustrates Piero's continuing study of the effects of light, his composition of space, and the beginnings of his system of perspective. Piero's interest in the materials of painting is evident in that he used a wooden base of chestnut for the *Saint Jerome*. It was extremely uncommon in the fifteenth century to use chestnut for paintings on wood. Moreover, the wooden foundation was slightly curved for a convex painting surface. Piero's purpose in his construction of a convex chestnut base is not known.

***

The 1440s may be termed Piero's lost decade because no painting is extant from those ten years. But that decade is lost only to us, as students of Piero. From his work in the

1450s and later, it is clear that Piero had absorbed a great deal from his residence in Florence, most importantly methods of representing the natural and man-made world in illusionistic three dimensions. Piero also had drawn from his experiences in Ferrara. This is seen especially in his experimenting with oil pigments as early as 1451. Given that this innovation was first used by Flemish painters, and given the presence of Flemish painters in Ferrara in the 1440s, we may assume that Piero discussed with them the use of oil as the base for pigments. He regarded perspective and oil as tools that he could choose to employ when he thought their use achieved his ends. Soon after Piero completed the *Saint Jerome*, he left Ancona for the flamboyant court of Sigismondo Malatesta in Rimini.

CHAPTER 3

Piero at the Court of Sigismondo Malatesta in Rimini

The date of 23 October 1446, when his brother Marco married, would prove to be an important day in Piero's life, even if he may not have been present for the celebrations.[1] Marco's marriage united the Della Francesca with the Anastagi family, one of whose members, Jacopo, was in Piero's youthful group. As discussed in Chapter I, the two youths shared a similar environment during their early years. After Ancona, Piero would go to Rimini to paint for Sigismondo Malatesta, the powerful ruler of the city and its region. Piero's Rimini work demonstrates several innovations: the use of oil as a medium for his colors, preparatory drawings applied to the painting surface, the use of a fully developed humanistic script for inscriptions, extensive spatial conceptions, and the ability to express a political ideology in traditional pictorial genres. His paintings for Sigismondo invite us to analyze Piero's representation of the Malatesta court's political symbolism and values. In this chapter I argue that Jacopo Anastagi was Piero's entrée to this court.

Jacopo Anastagi

We know that Piero was in Rimini by 1451 because he dates a painting there in that year. His movement up the Adriatic coast from Ancona in late 1450 or early 1451 was prompted by the presence of Jacopo Anastagi in Sigismondo's court. As noted earlier, the social and familial networks of Sansepolcro remained decisive throughout Piero's life. His commissions, perhaps excluding those in Arezzo and Urbino, are best explained and understood as deriving from patrons or supporters from his native town. Early modern historians have shown how migrants retained social relationships and ties with others from their native towns and villages after years in the larger urban centers to which they had moved. Individuals from a town or village would settle in one neighborhood of an urban center and exchange various forms of support, including making recommendations for employment (in an age without newspaper want-ads or internet agencies).

Thus when the family of Jacopo (who was by then well established in Sigismondo's court) and that of Piero became united through marriage—Jacopo being the cousin once removed of Marco's bride, Giovanna—we can assume that Jacopo would have sought to promote Piero in Sigismondo's court. The marriage process customarily involved the male heads of Renaissance families in lengthy negotiations; these premarital consultations demonstrate how marriage joined not just the spouses but both families. Consultations between Marco and his father on the one hand and men of the Anastagi family on the other doubtless had taken place over months if not years prior to the marriage. In the church of the Badia and in the presence of representatives of the town's leading families (Cattani, Graziani, Carsidoni, Pichi), these negotiations led to a legal agreement between the men of the families specifying that the bride's father Antonio Anastagi would gain his daughter Giovanna's assent to marry Marco della Francesca. The men established Giovanna's dowry at 750 lire. They also agreed that the marriage would be under Roman law, which required the husband to provide a small reverse dowry (*donatio propter nuptias*). The bride or her family would receive the *donatio* as well as having her own dowry returned should Marco die first and without children. The negotiations then shifted to the Anastagi house near the Graziani Crossing, where the marriage was celebrated. Here Giovanna and Marco mutually swore before the notary that they desired to be married and then exchanged rings. We may assume there were festivities in the bride's home before Marco led Giovanna in a circuitous route to the Della Francesca home, a hundred yards from that of Giovanna, where the marriage would be consummated. This series of events united the Della Francesca and Anastagi families in an alliance, a *parentado*, in which each family recognized that it was in its interest that the other family prospered.

Jacopo Anastagi was not only Giovanna's cousin but also the most celebrated man in fifteenth-century Sansepolcro. This doctor of civil and canon law served as a close adviser and secretary to Sigismondo Malatesta, the lord of Rimini.[2] Hence, Jacopo was well placed to aid his fellow Sansepolcro citizens and especially family members. My reconstruction of the relationship between Jacopo and Piero can be summarized most economically in the following propositions: firstly, Jacopo introduced Piero to the Malatesta court in Rimini by commissioning Piero's *Saint Jerome and a Penitent* (see Pl. II). He then aided him in gaining the commission from Sigismondo to paint the young lord's portrait (see Illus. 4) and the fresco entitled *Sigismondo Malatesta Before His Patron Saint Sigismundus* (see Pl. III). The importance of Jacopo to Piero is immortalized in Piero's use of him as the model for a figure that recurs in *Saint Jerome and a Penitent*, the Misericordia altarpiece, *The Flagellation of Christ*, and the frescoes in Arezzo.

Jacopo's father and grandfather were notaries. Writing his last will just before his death in 1413, Jacopo's father made the fetus in his wife's womb, if male, his principal heir. As this heir and with no brothers, Jacopo had sufficient wealth to attend university (though which is not known), where he studied civil and canon law around 1430 and, although apparently absent from his birthplace, entered its guild of notaries and lawyers as a notary by 1432 and a doctor of law by 1435.[3] By late in that decade he had entered the Malatesta service, either that of Sigismondo Malatesta in Rimini or of Sigismondo's brother Malatesta Novello (Domenico) in Cesena. In 1442 Jacopo's prestige in Sansepolcro led him to be named one of the fifteen men heading the lists of members of the council of the people, though he seldom, if ever, participated actively in the politics there.

Jacopo Anastagi had entered the Malatesta circle as one of several notaries and civil lawyers competing for offices and for the favors of the brothers Sigismondo in Rimini and Malatesta Novello in Cesena. By the early 1440s Jacopo had become a permanent member of the Malatesta "family" in both cities. The competitiveness of the members of the court is evident in the chronicle written by one of these men, Gaspare Broglio Tartaglia, who identified Jacopo as his chief rival for influence over Sigismondo and as the architect of Sigismondo's foreign policy and eventual decline.[4]

Piero's New Stage: The Court of Sigismondo

Piero's work in Rimini is best evaluated in the context of the extraordinary court to which Jacopo introduced him. The Malatesta had ruled the city of Rimini on the eastern shore of Italy and much of the surrounding parts of Romagna and the Marches from at least the early thirteenth century as agents of the papacy, who claimed sovereignty over much of eastern central Italy in addition to Rimini itself (see Map 1). Sigismondo's uncle Carlo Malatesta had served as lord of Rimini in the name of the popes in the first quarter of the fifteenth century, balancing political exigencies with loyalty to the Church. He played an important role in resolving the division, or Great Schism, in the Christian Church, providing refuge for one of the men, Gregory XII, claiming to be Pope, and then persuading him to abdicate, thereby paving the way for the reunification of European Catholicism in 1417. Because Carlo had no sons to succeed him as papal representative and ruler of Rimini and nearby areas, he used his positive relationship with the Church officials to persuade the new Pope, Martin V, to legitimize his brother Pandolfo's sons: Galeotto Roberto, Sigismondo, and Malatesta Novello, who as bastards could not otherwise have received papal grants of political authority. Control of Rimini could thereby pass in 1429 to Pandolfo's oldest son Galeotto Roberto. Known more for his spirituality than his political success, Galeotto Roberto died in 1432. Authority over the region then passed to fifteen-year-old Sigismondo, who became lord of Rimini while his brother Malatesta Novello was apparently content to rule Cesena.

Sigismondo played a decisive role in Italian politics as a *condottiere* (mercenary military commander) before his miscalculations of political forces led to the waning of his power in the 1460s. Sigismondo forged a regional state in Rimini and its territory. He also supervised the reconstructions of Rimini's castle into the Rocca Malatestiana and of Rimini's church of San Francesco into a Christian temple with classical architecture, hence known today as the Tempio Malatestiano. Even before he took up his position as ruler of Rimini, Sigismondo had gained military successes as a twelve-year-old against local rebels in Cesena and towns near Rimini. When Sigismondo inherited Malatesta territory, Pope Eugenius IV confirmed him as the papal vicar, whereby he could exercise judicial, legislative, fiscal, and financial authority in Rimini, Fano, and nearby smaller communes. The year after Sigismondo gained control of Rimini, the Holy Roman Emperor, Sigismund, invested his young Malatesta namesake with the title of *cavaliere*.[5] In 1435 Eugenius IV appointed the seventeen-year-old Sigismondo one of his mercenary commanders. Sigismondo has been viewed as immoral and given to capricious violence by many of his contemporaries and subsequent historians. Still, his subjects apparently supported him in defeats as well as victories. His character cannot be easily determined, and we can only say that, although Pope Pius II damned him to hell while he was yet alive, Sigismondo's violence and apparent faithlessness to wives and allies were only slightly more flagrant than that of other *condottieri*-rulers of the Renaissance.[6]

Since he spent his childhood and youth in northern Italian cities, it is not surprising that when he attained power Sigismondo sought to model his rule and court on the successful examples of northern Italy, especially that of Ferrara. The men of these courts were captivated by the Gothic culture of France. The Malatesta linkage to Ferrara manifested itself in 1434 when Sigismondo married Ginevra, the daughter of the ruler of Ferrara, Niccolò d'Este. More importantly, he imitated the refined and elegant court of Leonello d'Este in the 1440s, borrowing men and practices first prominent in Ferrara. Tangible evidence of this is Sigismondo's commissioning of a medal from Pisanello (Antonio di Puccio Pisano) after that painter had coined one for Leonello d'Este. Sigismondo's admiration for the Gothic elegance of the court culture of Ferrara was defining and continued through to his death in 1468. The men of the court imitated French taste for romance and the courtly, exhibiting scant interest in the Florentine artistic revolution in the representation of space.[7]

It would be a mistake to look for a rational and consistent pattern in the life and acts of this boy-prince. As the *condottiere* Francesco Sforza remarked, Sigismondo habitually sought "new things."[8] That may mean nothing more than that he was capricious, and it is true he maintained the earlier Malatesta preference for the courtly and the Gothic. This identity as a courtly prince became a permanent part of his self-presentation to his subjects and other cities. But Sigismondo also sought inspiration from another cultural tradition, that of Roman history. He viewed himself as a descendant of the Roman general Scipio "Africanus"; on one occasion he saw an eagle on his tent and encouraged his soldiers into battle by explaining that in ancient Rome this portended victory and that its appearance derived from his ancestral relationship to Scipio.[9]

The lord of Rimini attempted to impress his subjects and visitors with his political and military power by restructuring and expanding the Rocca Malatestiana. In the fifteenth century an incoming ruler would often construct or reconstruct a castle or fortified palace in his most important city as a bulwark against invaders but also as protection against possible rebellions from his subjects. Even more important was the symbolism of the Rocca. It represented the power of the lord, and it is no accident that Sigismondo's Rocca carried a variant of his name. The castle represented the person of the lord of the city. Sigismondo commissioned the forging of a large number of coins, most associating him with the Rocca Malatestiana rather than with the Tempio. He also sought to have his image and deeds recorded in medals and paintings as a means of bringing him renown in his day and beyond.[10]

Sigismondo's world of knightly success on the battlefield and a warrior's life in the castle and court imitated many of the narrations of the medieval knightly romances. The lord's amorous adventures were exemplified in his relations with Isotta degli Atti, with whom he associated even before the death of his second wife. He and Isotta eventually married. In the 1440s Sigismondo, still in his twenties and early thirties, was the most sought-after mercenary commander in Italy. In a war between Florence and Venice on one side and an alliance led by the king of Naples on the other, Sigismondo initially fought with the latter group. But he soon abandoned his powerful patron Alfonso of Aragon, king of Naples, and changed sides to become the general of the Florentine army. Sigismondo's victorious campaign for Florence over Alfonso at Piombino (1448) enraged the king of Naples, whose enmity toward Sigismondo became a permanent part of the foreign policy of the Kingdom of Naples even beyond Alfonso's death in 1458.[11] During the triumphant campaign of 1447–48 Sigismondo apparently vowed to build a chapel in honor of his patron saint, Sigismundus, which led to the rebuilding of the church of San Francesco as the Tempio. Despite the fact that Sigismondo would construct a court of humanists, painters, architects, poets, and lawyers, and that he supported a specific form of humanist culture that emphasized astrology and neo-Platonic symbolism, the lord and patron at the center remained close to medieval myths of the brave warrior.

Sigismondo encouraged intense discussions on the architecture and iconography of the Tempio and especially on its chapels. One of his courtiers, Roberto Valturio, wrote that the participants in the discussion had been informed by "the deepest secrets of philosophy."[12] Many have asserted that Leon Battista Alberti served as Sigismondo's architect for the Tempio, but that remains unproven. It is only certain that Alberti participated in discussions with Sigismondo after the external portion of the Tempio had been completed. The building of the Tempio and the iconography of the chapels would have been supervised by Sigismondo, but the court group, consisting of Valturio, the Florentine sculptor Agostino di Duccio, the architect Matteo Pasti, and the poet Basinio, discussed many aspects of the building and decoration of the Tempio. This is confirmed in letters to and from Alberti on the construction of the interior and on structural problems within the Tempio in the mid-1450s. Piero entered Sigismondo's court in 1451 and could not have been expected to ignore the values of Sigismondo and his entourage. Whether he admired Sigismondo or his construction of his domain and persona, we cannot say, but Piero was drawn into this court with its mixture of several cultural traditions and the drive of its lord always interested in new things. Piero would have been expected as a painter to celebrate in images the political propaganda first conceived by Sigismondo and his court.[13]

By 1451 Piero's relative by marriage, Jacopo Anastagi, had become an important member of Sigismondo's court and administration. In 1440 Sigismondo had appointed him as his supervisor for the *gabelle* (a form of sales tax) in the town of Fano. By 1448 Jacopo was advising Sigismondo as a member of his court and was also in charge of the *gabelle* in Rimini. He retained the latter position at least through 1456, but already in 1451 he held the office of judge of the *gabelle* and appeals in Rimini, and he was "counselor and chief secretary" in Sigismondo's court.[14] This suggests that by 1451 Jacopo was in constant contact with Sigismondo. Even Jacopo's harshest contemporary critic and rival for influence with the ruler, the aforementioned Broglio Tartaglia, named Jacopo as Sigismondo's "intimate secretary."[15] Jacopo appears also to have been close to Isotta, serving as a witness when she purchased a large farm near Rimini in 1452.[16] As an example of his influence with Sigismondo and support of his family back in Sansepolcro, in late 1449 Jacopo persuaded Sigismondo to appoint his kinsman Anastagio Anastagi (his cousin once removed) as chief judge of the town of Pergola in the Marches, which was under Malatesta rule.[17] In this same period Sigismondo was searching for a painter, and it has been suggested that Jacopo recommended his fellow townsman and in-law, Piero della Francesca, to paint in the church of San Francesco in Rimini, which Sigismondo was in the process of transforming into a Renaissance *tempio* and symbol of Malatesta dynastic ambitions.[18]

Piero painted at least three works in Rimini in 1450–51, I believe, in the following order: *Saint Jerome and a Penitent* (see Pl. II), a portrait of Sigismondo (see Illus. 4), and the fresco of *Sigismondo Malatesta Before His Patron Saint Sigismundus* (see Pl. III). Further, it seems likely that Jacopo commissioned the earliest of the three as a means of demonstrating Piero's artistic excellence to Sigismondo.

Saint Jerome and a Penitent

The painting of *Saint Jerome and a Penitent* depicts the kneeling penitent, Jacopo Anastagi, on the right in profile with Jerome on the left, who turns his head at three-quarters to gaze sternly and accusingly at the penitent. Meanwhile, the penitent concentrates his attention on the cross. The diminutive size of the panel suggests that it was prepared for a small altar of a private chapel or a portable altar and probably was not intended for a public place. The penitent wears an elegant scarlet gown and appears anything but penitent. Though his palms are joined in prayer and he is kneeling, he conveys a sense of power and the vigor of young adulthood, more capable of addressing problems of this world than denying earthly ambitions. His clothing implies important social and political status rather than modest merchant activity. An intimate rapport is depicted between the penitent and the saint that emphasizes the penitent's deference but also his "confidence."[19] Piero portrays an important personage rather than a tortured penitent seeking release from spiritual anxiety and past sins.

Jacopo Anastagi should be regarded as the patron depicted in *Saint Jerome and a Penitent.* The identification of Jacopo as the patron-penitent is tied to arguments about his appearance in later paintings, but we need only consider here the evidence that points to Jacopo as the most likely person to have commissioned and to be represented in this panel. First, at the center of the panel is a view of a walled town that is generally agreed to be Sansepolcro, in part because Piero has painted the quadratic town as on one plane but nestled within the hillside. Sansepolcro was not the only small town with these characteristics, but Piero's depiction eliminates towns that were situated on the tops of hills, set on several uneven hills, or full in the valley. Piero also has placed a castle with a tower outside the city walls—a castle to be found in other paintings of his in which his native town appears.[20] The prominence of the town is a near certain indication that the patron-penitent was born in Borgo. A patron would want his town represented along with his likeness in a small altarpiece intended for his private room or chapel.

In the lower left-hand corner Piero placed an inscription, "Work of Pietro de Borgo San Sepolcro," suggesting that he painted it in a place other than Borgo.[21] Two of the other three paintings carrying Piero's name and "Burgo" (the Berlin *Saint Jerome* and *The Flagellation of Christ*) were painted outside of Sansepolcro, or at least they were never located there. The combination of the inscription of Piero's birthplace and his depiction of Borgo in *Saint Jerome and a Penitent* leads to the conclusion that the painting was commissioned by a person from Sansepolcro but not resident there when the painting was commissioned. This describes Jacopo Anastagi precisely.

Second, the *parentado* (family alliance) that resulted when Piero's brother Marco married Jacopo's cousin carried obligations for each family to aid the other. Marco's wife, Giovanna Anastagi, was a cousin once removed of Jacopo, but Jacopo made it clear in his last will that he regarded her brother Anastagio as his nearest kinsman. Anastagio was in fact the only male among the Anastagi (other than Jacopo and his sons). In his testament Jacopo wrote that, should he die with no living son, his palace in Sansepolcro should go to Anastagio.[22] Just as Jacopo in 1449 secured from Sigismondo the position of judge for Anastagio in Pergola, he would also promote the interests of his in-laws, the Della Francesca, by encouraging Piero to come to Rimini to take the commission to paint him with Saint Jerome.

Third, the representation of the kneeling man in the Venetian *Saint Jerome* indicates Jacopo as the penitent and thus the patron. In the early 1450s when this panel was painted, Jacopo would have been in his early forties (which appears to be the approximate age of the figure in the painting) and the leading figure in Sigismondo's court as judge and counselor. The penitent is not a weak, spiritually tormented sinner, but an active and powerful man of affairs. Piero endowed the penitent before Saint Jerome with a gown including professional insignia that serve to identify the person. The gown is scarlet, and a scarlet strip of cloth hangs from the right shoulder of the figure. The strip's short end can just be seen curling on the ground in front of the figure. This scarlet strip appears again in *The Flagellation of Christ* (see Pl. VIII) on the figure on the extreme right among the three men in the foreground, and it has attracted a great deal of attention. Why did Piero include this subtle touch of the scarlet strip on the figure in both paintings? One might respond that in painting the strip of slightly different scarlet, with perhaps more yellow in the scarlet than the figure's cloak in the Venetian *Saint Jerome*, Piero wanted to display his virtuosity in painting colors. But the same strip appears in *The Flagellation of Christ*, in which the figure's cloak is composed of totally different colors. The more probable answer is that he wanted to specify the professional status of the figure as a means of identifying and pleasing the patron. This scarlet strip designated a university graduate in either medicine or law. As mentioned above, Jacopo Anastagi possessed a degree in civil and canon law.[23]

A fourth argument that substantiates Jacopo as the patron is based on what might otherwise be conceived as a problem. Why did someone named Jacopo order a painting with Saint Jerome rather than a painting with his namesake San Jacopo (Saint James or Jacob)?[24] When one commissioned a devotional panel in the Quattrocento, the patron customarily appeared with his or her patron saint. First, it should be said that there were two saints with the name Jacopo, and neither was often seen as a patron saint unless it involved a pilgrimage. In addition, Saint Jerome was a favorite of humanists, and Jacopo purchased manuscripts by ancient authors and fifteenth-century humanists for his library, indicating his own interests in humanism. Thus Jacopo could be said to have two patron saints—one of the two disciples named James and also Saint Jerome. Jacopo identified with the latter and sought his intercessory powers, which were linked to Jerome's penitential vocation but also to his scholarly life in the desert.

The commissioning of Piero to paint the *Saint Jerome* panel fits a pattern of the last two decades of Jacopo's life (he died in 1465) whereby he imitated the behavior of his Malatesta masters. Sigismondo vowed to build a chapel in honor of his patron saint, which led to the chapel of San Sigismondo and ultimately to the restructuring of the church of San Francesco. Jacopo Anastagi apparently took a penitential vow leading to his commissioning Piero to paint the *Saint Jerome* panel. Sigismondo commissioned a funeral chapel for himself, and Isotta did the same. In this period Jacopo sought the identical form of commemoration in Sansepolcro as the Malatesta had done in Rimini. In 1453 "the most celebrated doctor of civil and canon law" Jacopo set aside 450 lire for a funeral chapel in the Badia of Borgo.[25] For this chapel, this time dedicated to San Jacopo, he provided a design for the builder, master Melchiore di Piero da Citerna. The design laid out precisely the form of the chapel. Within three years, Jacopo wrote to his representative in Borgo that he was concerned about the ability of the slender columns to support the weight of the upper part of the chapel.[26] It is intriguing that in late 1454 the builders of the Tempio were discussing an analogous weakness of the walls or arches of the chapels in the Tempio to support the weight of elements above.[27] Jacopo believed the planning and building of his chapel needed his supervision, exactly as Sigismondo supervised the construction of the chapels in the Tempio in Rimini.

As mentioned above, Sigismondo reconstructed the Rocca Malatestiana as a residence and a defensive castle for his family and for Rimini.[28] Jacopo Anastagi likewise reconstructed his family palace for himself and his family in Sansepolcro. In March 1460 Jacopo sent two stone carvers, who were working in Rimini on the new façade of the Tempio, to make a new façade for his palace in Borgo. Jacopo contracted with the masters of stone Antonio and Giusto, both sons of Giovannozzo from Settignano (the center of stone carvers near Florence), for a design on which he had written "it pleases me, it pleases me." The patron commissioned two windows, each with fluted columns, perhaps pilasters, with "worked" capitals. For this the stonemasons were to receive 22 florins. In a separate part of the contract masters Antonio and Giusto also agreed to construct two cornices and a third window on the façade of Jacopo's palace for an undetermined fee according to a design provided by "maestro Ottaviano," also in Rimini.[29] This Ottaviano was to determine the appropriate payment for the artisans. In a later document we learn that Antonio and Giusto constructed two more windows on an upper floor and completed the cornices.[30] Sigismondo and his counselors had designed a shell for the existing church of San Francesco as a way to construct a classical temple; Jacopo thereafter decided to immortalize himself in his own tomb and to classicize his existing palace with specific Roman architectural elements, columned windows and cornices.[31]

Finally, Jacopo also imitated the Malatesta brothers in creating a library in his palace in Sansepolcro. Malatesta Novello's most significant achievements were his creation of an elegant library building and a collection of manuscripts. The Biblioteca Malatestiana in Cesena was constructed in the period 1447–54 by Matteo Nuti, probably to designs by Alberti. Malatesta Novello commissioned and accumulated some of the most beautiful manuscripts of the Quattrocento.[32] Sigismondo also planned a library, but it was dispersed, probably to the Franciscans, and little can be known of its contents, except to say that it appears to have concentrated on manuscripts of authors in his court, especially the works of the humanist poet Basinio Basini and the military author Roberto Valturio.[33] In these same years Jacopo Anastagi imitated his Malatesta masters in forming a library of valuable manuscripts. Jacopo was a member of the inner intellectual elite of the court in Rimini, and his manuscripts indicate his powerful humanistic interests.[34] He possessed one of the largest libraries in Italy in the 1450s and 1460s with nearly two hundred titles. Over half of them were related to his study and practice of law, but the other titles show a broad knowledge of ancient writers and Quattrocento humanists. Among the ancient texts we note the authors who were largely unknown in the Middle Ages: Quintilian, Suetonius, Xenophon, Livy's *Decades*, Tacitus, and the epistles and *On Duties* of Cicero. Renaissance authors in Jacopo's library included Giovanni Boccaccio (*Genealogy of the Gods*), Francesco Filelfo's translation of the *Lives of Plutarch*, Petrarch's sonnets, triumphs, and epistles, Poggio Bracciolini's *On the Misery of the Human Condition* and *Book of Jokes*, as well as Leonardo Bruni's translations of Polybius and an epistle of Plato. Titles from the Rimini court include Filelfo's *Eulogy* of Sigismondo and Giannozzo Manetti's oration in 1453 as a Florentine ambassador to Sigismondo and his troops in Sant'Angelo in Vado.

The Portrait of Sigismondo Malatesta

At the time that Piero was painting *Saint Jerome and a Penitent* for Jacopo Anastagi, it is highly probable that Sigismondo commissioned him to paint his portrait in Rimini. In this year (1451) Sigismondo was at the height of his power: his Rocca Malatestiana had taken definitive form after more than a decade of construction; as *condottiere* he had led Florentine forces to victory over King Alfonso of Naples; he had been confirmed in his authority over Rimini by Pope Nicholas V in 1448; and he had begun the transformation of the church of San Francesco into the Tempio. Sigismondo wanted his earthly achievements to be celebrated and his image immortalized.[35] To this end, he commissioned a portrait of himself (Illus. 4).

The Sigismondo portrait is done in a mixture of the traditional egg tempera and oil as carriers of the pigments.[36] This is the first known instance of Piero's use of oil in his paintings. As noted earlier, Piero adopted this novel practice from Flemish painters, at

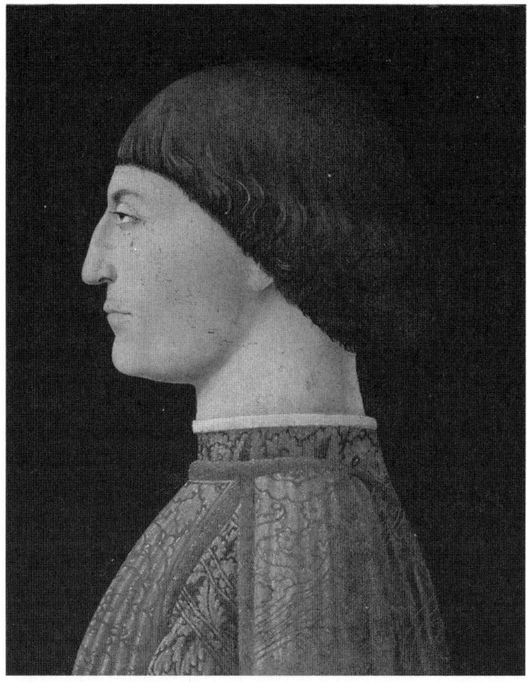

ILLUS. 4 Piero della Francesca, *Portrait of Sigismondo Malatesta*, 44 × 34 cm. Musée du Louvre, Paris

least one of whom, Roger van der Weyden, was present in Ferrara in the late 1440s. In the *Baptism* and the two paintings of Saint Jerome (in Berlin and Venice) Piero painted exclusively with egg tempera.[37] Indeed, one of the markers for the movement to the second phase of Piero's career is the introduction of oil-based paints to his palette. However, this raises a question: if Piero had come in contact with the use of oil in Ferrara in the late 1440s and employed it in the Sigismondo portrait (dated here in 1451), why did he not use the oil in his two panels of Saint Jerome, which carry the dates of 1450 and 1451? Given the current state of research, the most that can be said is that when Piero found a need to increase the luminescence of Sigismondo's presence in the portrait, he recognized that a mixture of tempera and oil could realize this enhancement better than the single base of tempera.

Piero has painted Sigismondo in full profile with finely etched lines to define his face, a cylindrical neck, and a crisp hairline curving around to the back of his neck. With his elegant doublet and rigid pose, Sigismondo appears as a young prince certain of his purpose and fully resolved to undertake difficult enterprises. Piero did not emphasize Sigismondo's military successes by clothing him in armor; instead, he chose to construct the portrait of a young lord emotionally untouched by his experiences of leading the armies of Venice and Florence to victories. Sigismondo's eye stares directly ahead so that he appears as fixed and as distanced as a figure on a medal.

The author of a study of the portrait in the Italian Renaissance, Joanna Woods-Marsden, has written eloquently on Piero's portrait of Sigismondo, noting the "volumetric substantiality" of the portrait that evokes the sitter's "determination and headstrong sense of self." Piero gave the young ruler "weight and gravitas by constructing his head as an almost perfect semicircle and by outlining his stern features starkly against a continuous black ground."[38] The portrait was probably intended to be seen by Sigismondo, visiting princes, the intimates of his court, and on a few occasions more publicly by his Rimini subjects. To facilitate this, it would have been placed in the Rocca Malatestiana, where courtiers and visiting dignitaries could see how Piero elevated his patron to the status of a prince—which dignity Sigismondo never in fact achieved—in a profile portrait that in the Quattrocento was associated with images of Roman emperors known from ancient coins.[39]

Piero used the same cartoon for the head of Sigismondo in the portrait and in the votive fresco (see Pl. III) in the Tempio, even if he had to vary the dimensions of the cartoon from the first of the paintings to the second. This adjusting of the proportions of cartoons from their exact or earlier dimensions became one of Piero's characteristic practices.[40] In spite of the alterations, the heads in both paintings have almost the same measurements. The art historian Michel Laclotte has argued most convincingly that the portrait was painted first based on the cartoon and then the cartoon was employed in the large fresco.[41] The close relationship between the two works is evident from the slight *pentimenti* (alterations) in the fresco. On the fresco Piero etched the same head from the cartoon (using a sharp implement), but when he painted Sigismondo's head he rethought the shape and extended the height of the skull or hair.

In an analogous *pentimento* on the fresco Piero readjusted his painting of the neck of Sigismondo's doublet, shifting it slightly, as is evident from an earlier outline that he left visible.

Sigismondo Malatesta Before His Patron Saint Sigismundus

This fresco was originally located in the Chapel of Relics, a small cell or chapel along the right side of the nave in the Tempio Malatestiana, but it has recently been detached and moved into the right transept (Pl. III). It is Piero's most important work in Rimini. By 1451, when he arrived in the town, Sigismondo and Isotta had already constructed their two large funeral chapels on the right side of the Tempio. In a 1449 letter to Giovanni de' Medici, Sigismondo had stated that "the chapels" were constructed but were not yet prepared for frescoes. They would have been by 1451, but by then Sigismondo had had a change of mind and had decided the two large chapels were not to be frescoed. Perhaps he followed Alberti's advice that chapel walls were better furnished with sculpture than with frescoes.

Piero instead painted in the small cell or chapel between the two funeral chapels. Why Sigismondo assigned Piero this small space once reserved for relics is unclear. It has been argued that Piero already had a design in hand for a large fresco in Sigismondo's funeral chapel, but when Sigismondo assigned the smaller space of the Chapel of Relics, the painter chose to use the design there. This would explain why Piero's fresco originally appeared somewhat crowded and why he could not fit all his painting on the horizontal wall of the chapel. His use of the pre-existing design forced Piero to place the upper horizontal painted cornice of his fresco above the chapel's vertical wall and on the curving lower portion of its barrel vault.[42]

The nature of court life and the role that Sigismondo played in his commissions may have complicated Piero's planning of the fresco. There is plentiful evidence that Sigismondo insisted on playing the defining role in the initial phases of his artistic commissions. Many of the decisions for the reconstruction of the Rocca Malatestiana were made by Sigismondo himself. In the Tempio's construction, Matteo Pasti was the architect, with Alberti as a late adviser. Agostino da Duccio was responsible for directing and creating the sculpture. However, many of the decisions for the Rocca and the Tempio were made by committee, with several men from the court involved in the complicated reconstruction of the church and the accompanying program of political propaganda and religious symbolism. As patron, Sigismondo doubtless did more than inform Piero of his desire for a fresco of himself and his patron saint. Although there is no documentary proof, Sigismondo probably demanded that his image be in the center of the painting and that the fresco include an image of the Rocca Malatestiana.

In the fresco Sigismondo Malatesta kneels before his enthroned patron saint, Saint Sigismundus, king of the Burgundians from 516 to 523. Piero heightens the significance of the figure by combining elements of this saint with those of the recently deceased

Holy Roman Emperor and king of Hungary, Sigismund (*d.* 1437), who had spent time in Italy in the 1420s and 1430s and had granted Sigismondo Malatesta the title of *cavaliere* (knight) in Rimini in 1433. Italians would have known the image of the Emperor Sigismund from his presence there and elsewhere in Italy. Combining attributes of two individuals or portraying an individual with the features of another was to become a common practice with Piero, expanding meaning by introducing ambiguity or double personages. Here the once prominent red in the badly damaged hat of the regal figure would have suggested imperial command, as would the globe in the figure's left hand that represented his theoretical universal authority. The shape of Sigismund's hat resembles the hat in a pencil drawing of the emperor attributed to Pisanello.[43] This shows the emperor with an ample but undivided beard; Piero also depicted a full beard in his fresco of Sigismundus but divided it from the chin downward in two parts. This split beard was to become a recurring motif in Piero's paintings.

In the pose of Sigismondo Malatesta kneeling before Saint Sigismundus with joined hands, Piero incorporates two iconographic traditions, one religious and the other political:[44] the religious motif of the figure entering a monastic order on the one hand and the political motif of the vassal proclaiming his subordination to his lord on the other. Images of this latter kind were usually horizontal, wider than they were high. Like the kneeling figure in the panel of the penitent before Saint Jerome (see Pl. II), Sigismondo displays little penitence. What is primarily represented here is (political) subordination rather than (religious) devotion or penitence. The positioning of Sigismondo's folded hands suggests that he is about to be granted a knighthood, that he is paying feudal homage to his patron. But Sigismondo's subordinate position is attenuated by his placement in the center of the picture frame; donors and subordinates were traditionally diminished in size and relegated to the side.[45] Though the fresco was originally located in the Chapel of Relics in the Tempio and therefore not easily viewed by his subjects of Rimini, it served to elevate Sigismondo's position from that of local lord to a princely figure associated with the emperor or the Burgundian king. The political reading of the fresco is confirmed by the oculus (round window) on the right, in which the Rocca Malatestiana is depicted asserting the power of Sigismondo. In the *condottiere's* reconstruction and in Piero's image the castle served as a residence, a refuge in time of invasion, but also as a symbol of Sigismondo's authority over his subjects.

In the religious iconographic tradition, painters depicted a donor kneeling in homage to his or her saint or the Madonna. This became one of the most popular devotional images of the Renaissance and had a religious significance. Painters of this tradition represented a smaller donor with a significantly larger saint in a hierarchical and vertical format. Despite our political reading of Piero's image, a fifteenth-century viewer would at least initially have seen a donor expressing devotion or beseeching the patron saint for aid. Piero brought these two traditions together, playing on the double or ambiguous meaning of the pose, heightening the political tradition with the powerful religious tradition. He mediates between the older vertical and horizontal traditions with a strong diagonal line demonstrating hierarchical relationships and faithfulness, which begins with the two dogs in the lower right and continues through the subordinate ruler of Rimini to the saint-king in the upper left.

There is an inscription on the lower cornice that identifies the two individuals present and proclaims Piero as the artist. He has painted the words "SANCTUS SIGISMUNDUS PANDULFUS MALATESTA PETRI DE BURGO OPUS MCCCCLI" ("St Sigismundus, Pandolfo Malatesta, work of Pietro from Borgo, 1451"). Instead of writing "Sanctus Sigismundus" and "Sigismundus Pandulfus," Piero chose not to repeat "Sigismundus," allowing the "SIGISMUNDUS" to serve a double function, designating both the saint and the lord of Rimini.[46] This would link the two men closely and remind viewers that the saint was reincarnated in his follower. In addition, in the circular cornice around the oculus with the representation of the Rocca, Piero has written "CASTELLUM SISMONDUM ARIMINESE MCCCCXLVI" ("Castle Sismondo of Rimini, 1446"). We should note that the castle of Rocca has its own name, a variant of Sigismondo's name, and that the date probably recalls the completion of the Rocca's reconstruction. All these letters are written in beautiful humanistic capital letters, each finely articulated in its own space. The lettering, the two square fluted pilasters, and the marble decorated cornices on the sides and above (complete with beautiful hanging garlands) all suggest a classical setting.

By 1452, after his presence in Ancona and at the courts of Ferrara and Rimini, Piero had developed several characteristics that were to reappear throughout the remainder of his career. Antonio Paolucci identifies his Rimini stay as a profound moment in Piero's painting of architectural elements. "The figures of Piero now found a fit ambience of columns, pilasters, and pediments of incomparable gravity and of proportioned beauty. His palate of color found a sufficient expression . . . in those geometric vestments of white marble, porphyry, green serpentine, destined to provide the setting, after Rimini, in many paintings."[47] As in painted architecture, so in more formal elements, Piero had become a mature artist, re-imagining iconographic traditions and combining two personages or poses in one portrait as a means of enlarging significance. His humanistic capital letters, as found in the two *Jerome* panels and the Rimini fresco, are employed again in *The Resurrection of Christ* (see Pl. VII) and *The Flagellation of Christ* (see Pl. VIII). Also in execution Piero employs new elements, for example using cartoons extensively for the first time. It was in this period also that he mastered the profile portrait and found a way to bridge the gap between naturalistic depiction and his patron's desire for political propaganda.[48] Acceptance and articulation of the prince's political program will appear again in Piero's paintings from Urbino. We have also seen that, along with his customary tempera, Piero introduced oil-based paints on the wooden panel of Sigismondo's portrait. His experiment with oil endowed Sigismondo's portrait with a high sheen and bestowed the ruler with great presence and vivacity. These experiments intensified hereafter, as Piero introduced oil onto frescoes as well as in paintings on wooden panels.

Piero's experiences in the two Adriatic cities also enriched his pictorial and intellectual imagination. His earlier painting of *The Baptism of Christ* addressed a traditional religious subject, while the three Rimini paintings embody wider and more secular concerns, especially representing the political propaganda of their patrons. Piero's associations with Sigismondo, Jacopo Anastagi, and perhaps others in Ferrara and Ancona seem to have challenged him to conceptualize his art in a broader framework of political ideas coupled with humanism.

***

In a letter to Giovanni de' Medici in 1449, Sigismondo suggested that he was prepared to pay a substantial annuity to retain a master painter for an extended period. Given this possibility and the success and excitement of Sigismondo's court, why did Piero leave Rimini soon after 1451? Assuming it was Piero's decision and not that of his patron, there are several possible explanations for his departure. Sigismondo appears to have accepted Alberti's earlier dictum forbidding frescoes in churches in favor of painted altarpieces and sculptural decorations. The ruler of Rimini did not commission a single fresco after Piero's in the Tempio; rather Sigismondo systematically added sculptural works to the chapels and nave of the Tempio. On the other hand, it is quite possible that, had he stayed in Rimini, Piero might have been commissioned to execute panel paintings for the chapels being constructed in the Tempio, as Fra Filippo Lippi was to be commissioned to paint the altarpiece for the Chapel of San Girolamo in 1454. Or Sigismondo might have retained Piero to paint an extensive fresco series in the Rocca Malatestiana, as others had painted in urban castles in Ferrara, Mantua, and elsewhere.[49] More speculatively, Piero may have found the hectic quality of the court where the ruler habitually sought "new things" no longer tolerable. Alternately, the commission to fresco the large high altar chapel (Cappella Maggiore) of the church of San Francesco in Arezzo may have been offered to Piero while he was still in Rimini. This commission would have been too large and significant for Piero to refuse. One or more of these explanations may aid us in understanding why he left the Malatesta court.

CHAPTER 4

Piero in Arezzo

The Legend of the True Cross

In late 1451 or 1452 Piero left the Rimini court for Arezzo. On his way, he may have passed through Sansepolcro and may have begun to prepare the Misericordia altarpiece or painted the *Saint Julian* fresco. Upon arrival in Arezzo, he began preparing a fresco cycle that surpasses all his other works in size and conception: *The Legend of the True Cross* in the high altar chapel (Cappella Maggiore) of the church of San Francesco (Pl. IV; see Illus. 5–7).[1] In these murals Piero demonstrates his mature ability to organize large spaces with multiple meanings and to conceptualize human and Divine history on an epic scale. In this he was aided by two visits to Rome that elevated both his formal and narrative abilities, carrying him into what I am calling the "second phase" of his development.

The Bacci Family and the Friars and Church of San Francesco

When Piero began painting the cycle in the 1450s the city of Arezzo was in a period of demographic and economic decline. For much of the fourteenth century the city had been independent, but Arezzo lost its political autonomy in 1384, when it was seized by the Florentines. Arezzo had been celebrated for its university, but the university no longer existed when Piero spent several years there in the 1450s and 1460s. Despite this, the town was the birthplace of many of the leading humanists of the century, probably the result of its excellent grammar school, similar but superior to the one in Sansepolcro.

The Franciscans had had a presence in Arezzo for over two centuries when Piero began painting in their church. In 1211 Saint Francis had witnessed the spectacle of devils in the sky above the town celebrating the civil conflict they had caused. He asked his companion Silvestro to exorcise these devils. Silvestro did so successfully, and the devils fled, leaving Arezzo in peace. Francis then saw a golden Cross in the heavens that encompassed the world with its arms. In the minds of contemporaries this vision established a close relationship between the symbol of the Cross and Saint Francis (and thus between the Cross and later Aretine Franciscans). Following the banishment of the devils from Arezzo, the saint established a community of friars just outside the city walls. Within a few years the Franciscans of Arezzo had been invited to take residence in the city, where they founded the present-day church of San Francesco. Building followed in spurts, in part because the apse was destroyed in the fourteenth century, necessitating a rebuilding of the area of the high altar chapel. Plans for frescoes for the chapel come into the historical record in the early fifteenth century when the Bacci family proposed painting its walls.[2]

Piero's activities in Arezzo revolved around the Bacci family and the Franciscan friars. The Bacci were one of the few wealthy merchant families in Arezzo, perhaps because Florence dominated the region's trade. They trafficked in spices, cloth, and doubtless other goods. They maintained close relations with the Franciscans throughout the fifteenth century, funding an annual meal on Saint Francis' feast day for them, donating oil and candles for Corpus Christi celebrations, and serving as lay supervisors and procurators for the church and convent. The patron of the chapel, Baccio (Bartolomeo) Bacci, produced cloth and owned substantial property in and around Arezzo. This wealth provided for the painting of the high altar chapel of the church of San Francesco. In his testament of 1416, Baccio required his sons Tommaso, Girolamo, and Francesco as heirs "to make to be painted and to be decorated honorably with figures the Cappella Maggiore of the church of San Francesco."[3] Baccio died soon after writing his testament, without indicating the exact amount he required his heirs to pay for the chapel, but the sons' later tax reports specified a total between 500 and 600 florins. Baccio's commission for the high altar does not appear to have been motivated by remorse or guilt for his merchant life (as was sometimes the case with other donors), nor was it the result of a vow. Baccio's gift can best be attributed to his devotion to Saint Francis and his friars, rather than to penitence.

Painting in the Cappella Maggiore began in September 1447, when Baccio's sons sold a vineyard from his testamentary bequest for 69 florins; "all the said [sum] has been given to the painter, which he has taken to paint our high altar chapel of San Francesco."[4] There is near unanimous agreement that the payment went to the Florentine painter Bicci di Lorenzo. Given his advanced age and that the painting was in the highest and most difficult place in the vault, it is probable that the pace was slow and the work largely in the hands of Bicci's assistants. The team completed the four Evangelists in the vault as well as a *Last Judgment* and prophets on the upper portion of the triumphal arch over the high altar. This initial phase ended in May 1452 with the death of Bicci, making this the earliest possible date for Piero to have begun his work in the Cappella Maggiore.

We do not know whether it was the Bacci family or the Franciscan friars who commissioned first Bicci di Lorenzo to paint in San Francesco and later Piero della Francesca to finish the project.[5] The question of how the Bacci or the friars heard of Piero and his abilities remains unanswered. Whatever link Piero may have had with someone in Arezzo, it was not so compelling that the Bacci or the Franciscans gave the commission first to Piero rather than to Bicci di Lorenzo.

Dating the Painting of the Arezzo Frescoes

Two fundamental questions confront us in considering Piero's painting of the frescoes in Arezzo. First, when did he begin the commission and when did he finish it? Second, are there two different phases of stylistic development exhibited in these frescoes? As we shall see, the question of chronology is intimately bound up with the second question: the evolution of Piero's style and techniques over this period.

The precise dates for the Cappella Maggiore fresco cycle are a topic of debate. But we do know that Piero's earliest possible start date is 1452 and that 1466 is the latest possible finishing date. In the later year officials of the confraternity of the Annunziata of Arezzo commented that Piero would be available for a commission because he had completed his work in the Cappella Maggiore of San Francesco.[6] It is now possible to shorten this fourteen-year time span to a more manageable period of 1452 to 1458 or early 1460, interrupted by Piero's two trips to Rome (1453–54 and 1458–59). This is possible because it is now generally understood that Piero began the project in the year of Bicci's death (1452). We then have documentary evidence suggesting that, after returning to Tuscany from a second trip to Rome in the summer or autumn of 1459, Piero proceeded to spend all or most of the next three years in Sansepolcro, which means that he could only have spent a few months in Arezzo over the winter of 1459–60 after returning from his second trip to Rome—enough, at most, to apply some finishing touches to his work there.[7]

Moreover, as we shall see, there is compelling evidence of a distinct development in Piero's style over the course of his work on this cycle. This change of style is most plausibly explained by the influence of the time that Piero spent in Rome during the 1450s. The majority of the cycle is painted in this new, more highly developed style that integrates elements from his Roman sojourn. It is hard to believe that Piero managed to complete all of this work in the few short months he spent in Arezzo in the winter of 1459–60, as some have asserted, after returning from his second trip to Rome and before moving back to Sansepolcro. It seems far more plausible that the new style in which the majority of the cycle is painted was the product of his longest sustained period in Arezzo, in the mid-1450s, between his two trips to Rome. This leads to the conclusion that Piero's first visit to Rome in 1453–54 was decisive, prompting the significant changes in his stylistic development that seem to have occurred during the painting of the cycle.

Looking at the Arezzo Frescoes

The chronology suggested above is in tune with the broad consensus of art historians, who now agree that Piero painted in the Cappella Maggiore in Arezzo before and after his mid-decade stay in Rome and that the substantial differences in the style of sections of the frescoes in San Francesco can be explained by what he absorbed in Rome, where he would have been exposed to the Eternal City's antiquities.[8] The art historian Roberto

Longhi sketched out in a few words "a certain evolution" between the scenes in the two lunettes (the uppermost sectors of the left and right walls) of the Cappella Maggiore and the lower remainder of the frescoes, especially those of the middle tier of the *Visit of the Queen of Sheba to Solomon* (Illus. 6). The lunettes of the *Death of Adam* (Illus. 7) and *The Restitution of the Cross* (Illus. 5), he said, retained "linear outlines having a distinctly Florentine cast" that are smoothed over in later lower frescoes with a "seamless conjoining of areas of color." According to this explanation, Piero integrated values and techniques garnered on his encounter with antiquity in Rome that are not evident in the lunettes but are in the lower scenes. Piero's close observation of Roman statues and buildings liberated him from placing architectural framing around specific scenes, taking from Roman public monuments an understanding of their compositional unity and from sarcophagi how scenes could be knotted together in a continuous narrative.[9] There are vast differences between the ways that art historians have viewed this evolution. For example, some believe that Piero's stay in Rome occurred after he had finished one lunette, but there is general agreement that either one or both lunettes were completed first and the lower parts of the cycle were finished later and that the two parts display different styles.

In addition to the stylistic evolution, changes in technique suggest a lapse of time between the execution of the painting in the lunettes and in the remainder of the chapel. In the earliest paintings (especially *The Restitution of the Cross* in the left lunette; see Illus. 5) Piero frescoed the sky with a grey base, and represented the clouds with white paint. In the remainder of the chapel he placed an azure tint on the white plaster to depict the sky and left clouds unpainted, thereby exposing the white *intonaco* (the uppermost stratum of the plaster). Another change occurred in the depiction of the leaves on the trees; in the *Restitution* lunette Piero placed a dark undercoating and then added green pigments for the leaves, all in "true fresco" (otherwise known as wet fresco, in which the pigment is applied to the plaster while it is still wet). On the other lunette and on the lower portions Piero painted *only* the trunk and branches in true fresco while adding the leaves *a secco* (a technique in which a mixture of pigments is applied to an already hardened layer of dried painted fresco).

Although there is not unanimous agreement on the nature of Piero's treatment of the frescoes, recent researchers have agreed that there were technical as well as stylistic changes after a Roman trip in 1453–54 interrupted Piero's work in Arezzo.[10] As we shall see in Chapter 6, Rome in the 1450s had begun to merge from its earlier stupor when violence was so endemic that popes were unable to live there. Piero was part of an influx in that decade of architects and painters from Tuscany, who transformed the urban structure and painting traditions by bringing Florentine ideas to the ancient city. Changes in Piero's style and technique in the Arezzo cycle suggest his presence in Rome, as does Vasari's assertion that Piero painted frescoes for Pope Nicholas V (*r.* 1447–55) on an upper floor of the Vatican and in competition with Bramante or "Bramantino"—Vasari used both names. Their frescoes were destroyed when Pope Julius II commissioned Raphael to paint in the so-called Stanze (Rooms). We know

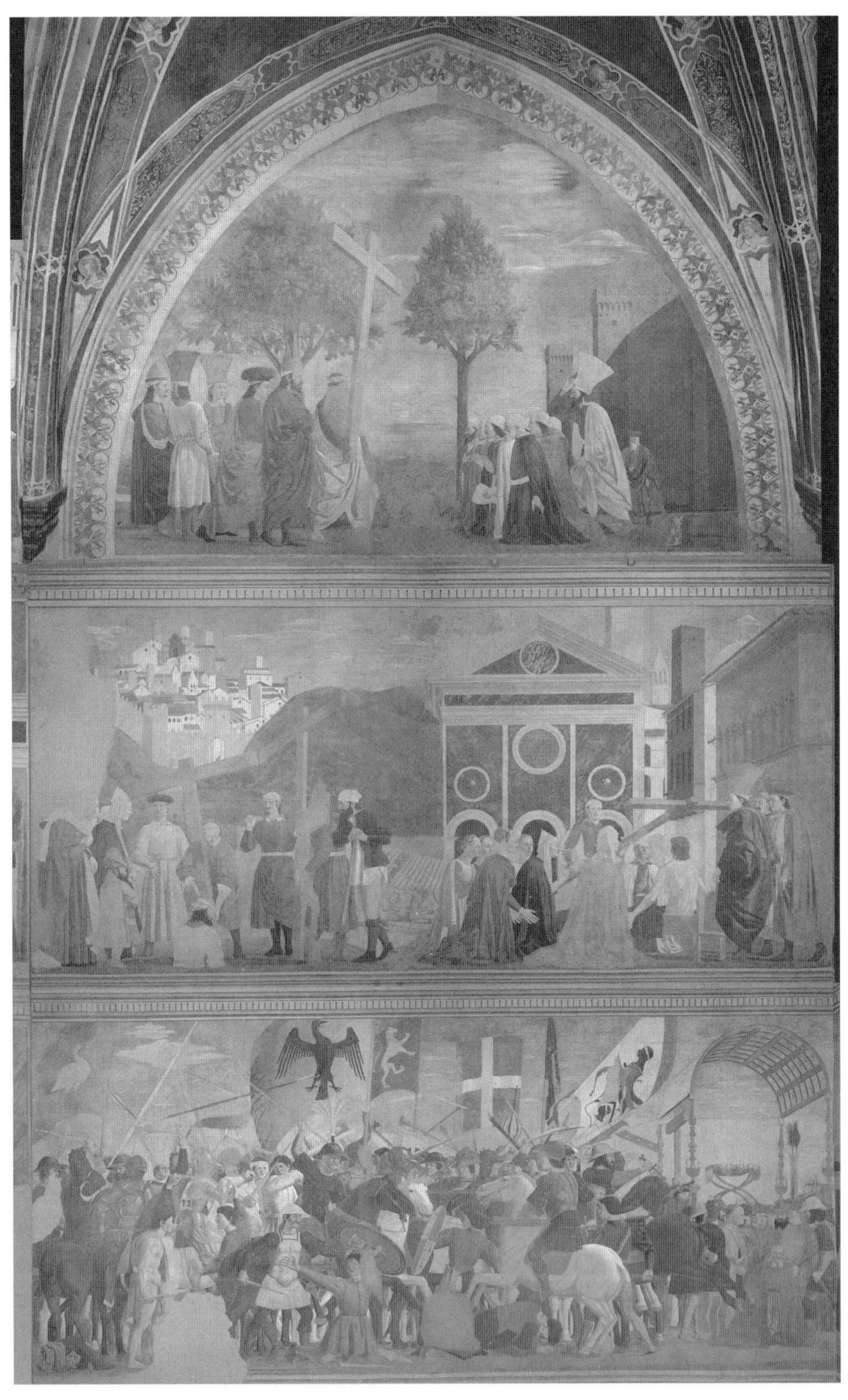

ILLUS. 5 Piero della Francesca, *The Legend of the True Cross*, High Altar Chapel, left wall, Church of San Francesco, Arezzo

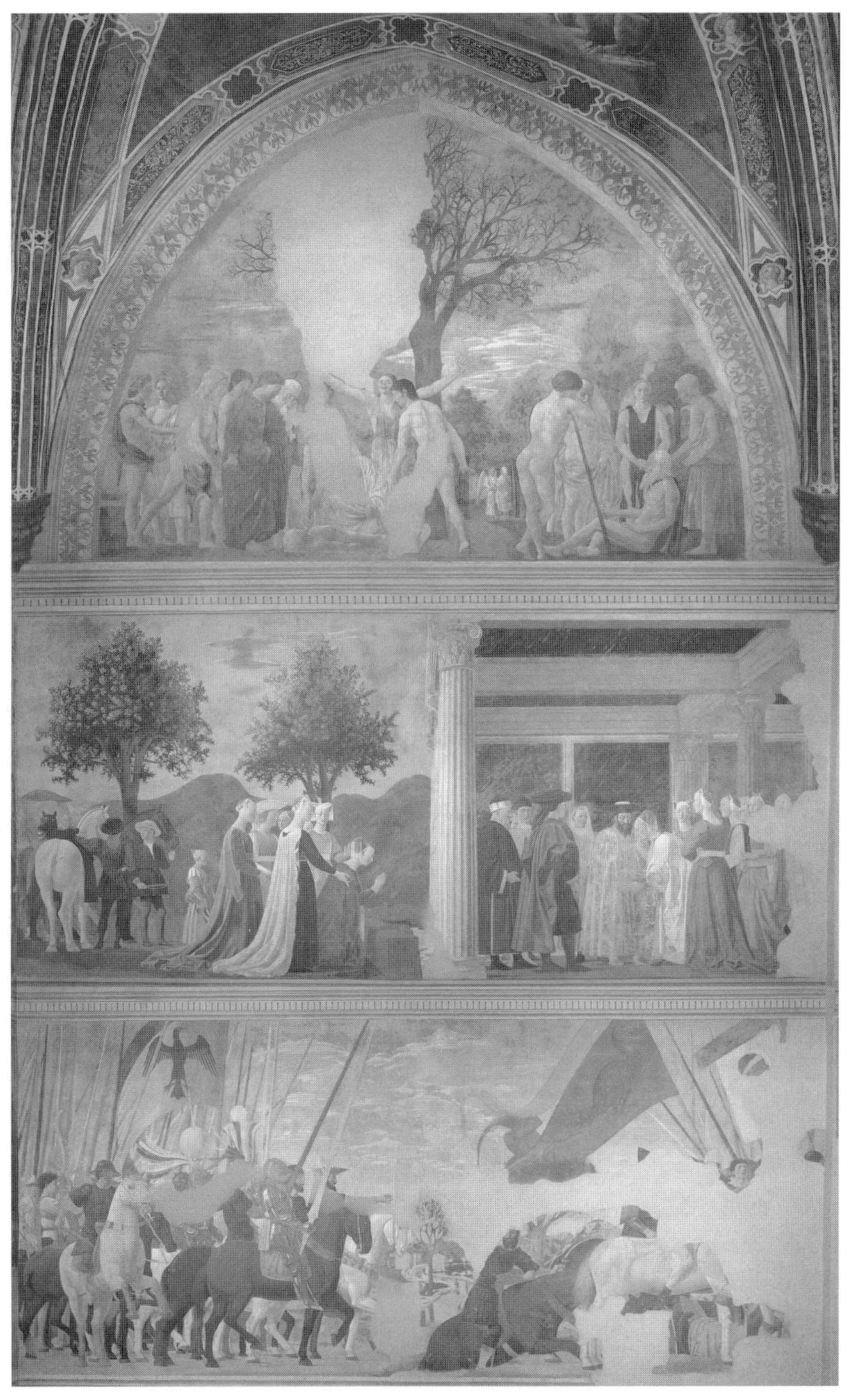

ILLUS. 6 Piero della Francesca, *The Legend of the True Cross*, High Altar Chapel, right wall, Church of San Francesco, Arezzo

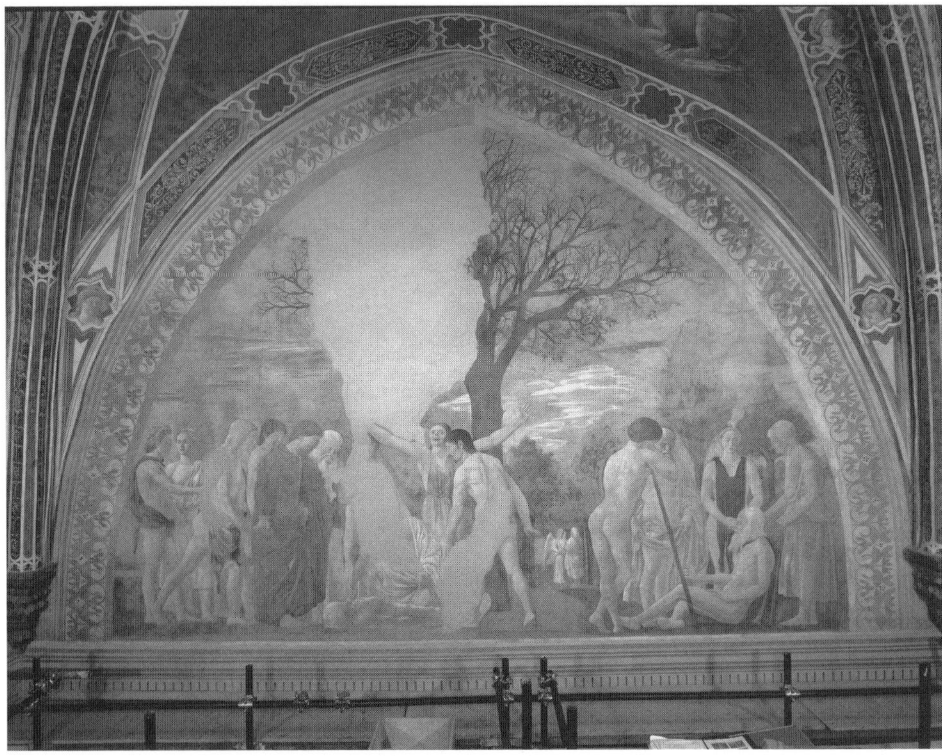

ILLUS. 7 Piero della Francesca, *Death of Adam*, *The Legend of the True Cross*, 3.9 × 7.47 m. Right Lunette, Church of San Francesco, Arezzo

nothing about what Piero was asked to paint, but we know that Bramante placed portraits of great men in one of these Stanze. Vasari's statement has often been discounted because of his lack of precision in identifying the "Bramante" or "Bramantino" that he mentions, and because the Bramante that we all know was much younger than Piero. It has therefore been assumed that Vasari misattributed Piero's documented later project for Pope Pius II in 1458–59 to Nicholas' period. However, an analysis of a list of the portraits of great men attributed to Bramante demonstrates that they all depicted friends and allies of Nicholas—and were either enemies of Pius or otherwise unrelated to him.[11] We can deduce from this that Vasari was accurate in his comments on the painter and, by implication, on Piero. The added fact that the shield of Nicholas survives in the Vatican rooms where Vasari said Piero and the portrait painter, (and eventually Raphael) worked leads many researchers to accept Vasari as accurate in stating that Piero painted for Nicholas in the Vatican Palace. Given his commissions elsewhere, Piero's first Vatican painting therefore occurred late in 1453.

It is probable that during this period Piero also frescoed the cross vaults of the chapel of Cardinal D'Estouteville (or the chapel of Saint Michael and Saint Peter) in Santa

Maria Maggiore, Rome (Illus. 8). The chapel's cross vault had fourteenth-century stone ribs that divided the space into four compartments. Piero painted each compartment with an azure blue sky, stars, and an Evangelist with his symbol. Other than Saint Luke, much of the remaining painting of the Evangelists is indecipherable. But what is clear is the overall geometrical planning within the pre-existing stone ribs, each decorated with a ribbon of leaves bordered by acanthus leaves. Piero's spatial imagination is evident in the overall design of the vault and in the substantial form of Saint Luke, who sits with his bull symbol on a cloud. The art historian Marilyn Lavin has commented on the experimental nature of the paint preparation, typical of Piero in the early 1450s, whether he was using oil (as in Sigismondo's Louvre portrait; see Illus. 4) or tempera *a secco* placed over frescoes, as in Arezzo. In the chapel of Saint Michael and Saint Peter there is liberal use of tempera applied to a ground composed of fine plaster, marble dust, and glue. This permitted Piero to depict fine details—as in the gold trimmings of Saint Luke's cloak and in the stylus and ink cup in his hands. Most critics suggest that Piero broke off this project and the painting was completed by one of his assistants or an Umbrian or Roman painter. In all probability, his early departure was due to the demands of the Pichi family that he return to Borgo to attend to his Misericordia commission.

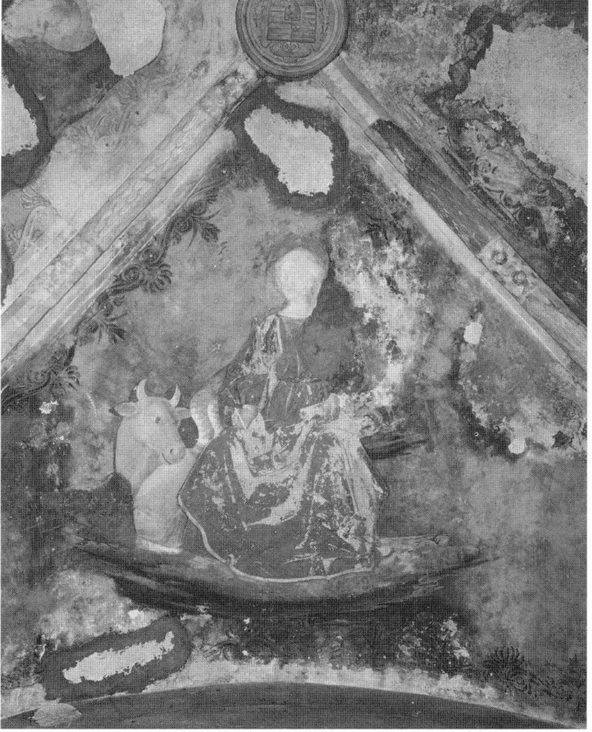

ILLUS. 8 Piero della Francesca, *Saint Luke*, Chapel of Cardinal D'Estouteville, Church of Santa Maria Maggiore, Rome

The art historian Antonio Pinelli has re-examined all the evidence on the dating of the Arezzo frescoes and has put forward a synthesis convincing in all respects but one. First, he accepts a date of 1452 as the moment Piero began the San Francesco frescoes. He follows Vasari's account that Piero painted in the Vatican late in the papacy of Nicholas V, and adds that Piero painted the Roman chapel of Saint Michael and Saint Peter in Santa Maria Maggiore in 1455 and then returned to Sansepolcro and Arezzo in that year. He believes that Piero finished the San Francesco frescoes by 1459. Pinelli examines a painting by Giovanni di Piamonte, an assistant to Piero in the Cappella Maggiore in Arezzo, who painted in the rural church of Santa Maria del Carmine in Morocco in Val di Pesa near Florence. In this painting Giovanni and his assistant demonstrated knowledge of Piero's frescoes in the middle and lower levels of the Cappella Maggiore in Arezzo. Pinelli concludes that it is most probable that Giovanni's painting dates from 1459–60 and hence that Piero had finished the Arezzo frescoes by that date.[12]

Pinelli's synthesis is compelling, except for his dating of Piero's Roman work to 1455. Pinelli maintains that Piero broke off his work in Santa Maria Maggiore in that year, when the Pichi family recalled the painter to Sansepolcro to work on the Misericordia altarpiece. In fact, it is now certain that the Pichi family recalled Piero to Borgo in January 1454, not 1455.[13] The problems in Pinelli's interpretation can be eliminated by moving the presence of Piero in Rome to 1453–54. We can organize all Piero's known activities in these years most economically and persuasively in the following statements: Piero would have started in Arezzo in 1452 and painted the lunettes there for a year until receiving a call to Rome by Nicholas V to paint in the Vatican and then in Santa Maria Maggiore. He would then have remained in Rome until he returned to Sansepolcro in response to pressure from the powerful Pichi family, who wanted the Misericordia project to be initiated or continued. Piero definitely appeared in Borgo by September 1454, when he contracted with the friars of Sant'Agostino to paint their high altar polyptych. The demands of the Pichi would explain why Piero left the frescoes in the vault of the chapel of Saint Michael and Saint Peter in Santa Maria Maggiore unfinished in early 1454. This dating of Piero's first presence in Rome to 1453–54 would allow for a change in Piero's style between that of the upper portions and of the remaining lower two-thirds portions of the Arezzo frescoes. Those who would hold that Piero went to Rome only in 1458–59 and then finished the fresco cycle are surely incorrect as there would not have been sufficient time for Piero to paint all the lower two-thirds of *The Legend of the True Cross* in the period 1459–60. As we shall see, Piero was occupied in Borgo in late 1460 and in the following two years. In my reconstruction Piero painted two-thirds of the *Legend* over the years 1454 to 1458 just after his first Rome visit, with some possible finishing touches over the winter of 1459–1460 after his second Rome stay.

Choices in the High Altar Chapel

Who chose *The Legend of the True Cross* as the overall subject and who chose the narratives of the specific scenes? In response, we can most probably eliminate the lay patrons (the Bacci). Had they taken the leading role in the conception of the cycle, we might have expected them to have recorded their choice of the chapel's subject in wills or other contracts that would have made their choices legally binding on the Franciscan friars. But no evidence for such legally binding documents exists. Instead, Bacci family members simply offered to pay someone for "works" and "to paint and make figures in the Cappella Maggiore" in the church of San Francesco. And they seem to have been content (or perhaps felt constrained) to entrust the choice of subject matter to the Franciscans and the painters. It is of course also possible that their decades-long close relations with the Franciscans assured the family that they would have at least an informal input.

Neither is there evidence that Bicci di Lorenzo or Piero chose the subject of *The Legend of the True Cross*. The mistaken notion that a painter could choose the iconography of important sectors of a church derives from romantic ideas of the role of the Renaissance artist. Recent scholarship has demonstrated that clerical communities assiduously defended their control over sacred space and the images that would be displayed there.[14] Piero and other painters had the fundamental role of taking oral or written formulations and traditional iconography and representing them in visual form; painters seldom possessed the privilege of choosing the subject matter of their paintings in churches.

This leaves the Franciscan friars. Elsewhere in Tuscany, Franciscan communities in Florence and Volterra had earlier chosen *The Legend of the True Cross* as a subject for their high altar chapel and a large oratory respectively. This control of the iconography continued throughout the fifteenth century. The best analogous example is in Piero's place of birth, where the Franciscans supervised the painting of the high altar polyptych of their church of San Francesco in the years from 1426 to 1444. In this, the most thoroughly documented altarpiece of the Quattrocento, the friars explicitly reserved to themselves the privilege of defining the iconography of their double-sided altarpiece in contracts to a carpenter and painters on four occasions. In the end the Franciscans and the painter Sassetta together sketched out the sixty iconographical subjects that were copied into a legal contract. It seems reasonable to expect that the Franciscans of Arezzo would have demanded similar control of the subject matter in the decoration of their high altar area.[15]

As one would expect if this were the case, the emphasis on the Cross in these frescoes derives from traditional Franciscan imagery and the specific history of the friars in Arezzo.[16] The Cross was venerated in all the religious orders, but, as previously mentioned, among the Franciscans above all, in part due to the founder's experiences in Arezzo. Most importantly, the signs of Christ's Passion on the Cross were implanted on Saint Francis' body, and in the authoritative biography of Francis, Saint Bonaventure tells us that the saint received the stigmata during the time of the liturgical celebration of the "Exaltation of the True Cross." In *The Legend* Piero depicts several scenes associated with this church festival.[17]

Fra Benedetto Sinigardi of Arezzo played an important role in the development of the Franciscan chapter in Arezzo and the friars' understanding of their identity. Converted under Saint Francis and leader of the convent in Arezzo, this friar became the provincial minister of the Holy Land in 1221. While there he performed miracles and participated in an attempt to unite the Greek and Latin churches. He returned to San Francesco in Arezzo where he died in 1282 and was eventually buried near the Cappella Maggiore. The Arezzo house of Franciscans venerated Fra Benedetto, and the friars retained an interest in the Holy Land into the Quattrocento. Closely related to the theme of the Cross was concern with crusades to rid the Holy Land of Muslim rulers. Already in the thirteenth century the Franciscans were well known for their preaching about the necessity of sending crusades to the Holy Land. In the 1270s Pope Gregory convened a church council in Lyon and made Saint Bonaventure, then leader of the Franciscans, a cardinal and nominal head of the Council. Under his leadership the Council sought to unite the Greek and Latin churches and succeeded in declaring a crusade against Islamic rulers. The Franciscan association continued in the fourteenth century when papal officials officially charged the Franciscans with juridical authority in the Holy Land and a direct responsibility for protecting and administering the holy sites, an authority that has persisted down to the present.[18] Hence Piero had ample precedents in local Franciscan association with the Holy Land and the Cross in the presentation of the scenes of the cycle.

Many of the subjects in the scenes of *The Legend of the True Cross* derive from two church feast days, the Feast of the Discovery of the True Cross (3 May) and the Feast of the Exaltation of the True Cross (14 September). Knowledge of these two feast days was found most easily in the narratives of the *Golden Legend* (*Legenda Aurea*), a thirteenth-century compendium of Scripture, saints' lives, accounts of the Church Fathers, and early medieval lore written or compiled by the chronicler Jacobus de Voragine. His texts for the feast days provide a multitude of events and images from which Piero and the Franciscans could choose for the murals. Even prior to the commission of the Cappella Maggiore granted to Bicci di Lorenzo, the Franciscans had doubtless chosen *The Legend of the True Cross* as the theme and had chosen several of the specific scenes. In all probability discussions between the friars (or a committee of them) and Piero ensued, with the painter providing suggestions as to which scenes would best satisfy the aims of the Franciscans. Piero may have presented the friars with preliminary drawings as part of these discussions. With the scenes decided upon, Piero, as the expert in the transformation of words into images, became dominant in representing the narratives on the walls. At some point in these discussions between the friars and Piero, we can also assume that either or both of the parties invoked the precedent of Agnolo Gaddi's *Legend of the True Cross* series (1380s) in Santa Croce in Florence as an example to follow, at least in part.

Conversations between Piero and the friars would have continued once he was on the scaffolding, with the painter arguing from his expertise and the friars from their knowledge of sacred history. Because Piero painted the first and last scenes in the cycle in the lunettes prior to finishing the medium and lower levels of the chapel and the narrative sequence was complex, he would have had to plan most, if not all, the scenes early in the process. This narrative sequence strikes many observers initially as obtuse or confusing, lacking in clear exposition. Marilyn Lavin has shown that medieval and Renaissance artists employed a variety of organizational schemes.[19] A modern Western "reading" of left to right and upper to lower had not yet become the norm. From early Christian and medieval precedents Piero and other Renaissance mural painters had many models from which to choose. Piero, perhaps together with the Franciscans, decided to pair scenes on the side walls of the chapel. He balanced the narratives on one side of the chapel with narratives on the other, thereby integrating what might seem to be incongruent scenes. Piero arranged scenes on the right wall of persons who were not or not yet Christians (including the emperor in *The Victory of Constantine*, Illus. 6) whereas those on the left wall were believers in Christ (Illus. 5).[20] He painted the tiers of the two sides with parallel narratives, most notably the procession of the Queen of Sheba with the entourage of the Empress Helena in the middle tiers, in which the queens recognize the significance of the Cross. Each side of these two scenes was divided into landscape and architectural settings. On the bottom tier, battle scenes are paired in which emperors emerge triumphant in battle through their adherence to the Cross. Piero again organized parallel components on the rear wall. To the left of the window in the middle tier, a Jew is dragged up out of a well, where he has been submerged, which is echoed on the right of the window, where the wood of the True Cross is lowered into the ground. To complete the parallelisms, on the back wall are two types of annunciation, one to Mary and the other to Constantine (see Pl. IV). But these pairings are only one component of a rich series of parallels of color, form, and personages that criss-cross from one side of the chapel to the other, all as a means of conferring formal importance and variety on the narrative. Because many viewers of the frescoes knew the narrative, Piero sought to multiply visual significance beyond the story, thereby engaging the viewer on several levels and stimulating participation and contemplation.[21]

Piero's Narration of *The Legend of the True Cross*

This is the sequence of the events depicted in the frescoes:[22]

1. Story of Adam
2. Visit of Sheba to Solomon
3. Burial of the Wood
4. Annunciation to Mary
5. Annunciation to Constantine
6. Victory of Constantine
7. Raising of Judas from the Well
8. Invention of the Cross (Finding and Proofing)
9. Victory of Heraclius: Death of Chosroes
10. Restitution of the Cross

Piero begins his *Legend of the True Cross* in the large lunette on the right in which he has depicted the origins of life just outside Paradise in a world marked by sin, which leads to the death of Adam (see Illus. 7). He has painted three scenes in the right lunette all under a blue sky marked by a large tree that, despite being damaged, integrates the episodes in an example of continuous narrative. The narrative starts closest to the viewer in the nave with the depiction of a dying Adam sitting upright surrounded by Eve and their three sons. In a small scene Piero depicts their third son, Seth, in the shadowy distance at the gate of the Garden of Eden seeking eternal life for his ailing father from the angel Michael, who sends Seth back with only a cutting from the Tree of Life. In the middle funeral scene Piero has painted a skillfully foreshortened body of the dead Adam with Seth planting in his father's mouth the seedling that will yield the wood for Christ's Cross. Among the mourners are a grieving female with her arms raised and two youths in the back corner, one clothed only in a lion's skin that presages Piero's later depiction of Hercules (see Illus. 22). Here Piero has not undertaken a rigorous system of linear perspective in the organization of the spaces.

The *Legend* continues on the middle tier on the right with the story of the Queen of Sheba and King Solomon (see Illus. 6). The Adam story above occurred in nature with early humans, half of whom were nude. The two scenes of Sheba and Solomon are in a completely civilized world of royalty. The first half of the tier is placed in a landscape in which Sheba has discovered and kneels before the now harvested tree, which serves as a bridge, and is placed perpendicularly to the picture plane. Sheba and her retinue are lavishly attired. The second scene in this middle tier depicts the encounter of Sheba and Solomon in which the queen informs the king that the wood of the Cross will destroy his dynasty. Piero has placed the ceremony within a finely constructed loggia in which fluted columns with Corinthian capitals separate this event from the former. The royal entourages are depicted in garments of rich cloth. In the queen's gown, under the white mantle, and in the king's cloak Piero has represented one of the most expensive silks of the Renaissance. This white "velvet cloth-of-gold" is patterned with stylized pine cones or pomegranates in gold, a pattern common for velvets and damasks in the fifteenth century for the elite, but the cloth-of-gold itself was associated with heads of government.[23]

In the retinue of the Queen of Sheba, Piero has again painted a representation of the man who appeared as the penitent in *Saint Jerome and a Penitent* and whom we earlier identified as Jacopo Anastagi. In this fresco Piero has conceived of his friend from childhood as the queen's counselor or perhaps chancellor and depicted him as a man of importance and of gravitas. In this period Jacopo served in the court of Sigismondo Malatesta, in the same role as that in which Piero represents him in the queen's service.

Piero's narration then moves to the middle tier of the back wall, to the right of the window, with the *Burial of the Wood* (see Pl. IV). To protect the reign of his heirs, Solomon commanded that the wood be buried. Here three men are in the act of placing the wood in a pool, most of which we have to imagine since we see only its edge. At the top of the scene Piero has painted a plank pushing on the wood, and we must imagine another man out of the mural assisting the three visible men as Piero expands the picture by invoking the viewers' imagination.

We now pass from events contemporary with the Hebrew Bible to the age of the incarnation of Christ. Piero moves our eye diagonally to the bottom level of the rear wall to the left of the window. Here, in the *Annunciation to Mary*, God the Father in the upper left-hand corner sends golden rays, representing the Holy Spirit, as well as the angel Gabriel with his news to Mary (see Pl. IV). A powerful figure in red and blue, Mary receives Gabriel in the portico of her Roman palace, unlike her simple Bethlehem house and unlike contemporary Arezzo houses. *The Annunciation to Mary* had not been included in earlier cycles of *The Legend of the True Cross*, but it is a rational inclusion as it completes the history of salvation from the Garden of Eden in the lunette to the Last Judgment on the chapel wall facing the nave. Piero matched the *Annunciation to Mary* with God's announcement to Constantine that the Cross would lead him to victory.

The *Annunciation to Constantine* was placed on the right side of the window on the bottom rear tier (see Pl. IV). Here as elsewhere throughout the chapel Piero has rationalized the source and play of light, which usually flows from the window. In this *Annunciation to Constantine* there is a slight dawn light in the sky, but a supernatural light emanates from the Cross that the angel holds out to show the future emperor the "sign with which you shall conquer." The light illuminates Constantine and the inside of his tent and backlights the soldier who looks toward Constantine. Piero introduces ambiguity into the scene as the angel with a left wing extended can almost be read as a descending bird with each feather finely articulated. In this image Piero demonstrates his mastery of light and how he could paint it to define surfaces and emphasize masses of color. Likewise, he uses shadows to articulate spaces and to show undulating planes.

The most recent restoration of the *Annunciation to Constantine* has revealed that Piero painted the stars in recognizable constellations, the Great and Little Bear for example. The stars have been positioned in their proper spatial relationships exactly as modern computer programs have projected for the middle of the Quattrocento.[24] This realistic depiction of the night sky and its stars is one of the earliest in Western art. But there is a complication. Piero's accurate representation of stars was not what a viewer on earth would see; rather, it is the view "from above"—what God would see from outside the earth. Why Piero so represented the stars is unknown. Perhaps a reversal of the cartoon occurred or perhaps he knew that Euclid had presented his illustrations of the stars from an external viewpoint. If the latter, Piero decided that Euclid's authority outweighed the painter's customary practice of representing what the eye saw.

The cycle now moves to the *Victory of Constantine*, in which Piero depicts the important battle for control of Rome between the generals Maxentius and Constantine (see Illus. 6). Located on the bottom tier on the right, the scene represents an historical event of 312 at the Milvian Bridge in Rome: the marvelous battle panorama of the flight of Maxentius' army on the right closest to the nave and the victorious Constantine in the saddle with the silvery white cross held before him centered in the painting. The victors are painted as if entering the grounds of a medieval tourney with a dominant flag depicting the imperial black eagle. The order and stateliness of Constantine and his mounted cavalry are contrasted with the chaos of Maxentius' army. The scene with its richness of detail in the steeds, armor, harnesses, and the meandering River Tiber as it unwinds in the distance celebrates the victory of Constantine and thereby, though understated except for the small cross, the victory of Christianity.

Piero introduced two scenes of Constantine into the cycle, whereas Agnolo Gaddi in his cycle of the True Cross in Santa Croce in Florence had not painted even one.[25] In the *Victory of Constantine* Piero placed the scene in Rome at the Milvian Bridge. Piero is historically accurate by choosing to depict the Battle of Milvian Bridge as the site of Constantine's victory over Maxentius and, according to early Christian historians, in showing that the victory was secured through the help of the Cross. It is significant that Piero chose a battle within Rome, a part of a civil war between two generals, both the sons of deceased emperors, and not a battle against an external and essentially "other" foe. Today historians of Rome view the battle as part of competition for control of the Roman Empire; Piero has represented the battle as a conflict between Christians, or proto-Christians as Constantine had not yet adopted Christianity, and non-believing Romans. One flag of Maxentius depicts an ugly dragon, a symbol of sin or evil, and another portrays a black-headed infidel in profile. Piero has also placed on Constantine the headgear associated with imperial authority.[26] The *Victory of Constantine* represents a conflict within Rome between Romans.

Following a chronological order, the narrative now moves to the back wall on the second level, where Piero returned to focus on the wood of the Cross (see Pl. IV). Helena, Constantine's mother, had gone to Jerusalem to look for Christ's Cross. She was informed that a young Jew named Judas possessed knowledge of the site of the Cross. Piero has assumed the viewer knew this part of the *Golden Legend* and that Judas had refused to reveal the location of the Cross, for which he was tortured by being lowered into a well. Piero depicts Judas being yanked from the well by his hair and by a rope on a pulley, outside the viewer's sight, attached to a three-legged frame. The young man pulling the hair of Judas has two symbols of his authority from Helena, his blue and white spiral-striped baton and a document stuck into his hat. This painting is usually credited to one of Piero's assistants and criticized because it is the only part of the cycle that does not show light flowing from the existing window. The way the light falls and the placement of shadow contradicts the other paintings in the cycle, in which the shadows fall in accordance with the light coming from the window at the back wall of the chapel.

The *Legend* continues on the left wall, second tier, with the *Invention of the Cross*, which, like its twin scene of Solomon and Sheba in the second tier of the right wall, is divided into two parts, again with one part a landscape and the other an architectural setting (see Illus. 5). The landscape portion depicts that part of the *Invention of the Cross* called *The Finding of the Cross*, in which Helena and her retinue and the bishop of

Jerusalem (Macarius) discover the Cross after being informed of its location by Judas, who has revealed that he is a Christian and explained that he had earlier feared revealing the location of the Cross lest it become bedeviled. In the upper portion of the discovery scene, Piero has painted the walled Jerusalem in the form of Arezzo, which is depicted on the slope of a hill in a receding background. Here Piero presents a wondrous play of geometric structures with the buildings, including the red-brick cathedral at the top, all bathed in defining sunlight.

The other half of the *Invention* recounts *The Proofing of the Cross*, in which Piero shows a foreshortened Cross being held over a man raised from the dead by its miraculous powers (see Illus. 5). Helena and her entourage kneel before the Cross as had the other queen, Sheba, on the paired scene on the right wall. Helena and her women are dressed elegantly but more simply than Sheba and her retinue, except for a woman in royal blue with her back to the picture plane, who adores the Cross as the Virgin would in a Crucifixion scene. The action occurs in a street where the buildings are dominated by a temple to Venus designed as a rectangle with a triangular pediment and divided at the ground level by three arches. Piero has simplified the classical architectural elements into a prototype of ancient buildings. The houses on the right follow a street receding in space, with a marvelously invented building in the distance capped by a dome culminating in a lantern of ten columns holding a perfectly shaped oval covering.[27]

The narrative continues below on the lower left tier in the *Victory of Heraclius: Death of Chosroes* (see Illus. 5). The *Golden Legend* states that the battle occurred in 615 (in fact 628) after the King of the Persians, Chosroes, had taken the Wood left by Helena in Jerusalem three hundred years earlier. The Christian Emperor Heraclius was determined to recover it and also to expel the Persians who earlier had sought to capture Constantinople. Whereas in the paired scene of the *Victory of Constantine*, Piero had depicted no violence because Constantine had won through the power of his brandished Cross, here the painter depicts a battle between the armies of Heraclius and Chosroes. All the elements—warriors with their horses, swords, and lances, but also colors and forms—are in conflict. Flags dominate the upper portion of the picture frame. In the center the black eagle standard of the emperor and the Christian flag with its Cross fly proudly, while on the right the flags of Chosroes are in disarray: one black standard hangs limply and a second of stars and the Turkish crescent descends to the horizontal to signify Chosroes' defeat.

The *Golden Legend* had recorded an earlier moment when a then ruling Chosroes had mocked Christian doctrine by representing himself as God the Father, a cross to represent the Son, and a cock for the Holy Spirit. On the extreme right of the battle, Piero has depicted the emptiness of Chosroes' mockery of the Christian Trinity with a cock, cross, and an empty throne covered by a canopy. In front of the throne Piero places a defeated Chosroes on his knees surrounded by the Christian victors. Heraclius, with his staff of command in hand, sentences Chosroes to death in the presence of the victorious soldiers and three men in fifteenth-century civilian dress, who Vasari believed were members of the Bacci family.

The events of the *Legend* conclude in the left lunette, where a grand sky has been encouraging the viewer's eye to ascend (see Illus. 5). The *Golden Legend* informs us that when Heraclius attempted to restore the Cross to Jerusalem its gates closed because the emperor had imagined his entrance as a victorious triumph, whereas he needed to enter the city as Christ had on Palm Sunday, barefoot and in humility. The viewer would have had to possess this knowledge in advance because Piero has chosen only to depict Heraclius' subordination of himself to the Cross. Heraclius enters Jerusalem barefoot with the Cross carried by one of his retinue. On the right Piero has painted a group of men of various ages, who kneel before the Cross, finally restored to its rightful place in Jerusalem.

Technical and Conceptual Accomplishments at Arezzo

Given the fact that the frescoes were painted over a period of six to eight years and given Piero's age at the time (he was in his forties), it is not surprising that he made dramatic technical and conceptual advances while in Arezzo. These advances signal his passage to a second phase of development, begun in Rimini, in which the most important advance in his pictorial technique was his extensive employment of cartoons. Piero's generation of painters in Tuscany had introduced the use of cartoons for large sections of their paintings, adding to the earlier practice of using cartoons exclusively for repetitive patterns,[28] as Piero did with small cartoons in his fresco of *Sigismondo Malatesta Before his Patron Saint* in Rimini in 1451 (see Pl. III). In Arezzo Piero's task of frescoing the grand spaces of the Cappella Maggiore led him to create large cartoons that were prepared for whole segments of the wall space. A portion of a large cartoon was then placed on the wet plaster and a powder pounced through holes pierced along the painting's contours, leaving an outline (*spolveri*) of a design for the painting. From the most recent restoration of the frescoes, we know that Piero prepared 230 *giornate* (a *giornata* is the area covered by fresh plaster to be frescoed in "a day," though often painted by necessity in two or three hours).[29] But his original cartoons were much larger than what could have been covered in a *giornata*. The existing frescoes demonstrate Piero's ability to organize vast spaces and integrate into his planning intricate questions of parallel meanings, colors, and solid forms, as well as an overall iconography across and around the chapel walls. As we have observed, Piero must have initially prepared an overall plan of the iconography for each of the architectural sections. Thus the cartoons take on great importance as an intermediate conceptual step in the process from Piero's mind to the frescoing of the scenes.[30] And this ability to conceptualize large spaces and organize a variety of narratives, forms, and colors in this space is a defining characteristic of Piero's art in this second phase of his development.

The Cappella Maggiore had ribbed vaults, cornices, lunettes, and a large window in the back wall within which Piero had to plan and execute his frescoes. To minimize these divisions and to present a large number of scenes from the episodes of the Cross, he borrowed the technique of continuous narrative from ancient sarcophagi or other ancient sculpture or from his memories of Florence—Masaccio's examples in the Brancacci Chapel and Ghiberti's on the Baptistery doors. Piero could have seen examples of this technique both in Rome and in Florence. Certainly, medieval narratives often mixed various moments from a saint's or Christ's life, but Piero's use of perspective and his memories or drawings of ancient sculpture and Florentine examples enabled him to guide the viewer through narrative passages, even though he eliminated all borders or fictive architectural structures.

In the Arezzo frescoes Piero magnificently demonstrated his ability to paint large spaces. A great deal of this was done in fresh plaster, where he had approximately three hours before the surface became too hard for integration of the pigments into the plaster. For this large-scale project Piero was compelled to adopt three procedures that were unusual for him at this point. In order to expand the period when the plaster was sufficiently soft, he placed wet cloths on the drying plaster as a means of preserving its ability to absorb the paints over a longer period. Secondly, he did resort at times to placing a layer of tempera paint (pigments in egg white or possibly oil) on the hardened plaster, a technique called *a secco*. Lastly, Piero employed two other painters to assist him, Lorentino d'Andrea d'Arezzo and Giovanni di Piamonte, the latter most prominently in the *Raising of Judas from the Well*. The latest preservation program has reaffirmed that Piero had minimal aid from either of these two painters. It is as well to note here that he seldom assigned significant proportions of painting to assistants.[31]

Piero had earlier developed a repertoire of methods to represent human, architectural, and spatial realities, which he now integrates with models adapted from classical history. Such a revolutionary change required close observation of classical forms; few artists have had a greater capacity than Piero for focused analysis of nature, of humans and their creations. In Arezzo he shows a new interest in representing the human body from classical models. Many have commented on the nude youth in the right lunette in the *Death of Adam*, where a son of Adam or Seth is represented with his back to the picture plane leaning on his staff (Illus. 7). Piero perhaps took this image from a class of antique statues in which a youth mourns or attends graves, or perhaps more precisely he borrowed from a copy of a sculpture by the Greek sculptor Scopas that was known and copied in mid-fifteenth century Florence.[32] Piero derived many of his human figures from observation of classical models. But he had by this stage already developed the ability to represent classical values in his paintings without a specific model, depicting persons as individuals in a variety of near-fixed poses, each isolated in his or her solid sculptural body. In this way he demonstrated a profound understanding of Roman statues freed from any close architectural setting.

In his groupings of individuals Piero demonstrates his grasp of classical spacing. Intricate linear perspectival schemes do not appear important in many of the scenes of the cycle. Certainly objects diminish in size the greater their distance from the viewer. Three-dimensionality, however, is created more from an overall spatial apportionment, the rhythm of objects, and the empty adjacent spaces than from etched orthogonals as a guide for painting. In many of the scenes of the murals the rhythm is achieved by alternating humans and space or by expressing mass by color. Piero took from Roman public monuments an understanding of compositional unity, and from sarcophagi he observed how scenes could be knotted together in a continuous frieze. In near mythic terms Roberto Longhi has described Piero's intuitive grasp of Egyptian and Greek space and depiction of monumental humans. Piero's understanding of Egyptian and Grecian forms, without having any known models, is inexplicable by usual art-historical methods, but many from Longhi to Bertelli have nevertheless attempted to give readers an appreciation of Piero's intuition and appropriation of the antique.[33]

In the Arezzo murals Piero continued his practice of depicting Roman architecture that had begun in the Rimini fresco of 1451 (see Pl. III). In the middle right tier of *The Visit of Sheba to Solomon* the painter has placed the two regal figures and their retinues under a portico supported by fluted columns with Corinthian capitals (see Illus. 6). On the left middle tier Piero paints the *Invention of the Cross*, in which he has three architectural portions (see Illus. 5). In the upper left corner Piero has represented the streets and buildings of Arezzo as Jerusalem in which, other than the city gates, all the buildings are rectilinear, an assortment of squares, triangles, and rectangles. In *The Proof of the Cross* in the temple to Venus, Piero further demonstrates his understanding and appropriation of classical architecture, especially in the marble facing of the temple and its pediment. Also striking in the upper right-hand corner is a beautiful domed temple on which Piero has constructed a "classical lantern resting on pillars." Ronald Lightbown sees this as one of the earliest images of a hemispheric dome in Renaissance painting.[34]

Piero's ability to imitate classical statues, spacing, and architecture matured after his 1453–54 visit to Rome, but Piero doubtless saw examples of classical remains in Florence, Rimini, Ravenna, and Arezzo, which could have provided for the occasional borrowing of a classical element.[35] But the profound appropriation of classical values in these three areas and the unity of his new vision of the world required a confrontation with antiquity that was all-encompassing and only possible by residence in Rome.

The Legend of the True Cross cycle is a lay epic freed from the variants and sometimes fairy-tale quality of Piero's *Golden Legend* source—a testament to his literary sophistication. Marilyn Lavin has described how Piero achieved a Christian epic that would fulfill the Roman poet Horace's criteria for the epic form. Piero's "individual compositions are grave and dignified; the figures are posed with decorum; emotional expression is strong but reserved; the scenes are filled with variety but not cluttered; the spatial constructions are rationally controlled, have balance and proportional harmony."[36] Despite the monumentalizing epic within which Piero's figures act, they are within the world of human possibilities. The men and women are solidly grounded and act out the ceremonies and events of fifteenth-century Italians in their "secular, profane life"; they participate in embassies, act as and meet dignitaries, die and are mourned, fight and conquer in battle.[37]

Piero invests this human world with muted supernatural significance, which has to be read into the narrative. Other than the appearance of God the Father in the *Annunciation to Mary* and the angels in the two Annunciations, there is no apparent supernatural intrusion in his historical account. In the *Death of Adam* sin is introduced into the world and in the *Annunciation to Mary* the Son of God is introduced into the world through the angel. Piero was freed from depicting the Crucifixion itself because there was a thirteenth-century Cross hanging over the high altar at Arezzo.

To conclude, Piero has shown in *The Legend of the True Cross* a conception of human history extraordinary in his age. The painter traces the episodes of the Cross as a means of integrating Divine purpose and human history that begins with the family of Adam discovering how disobedience to the Divine results in weakness and death of the human body. But the seedling, placed in Adam's mouth, holds the promise that in its maturity the wooden Cross will provide the means for Divine redemption. Into this narrative Piero weaves the stories of biblical monarchs, early Church history, Roman emperors struggling for power, and conflicts between Byzantium and eastern rulers. Piero never again received a commission that required a series of narrative panels or frescoes on these or similarly profound questions of human origins and destiny.

***

While Piero labored in Rome and in the chapel of the high altar of San Francesco in Arezzo, his commission to paint the panels of the polyptych of the Misericordia confraternity remained incomplete, leading him to return to Sansepolcro by the fall of 1459 and live continuously there from 1460 to 1462. This we shall observe in Chapter 7, though first we must examine his painting of the Misericordia altarpiece and then accompany Piero on his visit to Rome in 1458–59 and explore his developing passion for Greek geometry.

CHAPTER 5

Creating the Sacred

Piero della Francesca's Altarpiece for the Confraternity of the Madonna della Misericordia

Piero worked on *The Legend of the True Cross* in Arezzo and the altarpiece for the lay confraternity of the Misericordia in Sansepolcro over much of the decade of the 1450s, with the latter finished only in the 1460s. As we have seen, the painting of both masterpieces was interrupted by Piero's trips to Rome, which had profound effects on the Arezzo frescoes. The Misericordia painting, in contrast, manifests no significant demonstration of the art of classical antiquity. The lack of Roman influence and a restrained realism in Piero's painting in the Misericordia polyptych doubtless resulted from his acceptance of the traditional preferences of the confraternal officials. Piero had to limit his naturalistic representation of persons, space, and background to satisfy his patrons. Instead, contractual and probable oral instructions required him to surround saints and the Madonna with gold. Gold leaf had been traditionally applied in the backgrounds of saints and sacred figures as a means of elevating them out of this world and suggesting Paradise as the altarpiece's setting.[1] The saints in the main tier of the confraternal altarpiece are isolated in their separate compartments and serve as intercessors and patrons of the viewer. The Virgin Mary, the mother of God and ultimate mediator with the sacred, had to be portrayed as larger than any other figure, suggesting her glorification rather than her human nature (see Pl. V).

The person of Mary held an elevated position in the imagination of Quattrocento men and women. She was the mother of God yet a Virgin, a persuasive intercessor with her Son, a protector from the wrath of God the Father, and a model of female virtue. Late medieval and Renaissance narratives abound with persons finding themselves in danger, appealing to Mary, and then receiving physical and spiritual salvation when she persuades God to intervene. Marian confraternities dedicated to charitable and devotional activities proliferated across Europe. Such confraternities took two forms. In one, men expressed their devotion by organizing into choirs that regularly assembled and sang praises to the Virgin and her Son (*laude*). In the second form, some Marian confraternities combined the practice of self-flagellation as an imitation of Christ's suffering with devotion to the Virgin. Many confraternities took the name of Saint Mary of Mercy or in Italian, Santa Maria della Misericordia, and their devotion to Mary led them to provide hospital care and burial services. Misericordia confraternities eventually were found in almost every Italian city and town as the confraternities' hospitals replaced clerical institutions in caring for the dying for administering—except extreme unction—and providing rituals for the dead. The distinguishing feature of all these confraternities was that, unlike the monks or the friars, they were associations of lay people (sometimes women, but usually men) who had not taken holy orders.

The Confraternity of Santa Maria della Misericordia

Piero's altarpiece is best understood in the context of the Misericordia confraternity of Sansepolcro and the members' devotional and charitable acts.[2] In the construction of their church and association the brothers addressed the problem of how they as laymen could participate in the realm of the sacred, which had for centuries been dominated by the ecclesiastical order. Laymen and women could not claim the sacred status that the clerics obtained through the sacrament of ordination. For lay people the presence of the holy in both their corporate and individual life had to be claimed by a variety of means. Primary among these were acts of charity and imitation of the clergy, for example self-flagellation, preaching, and singing praises to Mary and Christ. As in other confraternal churches, the Misericordia men in Sansepolcro reproduced the architectural and decorative aspects of the churches constructed under clerical auspices. From the inception of confraternities in urban settlements in the late thirteenth century, the creation of monumental images of the Virgin appeared as palpable embodiments of the sacred in their buildings. In fulfilling the contract for the Misericordia polyptych Piero was not only painting an image of Mary, but, through his abilities to give visual shape to theological concepts and devotional feelings, he was assisting the brothers and other visitors to contemplate and adore the sacred.

From its founding in the fourteenth century the Misericordia church and its hospital in Sansepolcro have been under constant reconstruction. Excavations begun in 2011 suggest that the church's original site was adjacent to and east of the sixteenth-century church that stands near the site today.[3] In the Quattrocento, the church consisted of a nave with a vaulted high altar chapel and at least one side altar. The high altar was the focal point of the sanctuary with an anteroom at the other end of the nave. From its beginnings the church would have had an image of the Virgin on its high altar, in the form of a processional banner. A 1428 document recounts that a processional banner, presumably with the Virgin on its front face, was on the high altar. Though its officials paid a priest to perform the sacraments in their church, the confraternity was not connected to any bishop, parish, or religious order.[4]

The anteroom to the confraternal church nave was a liminal or transitional space in which the brothers cast aside their worldly personae and statuses, most easily seen in their donning of their black robes and capes (see Illus. 9). There is no documentary evidence that in the Quattrocento the bishop of Città di Castello or the abbot of Sansepolcro ever consecrated the confraternal church, demonstrating at the least that the confraternal officials did not celebrate a sacredness deriving from an ecclesiastical visitation. It was the building, the brothers' activities there, and eventually Piero's image of the Virgin that contributed to making the space and building sacred. The nave would have been filled with benches or chairs and the high altar adorned with their processional banner, with the Cross prominently above or on the high altar table. All this was in imitation of and in accord with the traditional ecclesiastic sanctuaries. In 1460 the confraternal leadership expended considerable financial resources in gaining a papal indulgence that recognized the confraternal building's sacred status by granting release from days and years of purgatorial punishments for those who visited the church.

The charitable activities of the men of the Misericordia that helped the group acquire a spiritual status focused on services to the community in connection with disease and death through the devotional act of public flagellation and through the administration of their hospital and other charitable activities. By the time of the Black Death in 1348, the people of the town associated death-related services with this confraternity. In ninety-seven extant testaments of 1348, forty-two testators of Sansepolcro bequeathed money or property to the confraternity. Some were members who chose to continue to support the brotherhood through bequests in testaments. Others were non-members who sought the honors accorded members at death, which included burial in a hooded confraternal cloak, a funeral cortege, candles, and the conveying of the body covered by the confraternal pall from the testator's house to the burial site. The deceased also received burial in the confraternity's common tombs in the Badia of San Giovanni Evangelista in the fourteenth century and San Francesco in the fifteenth century, as well as inclusion in corporate perpetual prayers and death Masses.[5]

The confraternal members supervised other charitable acts, many linked to their hospital adjacent to their church. Here grain was stored and sold or given to the poor. The brothers divided the hospital into male and female wards. Many of the expenses of the confraternity revolved around the care of patients, providing sugar, eggs, capons or pigeons when they were ill, oil for the lamps of the hospital, wood to heat the wards, and payments to priests and gravediggers when the patient died. Related charitable activities included care and supervision of orphans (usually only one at a time), dowries for poor young women, and food for prisoners or money for their release.[6] The brothers seldom if ever provided personal service for the individuals in the confraternal beds. Even the *spedalieri*, members elected to oversee the care of the sick and the dying, did not attend personally to the needs of the patients. Thus when Piero's brother Marco served as one of the two *spedalieri* in 1442, we should not assume that he gave day-to-day care to patients in the hospital. This was the task of employed nonmembers.[7]

The confraternity's sacramental and spiritual activities included participation in the Marian feast days, which until the end of the 1450s centered on celebration of the Birth of Mary in September. For the celebrations the confraternity paid for the presence of a priest and for wine. By 1460, however, the brothers chose or were encouraged to change their principal feast to the Annunciation to Mary on 25 March. The change may have been part of the decision to seek an indulgence from the papacy or the result of pressure from their political superiors in Florence, who made the Annunciation one of their principal feast days and who began their year on that day. The confraternal members also participated in the celebration of the feast of the patron of other confraternities, and on All Saints Day had Masses said for the dead.[8] Misericordia members participated in a regular round of rituals to maintain their purity, most importantly flagellation and confession.

The Della Francesca family was associated with the confraternity of Santa Maria della Misericordia from at least 1389, when "Monna Cecha [Francesca] de Benedetto della Francescha," Piero's great-grandmother, bequeathed olive oil to the brotherhood. The following year her son Pietro made a testamentary gift of 5 lire to the Misericordia, which his son Benedetto eventually paid for him later in the 1390s. This Benedetto, the painter's father, became a member of the brotherhood and served as one of the supervisors of the hospital (*spedaliere*) and as treasurer (*camerlingo*).[9]

The Pichi Family

The Pichi family played a complicated role in the planning of Piero's painting and in paying for it. They were a large and wealthy merchant family with several urban palaces and vast agricultural estates.[10] In the Quattrocento there were several branches as they had a prolific male offspring. Bequests from two men of the Pichi family provided much of the funding for the commission to Piero, but the confraternal leaders maintained control of the production of the altarpiece. The Pichi were not permitted to place their coat of arms anywhere on the polyptych; instead, the abbreviated confraternal name, *MIA*, appears twice at the base of the columns.

In 1422 the merchant Urbano di Meo Pichi bequeathed 60 florins to the Misericordia confraternity for "making and painting . . . an ornate altarpiece for the high altar" of the confraternal church. In 1435 another Pichi, Luca di Guido, set aside 50 florins that eventually were allocated to the Misericordia "for making and painting a polyptych for the high altar" of their church.[11] Even before this second allocation the confraternity commissioned the carpenter Bartolomeo di Giovannino d'Angelo to construct a wooden altarpiece and paid him 25 florins at its completion in 1430. The confraternal leaders provided Bartolomeo with a design for the altarpiece, which they had obtained from the noted painter Ottaviano Nelli from Gubbio. What happened to this wooden structure and whether it was ever painted is unknown. It is significant here only because, according to the commission, Piero was required to replicate the dimensions of the earlier altarpiece. This would include the provision in the earlier contract to the carpenter Bartolomeo "to fabricate an altarpiece from wood for the altar of the said society so that it [the wooden structure] holds the altar with the legs of said altarpiece, which legs will come outside the altar so that it [the altar table] ought to be included within said legs." These "legs" were vertical columns, now referred to as lateral piers, which extended from the top of the altarpiece to the floor and served as stabilizers of the large altarpiece, providing as well space for additional saints.[12]

The Misericordia Commission

Four decades were to pass between the first documentary note mentioning the altarpiece and its completion in 1462. The commission itself was given on 11 June 1445, in which the confraternal leaders contracted with Piero:

> to make and to paint an altarpiece in the oratory and church of said confraternity in the form of the altarpiece that is there now with all its wood and all its materials and expenses, of its furnishings and ornamentation of the painting and the positioning and installation in said oratory; with those images and figures and decoration, which the above said prior and council expressed to him or will be expressed by their successors in office and by said others upon their election, and [to be] gilded with fine gold and painted with fine colors and especially with ultramarine blue; with this condition that said Piero is held to repair at his expense for ten years all defects of said altarpiece deriving from the wood or Piero himself. And for all above stated they agreed to give him 150 florins computed at 5 lire and 5 soldi per florin. Of this they promised to give immediately at his petition 50 florins and the remainder at the completion of the altarpiece. And said Piero promised to make, to paint, to decorate, and to assemble said altarpiece to the same width and height and form as is that altarpiece of wood which is now there, and to deliver it completely assembled and set in place within three years, with those above written conditions, and qualities and fineness of colors and gold, and that no other painter is allowed to apply his brush except Piero. And for the same Piero, Benedetto his father agreed to guarantee all the above stated conditions on his part that said painter promised.[13]

The contract has customary clauses but includes additional provisions from the confraternal officials, who wanted an altarpiece that would serve several functions. The image should be seen as sacred and worthy of reverence; to provide a site and a stimulant for the brothers as individuals and as an organization to appeal for the Madonna's mediation with her Son; to intensify the members' devotion, especially during Mass; and, eventually coupled with an indulgence, to stir the interest of the people of Sansepolcro to visit the church. The confraternal officials and their successors retained the right to instruct Piero on "images and figures and decoration," thereby excluding the Pichi family from substantive involvement in the painting's iconography. We can imagine the confraternal leaders instructing Piero to present the Madonna in her traditional unnatural oversize and specifying which saints should be painted on the main tier, gables, and lateral piers.

The sacred perhaps cannot be prescribed in a contract, but Piero was required to use painting materials that had been traditionally employed to suggest it. Twice in the contract the patrons specified the use of the finest of colors, obligating Piero to purchase ultramarine blue, traditionally used for the Virgin's mantle. They also twice instructed Piero to purchase fine gold. The richness of the colors and gold were traditional symbols of an eternal reality that were often antithetical to naturalistic representation. The requirement to follow the form and the size of the pre-existing carpentry predetermined much of the eventual overall appearance of Piero's altarpiece, particularly the division of the lateral saints of the main pier into compartments. The wooden carpentry of the altarpiece, which Piero was required to have made, survives to this today, but without most of its framing elements. The original wooden structure must have been substantially ornate given the price of 25 florins for the identical pre-existing altarpiece.[14]

It is not clear why the leaders of the confraternity included the unusual contractual obligation that made Piero responsible for ten years for any damages that might develop in the wood or derive from his painting. This suggests a problem either with Piero's painting or else the carpentry in an earlier work. The only securely identified painting by Piero prior to 1445 is his *Baptism of Christ*, prepared for the church of San Giovanni Battista (or d'Afra) in Sansepolcro, and it shows no defects. It would have been conventional for Piero to have painted the other saints of the San Giovanni Battista polyptych, but these other parts were completed later by Matteo di Giovanni (see Illus. 2). It is possible to propose that the preparation of the wood or Piero's painting of the other panels had become defective in some way, necessitating the commission to Matteo di Giovanni and the clause in Piero's contract. This would also explain why his father Benedetto della Francesca was brought into the contract, to guarantee the promises made by his son. Benedetto was responsible for Piero's contractual obligations because the Della Francesca was a unified family in which the patriarch was responsible for all the actions of its members, adult or minor. If the father, as the patriarch, was responsible for his son in any event, why did the confraternal officials require Benedetto's presence and his assent to all of Piero's promises in the contract? Certainly the officials wished to intensify Benedetto's sense of responsibility, but what induced them to think there might be a future defect that required the father's guarantee? The two unusual provisions raise intriguing questions that are as yet impossible to answer.

The Misericordia Altarpiece

The Misericordia altarpiece served several traditional liturgical purposes (Pl. V, Illus. 9). Some interpret the altarpiece as having provided a site for Masses and other sacramen-

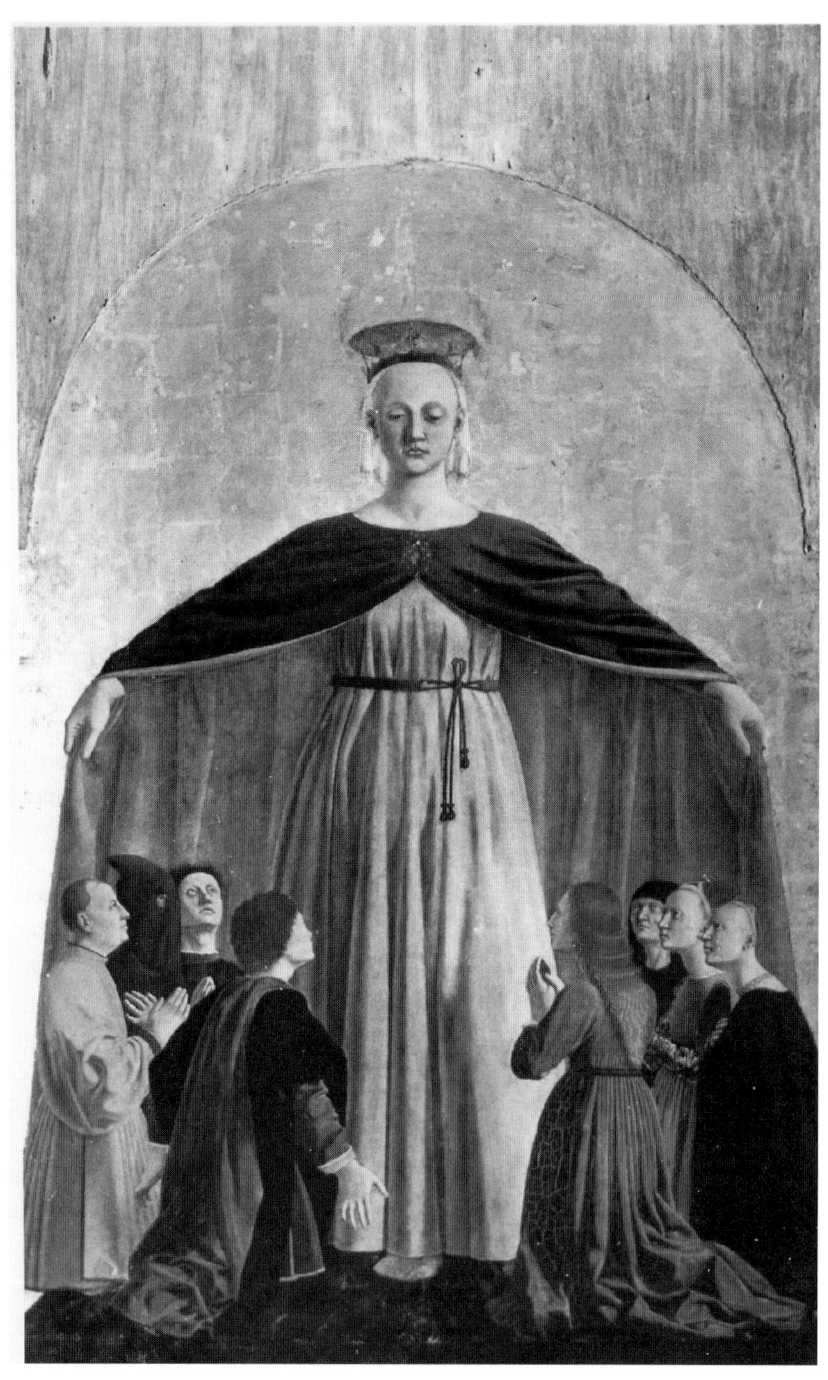

ILLUS. 9 Piero della Francesca, *Madonna della Misericordia*, detail of the *Misericordia Altarpiece*, 168 × 91 cm. Museo Civico, Sansepolcro

tal Eucharistic purposes and doubtless it did, but it is improbable that the confraternal brothers regarded the altarpiece's primary purpose as that of providing a site for Masses. The processional flag or statue of Mary on the confraternal high altar could serve that purpose. To conceive of Piero's altarpiece as focusing on the Eucharist places too much importance on ecclesiastical participation and the Mass. In fact, often there was no priest present for confraternal services. The altarpiece was regarded as sacred in itself and served as a focal point for many activities: as a site to present gifts, to offer up private prayers and votive appeals.[15]

One of these devotional purposes becomes particularly evident with a grant of a papal indulgence to the confraternity at the moment in which Piero was completing his work on its altarpiece. In June and July 1460 the officials of the Misericordia worked with one of Piero's youthful group, Malatesta Cattani, to persuade Pope Pius II to grant their church an indulgence, which would reduce a person's penalities for confessed sins in this world and in Purgatory. The Cattani were one of Sansepolcro's most eminent families, and Malatesta Cattani had a significant position in the ecclesiastical hierarchy. In 1460 he was bishop of Camerino and *referendario*, which position, according to the confraternal scribe, made him supervisor of the papal chancellery. Malatesta had studied canon law at the University of Siena and had lectured there on that subject in the late 1430s. He had also served in the chancellery of Pope Eugenius IV, whose funeral oration he had delivered.[16]

The confraternity appointed an ambassador, Roberto Nanni, to go to Siena with confraternal authority and a supportive letter from Borgo's communal government. Nanni met with Bishop Cattani and together they went to "supplicate" Pius II to gain as "large and better" an indulgence as possible for the confraternal church. Pius was in Mantua to persuade Italian leaders to undertake a mission against the Turks, but he found time to grant an indulgence that was conveyed to Sansepolcro through Cattani and Nanni. However, the indulgence lapsed after three years, which the confraternal ambassador found insufficient, and he persuaded Cattani to supplicate the Pope again. Since Cattani was recorded to be in Siena and Pius in Mantua, it is not clear how the negotiations were carried out, but what was important for the confraternal members was that the Pope eventually granted a perpetual and plenary indulgence. Granted a perpetual indulgence, the confraternity retained the privilege without a temporal limit. A plenary indulgence meant that whatever man, woman, or child worshiped in the confraternal church in a contrite spirit after having confessed on the day of the feast of the Annunciation and made a contribution to the church of Santa Maria della Misericordia would have full release from seven years of temporal punishment on this earth and in Purgatory. Moreover, whoever entered the church on any Saturday under similar conditions would receive forty days of release from similar punishment.

For Piero's altarpiece the confraternal officials chose conventional saints and a Madonna. As Piero did in Rimini, here again with the Madonna he combines two traditional ways of representing her. For altarpieces confraternal leaders had usually commissioned an enthroned Mary with Child, whereas for their processional banners they chose instead images of the standing Misericordia Virgin (i.e. the Virgin sheltering humans under her outstretched cloak). Piero combined the two traditions. He constructed his polyptych by using the image of the Madonna della Misericordia, typically found on cloth processional banners, as a panel painting for the confraternity's high altar. This combination of the two traditions demonstrates the confraternity's concentration on Mary as their patron and as one whose mercy prompted their charitable activities. Compared with contemporary images of the *Madonna della Misericordia* in the Marches and Umbria, especially those on processional flags, Piero's central figure reduces Mary's role as a protectress from Divine wrath. Instead of deflecting the arrows from a vengeful God the Father directed at sinful humans, as we see in these processional flags, Piero's Madonna serves as an intercessory with the Divine. Protection from Divine vengeance for the sins of individual humans may be one of her acts of intervention, but she, like the confraternity itself, had several means to aid and to comfort the sundry needs of her confraternal devotees.[17]

Under the open mantle of the Madonna, Piero has depicted individuals who are representative of groups in Quattrocento society. Under her left arm are four women at various stages of life from an unmarried young woman to two married women, and in the rear a widow.[18] The Virgin's right arm protects an elegantly dressed young man in the foreground, a middle-aged man in a vermilion *lucco*, a hooded member of the confraternity, and a fourth undefined male in the rear. We have encountered the man in vermilion as Jacopo Anastagi in the Rimini panel (Pl. II) and the Arezzo *Legend of the True Cross*, and shall encounter him again in our discussions of *The Flagellation of Christ*.

The saints in the main tier and gables are appropriate for a town in which the Franciscans (together with the Camaldolese monks) had the greatest religious influence. In fact, they correspond to the favored saints in confraternal account books, such as that of 1458 which invokes the "advocates," Saints Mary, John the Baptist, John the Evangelist, Francis, and Bernardino (all of whom are present in Piero's main tier and gables), along with Saints Peter and Paul.[19] The presence of Saint John the Evangelist to the right is not surprising, as he was the titular saint of the Camaldolese Badia and patron saint of the town.[20]

Saint John the Baptist held the place of greatest honor on the Virgin's right hand. The historian Franco Polcri has seen the choices of these saints as part of a new Franciscan spirituality in Sansepolcro in the middle decades of the Quattrocento.[21] John the Baptist was a highly favored intercessor and was, after the Virgin, the most appropriate saint to receive the highest honor in a flagellant confraternity on account of his traditionally recognized penitence and his powers of supplicating the Divine.

The placement of the *Annunciation* on pinnacles above the main register was a recurrent element in altarpieces, but it also has a special significance within the confraternity's devotions to the Madonna. This is especially true after 1460 when the Marian feast of the Incarnation became the central event in the confraternity's annual round of feasts. The *Crucifixion* in the central gable together with the scenes of the Passion in the predella chronicle Christ's final moments. Despite the proximity of the confraternity's church to its two hospitals, the church and the altarpiece did not exist for the primary purpose of providing religious services to the patients in the two hospital wards. Doubtless individual patients or groups would have entered the church and prayed before the altarpiece, but the available evidence all points to the altarpiece as serving the ritualistic and devotional purposes of the confraternal members themselves, and more generally the town community.

The predella of the altarpiece has presented several problems of interpretation. Most researchers hold that an assistant of Piero della Francesca painted the five narrative panels, although Piero had laid out their overall design. On stylistic grounds Mario Salmi argued seven decades ago that the Camaldolese monk and miniaturist Giuliano Amadei from Florence painted the predella narratives and the saints on the piers. Recently discovered documents confirm Amadei's presence in Sansepolcro in the late 1450s and early 1460s, when the confraternity received its indulgence and Piero completed the main tier and gables of the altarpiece. In 1460 the confraternal leaders commissioned Giuliano to paint their sign of *MIA* on a stone in the façade of their church to commemorate the indulgence obtained that year; it is similar to the *MIA* at either end of the predella. So Salmi's hypothesis appears to be accurate.[22]

A technical examination of the physical structure and wood grain of the predella panels in 2009–10 has revealed that they are arranged in an unconventional sequence. The narratives of most Renaissance predellas read from left to right in a chronological sequence, and for a century museum officials have chosen to display Piero's Misericordia predella in this conventional manner. When Piero and Giuliano Amadei prepared the predella it was one horizontally grained plank, but when the altarpiece was disassembled in the seventeenth century the plank was cut into five pieces; thereafter its scenes could be arranged in a variety of sequences. From the grain of the wood it is evident that Piero had planned and arranged the predella with an unconventional narrative sequence going from right to left.[23]

The five narrative panels of the predella recount the Passion of Christ. Arranged in the chronological order in which they appear in the four Gospels, the scenes are:

1. The Agony in the Garden
2. The Flagellation
3. The Deposition (Entombment)
4. Noli Me Tangere ("Touch me not")
5. Three Marys at the Sepulcher

The Deposition (*Entombment*) has to be in the middle under the Madonna because it is wider (81 cm) than the other four panels (33–35 cm). It is also under the *Crucifixion* in the central gable, which completes the Passion cycle. The wood grain indicates that the panels were arranged chronologically from right to left with the earliest, *The Agony in the Garden*, on the extreme right, followed by the *Flagellation*, with *The Deposition* in the center, and finishing with the *Noli me Tangere* and *Three Marys at the Sepulcher* on the extreme left. Machtelt Israëls has demonstrated that Piero's unconventional reading was not singular for predellas and that he organized the altarpiece to emphasize the Passion.[24] As a means of challenging his viewer to emphasize the *Crucifixion* in the reading of the predella and gain more narrative power, Piero broke with a conventional left to right reading.

The Pace of Painting and Payments

It has been assumed that Piero began painting immediately after receiving the commission in 1445, but several recently discovered documents suggest that he did not commission the construction of the altarpiece to a carpenter until later, and hence actual painting only began in the 1450s. We can assume this because the commission reads that Piero was to receive 150 florins for constructing the altarpiece, applying the gold background, and painting the altarpiece, with 50 florins "immediately at his petition" as his initial payment. We know the carpentry of the earlier altarpiece cost 25 florins—as Piero's would have—and the extensive gold of Piero's altarpiece could easily have required an equal amount. Thus the 50 florins could well have been expended in the preparation of the altarpiece; Piero would not want to execute these preliminary stages without first having received that payment. The documents indicate, however, that he did not receive the 50 florins immediately. The priors of the Misericordia conveyed approximately 20 florins to Piero's father Benedetto for the painter in January 1446. This suggests that Piero was not then present in Sansepolcro, but had departed. I cannot find any indication that he was in Borgo between 1445 and 1454, although he may have returned for short periods. In 1450 his brother Marco received approximately 10 florins from an agent of the Pichi family "for part of the payment for the labor of constructing the altarpiece in the oratory" of the Misericordia. This did not complete Piero's initial payment of 50 florins, but it is clear that a payment or payments of the remaining approximately 20 florins of the advance occurred before or after 1450. Early in 1454 members of the Pichi family warned Piero's father that if the painter did not return to his native town by the end of Lent of that year to make the altarpiece, punitive measures specified in the Misericordia commission would be applied.[25] Had Piero received his full 50 florins much earlier in the 1450s, the Pichi family would presumably not have waited until 1454 before demanding that Piero return to Borgo. Equally, only when Piero had the advance of 50 florins in hand was he obligated to begin the carpentry of the altarpiece.

In these documents of 1450 and 1454, the notary employs the gerunds "constructing" (1450) and "making and building" (1454), but not past participles that would imply a completely carpentered wooden altarpiece.[26] Moreover, no word even implying painting the altarpiece is mentioned. Finally, other than in 1454 and 1458, there is no firm evidence of Piero in Sansepolcro between 1445 and 1459.[27] All this calls into question the earlier assignment of much of the painting on the Misericordia altarpiece to the 1440s and the early and mid-1450s.

According to the contract of June 1445, Piero was to receive 100 florins when he had finished painting and had mounted the polyptych on the high altar of the confraternal church. In the period after August 1461 documents show most of this sum being paid. These payments indicate that the altarpiece's painting was completed in 1461 or 1462. Moreover, we know from other documents that Piero was in Borgo at exactly this period (1460–62).

From the payments in Table 1, we can see that the confraternity and the Pichi paid Piero in two different periods. With the first payments of 1446, 1450, and at least one other totaling about 20 florins prior to 1454, the patrons of the altarpiece had conveyed the initial payment of 50 florins to Piero. With the completion of the payment of 50 florins, Piero was obligated to begin constructing the altarpiece, which would explain his return to Sansepolcro in 1454.

In September of that year Piero accepted the commission to paint a polyptych for the high altar of Sant'Agostino in Sansepolcro. It would have been during this period that he constructed and gessoed the Misericordia altarpiece, as well as starting its gilding and painting. Which particular elements were painted in this period may be determinable by stylistic and technical analyses, but I shall leave this as a mystery to be solved by others more skilled in these forms of analyses. I conclude that Piero may have finished the preliminary work of the carpentry and the gilding and perhaps had begun some painting in 1454, but that the majority of the painting took place in 1460–61. It is also in this period that the confraternity sought and gained its papal indulgence.

Piero left Sansepolcro soon after receiving the commission for Sant'Agostino. On 12 December 1454 the patrons of that altarpiece conveyed 50 lire to Piero's brother Marco, suggesting that Piero had departed. Piero's absence is confirmed by the stipulation of

Table 1: Payments to Piero della Francesca for the Misericordia Altarpiece from the Confraternity and the Pichi Family[28]

Date	lire	sol.	den.
10 January 1446 (MIA)	100		
29 April 1450 (Pichi)	53	10	
5 June 1461 (MIA)	275		
January 1462 (MIA)	15		
pre-20 February 1467 (Pichi)	183	6	8
pre-20 February 1467 (Pichi)	15	17	3
Total	641	33	11 =
	642	13	11 =
122.5 florins			
Contract: 150 florins at 5 lire and 5 soldi =	787	10	
Undocumented payments 27.5 florins	144	16	

the Augustinian patron, forcing Marco, his brother Antonio, and their father Benedetto, in the name of Piero, to agree that the 50 lire would be returned under certain circumstances. The notary entitled the act a *quietatio*, which is a quittance or a receipt for a sum received. A set of conditional clauses are highly unusual in this type of document, and their presence here indicates the patron's uncertainty whether Piero would be present to complete the commission. Marco received 50 lire but had to agree to return it (as well as a piece of land given later) if Piero failed to undertake the commission due to his death or any other fortuitous occurrence. And if Piero only completed a portion of it, then an amount proportional to that which was not completed would be returned to the patrons. These conditions appear to be a commentary on Piero's slow fulfillment of the Misericordia commission. At the least the patrons show they are aware that some "intervening impediment and fortuitous inability" might hinder Piero from completing the commission.[29]

Between September 1454, when he received the Sant'Agostino commission, and September 1458, when he appointed a procurator to act legally on his behalf, there are no documents as to Piero's whereabouts. I am in accord with the majority of researchers who believe that from 1455 to 1458 Piero worked on the frescoes in San Francesco in Arezzo. Since Arezzo and Sansepolcro are separated by only 26 miles, Piero probably returned to his family home and may have painted parts of the Misericordia altarpiece in spurts, most likely in the coldest winter months when panel painting is less difficult than frescoing. But the Arezzo project required his sustained attention, which probably permitted only short visits to Borgo or anywhere else in these four years. In one of these visits Piero undertook a commission for the Observant Franciscan friars and lay supervisors of the recently constructed church of Santa Maria della Neve, located outside the walls and the Porta Castello in Sansepolcro. This we know because Piero appointed Marco as his procurator to negotiate with the church's supervisors. Unfortunately, the notary did not complete the procuration act so we do not know exactly the nature of Piero's relationship with this church of Observant Franciscans, but often a procurator was appointed to obtain a payment. As a recently constructed church, it would have required a variety of altarpieces and frescoes; we can only imagine a commission to Piero for this church, which was destroyed in the sixteenth century.[30]

Most scholars agree that Piero designated the procurator because he was leaving for Rome, where he is documented in 1459. He may have returned to Sansepolcro for the final days of his mother Romana's life or soon after her death in November of that year. The painter is documented in Borgo in 1460 and through to 1462. As is evident in Table 1, Piero received a large part of the payments for the Misericordia altarpiece in these years.[31]

Piero labored on the Misericordia altarpiece over an extended period of time. Unfortunately, the ornamentation of its carpentry is lost so that many aspects of the work are difficult to evaluate. The altarpiece appears on first view to be an old-fashioned Gothic polyptych, but Piero's organization of the Madonna, saints, and scenes, his rigor in rendering the Virgin, and his attention to lifelike detail show a mind integrating the patron's wishes with his own evolving practices. The primary example of this is the central panel (see Illus. 9). The original commission for the work suggests that the confraternal officials preferred the customary image of the Madonna della Misericordia as a means of visualizing its identity as a Marian confraternity of Mercy. Piero integrated this with his close observation of nature and accepted his patrons' wishes that the Madonna be represented as larger than her devotees, while endowing her with the fully realistic features of a young maiden of Sansepolcro. At the same time the eight individuals under her cloak are themselves represented as citizens of the town without any jarring sense of contradiction due to the difference in scale between them and the Madonna. Above all, Piero eschewed any suggestion of giving otherworldly attributes to his Mary and did not, for example, show her deflecting arrows sent by God the Father against a sinful humanity, a trope that might have been expected in such a work.

Technical analyses of the Misericordia altarpiece have revealed the experimental character of Piero's approach to its preparation and painting.[32] Piero made at least two important innovations in his materials. For panel paintings the artist or his assistants customarily applied several layers of animal glue, usually made from the skin of rabbits, as well as gesso to the wooden surface as a means of obtaining a smooth and secure surface for the paint. In contrast, Piero or the carpenter experimented with the preparation of the planks for his Misericordia altarpiece by placing carbon black on the wood prior to the animal glue.[33] Piero apparently thought that this preliminary layer would provide a more secure adhesion of the animal glue, gesso, and paint layers to the wood. Secondly, he experimented with a form of oil paint in addition to egg tempera paint as the medium for his painting of the two saints on the right of the main register, Saint John the Evangelist and San Bernardino, as well as a portion of the mantle of the Madonna. In Rimini, Piero had already successfully, and without subsequent damage, used oils in his portrait of Sigismondo Malatesta for the specific purpose of enhancing the lifelike quality of the ruler of Rimini (see Illus. 4). For the two saints and the Madonna in the Misericordia altarpiece he applied oil as a carrier of pigments over a more general area. The areas where the oil was employed have suffered damage and appear with substantial cracks. Whether it was a problem of Piero's technique or damage from some other later source remains a mystery.[34]

A summary of recent technical studies suggests Piero changed his procedures for the preparatory layers of his panel paintings. In the paintings of *The Baptism of Christ, Saint Jerome and a Penitent, Portrait of Sigismondo Malatesta*, and at least parts of the Misericordia altarpiece, Piero applied a final preparatory layer of *colla* (animal glue). From other forms of analysis we have dated these works as Piero's earliest ones. For the panel painting of the archangel Michael in the Sant'Agostino altarpiece and the panels of the polyptych of Sant'Antonio in Perugia, both usually dated to the late 1460s, Piero employed a mixture of oil and resin for the final preparatory stratum.[35] Hence, the technical analyses are in accord with conclusions on dating panel paintings derived from other types of evidence and together confirm my dating of Piero's panel paintings.

***

In the midst of his preliminary preparation of the Misericordia altarpiece and nearing the completion of the Arezzo frescoes, Piero received a call to Rome to paint for the newly elected Pope Pius II. As we shall see in Chapter 6, the commission in Rome brought Piero into contact with papal and humanist projects relating to the recovery of Greek mathematical texts, which would significantly enlarge his interests in geometry and prove transformatory to his later development and achievements.

CHAPTER 6

Greek Geometry in Rome and Piero's *Trattato d'abaco*

In this chapter we finally examine Piero's heralded knowledge of mathematics. As we have seen, in his early life Piero had no formal mathematical training in Sansepolcro or elsewhere, and there is no evidence suggesting that he learned any systematic knowledge at the feet of a learned humanist, mathematician, or *abaco* teacher. Piero did familiarize himself with the latest sophisticated mathematics of the university-trained elite, but he appears to have been self-taught, an autodidact who derived his knowledge from books rather than from a master's lectures. Of course, we can be confident that here and there he picked up ideas from the comments of artisans and learned persons, but these oral sources are beyond our ability to know. In his book on commercial mathematics (*abaco*), Piero reproduced a large number of examples of merchants' problems identical to those in earlier *abaco* texts. We assume that he copied these from books instead of from a teacher's lectures, because during Piero's youth and early adulthood Sansepolcro, as was true of the nearby towns of Città di Castello and Arezzo, had no school of *abaco*.

In the 1440s and 1450s Piero accumulated ideas and deepened his understanding of two parallel but largely separated systems of mathematical procedures and knowledge: a vernacular system related to commercial activity and a Latin university system based on Greek mathematics. Piero in all likelihood deepened his knowledge of *abaco* in Arezzo, while familiarizing himself with Greek-based geometry during his time in Rome. In his *Trattato d'abaco* (*Treatise on Abaco*) Piero brought together these two traditions, the vernacular tradition of *abaco* and the learned Latin tradition of geometry. This uniting of the two mathematical traditions is evident in his book *De prospectiva pingendi* (*On Perspective in Painting*) and finds its consummate expression in Piero's third book, *Libellus de quinque corporibus regularibus* (*The Little Book on the Five Regular Bodies*). Piero composed these three books over many years,

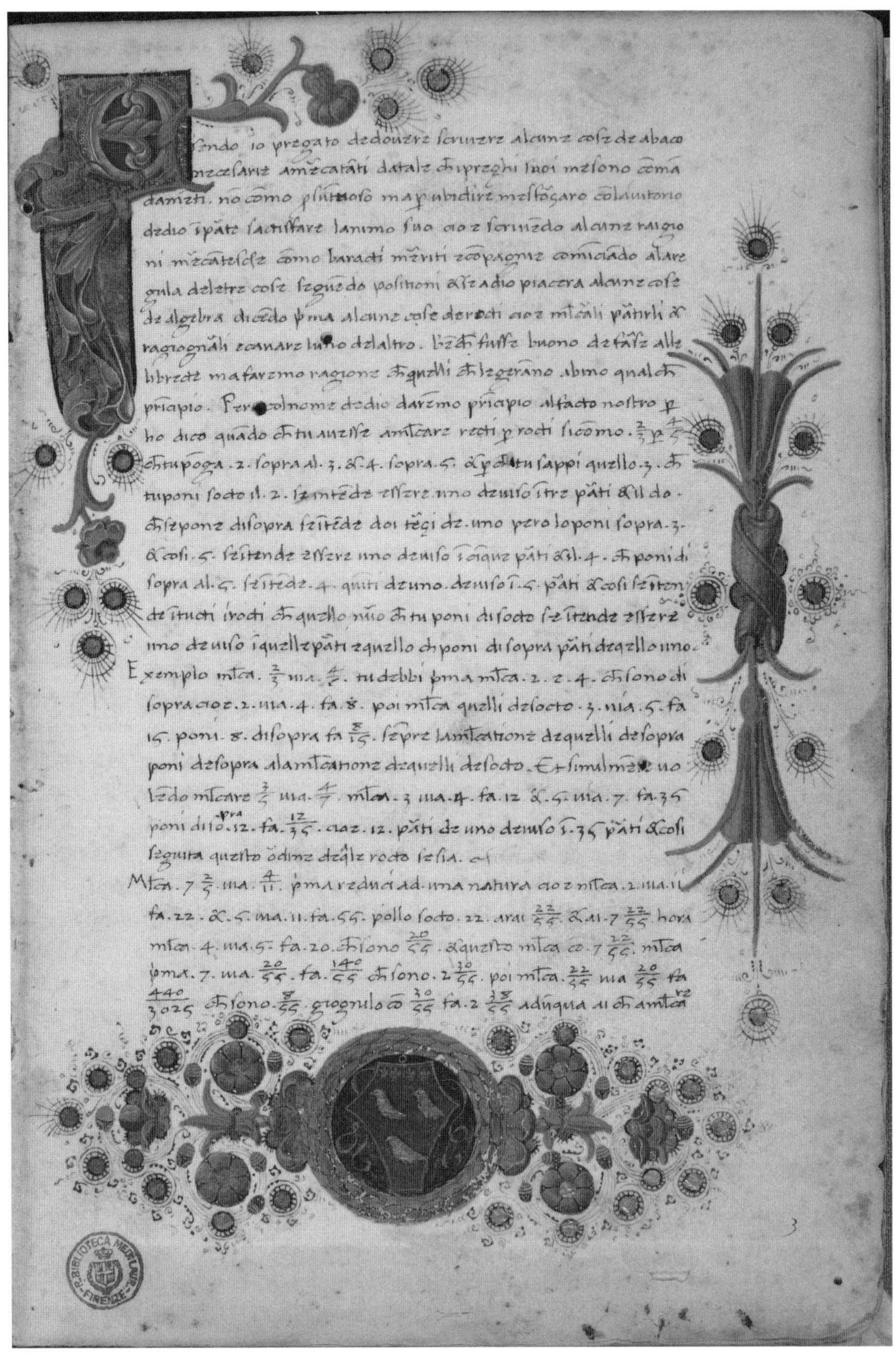

ILLUS. 10 Piero della Francesca, *Trattato d'abaco*, Ashburnhamiano 280 (359*–291*), fol. 3r, Biblioteca Medicea Laurenziana, Florence

the first two probably over decades. In this chapter, we concentrate on his *Treatise on Abaco* (Illus. 10).

For this treatise Piero read earlier *abaco* works, as well as Euclid's writings and medieval commentators on Archimedes. The extensive use of these sources and the necessarily long period of his exposure to them—in order to absorb the Greeks' knowledge evident in his writings—suggest that Piero either was in possession of these manuscripts or had continued access to them in someone's library. Like other writers on commercial arithmetic, he borrowed from Leonardo Fibonacci's widely available work from the thirteenth century that conveyed Arabic mathematical knowledge to Europe, or from one or more of the many subsequent treatments of the *abaco* teachers who usually reproduced Fibonacci's teachings faithfully. Piero shows the greatest familiarity with Tuscan writers on *abaco*, in particular the fourteenth-century masters Gilio from Siena and Paolo Gerardi from Florence, so probably he gained his mathematical knowledge either in Sansepolcro or Arezzo.[1] In the Quattrocento, Sansepolcro had no formal instruction in *abaco*, and Arezzo had no master of *abaco* for much of the first two-thirds of the fifteenth century, but from 1446 to 1456 the commune of Arezzo paid five *abaco* masters for formal public education in commercial mathematics. None of these masters is known to have written an *abaco* work, and each probably relied on one or more of the older textbooks on commercial arithmetic for his instruction. Given Piero's documented residences in this period and his work in Arezzo in the church of San Francesco during the mid-1450s, he may have had contact with one or more of these *abaco* masters. I would suggest master Piero da Montepulciano who taught in Arezzo from 1452 to 1455. Our Piero may have had conversations in Arezzo on *abaco* with this master Piero, but it is clear that he did not receive later formal study in *abaco* there as the town had no public school of *abaco* or full-time master from 1457 to 1484, the latter date being well beyond Piero's latest period of residence in the town.[2]

Piero only slowly developed his interest in classical mathematics, perhaps because he had no formal education beyond a few years in grammar school. No one knows when and where he gained the capacity to read complex geometrical books in Latin, but in his books Piero demonstrated that he had consulted Euclid's *Elements*. Manuscripts of this classic Greek work were not common or even to be found in libraries of many of the most learned men. The historian of science Pier Daniele Napolitani has emphasized the difficulties in comprehending and utilizing the complicated assumptions, procedures, and proofs of Euclidean geometry, which employed a theoretical-deductive procedure based on reasoning logically from general statements. Because Greek mathematics lacked the zero and negative numbers and derived from a rhetorical culture as well as from discussions of natural science, the geometry of Euclid was constructed on the basis of concepts and on magnitudes, not numerical quantities.[3] Proofs in Euclidean geometry were established by demonstrating proportionality, congruity, similarity, and "exhausting" proofs. This complexity would have slowed any person's grasp of Greek geometry, however equal they were to Piero in their natural intellectual abilities.

Euclid's procedure in the *Elements* was to begin with a series of definitions, for example in Book I definitions of a point and a line. This was followed by a series of postulates or axioms that were asserted without proof. Then there were common notions, for example (again from Book I) things that equal the same thing also equal one another. Finally, there are the theorems or propositions to be proved by geometrical constructions. An example from Book I states that if a straight line stands on another straight line, then it makes either two right angles or angles whose sum equals two right angles. These rules may seem elementary and they are, but they are only the basis for far more complicated geometrical constructions. To take the least complex example in Book XII (Proposition 10), Euclid shows that a cone's volume is one third of that of a cylinder, assuming the two shapes are equal in base and height.

At some point Piero came into possession of a Latin copy of the *Elements* of Euclid. This we know from the fact that in all three of his books Piero cites directly from the text and not through an intermediary. He cites Euclid and the *Elements* twelve times in the *Treatise*, seven times in *On Perspective*, and fifty-two times in the *Little Book*. Piero numbered the propositions he borrowed from Euclid's *Elements* differently from the numbering found in most manuscripts of the *Elements*. Because he was consistent in this numbering in all three of his works, Piero would have possessed the same rare manuscript of the *Elements* in the decades when he composed his three books and held it in hand for consultation as he wrote them.[4]

In the fifteenth century most people with an interest in Euclid derived their knowledge from instruction in a university. Their interest was largely theoretical and text-based, rather than in the application of geometry to practical problems. In contrast, *abaco* writers were fundamentally practical, and their instruction focused on surveying and using geometry to solve problems deriving from merchant exchanges. As we have seen, Piero did not attend a university, and no mathematician or professor systematically instructed him in geometry. As in his learning of Latin, Piero taught himself the intricacies of geometry through a study of Euclid, as well as the arithmetic in the *abaco* tradition, over an extended period of time. Piero's striking combination of the two traditions of *abaco* and Greek geometry in the *Treatise* may be best seen in his integration of the Greek verbal constructions with arithmetical representation of the proofs; Piero used numbers and arithmetic that he learned from the *abaco* tradition to express the proofs of Euclid that the Greek expressed only in sentences and magnitudes.

Piero's mastery of Greek mathematics and geometry, acquired through non-formal means, was further stimulated by his presence in Rome in 1453–54 and 1458–59 where he gained access to the Greek scientific manuscripts in translation. Until the 1450s Rome was a backwater, a relatively small city racked by the conflicts of its leading noble families. The violence in Rome had led the popes to migrate to Avignon under the protection of the French kings for the greater part of the fourteenth century. When the papal Curia returned to Rome in 1377, the French cardinals so feared the Roman crowds that they returned to Avignon and elected another Pope. This led to the Great Schism (1378–1415), with popes in Avignon and Rome both claiming to be God's representative on earth. After this conflict was solved with the selection of Pope Martin V (1417), he and his successor Eugenius IV (*r.* 1431–47) often were forced to live outside Rome. It was only with the election of Pope Nicholas V (*r.* 1447–55) that Rome was sufficiently safe for the popes to remain within the city. Nicholas began a conscious project to pacify and reconstruct Rome as the capital of Christendom with building projects and commissions for artists, architects, and humanists. He replaced Saint John Lateran with the Vatican as the center of the papal Curia. He brought Tuscan painters, Fra Angelico and Piero for example, to decorate the Vatican Palace, itself in the process of transformation. He supported new constructions and received Leon Battista Alberti's first version of *Ten Books on Architecture*, and perhaps accepted ideas on urban renewal from this Florentine humanist. He also advanced a program for the revival of classical culture by supporting humanists and commissioning works, especially translations of Greek works into Latin.

Exposure to these translations of Greek mathematical works proved to be crucial for Piero. In Rome, Piero shared an interest in these texts with his cousin once removed Francesco del Borgo, whom we saw earlier as a member of Piero's youthful group. Recent scholarship has shown the importance of Francesco del Borgo, who served in the Curia of four popes and by the late 1450s and 1460s had become the architect of the most innovative buildings in Rome.[5] Despite the ground-breaking research of Christoph Frommel on Francesco del Borgo's accomplishments in architecture, little has been known of his attraction to classical culture. He and Piero apparently encouraged each other in their study of Greek geometry and its visual representation; they both pursued interests that were fundamentally different from those of most humanists of their day. Humanists of the first half of the Quattrocento focused on rhetoric and grammar, pursuing the revival and critical editing of Roman and Greek historical and literary texts. About these endeavors neither Piero nor Francesco ever showed any curiosity. They were much more interested in reviving the *scientific* texts on geometry and optics left behind by the Greeks as well as in replicating ancient lettering, drawings for buildings, and the use of geometrical designs as proofs.

Francesco del Borgo and Greek Geometry

Piero's presence in Rome in 1458–59 is best understood in the context of this relationship with Francesco di Benedetto d'Antonio Cereo (or del Cera), usually identified as Francesco del Borgo.[6] Francesco's father had married Piero's cousin, Agnola di Niccolò di Zengho, thereby establishing a family connection between Piero and Francesco. It is near certain that Francesco was instrumental in introducing Piero to Greek scientific texts in Rome. As discussed in Chapter 3, migrants to larger cities from the same rural area or small town normally settled together in their own neighborhood, with earlier migrants aiding fellow townsmen and family members in finding residences and employment. These obligations intensified when the newly arrived was from the same family network. Francesco del Borgo probably encouraged papal officials to offer Piero commissions; in any case, Piero would have sought out his cousin once removed for advice in understanding and using the intricate networks of the papal Curia. And Francesco del Borgo may have been the most successful navigator of the papal bureaucracy in the mid-fifteenth century, until charges of misusing papal funds led to his trial in 1467 and death the following year.

The linkage of the two men can be determined by analyzing Francesco's career through 1459. Approximately the same age, Piero and Francesco shared a childhood in Sansepolcro and probably studied together in the town's grammar school.[7] By the 1450s the two men were among only a few Quattrocento Europeans to share an interest in classical manuscripts on geometry and mathematics. Even had they not been cousins once removed and former residents of the same quarter in Sansepolcro, this common interest would have drawn them together when Piero was resident in Rome.

Francesco appears in Città di Castello in 1449, where he received a commission by the city government to write and record the property tax (*catasto*).[8] This Umbrian city, ten miles from Sansepolcro, had excellent relations with papal Rome, and Francesco transferred there soon after. The earliest document in which he appears in Rome shows that he was working as a notary in the papal Curia, recording the income taken by papal officials in the form of customs tolls on imports entering the city along the River Tiber. From May 1451 Francesco managed these accounts books and a "secret cash box" of the papacy, taking taxes from the Tiber customs and assigning them to the necessities of the papal household. More importantly, he distributed income for construction projects on the Capitoline hill, Santa Maria Maggiore, and elsewhere. This foreshadowed his service to future popes as supervisor and architect of papal constructions in Rome. As a member of the Apostolic Camera, an intimate of the popes, and interested in construction, Francesco would have been in contact with Bernardo Rossellino, the official papal architect in 1453 and 1454, and probably with the humanist architect Leon Battista Alberti. Although Francesco's achievements in architecture are beyond the scope of our story here, his importance is evident from the fact that he designed the Piazza in front of Old St Peters and the Loggia of Benediction beside the church, in addition to redesigning the church of San Marco and the Palazzo Venezia.[9]

Evidence of Francesco's familiarity with humanistic practices can first be seen in his account book that recorded large payments from various cities to the papacy and expenses for its military captains in 1454.[10] Francesco wrote in an elegant minuscule humanistic hand with both letters and numbers spaced in near-perfect proportion and with rounded capitals and small letters. The use of this hand was unusual in account books; Francesco probably decided to employ this more elegant hand as a means to demonstrate his superior knowledge, to show members of the Curia that he was prepared to move from being a notary to becoming a member of the prestigious College of the "Writers of Apostolic Letters," a status that he had achieved by 1457–58, but only after having taken holy orders as well. This humanistic hand had earlier been introduced by Niccolò Niccoli and Poggio Bracciolini in Florence, but by mid-century there were practitioners of the hand in Rome.[11] Piero himself was in the process of adopting the capital letters of this style (known as the majuscule humanistic alphabet) in several of his paintings in the early 1450s.

The range of Francesco's interest in the new humanistic learning is evident in his involvement in the revival of Greek mathematics, optics, and geometry. Francesco commissioned three copies of Latin manuscripts of Greek mathematics. In line with Pope Nicholas' attempt to revive the study of Euclid, Francesco commissioned an exquisitely illuminated manuscript of Euclid's *Elements* in Latin with geometrical drawings (Vatican Library, Vat. Lat. 2224). Francesco's second commission was a copy in Latin of Euclid's *Optics*; this manuscript also included Ptolemy's *Sphera* and a work on algebra by the Arab writer Mohammed Ben Musa Al-Khawarizmi (Vatican Library, Urb. Lat. 1329). In this latter manuscript, according to Frommel, Francesco drew the geometrical illustrations.[12]

The two Euclidian manuscripts have several features in common. At the end of the Vatican manuscript of the *Elements*, the French scribe Michael Foresius recorded that he had written "the *Geometria* [*Elements*] of Euclid . . . in the city of Rome in 1457 for don Francesco da Borgo San Sepolcro, apostolic scribe and familiar of Pope Calisto III." At the end of the *Optics* manuscript Foresius concluded that he had written "this book for don Francesco, apostolic scribe from Borgo San Sepolcro in the city of Rome, 24 October 1458." Thus both manuscripts were commissioned by Francesco and written by the same French scribe. The two manuscripts contain miniatures as well as geometrical drawings.[13]

Attesting to the "avant-garde" nature of these manuscripts is the fact that the miniaturist who decorated Euclid's *Elements* (Vatican Lat. 2224) painted a realistic view of Rome that derived from Leon Battista Alberti's drawing in his *Delineation of the City of Rome* (*Descriptio urbis Romae*). In that work Alberti had combined a circular map with a polar coordinate system in a new mode for depicting cityscapes that included an accurate representation of building sizes and distances. The miniaturist in Vat. Lat. 2224 adopted Alberti's system and his characterization of Roman features, including errors in Alberti's cityscape.[14]

Meanwhile, Pope Nicholas had sponsored a translation of the works of Archimedes from Greek to Latin by Jacopo da San Cassiano (Cremona). Jacopo was a student of the Mantuan humanist Vittorino da Feltre and succeeded his mentor as tutor to the children of the Duke of Mantua, Ludovico III Gonzaga.[15] Jacopo had finished the original working copy (*primum exemplar*) of his Latin translation of the works of Archimedes by 1453.[16] The Archimedes manuscript was sent to Cardinal Bessarion soon after it was translated, and he returned it to the Vatican Library, but by 1458 Francesco had taken it from the library without leaving the customary note indicating that the manuscript had been borrowed. He then placed it in the hands of a scribe who produced a beautiful copy (Vatican Library, Urb. Lat. 261). At the end of the manuscript the unnamed scribe recorded that "Lord Francesco del Borgo ordered" that the books of Archimedes be transcribed.[17] That the manuscript was prepared for Francesco's library is evident because half hidden in a miniature of a letter that introduces Archimedes' discussion of the "Quadrature of the Parabola" the miniaturist or scribe wrote "D[ominus] Francischus de Bourgo."[18] With Francesco's name painted into an illuminated letter, it is doubtful that the manuscript was prepared for anyone else. In an inventory of his possessions after his death there is a list of around twenty manuscripts with elegant bindings.[19] Although none of the manuscripts was specifically identified, it is evident that Francesco retained many of his books to his death in 1468. This manuscript of Archimedes is beautifully written and illuminated with precisely drawn geometrical figures to illustrate the Greek's geometry.

Jacopo da San Cassiano's original translation of Archimedes that Francesco borrowed from the Vatican Library to be copied apparently was never returned by him to the Library. He seems to have retained the Archimedes manuscript in his possession, probably until his death for it never appeared again in the Library. The original Jacopo translation has a title written in a hand different from that of Jacopo's found throughout the text. The title states: "Archimedes *On the sphere and the cylinder*, book one interpreted [*interpetre*] by Francesco Cereo from Borgo San Sepolcro."[20] Cereo was the family name used by Francesco's father, so the manuscript somehow is linked to Francesco del Borgo, but the meaning of the word "interpetre" (probably a misspelling of the Latin "interprete") has caused confusion. Perhaps the writer intended to say that Francesco del Borgo had translated Archimedes' work into Latin. But the fact that the writer of the title knew Francesco's family name Cereo, which is not found otherwise in these manuscripts, suggests that this writer was from Sansepolcro and knowledgable about the manuscript's composition, and was taking pride in his co-citizen's participation in the construction of the manuscript.[21] Frommel's suggestion that Francesco had drawn the geometrical models in one manuscript leads us out of this conundrum. The writer of the title, in saying that Francesco "interpreted" Archimedes, clearly meant that Francesco had drawn the geometrical figures. In this manuscript the geometrical figures are precisely constructed geometric illustrations, frequently following the mathematical rules of perspective. Given that the writer of the title was probably from Sansepolcro and that Piero later came into possession of a copy of the Archimedes manuscript, it seems reasonable to conclude that the manuscript was sent with Francesco's other manuscripts to Borgo on his death.

Piero in Rome, 1458–59

I hold that Piero left Sansepolcro for Rome on or soon after 22 September 1458, having made his brother Marco his procurator in a dispute with the Franciscan Observant friars in Borgo. Most researchers place Piero in Rome in late 1458 and 1459 because in April 1459 he received 150 Vatican florins from papal sources in part payment for a painting in the papal palace.[22] This places Piero in Rome at exactly the moment that Francesco del Borgo had taken the manuscript of Archimedes from the Vatican Library and commissioned a copy (Vatican Library, Urb. Lat. 261), whilst organizing as well the copying of the two Latin manuscripts of Euclid. At some point in the remaining three decades of his life Piero was to deal in detail with three of the four manuscripts discussed above (the two of Archimedes and Euclid's *Optics*). His astounding persistence in gaining possession of these three manuscripts, all central to the fifteenth-century revival of Greek geometry, is the story for later chapters (see Chapters 13 and 14).

The papal payment of 150 florins for Piero's painting in the Vatican Palace indicates that he began painting it soon after having left his native town in September 1458. Because the 150 florins was only a part payment for his labor, it is probable that he painted at least until the summer of 1459. Little is known of Piero's painting in Rome beyond the payment and the ambiguous statements of Vasari. In the 1550 edition of the *Vite*, Vasari wrote on Piero's paintings in Ferrara: "These works made him known to Pope Nicholas V, who, having brought him to Rome, commissioned him to paint in the Palace two historical scenes in the rooms on the upper floor in competition with Bramantino of Milan. These paintings together were demolished by Pope Julius II to permit Raphael of Urbino to paint there his *Liberation of St Peter from Prison* and the *Miracle of the Mass of Bolsena*." Later, Vasari wrote of Piero that "having finished his work in Rome, he returned to Borgo for the death of his mother." The 1568 edition changes only the last sentence: "Having finished work in Rome he returned to Borgo his mother being dead." It is impossible to know whether Piero returned to Sansepolcro before or just after his mother's death on 6 November 1459, but it is almost certain Piero departed from Rome at this time.[23]

The April 1459 payment conveys important information. It reads: "We paid 150 florins of the treasury, by the command of the vicar of the vice treasurer on day 7 [April], to Piero from Borgo, painter, for part of his work of certain paintings he is doing in the room of the Holiness of Our Lord Pope."[24] The document suggests that the payment to Piero was for ongoing work with the Italian verb *fa* ("is doing") in the present tense. Unfortunately, there is no other document of payment to Piero, despite the document's statement that 150 florins were for "part of his work of certain paintings." But by combining information from documents about Piero's presence in and probable departure from Sansepolcro on 22 September 1458 with that found in the payment document, we can be confident that Piero was in Rome painting for Pope Pius II from the fall of 1458 to some time after April 1459—and through November of that year if Vasari's statements are accurate.

But where exactly was Piero painting? Vasari stated that Raphael's frescoes replaced those of Piero and Bramantino. If accurate, this would place their paintings in the Stanza d'Eliodoro on the third floor of the north wing of the Vatican Palace. But in our discussion of Piero's earlier visit to Rome, it was argued that since Pope Nicholas' coat of arms were in the room where Raphael later painted, it is more likely that Piero painted there in 1453 for Nicholas, and then painted elsewhere in the Palace in 1458–59 for Pius II. And since there is evidence of a building project for Pius II at this time in the west wing of the Palace, it is probable that Piero painted there.[25] But on the precise location and the subjects of Piero's painting in the Vatican Palace, to say less may be better than offering new hypotheses. We can be more confident in the extant documents that locate Piero only in Sansepolcro and Arezzo in the years from 1460 to 1467. It was in these years that he wrote his *Treatise on Abaco.*

Piero's *Treatise on Abaco*

Most researchers agree that Piero's *Treatise on Abaco*, *On Perspective in Painting*, and *The Little Book on the Five Regular Bodies* were written in that order. The greater geometrical sophistication demonstrated in the *Little Book* compared to the *Treatise* suggests the latter as the earliest text. Moreover, it has been demonstrated that Piero utilized medieval sources for his knowledge of Archimedes in the *Treatise*, but that in the *Little Book* he borrowed directly from the 1451–53 Latin translation of Archimedes by Jacopo da Cassiano. Arguments found in both the *Treatise* and the *Little Book* are expressed more economically in the latter, again pointing to it being the later work. Finally, Piero dedicated his *Little Book* to Duke Guidobaldo da Montefeltro after the death of the Duke's father Federico in 1482, which suggests that it was not finished until at least that date. Less conclusive is the evidence as to when Piero published his *On Perspective in Painting*, but most agree that it followed the *Treatise* and preceded the *Little Book*.

Their order is fixed; the dates of composition of the works are more difficult to determine. The most common estimates are from the 1450s to the 1470s for the *Treatise*, a date in the 1470s for *On Perspective in Painting*, and for the *Little Book* the 1480s. Piero spent many years composing at least the first two of these works, in the same protracted manner in which he executed several of his paintings. Evidence for an extended period of composition for the *Treatise* is suggested by his consulting of many *abaco* texts and by the repetition of several algebraic problems in his work. A short period of systematic composition would have shown less familiarity with many works of *abaco* and would probably have avoided the repetitions. Piero copied problems and examples from a variety of earlier *abaco* manuscripts.[26] It is certain that he would not have had several of these works in hand at one time or in one place. In their analysis of Piero's mathematical works, Enrico Gamba and Vico Montebelli conclude that the first two were the "fruit of the mathematical maturity" of Piero and derived necessarily from his research "conducted along an arc of decades."[27]

It has been asserted that Piero published the *Treatise on Abaco* in the early 1450s, although there is no evidence for this.[28] The date of composition is important as we are trying to represent Piero's painting and writing as evolving within specific time and space coordinates. Because Piero did not sign the manuscript, it was only in the early twentieth century that it was recognized on the basis of its handwriting (which was identified as Piero's) that he had ever even composed this work on *abaco*. The manuscript is also undated. It is therefore very difficult to assign a credible period, much less a specific year, for Piero's composition of the *Treatise*.

We do nonetheless have clues left by Quattrocento papermakers that assist us in estimating the date of Piero's first book. The fifteenth century witnessed a dramatic increase in the amount of paper produced and used. Papermakers placed watermarks on their paper as a form of copyright and advertising. They changed their watermarks over time, and companies of papermakers proliferated, so watermarks multiplied. The filaments of fine wire that formed the watermark image deteriorated after being used for three or four years. The papermaker might then replicate that original design for a new period, but the subsequent one would have differences, some slight and others marked compared to the earlier. The papermakers used images of horses, hats, letters, daggers, and myriad other objects. Watermarks can provide an indication of when writers set their quills to paper by matching watermarks in an undated manuscript to the same watermarks in other dated manuscripts from the same general area. Precise research is required to prove a match of a specific watermark in two manuscripts.

It is fortunate for us that in the case of Piero's *Treatise* we do not need to match specific watermarks found in it to ones in dated manuscripts, because for this manuscript Piero used paper that was first produced in Italy at a readily identifiable date.[29] In fact, we can show that the watermarks of Piero's paper first appeared in Italy in the mid-1460s. In an earlier study I took evidence from the three large collections of thousands of watermarks by Briquet, Picard, and Zonghi, and added my examination of paper and the watermarks of the notarial registers where we know Piero lived in the 1460s (Sansepolcro, Arezzo, Urbino), and compared these watermarks with the three in Piero's *Treatise*.[30] The paper of Piero's work on *abaco* has watermarks of a *balestra* (crossbow) in a circle, a hand, and a balance or scales with concave-shaped weights within a circle. The evidence from the three large collections and my research in specific notarial archives is conclusive and congruent. Piero's paper with its three watermarks did not appear until the mid-1460s in central Italy and specifically in the three towns where we know he lived. We may conclude that Piero and the notaries of Arezzo and Sansepolcro received paper with the three watermarks at approximately the same time and set pen to paper. This establishes the earliest possible years when Piero could have purchased the paper on which he recorded his *Treatise on Abaco*.[31] The watermarks do not exclude the possibility that he could have written it after the mid-1460s because the three watermarks are often present after 1470, at least in Sansepolcro. But it is doubtful that Piero wrote his *Treatise* after the mid-1460s because it precedes his other two books, and we can establish that Piero wrote his *On Perspective* in the 1470s.

The evidence from the watermarks also indicates where Piero wrote his *abaco* book. It is only in the Tuscan towns of Arezzo and Sansepolcro that these three watermarks of the paper used by Piero in his book are found. All three appeared in the years 1462 to 1468, with the greatest concentration of the three marks in the years 1466 to 1468. I suggested above that Piero came in contact with the Tuscan *abaco* tradition in Arezzo between 1452 and 1455, with the *abaco* master Piero da Montepulciano.[32] The hypothesis that Piero composed his *Treatise* in Arezzo or Sansepolcro, or both, fits well and independently with the fact that Piero borrowed extensively from Tuscan *abaco* writers for the first arithmetic portion of his treatise.[33] In summary: Piero wrote his final draft of the *Treatise* from approximately 1464 to 1468, while in Sansepolcro or Arezzo, or in both cities. Independently of watermarks and Piero's sources of knowledge of *abaco*, extant documents locate Piero only in Sansepolcro and Arezzo in the years from 1460 to 1466, as we shall see in subsequent chapters. We turn now to a more detailed description of Piero's first treatise for what it teaches us about Piero and his extraordinary mind.

The only complete manuscript of the *Treatise on Abaco* was written by Piero in a minuscule script.[34] Unlike other *abaco* treatises, Piero's work was not intended for students, and the existing manuscript is not a copy by a student of a master's lectures. Piero addressed an adult merchant, although the tone and familiar address to the reader reflects the *abaco* tradition. At the beginning of the work Piero states: "Since I was requested that I should write something concerning *abaco* necessary to merchants, by one whose requests are to me commands, not to be presumptuous but in order to obey, I endeavor with the aid of God, in part to satisfy his mind [*animo*], that is by writing on some commercial problems as barter, prices, and companies."[35] Piero referred here to someone who requested the book. Given that Piero's autograph work has the shield of the Pichi family of Sansepolcro, it has been assumed by all that it was a member of this family who placed Piero under the obligation of writing his *Treatise.*[36] The Pichi family was large and wealthy, with many men active in politics and commerce, but in the 1460s none was particularly learned. If Piero refers here to a Pichi, perhaps it was the notary Francesco Pichi, whose shop abutted the workshop of the Della Francesca. If someone other than a Pichi requested Piero to write a work on commercial arithmetic, Francesco del Borgo is a possible candidate given his ownership of books, his interest in mathematics, and his stature as a papal official, all of which would lend him the authority that is implicit in Piero's statement. But one wonders whether Francesco would have recommended to Piero anything other than a work based exclusively on Greek geometry. The question for whom Piero was writing remains open.

In both the arithmetic and geometric sections of the *Treatise on Abaco*, Piero went beyond practical commercial merchants' needs as well as beyond earlier and contemporary writers in the tradition. The work contains 480 problems, the majority of which are typical of those found in *abaco* textbooks, with the remaining 30 percent dedicated to geometry. Of the 480 total problems covered in the *Treatise*, Piero reconsidered 83 in the *Little Book*. He drew 132 geometrical designs in the *Treatise*, at times employing a compass and a dry-point scribe.[37] The *Treatise* opens with a discussion of fractions and then goes into an extended discussion of the "Rule of Three." This "rule" today would be set up as "a is to b as c is to d" or a:b = c:d. Piero discusses it in verbal phrases, writing:

> The Rule of the Three says one should multiply the thing one wants to know by that which is dissimilar to it, and one divides the result by the remaining thing.

> And the number that comes from this is of the nature of that which is dissimilar to the first term, and the divisor is always similar to the thing which one wants to know about.
>
> For example: 7 bracci of cloth are worth 9 lire, what will 5 bracci be worth?
>
> Do it like this: multiply the quantity you want to know by that quantity which 7 bracci of cloth are worth, that is 9 lire. Five times 9 makes 45, divide by 7, and what comes out is 6 lire, remainder 3/7 . . . [or] 6 Libre, 8 soldi, and 6 6/7 denari.

It is a simple proportion to which Piero devotes a long discussion with many examples.[38] Much of the discussion involves explanations of how to reduce complex problems of barter and shareholdings in merchant companies to a series of proportions. Piero has included an extended discussion because such proportions were fundamental to his arithmetic and geometry.

Piero then produces an arithmetic procedure called the "Rule of Double False Position," which is a means of finding a solution to equations with one unknown without using algebraic notation. His first step was to make an estimate and find the size of the error and then make a second estimate and again find the error, culminating with a calculation that relates the estimates to the errors. The first estimate is multiplied by the second error, which is subtracted from the second estimate multiplied by the first error, which is then divided by the remainder of the second error minus the first error. As if by magic, the calculation solves the equation. Piero presents many examples of this ancient method, known by both the Egyptians and Chinese and conveyed to Europeans by the Arabs. Piero's easiest example asks the reader to calculate the weight of the parts of a fish if in total it weighs 60 pounds with the head weighing 3/5 of the body and the tail 1/3 of the head. Piero begins by estimating that the body weighs 30 pounds and then applying the fractions to the estimate; this estimate yields the three parts as 30 (body) + 18 (head) + 6 (tail) = 54. This answer is not correct as it is not 60 pounds, and it has an error of 6. A second estimate of 25 for the body yields 25 + 15 + 5, and thus another incorrect total of 45 pounds and an error of 15. But we now have sufficient information to solve the problem by applying the formula to the calculations, which is expressed as:

$30 \times 15 = 450 - 25 \times 6 = 150 = 300$
$15 - 6 = 9$
300 divided by $9 = 33\frac{1}{3}$
For the head, $\frac{3}{5}$ of $33\frac{1}{3} = 20$
For the tail, $\frac{1}{3}$ of $20 = 6\frac{2}{3}$

Now the solution: $33\frac{1}{3}$ (body) + 20 (head) and $6\frac{2}{3}$ (tail) = 60.[39]

Piero then introduces algebra with a discussion of square roots:

> And now I intend to say a few necessary things about algebra, which addresses fractions and integers and of roots and squares, or of simple numbers. When

> numbers are multiplied by themselves, then those numbers are called roots, and the products which come out are called squares. And when the numbers are considered neither roots nor squares, then they are called simple numbers. Thus, according to this definition, all numbers are sometimes roots, or squares, or simple numbers.[40]

From here he proceeds to define the forms of equations and gives examples. His primary source, Leonardo Fibonacci, discussed six forms of equations, whereas Piero introduces a total of fifty-five, including cubic equations, biquadrate equations, and equations in the fifth degree.[41]

In the last third of the work Piero shifts to a discussion of geometry. Of geometrical problems, eighty-four can be categorized as dealing with plane geometry and fifty-six with solid geometry. He begins conventionally with discussions of plane geometry worked in a problem-solving form, specifically how to find heights and areas of triangles. Here he discusses many of the same types of examples as earlier *abaco* writers; like them, Piero introduces problems deriving from conventional methods of measuring land, distances, heights, and containers through computations of wells, towers, barrels, and walls. He distinguishes himself from the *abaco* writers by concentrating on abstract figures of plane and solid geometry.[42] Piero was drawn to the geometrical shapes themselves and not the everyday objects to which they referred or corresponded. In this, his first written work, Piero already demonstrates a firm grasp of complicated Greek propositions and the ability to appropriate these propositions into the traditional *abaco* numerical proofs.

A few of the earlier and contemporary *abaco* writers pointed out that solids have length, width, and depth or categorized objects as columns or pyramids. Certainly, Fibonacci had already considered many geometrical problems in his *Practice of Geometry* (*Pratica geometria*) in the thirteenth century. Piero's discussions of polygons and polyhedra, however, show a fascination for plane and solid objects, their lines, their surfaces, and their depths. Whereas the *abaco* writers and Fibonacci in his geometrical work may mention an abstract shape, they returned quickly to objects of daily life. Piero, on the other hand, constructs an abstract world of triangles, squares, pentagons, cones, and cubes. Despite the simplicity of expression and detailed constructions, one sees in his work the play of his mind and his single-minded concentration on the propositions and their proofs. This is especially true of his plane geometry and the measurement of polygons. In the measurement of triangles, Piero often employs the Pythagorean Theorem, which holds that in a right-angled triangle the sum of the square of the side opposite the right angle (the hypotenuse) is equal to the sum of the squares of the other two sides. In many propositions Piero solves problems by dividing complex geometrical figures so that there is a right-angled or equilateral triangle, from which he then deduces the measurements and areas of the more complex figures.[43]

Piero then moves on to polyhedra.[44] His most sophisticated geometrical thinking in the *Treatise* is seen in his discussion of the five "regular" or Platonic bodies (Fig. 6.1) and

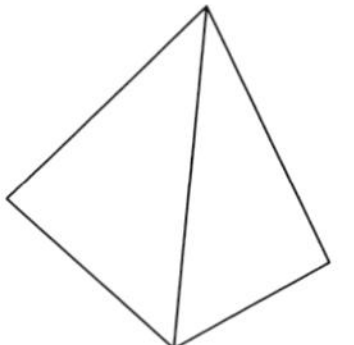
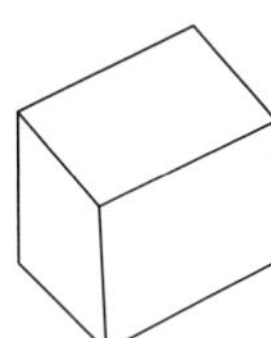
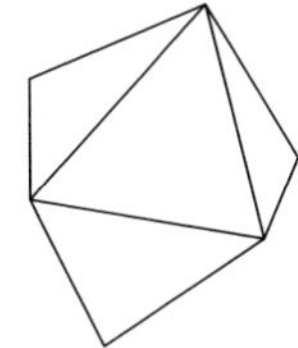
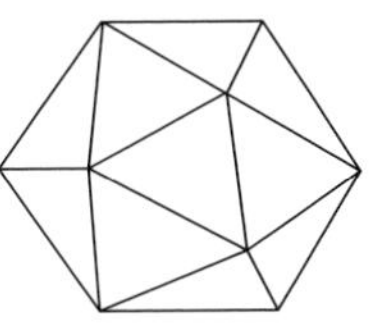
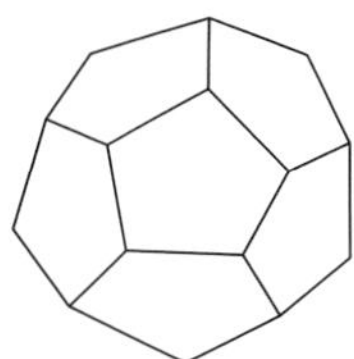

FIGURE 6.1 The Five Regular Bodies (Platonic Solids)

the "irregular" or Archimedean bodies. The five regular bodies (polyhedra) are three-dimensional solids in which each is composed of one type of polygon having equal angles and sides. The five are: the pyramid or tetrahedron composed of four equilateral triangles; the cube or hexahedron composed of six squares; the octahedron composed of two pyramids attached at their square bases, yielding eight sides of equilateral triangles; the dodecahedron that presents twelve faces, each a pentagon equilateral and equal angled; and finally the icosahedron of twenty equilateral triangles. Piero surrounds each of the regular bodies with a sphere, with each vertex of each polyhedron touching the curved surface of the sphere. The five regular bodies were often discussed in the ancient world, and Piero found a thorough discussion of them in Book XIII of Euclid's *Elements*. But we should note that Fibonacci had discussed three of the five, so their existence was known by a few medieval writers.

In the *Treatise* and in the *Little Book* Piero showed an uncommon facility with six of the thirteen Archimedean or semi-regular solids, which are much more complex than the five regular bodies. The defining properties of these polyhedra are that for each "every face is completely visible on the outside of the solid and... every vertex of the solid is surrounded by regular polygons arranged in the same way."[45] These polyhedra are solids in which each of the thirteen has two or three types of polygons, each of which is equilateral and equiangular. One of Piero's more complicated Archimedean polyhedra is the truncated icosahedron, which has thirty-two faces and sixty vertices and is composed of twelve pentagons and twenty hexagons.[46] Piero goes far beyond his medieval predecessors or contemporaries, whether in the *abaco* tradition or in the universities, in his knowledge and manipulation of the Archimedean or irregular solids. In the *Treatise* Piero discussed two of these, the truncated pyramid and the truncated cube. Let us examine the simplest of the thirteen, the truncated cube, which is constructed by cutting the eight vertices of a cube halfway down the cube's sides. The result is a solid of six octagons and eight triangles, of course adhering to the definition that each octagon and triangle has equal angles and sides. The other irregular solids are constructed in an analogous way but with more complex truncating of the other regular bodies. Piero finished his discussion in the *Treatise* after the first two irregular solids; in his *Little Book* he deals with four other Archimedean solids, as we shall see in subsequent chapters where we analyze Piero's later work.

To solve several problems in the *Treatise*, Piero had to borrow another important geometrical concept from the ancient world, the Golden Section or Divine Proportion. He did not use these terms, the second of which Luca Pacioli popularized in his 1498 and 1509 works entitled *Divina proportione.* Piero preferred to borrow from Euclid the phrase "the extreme and mean ratio." Fibonacci also used this concept, which is applied by taking a line or a rectangle and dividing it so that the ratio of whole line or rectangle to the larger part of the divided portion is identical to the ratio of the larger divided portion to the smaller. This relationship cannot be expressed in whole numbers, as it is an irrational mathematical constant. In other geometrical concepts Piero was prompt to find an exact whole number equivalent, but here he could not. He solved problems involving the pentagon and hexagon by employing the extreme and mean ratio, as well as using it in constructing the dodecahedron (twelve pentagons). No other known author of an *abaco* treatise possessed and solved geometrical problems in the sophisticated manner of Fibonacci or Piero, but Piero introduced geometrical problems not known to Fibonacci or others of the period.[47]

Piero ignored or failed to find exciting more speculative notions proposed by others in their discussions of the regular bodies and the mean and extreme ratio.[48] In his *Timaeus* Plato had identified the five regular bodies as the basic units of the universe. These five regular bodies are for the Greek philosopher the basic components of the universe: earth (hexahedron), air (octahedron), fire (tetrahedron), and water (icosahedron), with the dodecahedron representing the ether of the heavens or the universe itself. Piero must have read this application of regular bodies to the cosmos in Book XV of the *Elements* because he took other geometrical propositions from it.[49] Piero chose to ignore the mystifying of the five regular bodies, even though he believed mistakenly that it had the sanction of his much admired Euclid. Nor does Piero share the great fascination of many late Renaissance writers with the Divine Proportion. He certainly used the geometrical concept but he did not mystify his writings by contemplating symbolic or more than geometrical significances of the mean and extreme ratio. This focusing on that which was evident and demonstrative was a constitutive quality of his work and his mind. I doubt that Piero was a committed Platonist, as some have claimed his paintings demonstrate. Certainly when he wrote on perspective and geometry, even on the five Platonic regular bodies or the mean and extreme ratios, he refused to extend his discussion into metaphysical or religious significances. Piero's consistent focus on purely geometrical propositions appears to be a precocious step in separating fields of phenomena from an overall metaphysical or religious superstructure. Here Piero in geometry paralleled Machiavelli in politics, Vesalius in human anatomy, and Copernicus in astronomy in carving out a specific set of phenomena as the subject of his examinations for which he set forth defining propositions.

The dating of Piero's *Treatise on Abaco* to the mid-1460s fits in well with his contact with Francesco del Borgo and Francesco's interest in Greek mathematics and science in the 1450s. In particular it would explain one of the extraordinary features of Piero's *Treatise.* The truly innovative aspect of his work is that its last third is devoted to geometry with only a few discussions related to any practical questions of measurements that one might have found in earlier and contemporary *abaco* treatises. This portion of the *Treatise* contains geometrical problems totally new to the *abaco* tradition and went beyond a common knowledge of geometry, demonstrating Piero's profound understanding of problems of perspective and geometry. Discussions with Francesco del Borgo and familiarity with recently available manuscripts of Greek works in Latin would have provided Piero access to the privileged and not widely dispersed mathematical knowledge circulating in Rome in the early 1450s.

Piero made his conceptual leaps in the *Treatise* by combining practices from *abaco* writers of arithmetic and the scholarly tradition of geometry. He tirelessly translated Greek geometric propositions from their verbal expression and statements of magnitudes to the numbers of the *abaco* tradition. Piero also carries with him an artisan practice in which the master proves himself through products of his hand. The most persuasive proofs in his work are geometrical drawings—just as a painter provided proof of his skill to his prospective patron through his drawings. And of course the language of Piero was the language of the artisans and commercial mathematical masters, a vernacular with local spellings from his home town rather than the Latin of those who customarily read Greek geometrical texts. He had also become a writer, a person who believed it was important to record one's understanding of phenomena and convey this to others. The historian of mathematics, J. V. Field, has rightly emphasized Piero's rhetoric as essentially that of a teacher or a master in a workshop, who presented example after example in the imperative and the familiar form of the *tu*.[50] The reader is instructed to do this and do that. For Piero the emphasis is on the doing and making; he seldom reflects on the relationship of this process to other systems of knowledge. He does not write that painting can be shown to be philosophy, as Leonardo da Vinci would later assert, or comment on how his geometrical discussions relate to religion.

In the *Treatise on Abaco* Piero brought together his knowledge of commercial mathematics and Greek geometry with the practical skill of drawing geometrical proofs. We now return to Sansepolcro and Piero's application of his visual skills in painting.

CHAPTER 7

Piero's Return to Patria and Family

Piero was in Rome in April of 1459, probably remaining there at least into the summer or fall of that year and then he is recorded in Sansepolcro in 1460. For the first time since the 1430s Piero remained in Borgo for an extended period. In this chapter we reconstruct his activities in the three years from either the fall of 1459 or the spring of 1460 through 1462, during which he painted four important frescoes—certainly the most intense period of painting of his life.

Sansepolcro, and especially the Della Francesca family, had greatly changed from what Piero had left some two decades earlier. In the meantime, the town had been integrated into the Florentine economy and territorial state. The Florentine government conveyed the mandates of its powerful guilds into regulations for the merchants of Sansepolcro, although, in a frontier town like Borgo far from the eye of their masters, they enjoyed considerable commercial freedom (see Map 1). Certainly there was a great deal of trade between Borgo and Florence; the most profitable export of the subordinate town was woad, the blue dye that the Florentine cloth guildsmen bought in great quantities. For example, in 1471 the Della Francesca family sold approximately 80,000 pounds of woad to the Rucellai family in Florence through a man in Anghiari.[1] Sansepolcro merchants customarily returned from the capital city with a variety of goods, most of all with cloth to sell locally. Borgo's merchants also traded regularly with towns on the Adriatic from Ancona to Venice. Venetian merchants in particular bought large quantities of woad transported there by the merchants of Sansepolcro.

Piero's family had likewise changed dramatically. When he returned from Rome, his mother was either on her deathbed or already deceased (6 November 1459). Although Piero's father Benedetto remained active in the town, witnessing contracts and sitting in communal councils, he was now in his mid-eighties. Many writers have noted Piero's love of his birthplace and his spurning of larger and more active cities and princely courts. However, he was seldom in Sansepolcro when he was in his thirties and forties. It was after the death of his parents that Piero found the rest of his family and Sansepolcro more congenial. The available evidence suggests that he had problems with the demands of his father. As the firstborn Piero would have been expected to follow his father into commerce and, when he had sufficient wealth from trade, to carry forward the Della Francesca name by marrying and fathering children. His marriage would have also linked his family to another, thereby extending the Della Francesca's influence. Piero failed to meet his father's and society's expectations of the firstborn son. He never married, never had children, and therefore could never fully replicate his father's position as the head of a patriarchal family.

Piero went even further than this in rejecting or ignoring expectations about his duties as the firstborn male. He likely disappointed his father by choosing an occupation that initially secured only modest prestige for himself and his family and promised a paltry income. There had never before been an important native painter in Borgo; rather, local painters eked out meager incomes from small commissions and repairs. As we have seen, a number of documents suggest that either Piero's local patrons or his father Benedetto were skeptical of his commitment to complete the terms of contracts. The reader will recall that Misericordia officials required Benedetto to guarantee his son's commission, and in 1454 the Pichi demanded that Benedetto persuade Piero to return to Sansepolcro. Likewise, the patrons and Augustinian friars were not sure whether Piero would be able or willing to complete their 1454 commission for the Sant'Agostino polyptych and obligated Benedetto and Piero's brothers to stand surety for any potential losses. We cannot be sure whether we are dealing with the patrons' caution, the father's insistence on controlling his son, or everyone's concern with what we might call an artist's single-mindedness.

As Benedetto grew older, supervision of the commercial activities and the management of property for the family descended into the hands of Piero's brothers Marco and Antonio. In the fifteenth century, unless sons were explicitly "emancipated" from their father's authority by a legal act, they were subordinated to him until his death. Benedetto never liberated his sons; as a result they pooled their assets in Benedetto's hands and lived with him in the substantial family house, even though Marco and Antonio had wives and children. The family accumulated considerable property through the second half of the Quattrocento. In notarial contracts Marco appears as the active purchaser of land in his, Antonio's, and his father's name, but not in Piero's name, until Benedetto's death in 1464. After the death of the father, the three sons, now including Piero, are said to be the purchasers, and occasionally vendors, of property. At the same time most of the family responsibilities passed to Marco, who married twice into important families, fathered numerous children, became a successful merchant, and held nearly every important social and political office in Sansepolcro, thereby fulfilling the expectations of Benedetto and the values encoded in Italian patriarchal culture. Only in the 1480s did Piero assume the role of the firstborn of the family and supervise the affairs of the Della Francesca.

Patriarchs as demanding as Benedetto were not uncommon in Quattrocento Italy, and sons were expected to accept and maneuver around paternal demands. Piero in his late twenties removed himself from the presence of his father for two decades, and only with the fatal illness of his mother and with his father nearly eighty-five years old did he make Sansepolcro his more or less permanent home. Perhaps Piero and Benedetto came to some sort of accommodation after his mother Romana's death; doubtless Piero's profitable commissions and his renown were now also speaking volumes to his father.

Once Piero had taken up residence in Sansepolcro again in 1459–60, his fellow citizens bestowed offices on him, several of which included significant obligations. These positions indicate that Piero had gained local fame from his commissions in Ancona, Rimini, Arezzo, and Rome. Individual citizens and the commune assigned tasks to him that imply knowledge of architecture and also a commitment from the painter that he would be in Sansepolcro for months or even years. Before turning to Piero's paintings of this period, let us examine the family's workshops and the social-political tasks he was assigned.

Workshops of the Della Francesca Family and Piero's Presence in Sansepolcro

From the 1440s through 1466 the Della Francesca family rented shops on Sansepolcro's central piazza. Renaissance shops (*botteghe*) often combined craftwork and sales, but it is likely that the Della Francesca or their employees performed only the ultimate decorative leather work in these central shops. The more basic phases of leather and woad preparation, including bathing of animal hides and the woad plant in malodorous solutions, would have been relegated to the town's periphery or along side streets with water sources. The family shops for the sale of merchandise were centrally located, one on the south side of the Piazza Comunale in the area around the Torre di Berta and the houses of the Fraternity of San Bartolomeo. A second was even more central as it was across from the entrance to the Badia of Sansepolcro and on the upper edges of the Piazza Comunale. In 1450 Benedetto and his sons Marco and Antonio moved into this workshop in the center of Sansepolcro. This shop became the focal point of their activities for a decade and a half. From here father and sons had access to the social, economic, and political discussions of the town. It was also a convenient place for notaries to draft contracts; Benedetto and his sons often served as witnesses for transactions requiring written formal representation.[2] They maintained this latter workshop until 1466, when the sons relinquished it because they had come into possession of a shop at the Graziani Crossing (see Map 2). Here the most prestigious families of Sansepolcro resided: the Cattani, Anastagi, Pichi, and the Graziani.

In 1460 on the north-west corner of the Graziani Crossing, Piero collaborated with his brothers and father to transform an urban building into a workshop for the family's commercial activities. At some earlier unknown moment, perhaps as payment for Piero's painting of *The Baptism of Christ*, the Della Francesca family had obtained joint ownership with the Graziani family of a large urban structure. In the spring of 1460 the two families decided to divide the property. The Della Francesca family designated their portion of the building as a workshop with rooms above, a base that would serve as the center of their economic activities from the mid-1460s to beyond the death of Piero, although their reconstruction of the site took several years to complete.

The earliest documentation of the division of the building dates from 30 April 1460 when a Graziani representative made a "pact of division" with Benedetto, and in the name of his sons Marco and Antonio.[3] Piero's name was not initially included in the agreement. The two families agreed that Marco would draw a design of the building and divide it into two parts. He had an incentive to make the parts as equal as possible because the Graziani had the privilege of choosing which part they wanted. A few days later Marco presented the design to the Graziani, with that family's most senior member, Benedetto di Baldino Graziani, observing the transaction as a witness. The other witness, doubtless called by the Della Francesca family, was Michelangelo Palamidessi, a leading citizen, bibliophile, and intellectual. More importantly, Piero was present with Marco to represent their family.

The Graziani made their choice of their section, and the parties agreed to construct a stone or brick wall to divide their respective areas. The divided building survives today with its configuration still recognizable from the documents, which describe a large building bordered by three streets. From later documents we know that the property was located at the intersection called the Cantone or Angolo dei Graziani and thus on the corner of the then via Maestra and via Borgo Nuovo (see Map 2). The existing building on the north-west angle of the crossing is bordered on a third side today by the via delle Campane that leads to the apse of the cathedral, then the Badia church. Marco had cleverly divided the property into a narrow strip on the corner of via Borgo Nuovo and via Maestra and a much larger building with frontage only on via Maestra, the principal street of the town. The Graziani chose the narrow strip in order, I believe, to possess space for sale shops on the corner and up via Borgo Nuovo. The Della Francesca workshop was located between the properties of the town's most powerful families; on one side the Graziani had their narrow strip (they also owned palaces across the intersection) and on the other side on via Maestra the Pichi owned a substantial building, which housed the workshop of the notary Francesco Pichi. Piero and his brothers frequently witnessed the contracts prepared by this notary, who also served occasionally as chancellor of Sansepolcro.[4] In the new workshop Piero's brothers would display wares and copy their accounts into ledgers, which were cited in contemporary contracts but are not known to be extant. If Piero established a workshop for painting in Sansepolcro other than in the ancestral home further up via Borgo Nuovo, it would have been here on via Maestra, where there were ample spaces for both his brothers' commercial affairs and for his painting workshop.

The document finalizing the division of the property places Piero in Sansepolcro in early May 1460. In late August he witnessed a quittance contract for a dowry between families otherwise unknown, but again the contract serves to locate Piero in his home town. More importantly, later that year in October, Piero participated in resolving a conflict between two families over the claims of a dowry. Two men were appointed as arbiters, who then chose Piero among eight "estimators," doubtless to evaluate land that had been part of the dowry. Again the families involved in the dispute have no known connection with the painter. Piero was chosen by either one of the arbiters as a mark of respect for him and his extramural renown.[5]

We have seen in Chapter 5 that in June and September 1461 Piero was involved with the Misericordia officials, finishing their altarpiece and garnering his payments from them for his work. Piero was also in Borgo in the spring and summer of 1462. On 20 April of that year he witnessed the reading of the testament of a man, who bequeathed funds for paintings in the church of the Pieve di Santa Maria. Here again Piero was in the company of master Michelangelo Palamidessi. On 4 May Piero, along with his brother Marco, witnessed another document of a land sale by the officials of the Misericordia confraternity. In still another document Piero was present for a contract of a sale of property. On 24 July 1462 he witnessed a sale of woad by the Pichi family valued at 1,015 lire. Piero probably chose to witness these sales because he anticipated that one or both would provide the funds for the final payments for painting the Misericordia altarpiece.[6]

Piero remained in Borgo until at least 12 August 1462, when he helped arbitrate a dispute between Giovanni Fucci, the archpriest of the church of Pieve di Santa Maria, and the goldsmith Angelo Antonelli. A chalice had been commissioned for the Pieve from the goldsmith, but the archpriest refused to accept the chalice, claiming that it was not "suitable" (*aptus*). Piero and another man were brought in at some earlier moment as arbiters and on 12 August their compromise between the parties was recorded by the notary. Piero and the other arbiter deemed the chalice not fully acceptable, apparently because it exhibited some defect of workmanship or quality. The arbiters decided that the archpriest could accept the chalice but pay 5 lire less than that agreed upon in the commission contract or that Antonelli had the choice of reworking the chalice and presenting it at the contracted price.[7]

From these notarial documents and assuming he was present at or soon after the death and funeral of his mother, we can say with reasonable assurance that Piero was in Sansepolcro in the summer and fall of 1459 (at the latest spring 1460) through at least the fall of 1462. By this period Piero had attained recognition for his work outside his birthplace, so that local individual and corporate patrons came to their renowned townsman with still more requests. In addition to completing his painting of the altarpiece for the confraternity of the Misericordia, he gained new commissions for the frescoes entitled the *Madonna del Parto*, *Saint Louis of Toulouse*, *Saint Julian*, and *The Resurrection of Christ*. Piero may have also started painting the polyptych for the high altar of Sant'Agostino in these years.

Madonna del Parto

Piero painted the *Madonna del Parto* in a small church located between Sansepolcro and Arezzo, just outside the small hilltop town of Monterchi (Pl. VI). In its original setting the painting suffered neglect, an earthquake, and a radical reconstruction of the church, which was diminished and reoriented by ninety degrees. The high altar was relocated such that Piero's fresco, formerly on a side wall, was repositioned in the apse. Twentieth-century visitors saw Piero's image as the focal point at the end of the chapel's short nave. Now removed to a former school in Monterchi, the painting is still the subject of an intense debate as to its future site.

Already in the early thirteenth century, the church of the Madonna del Parto existed under the name of Santa Maria di Momentana. An unknown fourteenth-century artist frescoed an image of a *Madonna and Child*, and Piero painted his fresco of the pregnant Virgin over the earlier image. It has been argued that Piero's image derived its popularity from a preceding fertility cult. This assertion is not provable, but it does raise the question of the image's role. Piero's *Madonna* became a devotional focus for local women, although it is not clear whether the image was thought to cure infertility or to assure a successful pregnancy, probably both. However, in several pastoral visitations of the sixteenth and seventeenth centuries the visiting bishops concentrated their attention on a lateral altar with a miracle-working wooden statue of the Virgin and Child that stimulated the devotion of the people of Monterchi, while Piero's image was mentioned only in passing.[8] It may be the bishops refused to acknowledge the popularity of a cult dedicated to the pregnant Madonna because the Catholic Church officials had discouraged its devotion.

No contemporary of Piero commented on his image of a pregnant woman nor is there any document indicating the patron or the painting's date. Some have assumed that Piero's image was related to a cemetery adjacent to the church of Santa Maria di Momentana, in which it was proposed that his mother might have been buried, and that this validates dating the *Madonna del Parto* to the period after the death of the painter's mother. However, we now know that the fifteenth-century church did not have a nearby cemetery; that was built three hundred years later. An image of a pregnant Madonna in a mortuary site is extremely rare or non-existent in Renaissance Italy, although this does not necessarily invalidate the hypothesis that Piero painted the image in Monterchi in honor of his deceased mother.

Piero's mother Romana can be linked to the general location of the *Madonna del Parto* because Monterchi was her birthplace, or at least where she lived in early life.[9] We know little of her father Renzo except that he lived in Monterchi with Romana and her five brothers. The family was not without means as is evident in a mercantile partnership in wool between Romana's brother Gasparre and a merchant of Borgo in 1408 in which the brother invested 100 florins. After Romana's death her natal family disappears from the historical record (except for one brother's labor for the Bacci family in Arezzo).[10] Romana gave birth to six children who survived to maturity.

Other than the death note of her burial on 6 November 1459, Romana appears in the historical record only in 1416, when she consented to the sale of land, perhaps the basis of her dowry, by her husband. What is lacking is any proof that Piero painted the *Madonna del Parto* in Romana's honor. It is reasonable to date the painting to the period after her death on the grounds of possible filial loyalty, but more assuredly on the style of the painting and the fact that he was in the area at this time. Piero was in Borgo, probably for, and definitely after, Romana's death, and the painting displays the mature powers he possessed by the early 1460s.

The most persuasive evidence for the placement of the *Madonna del Parto* in this period is Piero's selection of methods that he had perfected over the previous three decades. First to be noted is the rapidity with which he frescoed the painting. Piero painted the image of the pregnant Madonna in only seven *giornate* (days), though doubtless preparation for the fresco and its cartoons required more time. The *Madonna del Parto* is distinguished by another technique, new for Piero, that definitely required much more time. Piero initially applied a relatively thin layer of fresh plaster in the areas of more detailed and complex representation. In these areas of the fresco, notably the Virgin, the wings of the angels, and the clothing, Piero purposely thinned the preparatory layer of plaster, the *intonaco*, which he frescoed with base color only, or left unpainted, in preparation for a subsequent *a secco* painting phase. On the other hand, in the larger areas that required less precise brushwork, he prepared with a thicker *intonaco* and painted immediately on the fresh plaster. As in the Rimini fresco of *Sigismondo* (see Pl. III) and then more often in the Arezzo cycle (see Pl. IV), Piero painted *a secco* upon the dried fresco stratum. Whenever he required extra time for the more difficult and more compellingly beautiful elements of the painting, he resorted to this technique of *a secco* painting. Given his intent to be more precise or to endow these portions with more detail, Piero did not employ cartoons and in these areas painted *a secco*, whereas he did use this method on those areas that needed less precise brushwork, such as the fresco decoration of the tent. For the areas painted *a secco*, especially the neck and contour of the Madonna, the hair of the angels, and the hands of all three, he etched an outline with his brush end or some sharp implement.[11]

For the modern viewer the *Madonna del Parto* is Piero's most eloquent painting. It "speaks" to moderns because of its combination of simplicity and majesty. Few images of Mary by Piero or other fifteenth-century painters possess the gravity of this young woman. The image seems to belong to no other narrative than that of a young woman managing her pregnancy with grace and poise. Here, as almost always, Piero endows human life with a seriousness and dignity, in this case in the form of a pregnant young woman from a country hill town.

Saint Louis of Toulouse

Whereas the evidence for dating the *Madonna del Parto* to the early 1460s is circumstantial, another important undertaking in those years—a painting of Saint

Louis of Toulouse to adorn the captain's residence in Borgo—is better documented. After Florence took possession of Sansepolcro in 1441, it sent a captain every six months to oversee its rule of the dependent town. The captain occupied approximately one half of the communal palace in what was called his residence (later Palazzo Pretorio). In addition to his living quarters and those of his horsemen, notary, and a judge of his choice, the captain had a large meeting hall, a chapel, a room where "justice was disposed," and on the ground level a loggia where taxes were collected and where weights and measurements of the town were made available for merchants under what was called the "Arch of Weights." This "Arch" linked his residence to the other half of the communal palace occupied by the conservators. Together these two residences in the communal palace were the center of political life in Borgo.

Ludovico Acciaioli, a member of an illustrious Florentine family, held the position of captain in the second half of 1460. While Acciaioli was in office, Sansepolcro introduced a reform of its laws. The captain aided Sansepolcro in proposing that the town imitate a crown jewel of the Florentine republican constitution, in which the chief executive was named the standard bearer of justice and he and the other executives lived in the communal palace during their term of office. Whether the town's governors or Acciaioli initiated the idea is uncertain, but it is clear that the town elite desired it. This reform would ally Sansepolcro more firmly with Florence, but it required the commanding city's approval. Either the Florentine officials initially granted the change in the constitution or Acciaioli and Borgo's governors thought they did, because Acciaioli was honored with the office of standard bearer of justice. However, it seems that around the beginning of 1461 Florence informed the town that it had either never approved of the change or else was withdrawing its previous approval. Only later, in 1467, did Florence grant Sansepolcro the privilege of possessing an executive structure similar to its own.[12]

Between 30 October 1460, when the communal governors and Acciaioli approved the law establishing the new office, and early 1461 when Florence chose not to approve or withdrew the law, either Acciaioli or the governors of Borgo commissioned Piero to paint an image of Saint Louis for the chapel in the captain's residence (Illus. 11). When the fresco was rediscovered there in the nineteenth century, an inscription was readable. It stated: "In the time of the governance of the noble and generous man Ludovico Acciaioli governor for the magnificent and excellent Florentine people and first standard bearer of justice of the people of the land of Borgo."[13] In this period the expenditures of the town were usually recorded in the chancellor's register, as were the proposals and the votes on the expenditure of even relatively small sums. There is neither a discussion of the communal government commissioning a painting nor an expense listed conveying a payment to Piero for his labor. Expenditures for the building of the residence of the town conservators were usually taken from the fines assigned by the judge of civil cases (*danno dato*), and these records have not survived for this period. Saint Louis of Toulouse was the

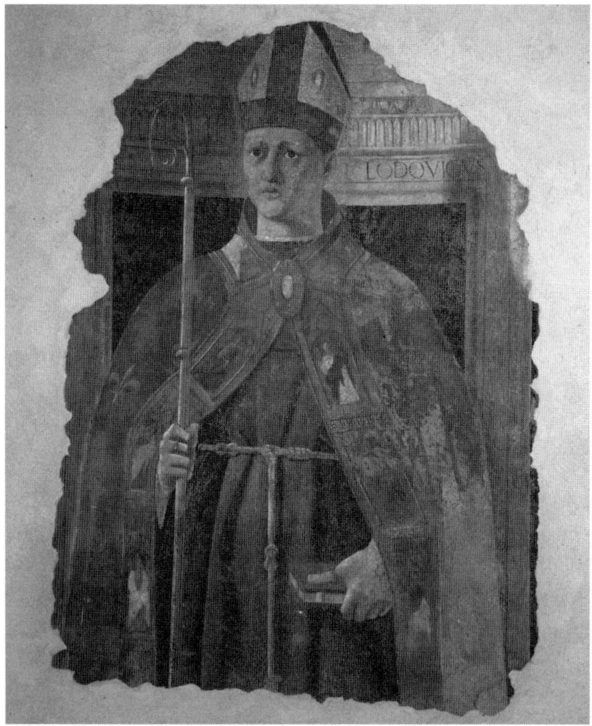

ILLUS. 11 Piero della Francesca, *Saint Louis of Toulouse*, 123 × 90 cm. Museo Civico, Sansepolcro

name saint of Acciaioli, and had the captain commissioned Piero he would have specified Saint Louis as the painting's subject. But we cannot determine whether Acciaioli personally or the local officials commissioned Piero.[14]

Piero would have played some part in the passage of the law establishing the office of the standard bearer of justice, for he was on the council of twelve when the proposal was first approved. This council worked closely with the conservators and the Florentine captain. Also as a member of the twelve, Piero would have been acquainted with Ludovico Acciaioli, since the councilmen convened with him on average once or twice a month. Piero painted the fresco of *Saint Louis of Toulouse* in the chapel of the captain's residence in November and December of 1460, as indicated by the inscription that included the title of Acciaioli as standard bearer. But in January 1461 neither the new captain Bartolomeo Martelli nor anyone else carried the title.

The fresco remained in the captain's chapel in his residence until 1846 when it was detached, suffering damage in the process, and transferred to another part of the communal palace, where it was stored until the building became the Museo Civico. Piero's image depicts Saint Louis as a young man with the habit of a Franciscan friar and with bishop's attire. This depiction is accurate. Born into the royal family of the Angevin rulers of Naples in 1274, Louis renounced his right to rule, joined the Franciscans, and in 1297 was appointed bishop of Toulouse, dying soon thereafter. By 1317 this royal personage was made a saint for his humility and learning.

Doubtless in 1439, when in Florence, Piero had seen Donatello's oversized statue of Saint Louis of Toulouse in one of the exterior niches of the church of Or San Michele. But Piero's *Saint Louis* is more finely wrought than the rugged bronze sculpture of Donatello. Many have commented on the similarities between Piero's painting in Sansepolcro and another of Saint Louis that Piero designed but executed with the help of an assistant in San Francesco in Arezzo. It is possible that he used the identical cartoon for both images, although reversing the cartoon in Borgo and adapting its size, as Piero did on other occasions when he employed cartoons for more than one painting.

Piero depicts the saint sympathetically but somewhat coldly. He emphasizes the symbols of the bishop's office with the pastoral crosier, a jeweled miter, and an ornate cope. The latter is decorated with scenes along its borders. Louis' beardless face is that of a young man—he died at twenty-three. The blue mantle is decorated with fleur-de-lis, alluding to the French origin of his Angevin dynasty in Naples. He holds a book in his left hand, commemorating the saint's devotion to studies. Images of the saint often had a crown at his feet as a visual reminder that he had renounced the Neapolitan throne, but the bottom of Piero's fresco is completely destroyed, so we cannot know whether Piero had in some way included the crown.

Even with the loss of the lower portion of the fresco and the general abrasion of the fresco's surface, Piero's painting demonstrates his fine sense of pictorial organization. Nineteenth-century sources mentioned that the fresco was originally placed in a shallow rectangular niche; Piero has also placed his *Saint Louis* in an illusionistic rounded niche with a circular architrave inscribed with the saint's name. Piero has designed the letters with care; his finely seriffed humanist capitals seem as carefully carved as in a contemporary humanist tomb. Despite Ludovico's youthful and slim body suggested by his columnar neck and the Franciscan habit underneath, the saint presents a substantial figure. Piero has integrated form and color in the image of the bishop-saint. The large blue cope with its now brown borders enlarges the slender figure, thereby giving great authority even to the young Saint Louis, and by extension to Ludovico Acciaioli. Piero has taken a relatively insignificant youth, though royal by birth and saintly by renouncing his royal birth, and imagined him as a grand officer of the Church. As with his portraits of Sigismondo Malatesta so here with Louis, Piero has taken a young man and endowed him with grandeur beyond that achieved in his life.

Saint Julian

In this same period Piero completed yet a third fresco, an image of Saint Julian, which was only discovered in 1954 in the church today known as Santa Chiara. The church, situated inside the walls of Sansepolcro, acquired that name in 1555 when Clarissan nuns were relocated there from their extramural convent and the previous community of Augustinian hermits were transferred to another church. I shall employ the fifteenth-century name of Sant'Agostino here and in Chapter 9, as it reminds us that in the Quattrocento it was occupied by the friars, who were subject to the rule of Saint Augustine.[15]

Piero frescoed the *Saint Julian* around 1460 (Illus. 12).[16] I would suggest Giglio di Bartolo di Cristofori Cresci as the patron who commissioned the fresco because he financed the construction of the chapel in which the image of this saint was eventually discovered. He bequeathed funds for a chapel dedicated to Saint John the Baptist in 1451, which would have been built not long before Piero painted the fresco of *Saint Julian*.[17] From a 1503 document, we know that this chapel was located to the right of the high altar of the church of Sant'Agostino, exactly where Piero's *Saint Julian* was found in 1954. This document confirms that the Cresci family possessed patronage over the chapel of Saint John the Baptist.[18]

The representation of Saint Julian provided Piero with many possibilities because the life of the saint was so eventful. A noble, born in France or in Macerata, Italy, Julian killed an unidentified beast that told him as it expired that he was destined to murder his parents. In another version of the legend, Julian's mother had a

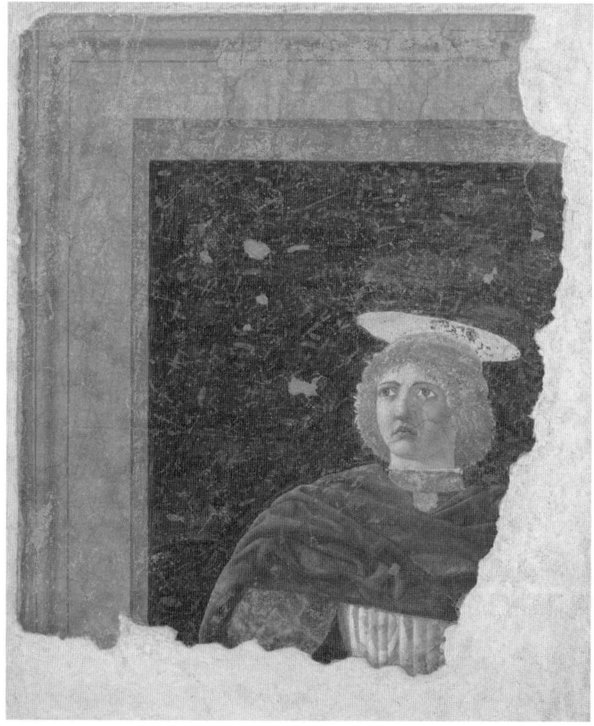

ILLUS. 12 Piero della Francesca, *Saint Julian*, 130 × 105 cm. Museo Civico, Sansepolcro

vision at her son's birth informing her that he would kill her and her husband. Learning about his destiny, the young knight fled his homeland and his parents, undertaking pilgrimages to Santiago de Compostela, Rome, and the Holy Land. In the Near East he emerged as a defender of the Cross against Muslim Turks. Returning to Europe, he married a rich widow, who one day in Julian's absence granted a traveling couple hospitality and allowed them to sleep in the conjugal bed. The future saint returned in the night and, assuming it was his wife who was in bed with a lover, stabbed them. When he realized he had killed his parents, he immediately resumed his penitential life. In time he set up a hostel along a river and aided people in crossing the water. After years as a hospitaller, he aided a nearly dead leper, who turned out to be an angel or Christ himself. Julian was forgiven for the murder of his parents.

Among all the possible representations, the patron asked Piero to depict Saint Julian as a knight and give him a prominent halo, thereby combining his noble origins and his sainthood. Originally, Piero's *Saint Julian* probably held a sword in his right hand—now invisible because of the loss of the lower half of the composition—that would have further emphasized his knightly identity, rather than other possible attributes from the penitential or care-giving phases of his life. These choices indicate an individual citizen as the patron rather than a corporate group; the patron wished to be associated with a knight rather than with an elderly penitent or hostel keeper. Piero has combined this military identity with the singular and striking gaze that one sees readily on the face of the saint. This gaze has been interpreted as Julian's horror of his destiny, the killing of his parents. Piero's *Saint Julian* stares into the abyss of his future with the forlornness of an already parentless child.

Piero painted on wet plaster without additions *a secco*. In the figure there are traces of *spolveri* from a cartoon. In addition, Piero employed, as he had often in the past, a direct scoring with a sharp instrument on the wet *intonaco* to achieve an outline of the illusionistic architectural elements.[19]

The Resurrection of Christ

In this same period Piero executed in the communal palace of Sansepolcro one of his most admired images: *The Resurrection of Christ* (Pl. VII). The dating of this masterpiece can now be correlated with a substantial addition to the communal palace leading in the late 1450s to a new name for the conservators' portion, "the new residence of the conservators." The communal palace had earlier undergone several phases of construction and decoration. In 1444, for example, Piero's early master, Antonio d'Anghiari, painted a *Madonna and Saints* in the "newly constructed and reconstituted auditorium of the councils" (*auditorio consiliorum*), where the council of sixty held their meetings.[20] This assembly hall was the large room next to the tower, in the portion of the communal palace adjacent to via delle Giunte. It has often been misidentified as the assembly hall where Piero painted the *Resurrection*.

An extensive building adjacent to the communal palace was obtained in the 1450s, and after its reconstruction the old and the new structures together were named the Residenza dei Conservatori. The new portion was located to the south of the older portion and doubled the size of the older palace.[21] The new half included the large hall in which Piero was to paint the *Resurrection*. In front of the external door of this new large hall of the new residence a loggia or porch was constructed. A sixteenth-century drawing shows a balustrade and columns framing a door leading into the hall of the *Resurrection*, or its anteroom.[22] This structure extended into the Piazza Comunale and had a stairway leading down toward the Arco della Pesa. All that remains of the porch today are the stairs leading to a platform and the platform itself, which in the Quattrocento served as a podium from where political leaders could address the townspeople. The loggia was constructed in 1458 under the Florentine captain Giovanni Lorini.[23] In 1468 the communal officials paid a local painter "for restoring and painting the shield and emblem of our commune, certainly the sepulcher of Christ, over the highest part of the door of the residence."[24] The conservators' new residence presented the communal shield of Christ's sepulcher at its entrance, and within its most important legislative chambers Piero's painting of Christ rising from the sepulcher was featured.

The building activity in the communal palace in these years should be related to an attempt by Borgo's political elite to elevate the importance of their local political officials. With their new enlarged residence, Borgo could provide dignified living quarters for the conservators. As we have just seen, in 1460 Sansepolcro's officials sought a law to establish a standard bearer of justice and to obtain the privilege for him and the conservators of eating and sleeping in the new residence. Piero's commission for the *Resurrection* should be placed in this context of the construction of the residence and in this period of 1459–62, when we know he was in Sansepolcro. To be as precise as possible, we can say that Piero painted the *Resurrection* either just before his departure for Rome in September 1458 or immediately after his return in 1459–60. Given the fact that the large auditorium was in the process of construction in the late 1450s, I am inclined to place the date of Piero's painting after his return. Moreover, in 1460 the communal officials allocated 100 lire for the unusual and unclear purpose of "the defense of the accounts of the residence."[25] That may or may not have been for part payment of Piero's honorarium, but it does suggest changes or additions in the residence.

Around 1600 an altar was placed in front of and below Piero's fresco, which probably explains why an inscription beneath the resurrected Christ has been almost completely obliterated and is now unreadable. In the Quattrocento there had been a chapel in a room adjacent to the hall of Piero's fresco for the private liturgical purposes of the town's executives. Thus in Piero's planning for his fresco he was not required to provide a space for Masses or sacraments. Rather, the *Resurrection* served a civic function, confronting the legislators whenever they considered what laws would promote the well-being of the townspeople of the Holy Sepulcher.[26]

There were various rooms in the communal palace where the several councils of the town government could meet; the largest was the rectangular space where Piero was commissioned to paint the *Resurrection*. The large auditorium was valued because here the council of sixty would congregate and vote on the legislative proposals from the conservators and the council of twelve; the room thereby served for the expression of the authority of the town's legislature. It was appropriate that the image of the resurrected Christ, already adopted for Borgo's coat of arms, should oversee the council's activities.

Piero's *Resurrection* has become renowned in part because of an essay in 1925 by the writer Aldous Huxley, who declared the fresco "the best picture in the world." Piero has painted Christ rising from the dead as the defining moment in Christian theology and belief. Christ emerges from the sepulcher as a triumphant warrior with the Christian flag held erect in his right hand. The figure stares directly ahead at a distant point with a gaze that powerfully engages the viewer in a hypnotic manner. One often hears it said that medieval art intended to establish eternal verities whereas Renaissance painting sought to depict a specific moment in time and in a specific place. Piero combines the two by catching the rising Christ at a precisely realized moment against the landscape of the painter's home town on Easter morning, but at the same time frozen into an iconic presence and retaining all the abstractness of a medieval Christ.

The hypnotic power of the image in part derives from Piero's construction of two systems of perspective. In one, Piero assumes the viewer to be placed low, seeing certain parts of the image from below, in a perspective called *di sotto in su* (from lower to higher). For example, the viewer sees the underside of the cornice above the obliterated inscription and cannot see any space within the tomb. On the other hand, the viewer engages with the figure of Christ and sees especially his eyes not from below but almost at the same level. This causes the viewer's eye to move from one system of perspective to the other and powerfully engages the viewer.

This is a good moment to consider two images in Sansepolcro that Piero would have seen already in his childhood.[27] In the middle of the fourteenth century, the Sienese artist Niccolò di Segna painted a *Resurrection* for the high altar of the Badia of San Giovanni Evangelista, and it remained there beyond Piero's death (Illus. 13). The central image of Christ resurrected was accompanied by four saints in the main tier, numerous smaller saints in the pinnacles, and with Passion scenes in the predella below. This *Resurrection* is represented with a powerful horizontal line in white that traces the top of the sepulcher and markedly divides the scene. Piero rejected many elements of Niccolò di Segna's image, including the crowdedness of the composition, the rapturous background with seraphim arranged in an almond-like shape, and the gold setting. However, he did take from this model a completely frontal Christ who stares directly at the viewer, the half-bared chest, the flag, and sleeping or reclining soldiers. Just as in Niccolò di Segna's depiction from more than a century before, Piero's Christ emerges from death with his left foot on the front parapet of the sepulcher.

The second image, a *Volto Santo*, is one of the oldest monumental wooden medieval sculptures in Europe. Piero would have seen this image of the crucified Christ in the church then known as the Pieve di Santa Maria. The Sansepolcro *Volto Santo* had

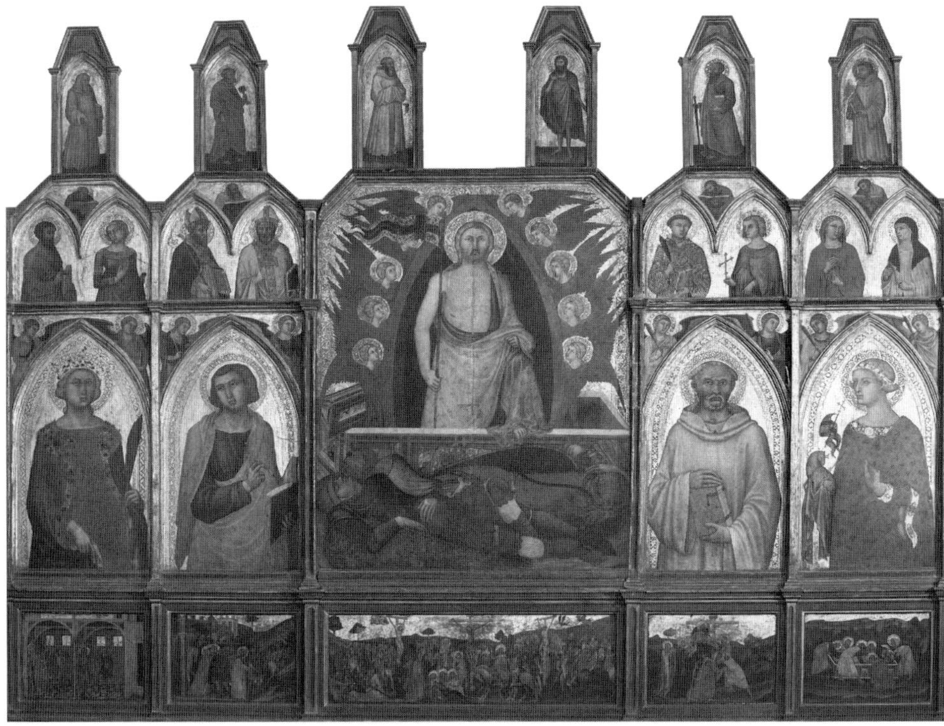

ILLUS. 13 Niccolò di Segna, *The Resurrection*, undetermined × 3.745 m. Cathedral, Sansepolcro

been sculpted in the period between 700 and 950 (Illus. 14).[28] The *Volto Santo* legend identifies the biblical Nicodemus as the original sculptor, with angelic assistance for the face (*volto*): hence the name *Volto Santo* ("Holy Face"). With a height of more than two and a half meters and an arm span of nearly three meters, the Christ of Sansepolcro, alive and regally dressed as he hangs on the Cross, makes a powerful impression on the viewer. The figure's tunic, originally in red, and his open eyes suggest derivation from the Byzantine "Pantocrator" iconographic tradition, which celebrates Christ triumphant as the ruler of the universe.[29] The *Volto Santo* has a full beard though divided into pointed halves, a form that Piero would often repeat, for example in the light beard of the Christ in his *Resurrection* (Pl. VII). Of greater significance is the iconic presence of the *Volto Santo* that Piero repeated in so many of his figures. It is not a simple feat to take the iconic qualities of images, expressive of social-cultural values of a previous historical epoch, and represent them convincingly for a later audience with different values. Piero appropriated this early medieval practice of making the Man-God sacred for a different historical world. He conceived his God in a naturalistic manner and in historical and earthly space. The frozen or static quality that so many have noted in Piero's art derives from the *Volto Santo* as much as from Piero's formal practices.

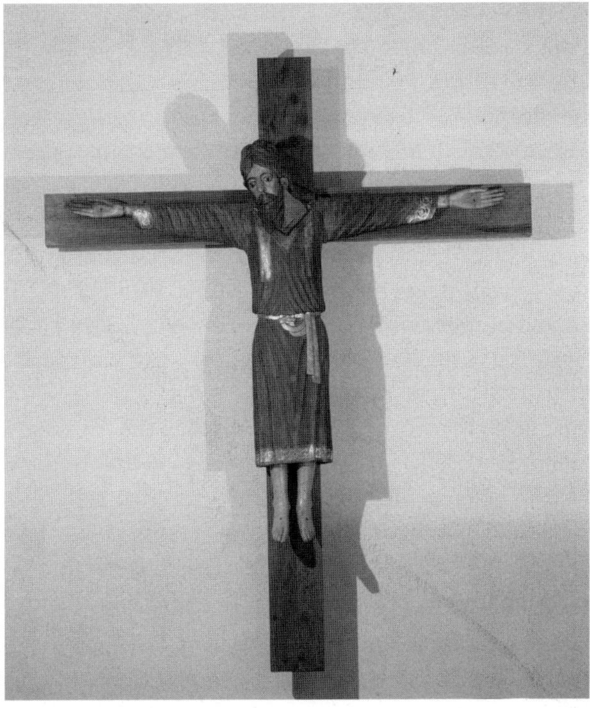

ILLUS. 14 Anonymous, *Volto Santo*, 2.7 × 2.9 m. Cathedral, Sansepolcro

We can see in *The Resurrection of Christ*, as in earlier paintings, how Piero multiplied significances in his art by uniting two iconographic traditions. In the *Resurrection* he combined a triumphant standing Christ with a seated judging Christ. Piero depicts Christ's right half as standing with his right hand holding the flag of Christianity as a victorious warrior against the forces of darkness and death, which we can see depicted in the lack of foliage on the trees behind the flag. Christ's left side is that of a judge, his left leg raised on the front portion of the sepulcher as if he were seated. The image of Christ in judgment had been often found in Byzantine and medieval art, especially in church apses. Renaissance artists represented the image of Christ as judge in frescoes and altarpieces. Piero's Christ is ruler and judge of the universe, conquering death and the devil's introduction of sin into the world of humans. In the context of the hall of the council of sixty, Piero has portrayed Christ the judge who with his powerful gaze reminds the legislators that he will judge them by their acts. Part of the power and continuing attraction of the image derives from this combination of warrior and judge.[30] The viewer's absorption with the image can also be traced to Piero's combination of these Divine qualities with a more human, almost an "everyman" form in the resurrected figure. Roberto Longhi wrote of a "nearly bovine woodland creature," and Kenneth Clark saw the figure as a "grim Umbrian peasant" of the Tiber valley. Others have viewed Piero as invoking a natural religion, basing this on the death of nature (the vegetation) on the left and its renewal on the right, coupling this rebirth with the morning sun. All this is subordinated to the story of Christian salvation, but these elements demonstrate clearly how Piero drew from many traditions as a means of enlarging the image's significance.[31]

Piero has placed the *Resurrection* not in the Holy Land but in the hills of the Tiber valley. His Christ is neither standing on the grave nor mystically levitating as he ascends above everyday reality, as in a Giovanni Bellini painting or a Michelangelo drawing.[32] Instead, Piero has caught Christ as he steps from the sepulcher in a realistic historical moment, without the event being infused with unnatural light. Piero's figure is completely triumphant and human, with his corporeality emphasized in his exposed chest. The dead will be restored to life not as spiritual entities but with perfected bodies, as in this image of Christ.

Piero's techniques in this fresco are similar to those in the Arezzo cycle. In setting up his composition, Piero has used a sharp instrument to etch into the *intonaco* many of the architectural forms. Occasionally he has snapped a cord into the wet plaster to construct straight lines, and perhaps he employed a compass-like device to outline the helmet of the soldier on the left, while he also used cartoons with which he transferred designs to the wall with *spolveri*. It is striking how Piero has attended to every major and minor element of the painting, no matter how insignificant. He applied fresh plaster on sixteen days or occasions, but he also added details *a secco*. Piero and other artists committed more time to painting faces than any other part of the body or any object, and our painter reflects this by devoting three of the *giornate* exclusively to faces, of course Christ's, but also the faces of the two middle Roman soldiers. Other peripheral elements have attracted Piero's keen attention. In the top right and left corners, there are small Corinthian capitals, where the acanthus leaves were drawn with the use of cartoons and with many perforations that permitted him to draw precisely the edges of the leaves.[33] Another example of Piero endowing significance to a relatively subordinate element is his use of color in the clothing of the soldier on the extreme right. For the tunic of this reclining man Piero has used the expensive ultramarine. Made from lapis lazuli, this pigment was usually reserved for the Virgin, but here the painter enhances a minor figure's presence with this deep blue color. Piero's concern to draw and to paint in detail and with precision these extreme corner objects or less than central figures, not to mention the folds in Christ's robe and banner with its ribbon, all point to Piero's practice of first drawing accurately every object and person and then painting them in a fully calibrated illusionistic three-dimensional space.

At the time when he was working on the *Resurrection*, Piero was nearly fifty years of age and his intellectual and technical capacities were fully developed. Not for the first time, in this painting Piero has taken traditional iconographical subjects and reinvented the representation of their meaning, placing this familiar event in the Tiber valley with a natural setting of hills and trees rather than the traditional gold background. For Piero, the Divine had to be on the plane of the human, the natural, and the historical. Christ appears in several of Piero's paintings, but the viewer always has to assume that he is

Divine and to imagine him as participating in a drama of sin and redemption; in the paintings, almost everything appears as a human historical occurrence. Here we are beginning to identify the elements of Piero's naturalism, and it is one of the areas where he comes to conclusions similar to those of the Quattrocento humanist historians, who banished the Divine from their portrayal of the historical world. To say this in a different way, Piero diminishes the immanence of God in the world and instead signals Divine transcendence to his viewer within an historical world.

Despite our attention to religious traditions and painting techniques we should remember that Piero painted the *Resurrection* for the town hall and that the image of the Resurrection was at this moment beginning to be valued as the emblem of the city.[34] Christ's gaze in the painting engaged Sansepolcro's legislators as they made laws. Piero's fresco is in that sense a civic painting. We can compare Piero's Christ with Simone Martini's early fourteenth-century *Maestà* in the communal palace in Siena, in which the Virgin directly admonishes the city's officials through written texts to rule righteously.

The period from 1459 to 1462, a time of intense activity as a painter and as a citizen in his home town, marks a watershed in Piero's life between the years of wide-ranging and frequent travel prior to 1459 and the remaining three decades of his life. As far as the documents and paintings can inform us, the artist restricted his work in these decades to Arezzo, Sansepolcro, and Urbino, with the exception of one project in Perugia and a year's residence in Rimini. We now move on to Piero's activities in Arezzo in the middle of the 1460s.

CHAPTER 8

An Arezzo Interlude

Thanks to the documents and paintings, Piero's life in Sansepolcro in the years from 1459 or 1460 to 1462 can be mapped out with confidence. In the next four years we cannot be as precise, although it is clear Piero largely limited his travels to within Tuscany, probably with brief residences in Perugia and Urbino after 1466. With the help of the surviving documents, we can securely place him in Borgo and Arezzo in 1464–66 and also assign several of his paintings within these years. From August 1462 to January 1464 his whereabouts are not documented, although in the latter month Piero is in Sansepolcro and thus may have been in his home town throughout 1463. In the years 1464 to 1466 records show his presence in or near Arezzo; however, we can assume occasional visits to Borgo, especially since he received a doctor's attention there in 1466.[1]

Two Lost Processional Banners

What we know of Piero in Arezzo in the middle years of the 1460s is based on records of commissions and payments made by two confraternities for their processional banners (*gonfaloni*), which unfortunately no longer exist. Confraternities commissioned these banners for liturgical purposes within their churches, with the flags serving as high or side altar pieces. More importantly, the banners heralded the confraternal corporate presence in town processions. Carried before the group as they paraded through the streets, each banner was painted on cloth (rather than wood) to lighten the load for the members carrying the large flag.

In July of 1464 the confraternity of the Holy Trinity (Santissima Trinità) in Arezzo commissioned Piero to paint a new processional flag and agreed to pay him 24 large florins (*fiorini larghi*), although from this sum he was to purchase the paint, including gold and fine ultramarine.[2] The contract required Piero to paint an image of the symbol of the confraternity, the Holy Trinity, no doubt on the front of the flag, for its processions. We know from subsequent documents that this banner had a reverse but separable cloth image, which Piero's younger contemporary Luca Signorelli may have painted. This would explain why Giorgio Vasari attributed this banner of the confraternity of the Holy Trinity to Signorelli.[3] The confraternal officials asked Piero to paint "the figure of the most Holy Trinity similar to the figure which is above the altar of our church." We do not know whether this figure above the altar was also a banner cloth or a traditional painting on wood. It was commonplace in commissions for patrons, especially corporate patrons, to include in contracts the provision that painters were to replicate a pre-existing image. By this means the patrons could convey their preferences to the artist and maintain continuity with traditional and recognized images. In the centuries before and after Piero's painting of the banner, the confraternity commissioned other artists to paint an image of the Trinity; on each occasion the image included three saints admiring the Trinity. A fourteenth-century fresco painting of this subject—perhaps by Spinello Aretino (*d.* 1410)—has survived in Arezzo and may have been the earlier model for Piero, though this example was painted in a tabernacle on the façade of the confraternity's oratory. Vasari himself painted a banner of the Trinity a century after Piero painted his. It is probable that the confraternal officials asked Piero to follow one of Spinello's depictions. Vasari's banner, also with saints adoring the Trinity, probably replaced Piero's.[4]

Piero signed the contract of commission for this banner in July 1464 in Arezzo and received his initial payment a month later. In April 1465 a second payment was conveyed to him, with a final payment in December of that year signaling the completion of the project. The payment of August 1464 was carried by a confraternal official to Piero in Capolona, about ten miles north of Arezzo.[5] This location is intriguing because his patrons for the commission of *The Legend of the True Cross*, the Bacci, located their country estate in Capolona. Perhaps the Bacci had commissioned Piero to paint in their church of Santa Margherita there or perhaps they were hosting him in their country estate. This link with the Bacci is further suggested by the name Angelo di Girolamo that appears in the initial contract of the commission by the confraternity of the Holy Trinity. Angelo served as Piero's guarantor and was the grandson of the original Bacci patron of the frescoes in San Francesco. In September 1466, Piero appeared in Angelo's workshop in Arezzo, where the artist, Angelo, and other Bacci agreed to resolve their disputes over payments for Piero's painting in San Francesco.[6]

For part of the period between January and August 1466, or perhaps only for October of that year, Piero resided in Sansepolcro. This we know because in late October the local doctor Domenico d'Arezzo brought Piero's brother Marco and Giovanni Onofro Nardi, husband of their sister Vera, to Borgo's civic court for failure to pay for medicines he had given when Piero and Vera were ill. The case was complicated because the defendants gave, or claimed they earlier gave, cloth to the doctor. The judge's verdict is not recorded.[7] Piero and Vera may have had the bubonic plague because the disease ravaged Borgo in 1466–68, when around 15 percent of the population succumbed to the disease.[8] The earlier attack of the plague would help explain why in 1468 Piero chose to reside in the country home of the Della Francesca in Bastia, just south of Sansepolcro.

The commission for the second processional banner signed in December 1466 puts Piero back in Arezzo.[9] The confraternity of the Annunziata had decided to replace their older processional banner with a new one and searched for a painter. Despite the fact that Piero had just completed the *gonfalone* for the confraternity of the Holy Trinity and the confraternal scribe noted that Piero had painted *The Legend of the True Cross* in the nearby church of San Francesco, the confraternal officials' choice of Piero was not uncomplicated. Before commissioning him, the scribe noted, they discussed the choice of a painter amongst themselves and sought the advice of unspecified persons in Florence.

The confraternal patrons laid out precise specifications for Piero. The banner was to be three and one-half *braccia* by two and one-half *braccia*, approximately two meters in height by a meter and a half in width. A processional flag customarily was bordered by a frieze, usually with geometrical or floral designs, and here the patrons further specified that the central image had to be three and one-quarter *braccia* in height and two and two-fifths in width. These measurements, as well as the images, were to be taken from a pre-existing processional banner. The confraternal officials bound Piero contractually to paint an image of Mary, saying that inside the frieze he was to "paint Our Lady already announced (*annunziata*) with an angel on one side and the other."[10] The confraternal officials also wanted a combination of expensive materials, ultramarine and other "fine colors," especially on the Virgin's mantle. The quantity of these fine colors and their distribution were left to Piero's discretion and were no doubt determined by the amount of his payment, but the patrons provided that the frieze and "the head of Our Lady and of the angel [were to be] gentle and beautiful with angelic faces," and painted with ultramarine and other fine colors.

These rather strict contractual provisions again set the overall appearance and colors for Piero. One other stipulation is unusual; the patrons required Piero to employ oil as the medium for the colors. As we have seen, Piero had used different types of oil for specific purposes in several earlier paintings, but here the patrons of Arezzo apparently realized that oil paint would be the best binder for the pigments on the linen cloth. Although we now know that Italian painters had been employing oils much earlier than previously thought, this is one of the earliest examples of a patron requesting an oil-based painting in Italy.

The contract also laid out the payment schedule. The confraternity agreed to pay Piero a total of 32 large florins. The painter had to pay for the gold, ultramarine, and other fine colors, but the confraternity provided the linen cloth. The contract stated that the patrons would pay 10 large florins immediately, 11 large florins in August 1467, and a final payment of a like amount when Piero finished, which he agreed would be within a year. Piero signed this contract dated 20 December 1466 and received the first 10 florins on 31 December, specifying that the confraternity had paid him. Piero did not receive the second payment scheduled for the summer of 1467, most certainly because he no longer lived in Arezzo and had made little progress on the banner. We can conclude this because he failed to complete the painting within the contracted year, was never documented in Arezzo after December 1466, and did not hand over the processional banner to the representatives of the confraternity until nearly another year had elapsed after the initial contract, on 7 November 1468. Moreover, the confraternal officials had to come to the Della Francesca's country house in Bastia to obtain the completed banner. The confraternal scribe stated that Piero had gone to Bastia to escape the plague.[11]

Saint Mary Magdalene and Other Commissions in Arezzo

At some point in the years 1464–68, while Piero labored on the two processional banners, he received a commission from an unknown patron to paint *Saint Mary Magdalene* in the Cathedral of Arezzo (Illus. 15). There are no known documents on this fresco, which is to the left of the high altar and squeezed between the portal of the sacristy and a large fourteenth-century stone sepulcher with panels recounting the military victories of a bishop of Arezzo. The lack of any evidence of Piero's patron or the purpose of the commission encourages us to concentrate on the image. Piero has represented Mary Magdalene as a mass of color and form. She is neither wasted by sin nor struck with guilt nor penitent for the life as a prostitute that medieval theologians ascribed to her. She holds a phial of myrrh that she will bring, or has brought, to cleanse the body of Christ. The undefiled physical beauty of the saint and the presence of the phial place her in the tradition of the *Myrophore* (from the Greek, meaning "myrrh-bearer").[12] This tradition recounts her as a "myrrh-bearer" and, as in Piero's image, emphasizes her youth and her undefiled body. Whether or not Piero has intended to depict Mary Magdalene in Paradise with her reconstituted pure body, as some assert, he does represent the saint as fully corporeal, wrapped in a large mantle, which is in bold scarlet on her left shoulder while the inner white lining of the mantle flows off her right shoulder. Here again when Piero had an opportunity to depict a body deformed by sin or in penitence, he refused to do so, choosing instead to endow the young woman with a fully sculpted body. To the left and right behind the saint's shoulders, there are hints of capitals and a parapet. The capitals must have had pilasters as there would be little reason for them otherwise. Thus the original image occupied a classicized area that at least to the left of the saint was altered when the bishop's tomb was moved there in the eighteenth century.

Vasari informs us that the Aretines commissioned three other paintings from Piero, which are no longer extant. Piero painted an image of the founding bishop of Arezzo, San Donato, in his episcopal garb in the cloisters of the church of Santa Maria delle Grazie, then on the outskirts of Arezzo. The bishop was presented in perspective, wrote Vasari, with a circle of surrounding cherubs. A second painting was located in a high niche in the church of San Bernardo; it was an image of Saint Vincent that, according to Vasari, the artisans of Arezzo much admired. The third work praised by Vasari was found in the Franciscan monastery church in Sargiano south of Arezzo;

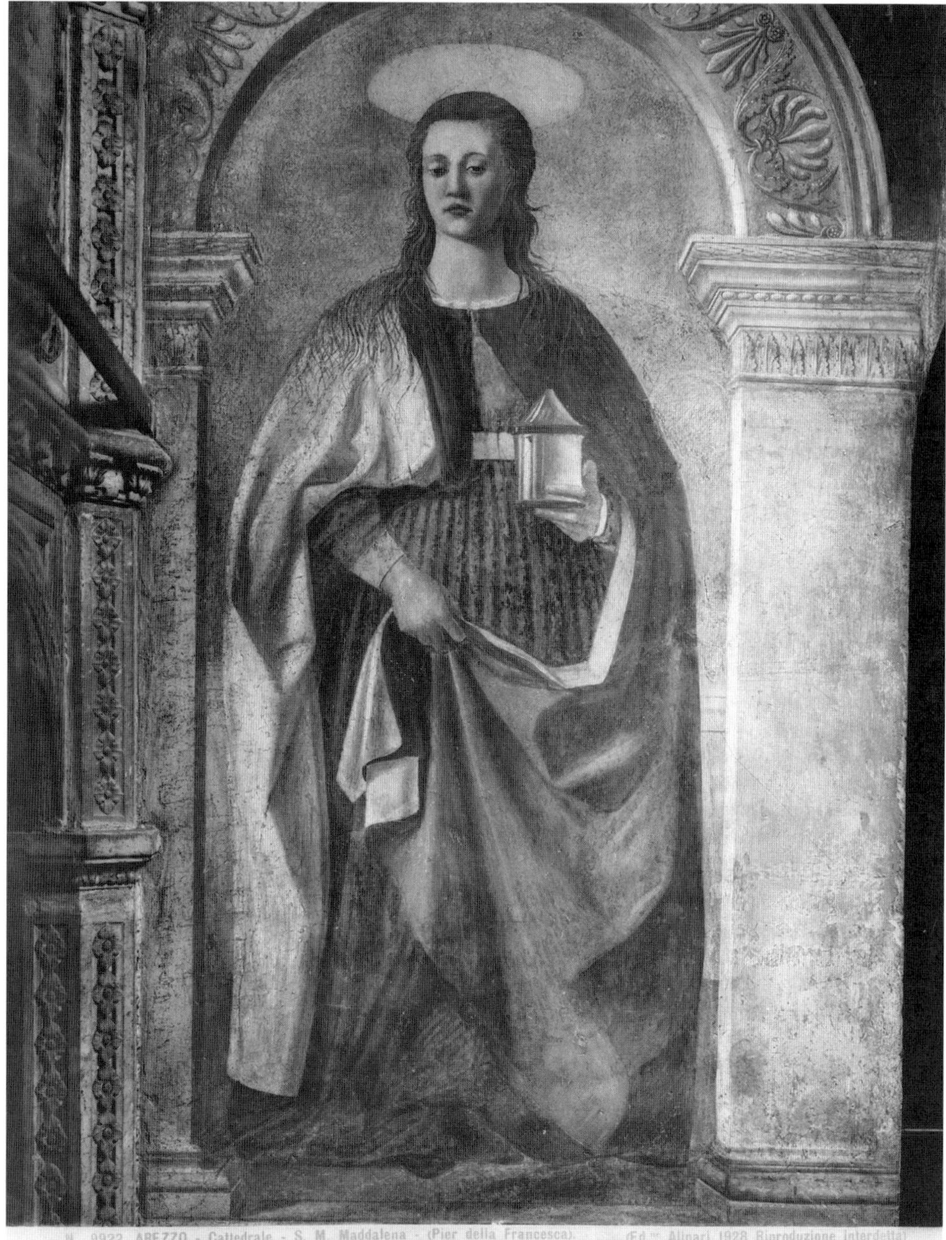

ILLUS. 15 Piero della Francesca, *Saint Mary Magdalene*, 190 × 80 cm. Cathedral, Arezzo

Piero decorated a Bacci chapel there with a night scene of a "beautiful" Christ praying in the garden before his Crucifixion. Were this painting extant, it would be instructive to compare it with Piero's night scene of Constantine receiving a Divine message in the frescoes of *The Legend of the True Cross.* The two were among the first night scenes in Western art.

***

The frescoes in San Francesco proved to be much admired by the people of Arezzo, witness the six commissions with which they honored Piero in the decade after the frescoes' completion. An indication of the reception of Piero's other images can be seen in the response of the worshipers in the church of the confraternity of the Annunziata. As noted above, a confraternal official brought Piero's processional banner from Bastia to Arezzo on 7 November 1468. Immediately thereafter, a confraternal scribe recorded the amount of money donated by worshipers after having viewed Piero's banner placed, between processions, on one of their altars. On Sunday 20 November many women, the scribe wrote, donated a total of five soldi "to see our new banner. And it was offered for the love of said banner."[13]

After this interlude of relatively minor or at least smaller works in Arezzo in the mid-1460s, Piero painted two major altarpieces in Perugia and Sansepolcro and *The Flagellation of Christ* in Urbino. It is to these that we now turn.

CHAPTER 9

The Practice of Perspective

The Sant'Antonio and Sant'Agostino Altarpieces and *The Flagellation of Christ*

We have seen how Piero painted *The Baptism of Christ* in the late 1430s, the Arezzo cycle in the 1450s, and *The Resurrection of Christ* around 1459–60, as well as lesser works in Sansepolcro and Arezzo through 1466. In the late 1460s he painted three additional works: the Sant'Antonio and Sant'Agostino altarpieces and *The Flagellation of Christ*. The three paintings exhibit Piero's classical style of fully sculpted monumental figures with more gravitas than emotion in a meticulously constructed perspectival space. They stand as the most complete realization of what I am calling the "second phase" of Piero's painting career. The exact sequence of creation of these three masterpieces is difficult to establish with certainty, and it is possible that Piero painted the Sant'Agostino altarpiece at intervals throughout the 1460s.

Piero may have returned to Borgo soon after receiving his initial payment in December 1466 for the second processional banner from the confraternity of the Annunziata in Arezzo, although from that month until November 1468 when he was in Sansepolcro there is nothing to indicate the painter's whereabouts. There are several reasons for thinking he was in Perugia in 1467 and Urbino in 1468.

The Sant'Antonio Altarpiece of Perugia

In configuration and experimentation Piero's altarpiece for the church of Sant'Antonio in Perugia is his most unusual painting.[1] Commissioned by the Third-Order Franciscan women of the church, the altarpiece is made up of a traditional main tier of a *Madonna and Child* with two standing saints on each side, with a gold background in all five panels and framed with carved or molded Gothic framing (Illus. 16). In many contemporaneous altarpieces, including Piero's Misericordia, there are two small panels above that depict the *Annunciation*. In Perugia, by contrast, Piero has constructed an *Annunciation* on one large panel with intricate classical architecture and deep perspective. The main tier of the Madonna and saints and the upper tier with the *Annunciation* are so different visually that many have asserted that the two elements were not intended to be integrated into one altarpiece, or that Piero had painted the two at different stages of his career. Recent technical studies have made both of those conjectures extremely improbable. Another unusual feature is the double predella (the series of smaller narrative paintings located below the main tier). The upper slimmer predella presents two female saints, each in an oculus (a circular eye shape), while the central panel under the *Madonna and Child* has been lost. The lower predella contains large panels with three scenes from the lives of the three Franciscan saints depicted above in the main tier. Here Piero experiments with the effects of low intensity of light and various brown hues, so uncharacteristic of him that one wonders whether he painted these panels.

In Quattrocento Italy, Saint Francis of Assisi's message still aroused widespread enthusiasm, and many men and women tried to structure their lives around it. There were a number of recognized ways to do so. As in the past, men could become friars of the First Order, entering a Franciscan convent, either under a relaxed (conventual) or more rigorous (observant) version of the monastic triad of poverty, chastity, and obedience. Women could enter what was known as a Second-Order house, taking vows to live under the Rule of Saint Clare. But the most rapidly growing religious groups were the Third-Order Franciscans, or tertiaries, lay men and women (many of them widows) who combined some degree of secular life (marriage, family, and work) with special dedication to the Franciscan ideals of penance and charitable service without, however, taking the traditional monastic vows. Female tertiary houses supported themselves by family bequests and begging for alms in the streets. In the fifteenth century these houses were becoming larger and more monastic, living by the rule promulgated by Pope Nicholas IV in 1289, and obeying an abbess-like leader called a *ministra*. While many of these women resisted the pressure of Church authorities to live in *clausura*, or full monastic enclosure, they worshiped in their own churches, with a portion of them living in common and adopting a standard habit (monastic attire).

In Perugia the Third-Order female Franciscans of Sant'Antonio had been organized from at least 1400 and grew in wealth and number, especially by recruiting widows and daughters of the elite.[2] In 1442 the women acquired a house and cloisters in the Porta Sant'Angelo district and through the remainder of the century progressively transformed the house into a convent with a church. Just after mid-century the women received papal permission to have Mass performed at their altar and to bury their dead in the convent. Although the women were occasionally referred to as nuns and their house as a monastery, they remained in the Third Order. The ambiguity of the women's status manifests itself in Piero's altarpiece in the selection of saints depicted, some of whom lived under a monastic rule, and at least one of whom was a Third-Order

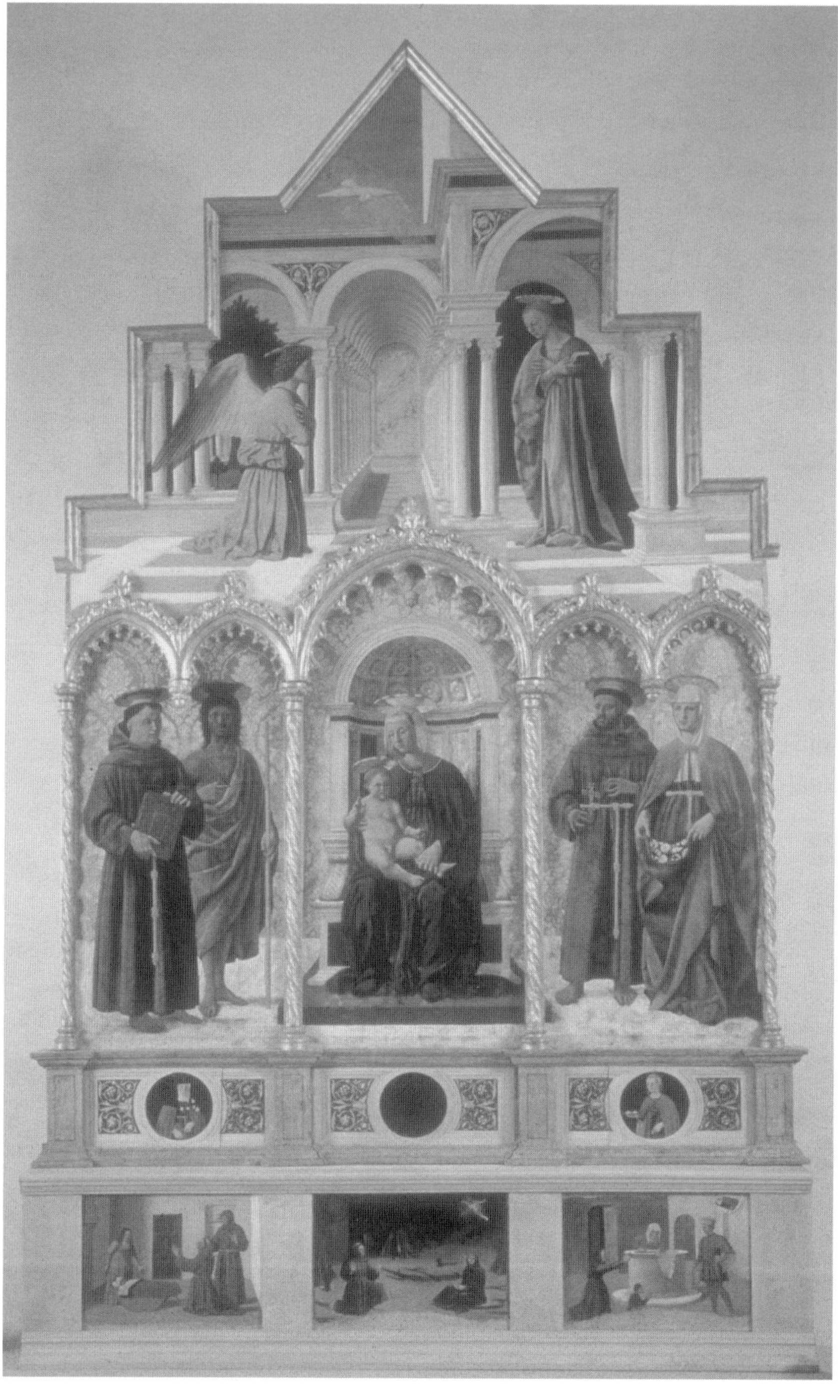

ILLUS. 16 Piero della Francesca, *Sant'Antonio Altarpiece*, 3.38 × 2.3 m. Galleria Nazionale dell'Umbria, Perugia

tertiary. The women of Sant'Antonio resisted local ecclesiastical efforts in 1469 to place them under the Rule of Saint Clare, and thereby under monastic vows of poverty, obedience, and chastity, but at the same time they chose many of the trappings of monastic life.

Given the relative proximity of Sansepolcro to Perugia and their frequent commercial relations, it is surprising that Piero had not previously received a commission from anyone in Perugia. Another link between the two towns was Borgo's availability as a refuge for members of Perugia's political elite during their recurring moments of political strife. This included the ruling family of Perugia, the Baglioni, who owned property in Bastia adjacent to that of the Della Francesca. The best evidence for dating the altarpiece derives from a contribution of the communal government of Perugia. In June 1468 the priors and council "were beseeched on the part of the Sisters of St Antonio of Padua of Perugia, gate of Sant'Angelo, who already for the reverence of almighty God made to be painted and to be fabricated an altarpiece and because of their poverty the women are not capable to pay the entire price ..." The Perugian governors agreed to pay 15 florins to the Third-Order women.[3] For most of the years 1467 and 1468 Piero's whereabouts cannot be documented. I believe he spent much of that time painting the Sant'Antonio altarpiece in Perugia.

The woman who undoubtedly led the tertiaries in securing the commission for Piero was Ilaria, daughter of the virtual lord of Perugia, Braccio Baglioni. Little is known of her except that she served as *ministra* of the tertiaries of Sant'Antonio in 1467–69, the years in which Piero executed the commission. Her father Braccio commissioned painters and builders, for example Domenico Veneziano who had painted (probably with Piero as his assistant) in Braccio's palace in 1438–39. The Della Francesca possessed property in an agricultural estate contiguous with that of the Baglioni in Bastia in the Tiber valley within view of Borgo. The Baglioni owned almost sixty pieces of land there as well as part of the Villa Bastia, where in November 1468 Piero handed over the processional banner for the Arezzo confraternity of the Annunziata. The Baglioni shared ownership of the Villa Bastia with the Della Francesca and others. From at least as early as 1463 there had been close relations between the Baglioni and the Della Francesca. In that year, Pantisilea, wife of Pandolfo Baglioni (cousin of Braccio), named Piero's brothers, Marco and Antonio, legal representatives for herself and her daughters, for loans and debts totaling over 300 florins. In April 1464 Marco and Antonio received from the *ministra* of the Third-Order Franciscans of Borgo two strong boxes (*forzerios*) and another container (*cassum*), all locked, which the *ministra* had received from Pantisilea Baglioni and her daughter Andronica. Marco promised to conserve the locked chests for the Baglioni women. In 1464 Pantisilea divided land and a pond in Villa Bastia with her sister-in-law, the widow of Galeocto Nelli Baglioni, and the widow of Gregorio di Domino Rogerio Antignalla of Perugia. The Antignalla family had owned land in Bastia since the 1430s and would challenge Marco's attempt to make additions to the Villa Bastia that the Antignalla, Della Francesca, and the Baglioni shared. In 1466 Marco was again made the legal representative of

Pantisilea, Angela, and Blannola (all Baglioni), and in 1469 when Marco pledged a ruby ring of Pantisilea's as a guarantee for a loan, probably without the knowledge of its owner. The relationship of the three families, the Baglioni, Antignalla, and Della Francesca, continued beyond Piero's death, as they all owned contiguous property in Bastia.[4] Obviously then, this relationship between the Baglioni and the Della Francesca preceded any specific commissioning of Piero for the Sant'Antonio altarpiece. Pantisilea must have known about Piero from his brother Marco, so that at any time after 1463 she could have recommended him to her niece, *ministra* Ilaria, the probable patroness of the Sant'Antonio altarpiece.[5]

The altarpiece of Sant'Antonio presents contrasting visual elements: a lower part consisting of the two predellas and the *Madonna and Child* with the four full-length saints set against golds and browns, and an upper tier of the *Annunciation* in full light that emphasizes the white of the marble architecture. The extraordinary shape of the altarpiece can partially be explained by the specific architectural space for which it was constructed. Although adapted from a prior structure and reconstructed after Piero installed his altarpiece, the high altar area of the church was enclosed in a small half-hexagon apse with Gothic vaulting overhead. This was the "external church," so-called because local lay people could enter and attend Masses conducted at the high altar. There was also an "internal church" with its own altar; a wall separated the backs of the two altarpieces. In the internal church the thirty or so women said their required offices and private prayers, the space functioning as a monastic choir. The back to back apses (the internal church received an altarpiece by Raphael around 1504–05) inspired the construction of an unusual feature of Piero's altarpiece. He constructed the now lost central rectangular panel of the upper predella so that there could be some form of communication or transfer of objects from the external church to the internal church through his altarpiece and an opening (still visible, though closed) in the wall behind.

The iconographic subjects requested from Piero by Ilaria and her tertiaries were primarily Franciscan. The only non-Franciscan on the main register is Saint John the Baptist, who is presented in the position of honor on the Madonna's right hand. Saint Francis as founder of the Order is on the Madonna's left. He wears the traditional brown habit and knotted belt. His feet are marked with dots signifying the stigmata, and his left hand opens his habit to show his wounded chest. Piero strengthens his references to the saint's defining experience by placing a transparent glass cross in Francis' right hand, reminding the viewer of the saint's special devotion to the Cross rewarded by the gift of the stigmata. Saint Anthony of Padua, second only to Francis in the Order, likewise is dressed in the Franciscan habit and corded belt. His distinctive feature is the large book that he presents frontally, signifying his call by Francis to teach as well as his published sermons. The three men are barefoot and are relatively young. On the viewer's far right, Piero painted Saint Elizabeth of Hungary as young (she died at twenty-four in 1231), and as dressed in a brown habit and with a brown overcloak. Elizabeth had been married to the ruler (Landgrave) of Thuringia in Germany and mothered three children. After her husband died when she was twenty, Elizabeth became famous for her charity, distributing her dowry and other wealth and becoming the first female tertiary in Germany. The roses Elizabeth carries allude to a tradition that on a day when she was carrying bread to the poor her deceased husband appeared to her and the bread was transformed into roses. Given her widowhood, her generosity to the poor, and her life as a tertiary, Elizabeth was an excellent example to be followed, for the majority of women in the house were widows.

The central panel of the *Madonna and Child* presents Mary in a rounded marble niche decorated with rosettes above and a minimal throne below. The niche-throne is of marble with panels of valuable stone. The Virgin with her attendant saints is set in her celestial court. It is probable that the women of Sant'Antonio commissioned a traditional main tier of a *Madonna and Child* and four saints in compartments, and that Piero sought to meet their requests and yet include elements of evolving polyptych design that integrated all the saints on the main tier into one integrated space. Piero has avoided any isolation of the saints in the main tier by bringing them into a sacred conversation in one space and forming them into a slight semicircle by moving the two outer saints slightly forward. The space is in perspective and integrated by a continuous and deep marble floor and a common gold background. The women of Sant'Antonio probably asked for a traditional background of real gold leaf, but Piero instead painted gold damask fabric with his favorite pattern for cloth, the pineapple or pine cone. Piero thus succeeded in incorporating the older with the newer elements. Were it not for the other parts of the altarpiece, these contradictions or mixtures on the main tier would probably elicit little comment. But many have noted the Gothic elements, however moderated by Piero, of the lower part of the altarpiece and contrasted it with the decidedly Renaissance character of the *Annunciation* above.

The upper of the two predellas presents two half-body portraits and would have included a middle panel (now missing) under the *Madonna and Child*. In the left portrait Piero has depicted Saint Clare with her book, thereby alluding to her rule for the Second-Order Franciscans, and flowers that emphasize her purity and chastity. Likewise in the other portrait, Piero has designed a half-length likeness of Saint Agatha of Catania, a third-century virgin whose breasts were cut off by a pagan admirer, who martyred her when she refused his proposals. The three female saints—Elizabeth on the main tier, Clare, and Agatha—presented apt models for the tertiaries, who dedicated their lives to charity and abstinence. Saint Elizabeth would have been a model for the widows because of her early exemplary family life as wife and mother and, with her husband's death, her commitment to a life of continence and charity. Agatha was not a well-known saint, but her breasts on a plate and Clare's flowers emphasize their lives as exemplars of continence and commitment to Christ.

As in many Quattrocento altarpieces, predella scenes presented narratives from the lives of the saints found on the main tier above. On the lower predella on the extreme left Piero has placed Saint Anthony praying over a dead child in a space with a portion of a fireplace on the left wall and a paneled door and classicized cupboard on the back wall. In the center panel Saint Francis receives the stigmata, and in the right panel Saint Elizabeth performs a miracle, reviving a drowned child in answer to the mother's prayer for the saint's intervention. Elizabeth is the half-figure in the upper right corner viewing the successful result of her intercession with the Divine. The figures in the three lower panels are less monumental and more colloquial than is usual for Piero, although the composition of the panels has the hallmarks of his customary classical design. As a consequence, it is possible that Piero had designed the panels but that an assistant painted them.

The *Annunciation* in the uppermost section of the altarpiece is one of the most beautiful and problematical paintings of the Italian Renaissance. In many ways it exemplifies Piero's transcendent pictorial practices. He has endowed the Virgin and the angel Gabriel with a quiet calm that is intensified by the overall composition with its white marble columns and arches. The white of the architecture and the blue of the sky, Gabriel's dress, and Mary's mantle serve to monumentalize the appearance of a kneeling angel and an obedient young woman. The inclusion of the *Annunciation*, and an unusually large one, was probably the choice of the women of the convent. For any woman and especially for those who dedicated their lives to Christ, the Annunciation depicted the most significant participation of a woman in the Divine plan of redemption. The Annunciation was the moment in which the Word became incarnate in the world, and a woman served as its agent. Piero depicts the Virgin as elegant but simple and with her slight bow, accepting her role. As we have seen elsewhere, Piero could take a common pictorial representation of a scene found in nearly every church in the period and endow it with immediacy and gravity. It was not uncommon for artists at the time to endow these events of sacred history with immediacy by placing them in environments peopled by commoners clothed in everyday dress. This is what Piero (or his assistant) chose to do here, in the scenes of the lower predella. Through Piero's representation of theological concepts, his sense of place, and his gift of rendering composure, he convincingly manages to depict a humble woman as the metaphysical mother of the God-Child. The tertiaries would have found in this representation a woman whose virtue, especially humility, obedience, and abstinence, could be both shared and emulated.

In no part of the altarpiece is poverty objectified, whether in the iconography or the representation of saints. Even Piero's Saint Francis does not "exemplify" poverty in any straightforward way. At times the lack of a particular element or iconographic sign is as significant as the presence of one. The women of the convent of Sant'Antonio in Perugia were at times called "little poor ones" (*poverelle*), but they, or Piero, in this case apparently chose *not* to emphasize poverty or any aspect of a life of denial except sexual abstinence. The art historian Ronald Lightbown has emphasized the importance of virginity in the altarpiece from the choice of female saints to the presence of the enclosed garden adjacent to the *Annunciation*. However, this is not quite to the point. Saint Elizabeth was a mother and many of the women of the house had been married and presumably were mothers.[6] For these women it was sexual abstinence that was raised as the moral ideal, not virginity per se.

There have been many criticisms of the *Annunciation* and its relationship to the other elements of the Sant'Antonio altarpiece (the main tier and the predellas).[7] Some writers have been critical of the placement of the colonnade, pointing out that it is not centered in the perspective of the polyptych and that the finial of the upper cornice of the *Madonna* is not centered under the colonnade of the *Annunciation*. Others have questioned Piero's choice of cutting off the architecture of Mary's house and garden. The arched room or loggia behind the Virgin is lowered on the right-hand side with the second floor of her house only partially visible. Some writers have even suggested that originally Piero had painted the whole upper pediment over the house and garden as a rectangle and that subsequent reconstructions had cut it down to its present triangular shape. But most historians today agree that the present configuration in all its elements is basically what Piero had constructed and painted. Portions of the main register and especially the lower predella may have been painted by assistants, but the overall construction and composition belong to Piero.

Piero's technical skills are especially evident in his transfer of his composition to the prepared surfaces of the panels. Given his elaborate preparation and use of cartoons in the Arezzo cycle, one might expect him to have employed cartoons and *spolveri*, or lines indicating orthogonals. In the Perugian altarpiece he did occasionally use these methods, but more often he incised lines directly on the gesso as a guide, especially in the architectural elements. In the *Annunciation* Piero used cartoons and *spolveri* only for the classical vegetative decoration in the margins of the arches, a minor element of the altarpiece, although he may have incised guiding borders through the pressure of a sharp instrument on cartoons in other areas as well. He painted with his brush most of the defining edges of the pavement, the bases of some columns, the hands, book, and some outlines of the Virgin's clothing. Most surprising of all, the intricate and extraordinarily beautiful colonnaded arcade has only guide lines for the plinth, the first arch, and straight lines as orthogonals demarcating the architrave. Otherwise Piero painted the columns with their intricate composite capitals and arches of the colonnade without any prior guidelines in an amazing demonstration of freehand brushwork.

Piero has depicted a powerful sunlight that floods the uppermost portion of the altarpiece. In the *Annunciation* the enclosed garden (*hortus conclusus*) represents Mary's virginity and her enclosed womb. Piero depicts the dove of the Holy Spirit conveying the seed of the Father to the Virgin as part of the light of the sun that illuminates the actual garden behind the angel Gabriel. The light comes from the left and plays most beautifully around the colonnaded arcade. The columns on the left of the arcade throw their rhythmic shadows on the red floor with the plinth's shadow covering a third of that floor. The columns on the right of the arcade are in light. Certainly the main tier has its light from the left as well, but it and the predellas are predominantly brown and gold. The browns fit well with the Franciscan context, but the browning of the faces is in part a result of Piero using oil as the basic medium for his paints. Over time this oil has darkened the faces in the predella and reduced Piero's customary luminescence, which only survives to a degree in the face of Saint Elizabeth.

The Sant'Agostino Altarpiece

We have seen in Chapter 5 how the Pichi family demanded in early 1454 that Piero return to Sansepolcro to fulfill his contract to paint the Misericordia altarpiece. He remained there at least through September when a patron and the hermitic friars of the church of Sant'Agostino in Borgo commissioned him to paint a large polyptych for the high altar of the church. In Piero's time this church included a large nave, a rood screen, a choir in front of the altar, and a wide triumphal arch over the high altar with a large apse or tribune behind it.[8]

The altarpiece had been in the planning for several years. The patrons were two brothers, Simone and Angelo, sons of Giovanni, and Giovanna, wife of Simone. The brothers were *asinarii*, mule drivers. This and their lack of a surname indicate modest social status, although as providers of the principal means of land transportation mule drivers played a vital economic and social role in pre-modern Europe. The testaments of Giovanna and Simone and the eventual payments of Angelo suggest the family possessed considerable wealth, as well as showing their deep devotion to the church of Sant'Agostino and its friars. In her testament of 1446 Giovanna bequeathed most of her dowry of 400 lire, to be augmented to 500 lire if her husband so desired, to the church for purchasing "beautiful and sumptuous" altar cloths and a cope.[9] In his 1448 testament Simone reaffirmed his wife's gifts and added bequests of land for the friars and for his chapel. He also provided funds for a stained-glass window in the large apse of the church, as did his brother Angelo in his 1459 testament.

Angelo had begun planning an altarpiece for Sant'Agostino as early as 1451. In that year he sold nearly 40,000 pounds of woad to Nardo Pichi for approximately 444 florins. From this sale Nardo was to pay in the name of Angelo 20 florins "for the wood or altarpiece of wood by him [Angelo] purchased from the friars of San Francesco which he bought and conceded to the friars of Sant'Agostino for the altarpiece of the church of Sant'Agostino." The purchase of the Franciscans' carpentered altarpiece brings us back to Piero's early career. In 1426 the friars had commissioned a carpenter to construct a double-sided altarpiece for the high altar of the church of San Francesco and in 1430 commissioned its painting to Antonio d'Anghiari. As we know (see Chapter 1), in 1432 master Antonio employed Piero to gesso this altarpiece. However, the commission was withdrawn from Antonio, and in 1437 the friars recommissioned the altarpiece to the Sienese painter Sassetta, permitting him to build a new wooden structure and execute the commission in Siena. As a consequence, the friars had the fully prepared wooden altarpiece of 1426 worth 50 florins on their hands.[10] They apparently kept it in storage until 1451 when Angelo purchased it for the high altar of Sant'Agostino for the bargain price of 20 florins. Thus Piero had a completed wooden and gessoed altarpiece, ready and waiting to be painted. The preparation of the wood under the gesso is similar to the preparation of the Misericordia altarpiece. On the wood and under the layers of gesso the carpenter Bartolomeo di Giovannino d'Angelo or Piero had applied a layer of carbon black.[11] Carbon black provided a smooth and strong underlayer that would even out any imperfections in the wood.

Today we have to recreate the form of the Sant'Agostino altarpiece because in the 1550s it was dismantled and moved to another church, and early in the next century at least parts of it were placed in private hands (Illus. 17).[12] The most important surviving pieces of Piero's altarpiece are four full-length saints from the main tier, Saint Augustine, Saint Michael, Saint John the Evangelist, and Saint Nicholas of Tolentino. Once upon a time these figures would have flanked the central panel of the altarpiece (its whereabouts

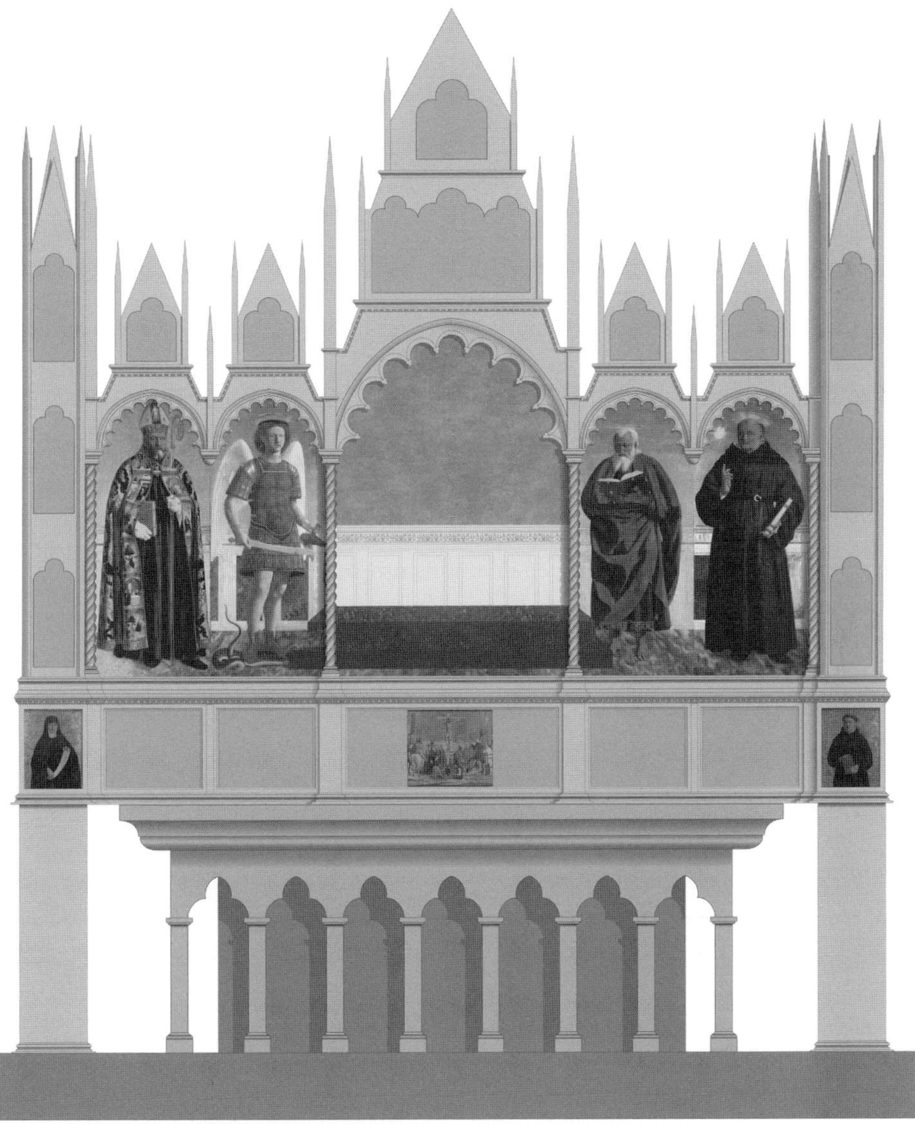

ILLUS. 17 Piero della Francesca, *Sant'Agostino Altarpiece*, frontal reconstruction, photomontage by Nathaniel Silver, Frick Collection, New York

are unknown and it may no longer exist). It was most likely an enthroned *Madonna and Child*.[13] Of the numerous other smaller panels that Piero painted for this altarpiece, only a Crucifixion and three saints are known still to exist. The Crucifixion, now cropped, is hypothesized as the central panel of the predella, with one Augustinian saint at the foot of each side column (the third saint is not shown in the reconstruction, Illus. 17).

Piero, the Augustinian friars, the *operari* (lay church supervisors), and Angelo di Giovanni signed a detailed contract of commission in October 1454, which reveals a great deal about this moment in Piero's life. Its basic provision called for him "to paint and to adorn and to gild [an altarpiece] with those images, figures, pictures, and decorations" that the painter and the patrons had agreed to and would be recorded on paper for the high altar of the church of Sant'Agostino. So, in addition to the contract, the patrons and Piero had written down the intended subjects and saints to be included in the altarpiece. The painter promised to deliver the completed altarpiece within an unconventionally long period of eight years, for which he was to be paid the substantial sum of 320 florins. A great deal of the contract specified the terms of payment, the burden of which was to be split between Angelo and the friars. In the names of his deceased brother Simone and his deceased sister-in-law Giovanna, Angelo agreed to deliver 100 florins at the painter's "petition and will," and a piece of land whose value was to be determined by mutually appointed estimators. Although unstated in the contract, these two values constituted the down payment, customarily one-third of the total fee for a painting. Angelo also agreed to pay Piero 50 florins at the time of the completion of the commission. The friars and the *operari* contracted to pay the remaining amount, uncertain at this point because the value of the land was unknown, up to the contracted sum of 320 florins, again upon completion of the painting.[14]

The patrons' agreement to allow Piero eight years to complete the altarpiece shows his esteem in the eyes of his fellow townsmen, as does his remuneration. The contracted term of eight years to complete the project as well as the fifteen years from the commission to the altarpiece's completion demonstrate Piero's crowded schedule in the second half of the 1450s and in the 1460s. In 1454 the patron, *operari*, and friars knew that Piero had not finished the Misericordia altarpiece and probably had only completed a portion of the Cappella Maggiore in San Francesco in Arezzo. Only this explains their willingness to give Piero eight years to execute the commission.

Piero painted the Sant'Agostino altarpiece at unknown periods in the 1460s, finishing it in 1469 when the patrons gave him substantial payments.[15] Piero was paid at the beginning and at the end of the fifteen-year sequence, so the payments give us little indication of the pace of his labor in Sant'Agostino. Let us examine the documents of payment, which will also shed light on Piero's absences from Borgo after 1454. In December of that year Piero's brother Marco received 500 lire (100 florins) for Piero from Nardo Pichi and his brothers, who were paying Piero in the name of the patron Angelo. This indicates the painter's probable absence from Borgo. The notarial contract states that if Piero does not begin or complete the painting, he and his family members were responsible for the repayment of the 500 lire.[16] As was usual practice,

Piero did not begin painting, in part because the initial payment was not available until December 1454. Angelo wrote his testament in August 1459 and recounted all his payments to Piero and the Augustinians. This included the land given in 1454, which he said was valued at 39 florins. The commission of 1454 required that Angelo pay Piero 50 florins at the time the altarpiece was completed. Angelo's total contribution to Piero should total 189 florins, with the *operari* and friars of Sant'Agostino paying the remaining 131 florins of the 320 florins that Piero was owed.

In late 1454 Piero or his family held 139 florins for the altarpiece, certainly more than the customary initial payment of one-third of the total commission. But there is no new payment for fifteen years. In November 1469 the *operari* and friars of Sant'Agostino conveyed a total of about 74 florins, including an estimate of the value of land to be given to Piero if the *operari* and the friars failed to complete their payment in coin. In the following year the land apparently passed to Piero, and Angelo's heirs conveyed 23 ducats (approximately 23 florins) to Piero's brother Antonio, who absolved the heirs from any further payment. This means that a payment of 27 florins is missing from the contracted total of 189 florins unless Piero waived that portion of his commission. The document of 1469 records that the Sant'Agostino altarpiece was "picte," a past participle meaning "painted." Another payment followed in 1470, and finally in October 1473 Piero's brother Marco gave a friar and one of the *operari* of Sant'Agostino a release from the debt of 320 florins for Piero's painting of the altarpiece.[17]

All this permits us to say that the Sant'Agostino altarpiece was painted at some time in the 1460s and finished by the end of that decade. Piero may have begun the altarpiece in the period 1460–62, when we know he was resident in Sansepolcro. From 1460 to 1468 the only places where his presence is confirmed are Arezzo and Sansepolcro. Piero is documented in Sansepolcro in 1460–62, 1464, 1466, 1468, and 1469; in any or all of these years he may have worked on the Sant'Agostino altarpiece.

The altarpiece demonstrates Piero's virtuosity as a painter and shows him in full command of all the skills of a Quattrocento painter.[18] Though it has a scant outdoor setting, the altarpiece is displayed in a powerful natural light coming from the right that illuminates the four saints of the main tier with a blue cloudless sky behind them. Behind the saints is a white marble wall with panels of varied precious stones that meets the sky. The sky, the wall, and a common floor served to integrate the saints into one space of sacred conversation despite the probable original presence of vertical moldings. Three of the four saints wear heavy cloaks that endow them with great bulk and substantiality. Piero never sought to display ascetic figures, even though the altarpiece was in the church of the Augustinian branch of mendicant friars. Each of the saints is individuated, three holding books to emphasize the learned aspirations of the Augustinian friars. Saint Augustine has a book, a jeweled miter, a glass crystal transparent staff, and a brocaded cassock with scenes on its borders. The young Saint Michael (Illus. 18) wears a short skirt and a transparent blue cuirass covering his chest and abdomen, with its clasps visible on his right side. This finishes in transparent lace at the neck, transparent fine cloth on the arms, laced red ankle-height boots, and a sword in one hand and the head of the dragon in the other. On the border between the leather protective skirt and the blue shirt Piero has painted in Roman capitals the phrase ANGELUS POTENTIA DEI, which can be translated "the Angel, God's power." It was most unusual for the angel Michael to receive the most honored position on the right hand of the Madonna in such a way. The honor has double significance: he was probably the patron saint of the donor of the altarpiece angelo di Giovanni, while the angel also honored the most venerated friar in the history of the church of Sant'Agostino, the Blessed Angelo (*d.* 1306) whose ascetic life became a model for later friars. His tomb had been under the high altar and probably remained there until the Augustinians were forced to leave their church.[19] Piero and the friars may also have wanted to honor Piero's cousin, the friar and sometime prior of the Augustinians, Angelo di Niccolò d'Aiuto.

Saint John the Evangelist wears a large red cloak around his ample body, which below his waist catches large shadows in the swirls of the cloth. His under-tunic has jewels interwoven on the bottom border. Less ornate and less animate than Saint Augustine

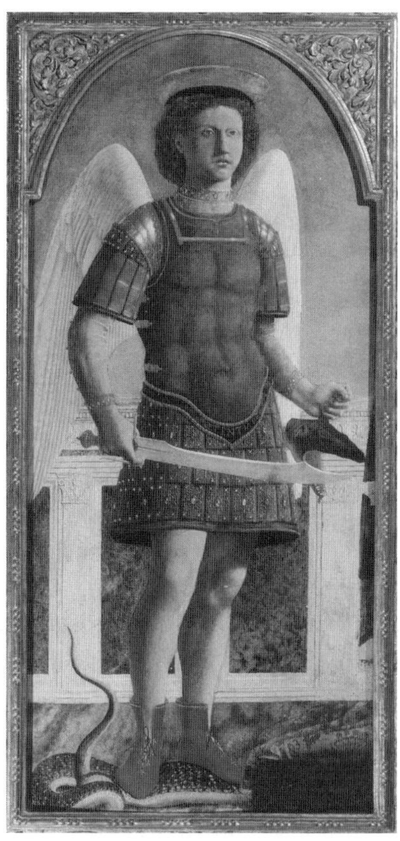

ILLUS. 18 Piero della Francesca, *Saint Michael*, panel of the *Sant'Agostino Altarpiece*, 133 × 59 cm. National Gallery, London

or Michael, John is occupied with the book he is reading. On the far right of the altarpiece the Augustinian Saint Nicholas of Tolentino wears the gray-black habit and gray belt of the order. He too carries a book and with his right hand points to his emblem of a bursting star at the height of his head. He is so corpulent that formerly historians thought the figure represented Saint Thomas Aquinas, renowned for his ample girth. Piero has chosen to ignore the extraordinary life of self-denial of Nicholas's biography. This figure is so different from the historical Nicholas that observers have suggested he was drawn from a contemporary friar of Sansepolcro, possibly the then current prior Francesco di Niccolò or Piero's cousin, Angelo di Niccolò, introduced above.[20]

One can only surmise that the lost center panel of the *Madonna and Child* would have been as beautifully imagined and painted as the other panels of the main tier. However, while every other piece of the main tier and predella came to be mentioned in seventeenth-century records of Sansepolcro, the elusive center panel seems inexplicably to have disappeared without trace. Perhaps the most likely explanation is that the *Madonna and Child* was separated from the other panels of the polyptych when the Augustinians were forced to leave their church and migrate to the church of the Pieve in 1555. The bishop of Città di Castello purchased some of the church's furnishings at this time; it is probable that the central panel ended up in his hands.

The Sant'Agostino altarpiece saints are dispersed in various museums; as a consequence, we see the surviving panels of saints as individual pieces of art. When the altarpiece was complete and in place, it must have been visually most impressive (see Illus. 17). A seventeenth-century source records a predella composed of four scenes: the Flagellation, Crucifixion (the only predella piece that survives), Deposition, and Resurrection, with a center panel under the *Madonna and Child* of an unknown subject. To finish the altarpiece Piero probably painted a second tier of smaller saints above the four major saints with some decorative saints and finials on top. The whole altarpiece would have been framed by columns upon which the three extant small standing figures of a male and a female Augustinian saint (Beato Angelo and Saint Monica) and Saint Apollonia were mounted. Piero prepared the altarpiece for a large nave and extraordinarily large apse, with a grand width of ten meters.[21] Over the high altar and Piero's altarpiece rose a large triumphal arch. A viewer in the nave would have seen the altarpiece glowing in its light and blue sky with space above and behind it. As Piero painted, the church was itself undergoing construction. Piero's patron paid for a new stained-glass window to be opened in the apse and commissioned the vaulting of the apse's circular structure. The friars, with a subvention from the town government, commissioned a new choir in front of the high altar from the carpenter Giovanni Bigio.

The loss of the central panel diminishes our ability to see the overall perspective of the altarpiece, but we can imagine from incised marks at the bottom of the *Saint Michael* and *Saint John* panels and from barely visible plinths on these two panels that orthogonals passed alongside the throne of the Madonna.[22] The perspective was heightened by slight changes in the four saints' panels. For example, in the painted rounded arches above the two outer saints Piero has narrowed the inner portion to give the illusion of distanced space. He has also used two mediums of paint, tempera composed with egg and with oil. We have seen Piero employing oil in the portrait of Sigismondo Malatesta (see Illus. 4), in the Sant'Antonio and in selective areas of the Misericordia altarpiece. In parts of the Augustinian altarpiece, over the carbon black and layers of gesso, Piero has introduced a thin layer of oil prior to the introduction of any paints. Despite several destructive cleanings, the sky has lively luminescence, due to the use of oil for its blue and to its being painted at two different times, with the second application performed with rapid strokes. In another technique, this one borrowed from Flemish painters, Piero has left unpainted a narrow space along the edges of the skin of the saints' faces and hands, thereby revealing the preparatory layer. This lighter strip intensifies the illusion of three dimensionality in the hands and faces of the saints. He employed cartoons and *spolveri* in these areas, as well as in the frieze and capitals of the balustrade. As usual he used his brush handle or other sharp tool to incise on the preparatory layers as a means to predetermine the boundaries of the architectural elements of the balustrade and throne (the corners of which are visible in the *Saint Michael* and *St John* panels) and the overall perspective of the altarpiece. Piero also drew directly on the preparatory strata and then corrected with the paints from his brush. Another of his techniques was to paint an element that would eventually be hidden by some object closer in the foreground and in the view of the observer. For example, in the *Saint Michael* panel, he drew and painted the saint's whole left foot and its boot even though eventually a plinth would overlap the toe; likewise, he has painted the lower jaw of the dragon, even though Michael's sword eventually covered most of it. Piero had used this technique from his earliest paintings, for example the lion in *Saint Jerome in the Desert* (see Ill. 3), as a means of creating depth and a more accurate space and perspective.

The Flagellation of Christ

To my mind, Piero painted the *Flagellation* (Pl. VIII) in either 1467–68 or 1470–71. The most convincing arguments for dating the painting in the late 1460s or the early 1470s are based on the fact that he was in Urbino in early 1469—and Urbino is where the painting was first located. Moreover, it is the moment in which Piero's theoretical interests in perspective intensified. His first treatise, the *Treatise on Abaco*, was completed and Piero had already begun, or was about to begin, his extensive analysis of the place of perspective in painting, the *De prospectiva pingendi*, completed in the mid-1470s. As discussed below, the painting would have commemorated the recent tragic deaths of Jacopo Anastagi and his son Carlo in Rimini in 1465 and 1467.

Most researchers agree that Piero executed the *Flagellation* in the 1450s or 1460s. Vasari suggests that Piero painted several times for Federico da Montefeltro, and the late 1460s would be the first possible occasion (other than 1463–64) for a residence of more than a few months in Urbino after 1450.[23] A document of 8 April 1469 records Piero's presence in Urbino in the house of Giovanni Santi, an important painter in

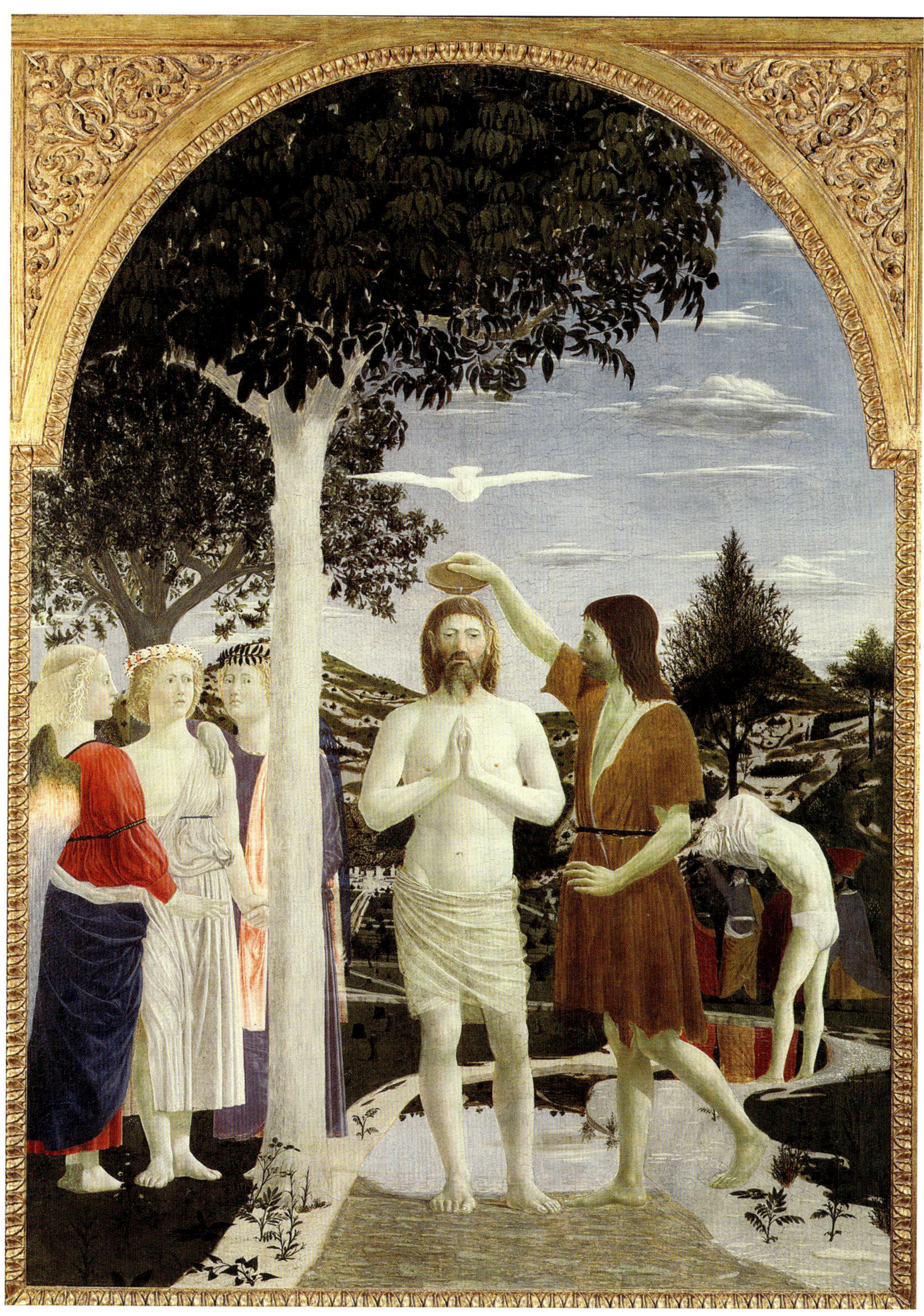

I. Piero della Francesca, *The Baptism of Christ*, 168 × 116 cm. National Gallery, London

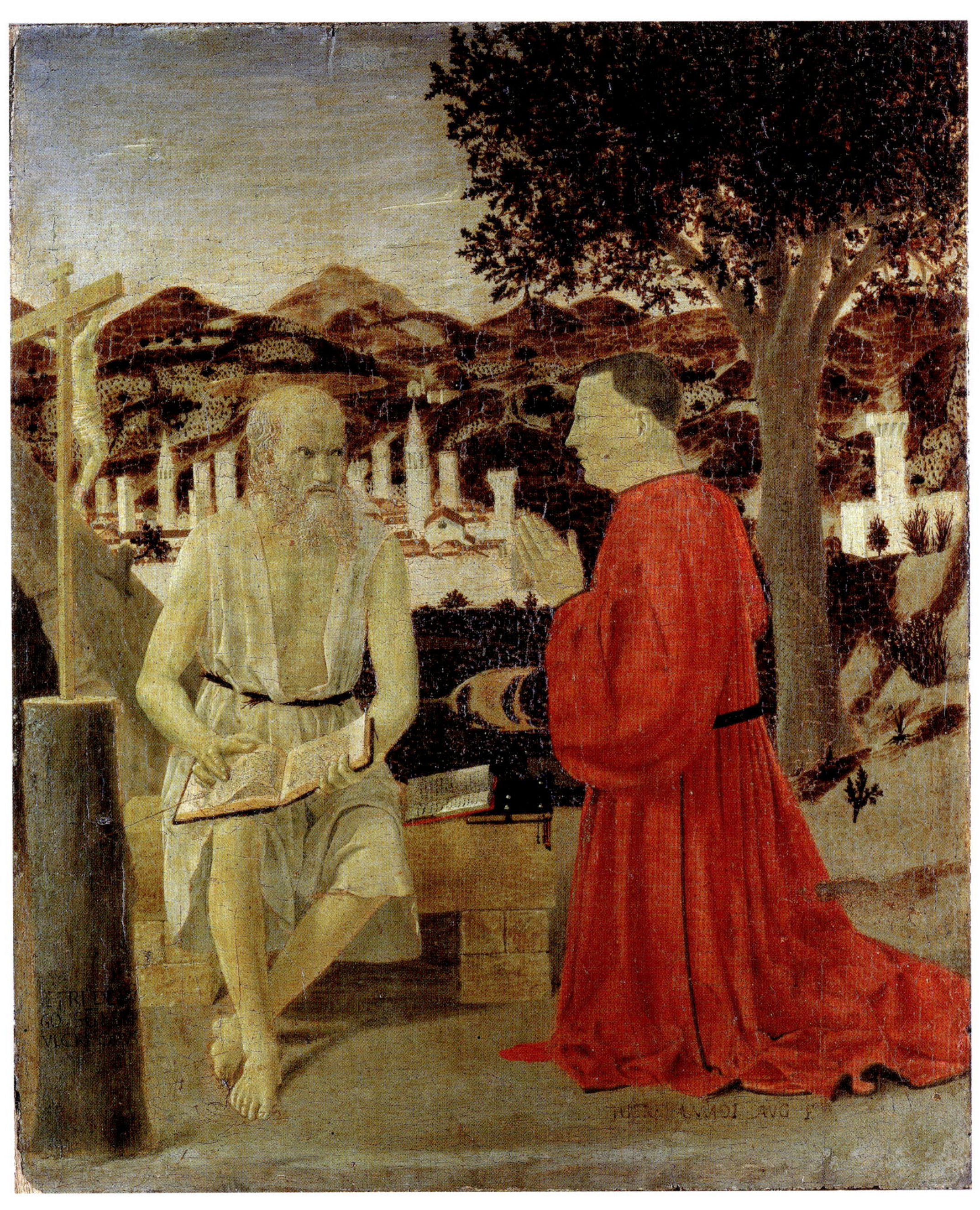

II. Piero della Francesca, *Saint Jerome and a Penitent*, 49 × 42 cm.
Galleria dell'Accademia di Venezia, Venice

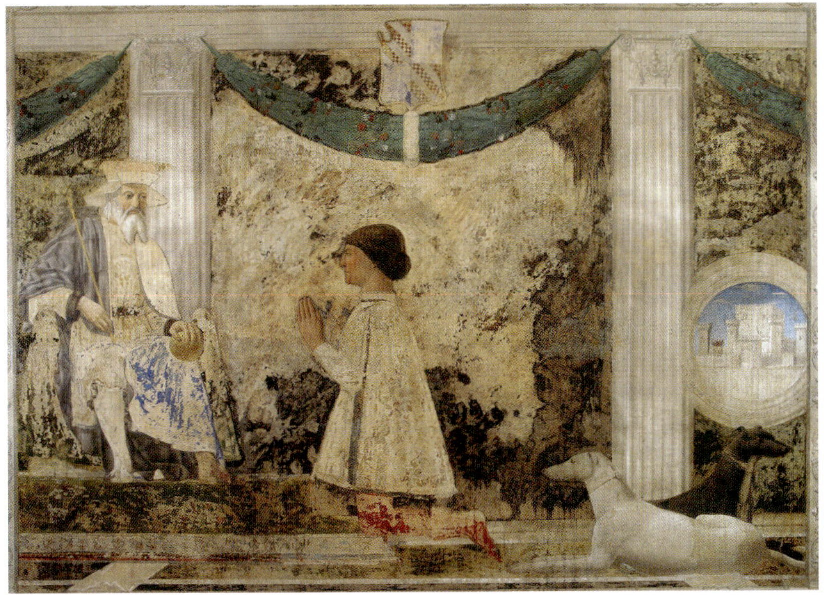

III. Piero della Francesca, *Sigismondo Malatesta Before His Patron Saint Sigismundus*, 2.57 × 3.45 m. Il Tempio (San Francesco), Rimini

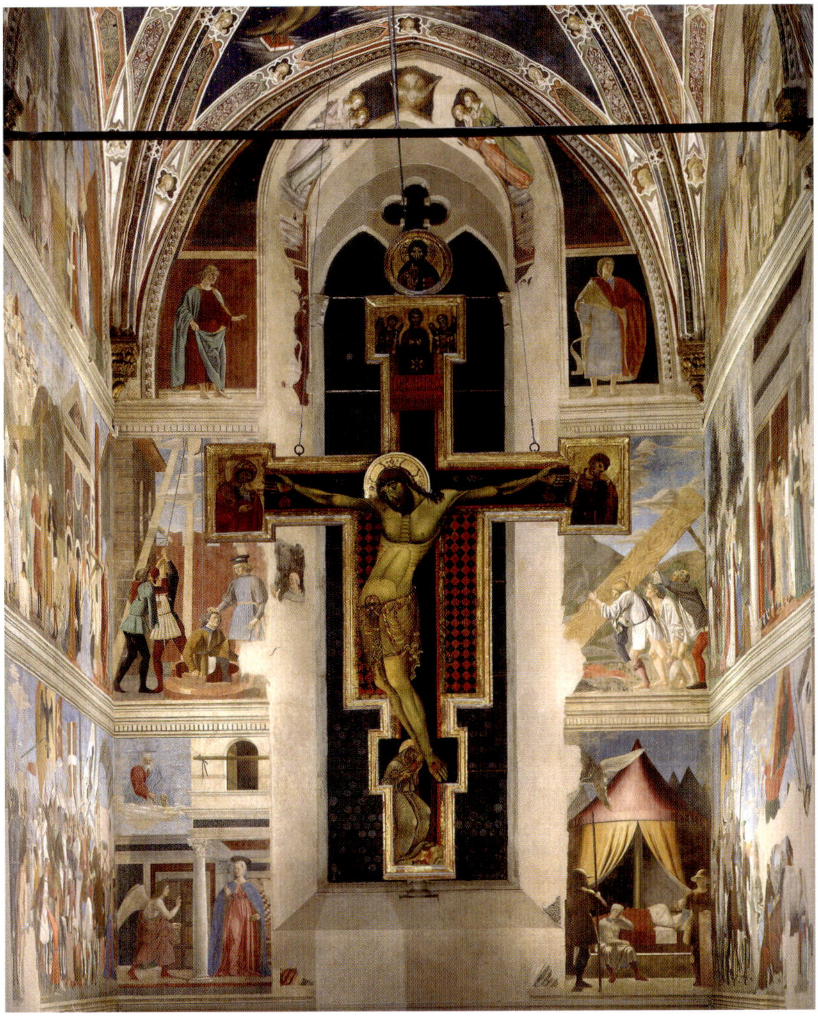

IV. Piero della Francesca, *The Legend of the True Cross*, High Altar Chapel, San Francesco, Arezzo

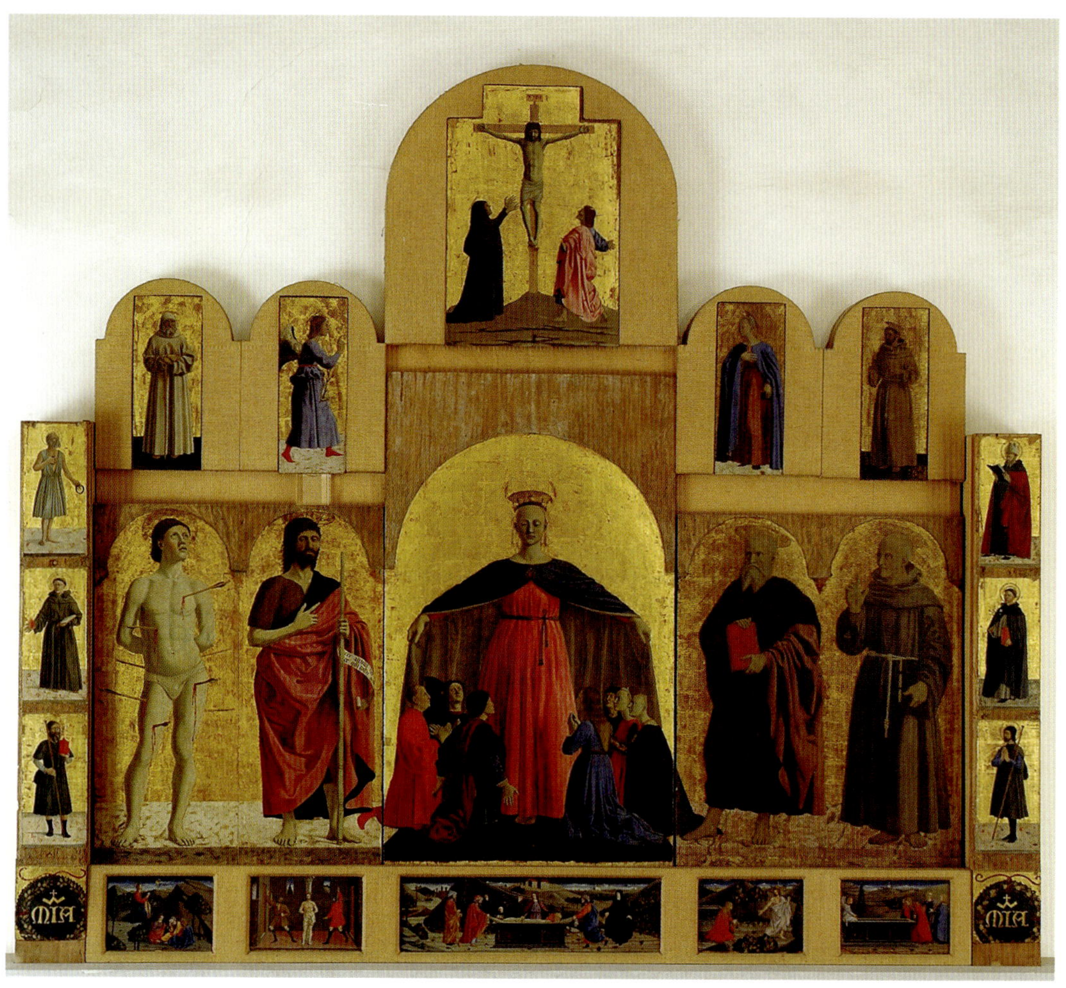

V. Piero della Francesca, *The Misericordia Altarpiece*, 2.73 × 3.3 m. Museo Civico, Sansepolcro

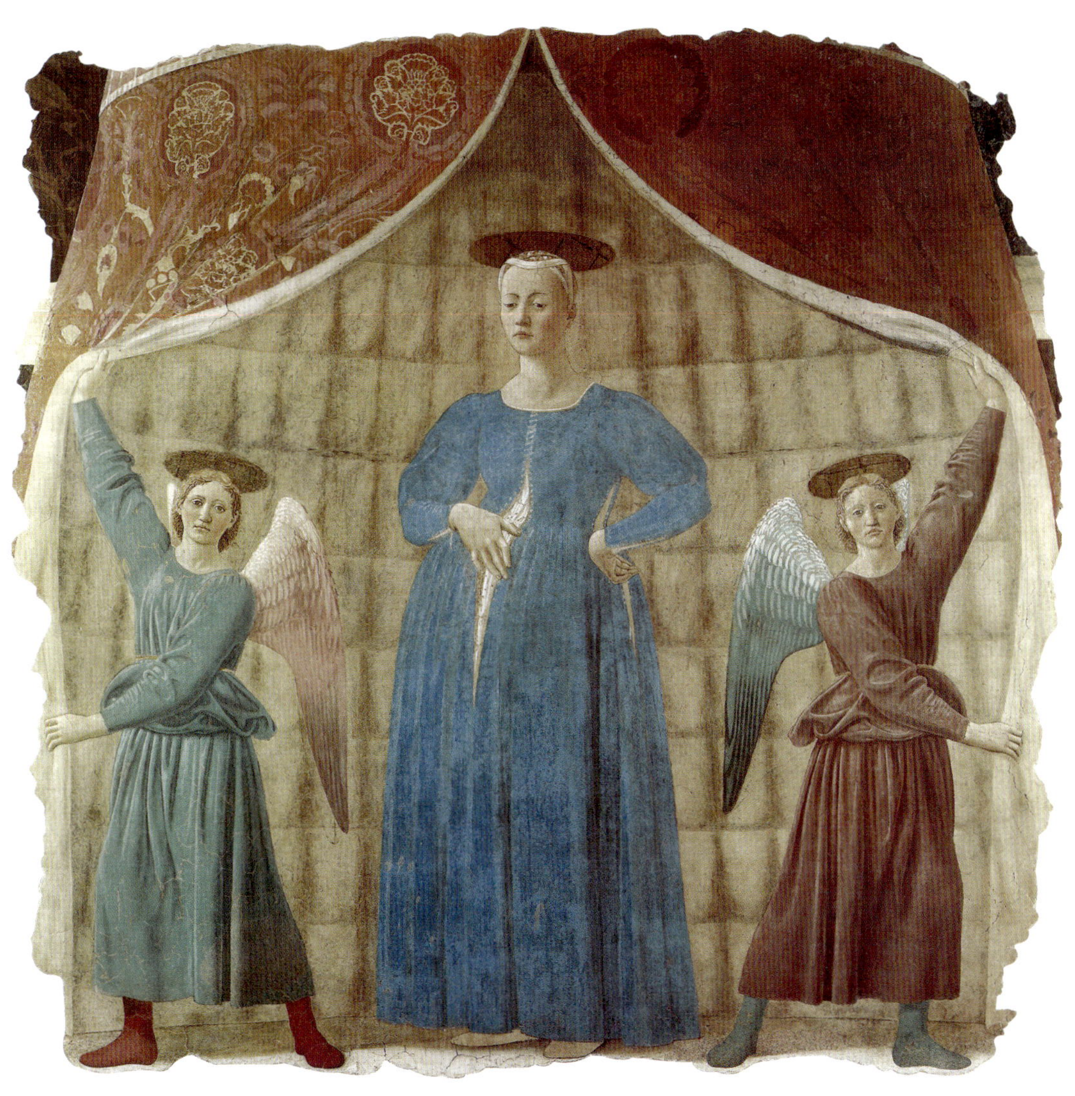

VI. Piero della Francesca, *Madonna del Parto*, Museo della Madonna del Parto, 2.6 × 2.03 m. Monterchi

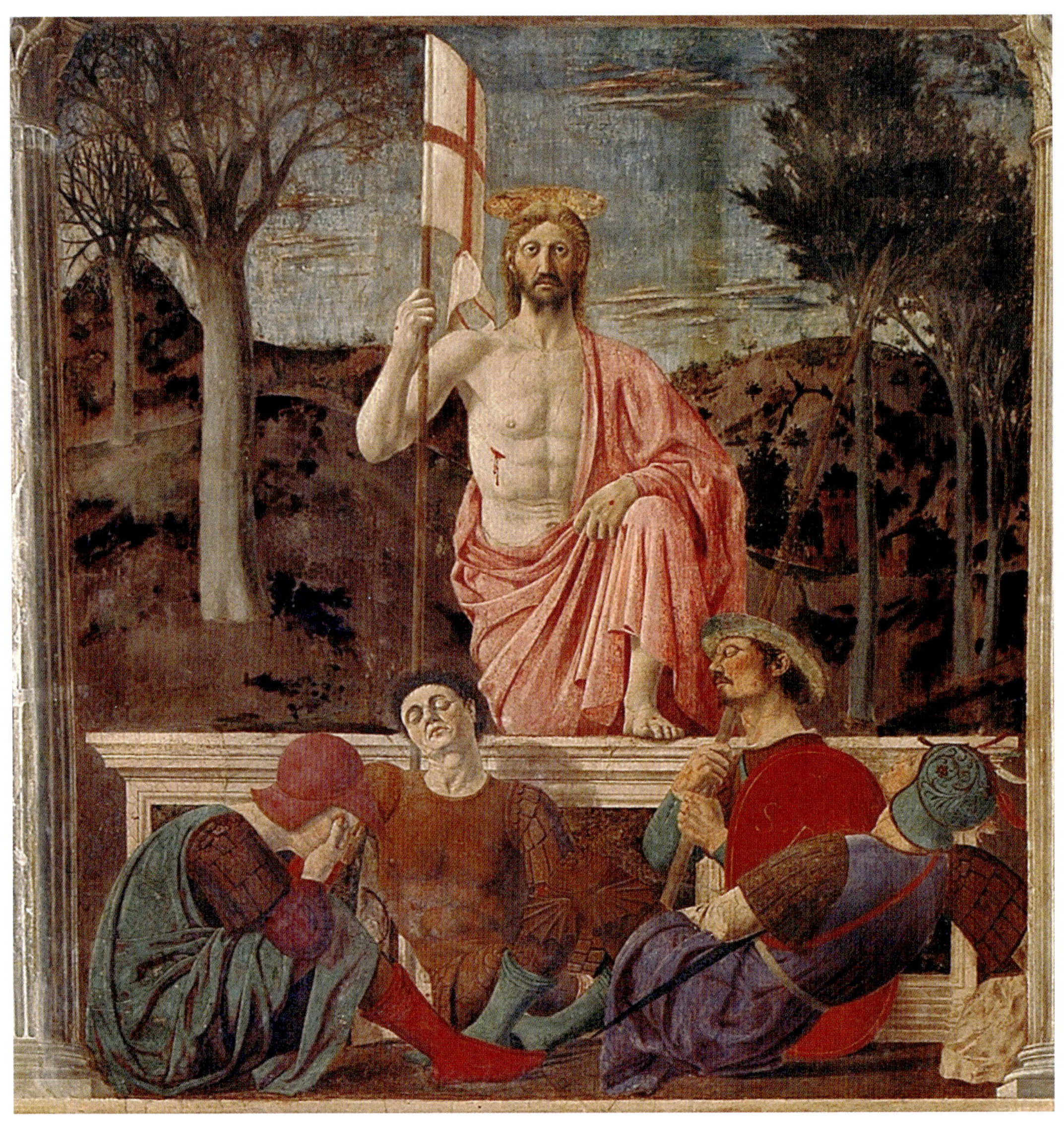

VII. Piero della Francesca, *The Resurrection of Christ*, 2.25 × 2.2 m. Museo Civico, Sansepolcro

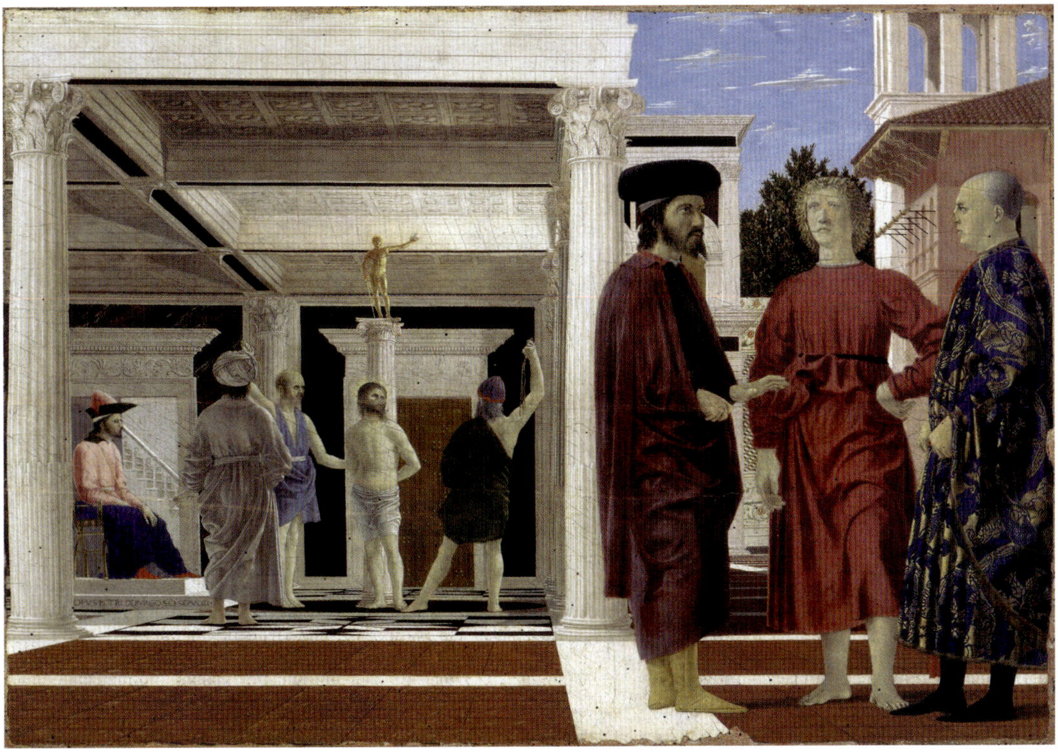

VIII. Piero della Francesca, *The Flagellation of Christ*, 58.4 × 81.5 cm.
Galleria Nazionale delle Marche di Urbino, Urbino

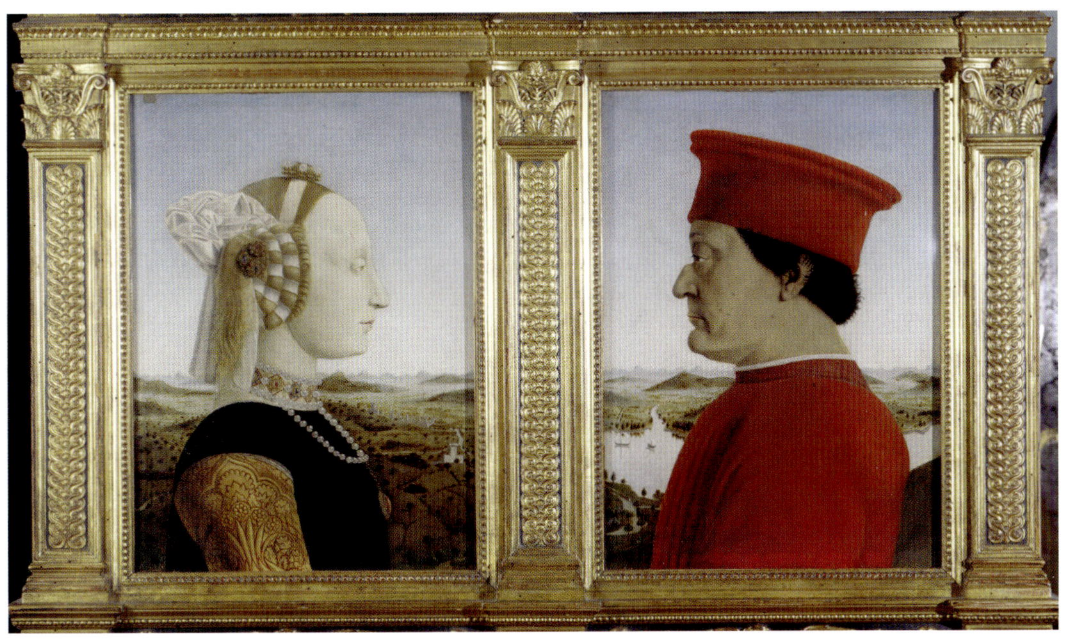

IX. Piero della Francesca, Diptych of *Federico da Montefeltro and Battista Sforza*, 47 × 33 cm each.
Galleria degli, Florence

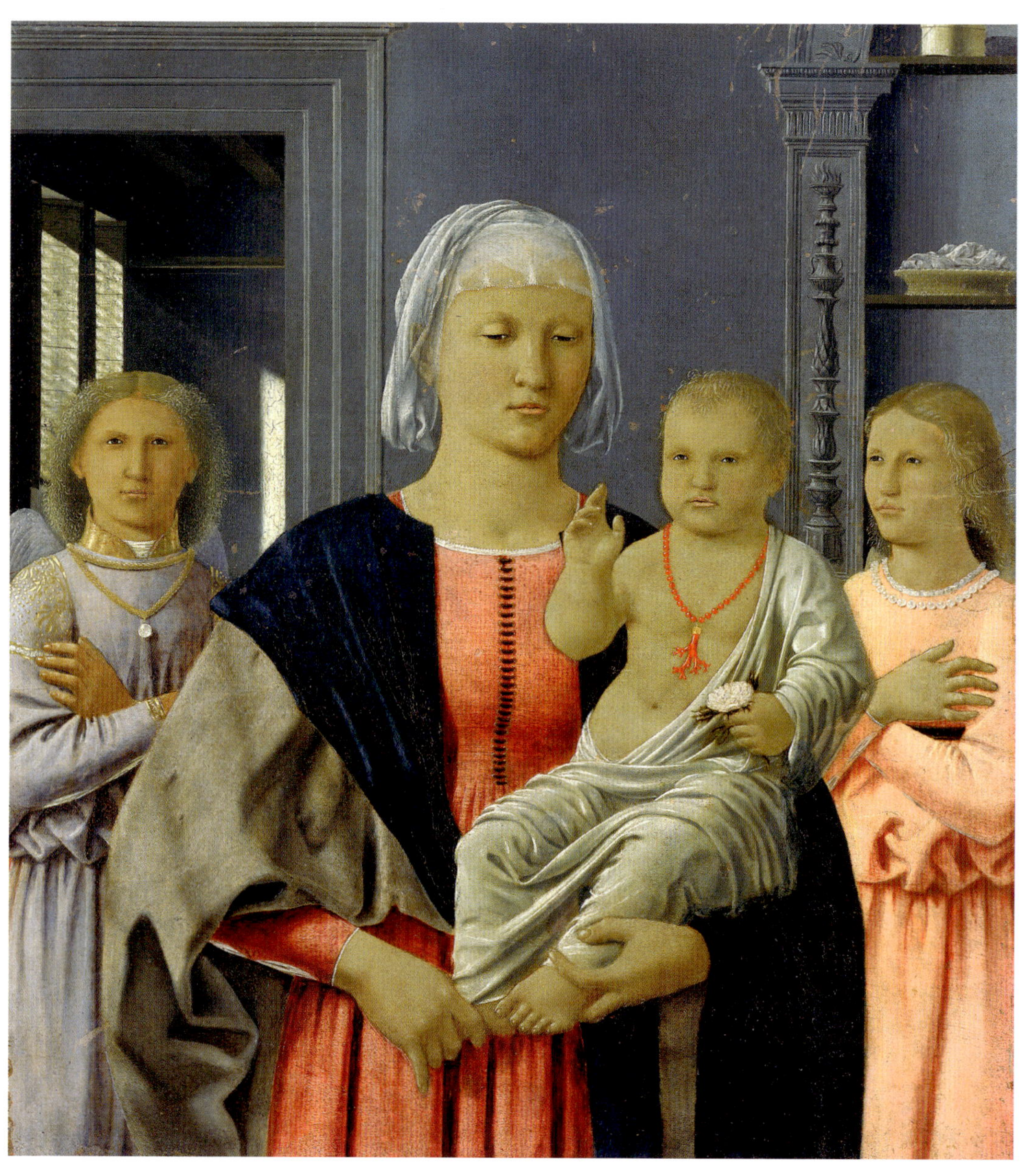

X. Piero della Francesca, *Senigallia Madonna and Child*, 61 × 53.5 cm.
Galleria Nazionale delle Marche di Urbino, Urbino

Urbino and father of Raphael. The document states that Santi was paid by the confraternity of Corpus Domini to host Piero who had "come to see the altarpiece that he will do for the Fraternity."[24] If Piero was offered the commission, he declined it because it is known that Justus of Ghent painted the altarpiece in 1474. We do not know why Piero declined (if he had in fact been offered the commission), but it is possible that he had other commissions to complete (the Sant'Agostino altarpiece) or to start. This is almost certain given the fact that, two months after having visited Giovanni Santi and Urbino, Piero had already returned to Sansepolcro.[25]

Piero's *Flagellation* has probably received more interpretations—now more than forty—than any other painting in Western art, and yet it remains a mystery. There is no general agreement on the occasion, the patron, the purpose, or the meaning of the painting.[26] Piero has painted an image with two focal points: on the left the traditional scene of Christ being flagellated before the enthroned Pilate and on the right three figures, visually powerful and distinctive as they are large and in the foreground. The modern viewer senses that the scene of the Son of God being flagellated is subordinate to the three figures on the right. The representation of the three men and the emphasis on perspective will be our principal concerns.

The *Flagellation* received no known attention in its day, unless Vasari was including it when he spoke of Piero's "many paintings with the most beautiful small figures" in Urbino. The painting is first securely recorded in an inventory of objects in the Old Sacristy of the Cathedral of Urbino in 1744. Piero in all likelihood painted the *Flagellation* for a patron from this town in the Marches. We may note here that, despite its powerful visual presence encouraging viewers of photographs to assume that the painting is large, it is relatively small (58.4 × 81.5 cm, or 23 × 32 in). Piero could thus have painted it elsewhere and carried it to Urbino from Sansepolcro, although we shall follow the most likely assumption that Piero painted it in Urbino for a local patron.

First we should note that formally the two portions of the painting are tightly related.[27] In the left in the center of an open loggia of Pilate's Praetorium (judgment hall), two men flagellate Christ while a third watches, with Pilate seated in the back left corner. The figures of Christ and the two men who flagellate him are formally almost identical with the three men on the right. The spacing between the men of the two groups is similar; the pose of Christ and the pose of the central man of the three men on the right are also similar. Piero intended the relationship of the two groups to be seen as more than casual. That relationship is part of the mystery to be solved by examining the painting closely and placing it in the context of Quattrocento events.

Interpretations of the three figures on the right can be divided into three groups. The first views the three men as contemporaries of the Biblical moment. Jews were not permitted to enter Pilate's Judgment Hall, and Piero—in this interpretation—has depicted three Jewish leaders who, it was said, conspired against Christ after his criticisms of Jewish institutions and his prophecies of imminent changes. Thus all the elements of the *Flagellation* involved men contemporary with Christ.

The majority of interpreters see the three men on the right as portraits of fifteenth-century individuals. If that is the case, the problem is to decode the painting as a means to explain the meaning intended by Piero and the person who commissioned him. This has led to widely divergent interpretations, from seeing the painting as a lamentation for lost opportunities to counter Muslim advances into Christian centers in an epochal conflict of civilizations, to the view that the scene is a subtle recalling of Federico da Montefeltro of Urbino's presumed murder of his half-brother Oddantonio in 1444. The earliest and most recurring interpretation of the mysteries of the *Flagellation* relates to the events of that year. Thus, it is said that the *Flagellation* depicts men involved in the events in 1444, usually with the young barefoot center figure interpreted as Oddantonio and as an innocent victim, analogous to Christ; the other two are seen as either the Duke's evil counselors or other members of the Montefeltro family.

The third group of interpreters sees the figures on the right not as portraits or contemporaries of Piero but as types of some abstract quality, and usually note as well that several earlier exemplars of the flagellation in Italian painting have placed men outside the Praetorium. This interpretation has been asserted rather than persuasively argued. The most powerful argument against this position derives from a consideration of the figure on the extreme right in the *Flagellation*. Interpreted variously as an aristocrat, a Venetian senator, or as one of several rulers, the figure could easily have been Piero's embodiment of a man of political and social distinction. However, the same man appears in several of Piero's paintings with the same features—and, most importantly, the figure ages from one painting to the next. Hence it is difficult to think of the figure as representing an abstraction. Let us examine the five paintings where the figure has appeared.

The earliest appearance of this figure (1451) is in the *Saint Jerome and a Penitent* (see Pl. II). In Chapter 3 this figure is identified as Jacopo Anastagi. Here Piero paints Jacopo as fully confident of his abilities and capable of absorbing Jerome's stern look without flinching or acknowledging any deficiencies or sins. This "penitent" is more in the foreground than the seated saint and, because of this placement, though kneeling, is taller than him. As a result, the saint appears diminutive while his interlocutor is large and visually assertive. The "penitent" is clothed in a bright red full-length overgown (*cioppa*), which endows his body with weight. Here we have an excellent example of Piero's integration of color and form. Piero intended to accentuate his patron's importance and dignity. The "penitent" can be judged as approaching mid-age, perhaps about forty years of age, and, though he has begun to lose his hair, there is no hint of gray. As in the other examples of this figure, the man's hair is cut very short. It is important to note that the patron has a most vibrant red strip of cloth visible on his back and curled in front of his knees. Piero, in choosing to add this barely visible red narrow strip of cloth to a man already clothed in a red cloak, must have intended to signal something about the figure. Since an identical strip appears in the *Flagellation*, it will be part of the discussion of that painting.[28]

This man appears again under the gown of the *Madonna* in the Misericordia altarpiece that we have dated to the mid and late 1450s (see Pl. V and Illus. 9). The man is again on his knees and wears an identical red *cioppa*; again the gown is lined at his neck and perhaps at the bottom by a narrow black trimming. He is again in profile with his head tilted back, enabling him to seek the face of the Madonna. We find the identical well-formed head with the same thinning and naturally dark brown hair as in the *Saint Jerome* (see Pl. II). We cannot say that he has aged much and could be judged to be in his mid-forties.

The figure next appears twice in the Arezzo frescoes of the late 1450s. He is in the middle tier of the right wall in the scene of the *Visit of Sheba to Solomon* (see Illus. 6). In the *Death of Chosroes*, he appears on the extreme right side of the *Victory of Heraclius* in the bottom register on the left wall (see Illus. 5). In the first the figure is again in his red overgown, here slightly darker in color compared to the earlier two images and trimmed in white. He also wears black leather boots. He is an important member of Solomon's entourage and carries an object in his right hand, perhaps a gift for the queen. We can imagine him as Solomon's chancellor or chief adviser. In the 1992 exhibition of jewels and clothes depicted by Piero in Arezzo, the curators of the exhibition named the figure a chancellor. He wears a cap so that it is impossible to see much of his hair or his hairline or to judge his age, but because the cap is scarlet and fur-lined, we know that he is a university graduate and, given his scarlet cap and scarlet gown, probably a civil-law graduate.[29]

In the scene of the execution of Chosroes in Arezzo, the man appears for the fourth time in profile. Piero has again represented this figure as an important member of a king's entourage. Though no longer in a red overgown, his position to the right of King Heraclius indicates Piero associated this man with juridical authority in this moment when Chosroes was condemned to death. Piero had to depict the execution of Chosroes as more than simply revenge or murder. The presence of an expert in law would legitimate the execution, which explains the inclusion of the figure. His hair is closely cropped and his hairline is both receding and gray, and he appears older than in the paintings in Rimini and Sansepolcro.

Finally, we return to the *Flagellation*. As in the earlier depictions of this man on the extreme right, he is again in profile, and his hair has receded further and is close-cropped and gray. He has aged and appears to be in his fifties. He wears the same black boots as in the Solomon and Sheba scene (see Illus. 5). His elegant blue gold-brocaded overgown (*vestito* or *cioppa*) is decorated with golden pomegranates and lined with fur. Silk brocades are seldom found in depictions of Venetians and Florentines because the rich cloth denied elements of their republican ethos. Rich and expensive silk appears more in courtly settings and on formal occasions. Certainly the Flagellation of Christ is not a celebratory moment; Piero must have had other reasons for enhancing the status of this man.

The figure in the rich blue and gold brocade has a crimson strip of cloth on his right shoulder that continues almost to his feet. It is identical to the crimson strip found in the earlier *Saint Jerome* painting. To repeat, the recurrence of this marker cannot be casual. This strip has been explained variously as that of a cardinal, a Venetian, and a Jew, but the historian of Renaissance clothing Jane Bridgeman has argued convincingly that the crimson strip signified a university graduate in law, medicine, or the arts. The man has often been identified as a prince of central or northern Italy, but there is not one royal or princely attribute. And this is true to say of all the other paintings in which he appears. The figure in Piero's *Flagellation* is highly similar to the painting of Nicolas Rolin (*d.* 1462), who appears in Jan van Eyck's *Chancellor Rolin and the Virgin* (the Louvre, Paris). Rolin was the chancellor for the Burgundian ruler Philip the Good. Van Eyck depicts Rolin as proud and powerful in his pomegranate-decorated brocade, despite being on his knees and with his hands folded as a devotee of the Virgin. Van Eyck celebrates the worldly success of Rolin by placing the richly attired chancellor in his grand palace with its expensive accoutrements. I am not suggesting that Piero had seen or was borrowing from Van Eyck's painting; rather, it seems that Van Eyck and Piero faced the identical problem of elevating a man of common birth who had assisted a prince and eventually exercised extensive delegated political power. Both painters gave their chancellors expensive cloth, an air of great confidence, and a fully articulated body.

In this discussion of the man whom Piero has depicted on five occasions we have been developing criteria by which to identify him. Some elements exclude certain categories of persons and others indicate certain categories of persons. Let us begin by eliminating certain categories of men. Inasmuch as not one of the five depicted figures has any royal or princely attributes and the figure twice appears as subordinate to royalty (Sheba and Heraclius), we can eliminate all kings and princes. Because he is portrayed under the mantle of the Misericordia Madonna and the men of the confraternity would not have accepted indiscriminately someone from outside Sansepolcro to be depicted with so great honor in their altarpiece, the man cannot have been born elsewhere than Sansepolcro. This argument, and the connection to Sansepolcro, is strengthened by Piero's decision in the *Saint Jerome* painting to place the figure representing the same person before a depiction of the town itself.

Let us note next the qualities that will enable us to identify the man in the paintings. He must have had considerable success exercising delegated political power, probably in the role of a chancellor or political adviser. Given his proximate age in the five paintings, the man was born in the decade of the 1410s. As the crimson strip of cloth on his right shoulder in the Venetian *Saint Jerome* and *Flagellation* paintings indicates, the figure was a university graduate, most likely in law. Because the figure is clothed in the *cioppa* in at least three of the paintings and this silk vestment cost between 20 and 100 florins, he would have been wealthy. So we have pieces of the biography: born in the decade of 1410 in Sansepolcro, he was wealthy though neither princely nor noble, and a university graduate who had exercised delegated political power.

Jacopo Anastagi

In Chapters 1 and 3 we introduced Jacopo Anastagi as a youth in Sansepolcro with Piero and as an adviser of Sigismondo Malatesta from the 1430s to Anastagi's death in 1465, as the patron and the figure depicted in Piero's Venetian *Saint Jerome and a Penitent*, and as a member of the family linked to the Della Francesca through marriage. Even though we do not have an example of Jacopo's appearance from a source other than Piero's portraits to solidify the argument, I would argue that the figure Piero represented five times is this same Jacopo Anastagi.

Jacopo meets all the positive criteria and is not excluded by any of the negative criteria. His birth in 1413 fits perfectly with the estimated ages of the figure in Piero's paintings.[30] At the time of the painting of the *Saint Jerome* now in Venice, Jacopo would have been thirty-eight years of age and fifty-five at the time of the *Flagellation*. He received his degree in civil and canon law in the 1430s and became an adviser to Sigismondo and, though the term "chancellor" was not used in the court of Sigismondo Malatesta, he served that function as "secretarius." Later he aided Malatesta Novello, brother of Sigismondo and ruler of Cesena, as counselor. He profited from his career in Rimini and Cesena, enriching himself and accumulating a great deal of property in Sansepolcro. Though Jacopo made Rimini and Cesena his residence until his death, he remained close to his native town, building a palace there and providing for a burial chapel in the Badia of Borgo. Hence the members of the confraternity of the Misericordia would have accepted his portrait in their altarpiece, just as the political elite of the town included Jacopo as a member of council of the people in 1442, in fact as one of the *capilista* who headed that council.

It should be kept in mind that Piero and Jacopo were approximately the same age. As children they lived within 100 yards of each other, and would have gone to grammar school together. Though not born to a noble family, Jacopo was regarded by his townsmen as the most eminent person born in the town in the Quattrocento. It should not be surprising that his image provided Piero with a prototype of a successful man of the world who exercised delegated political power. Piero marks Jacopo's success by presenting him in the expensive *cioppa* in at least three of the five portraits. We now know that Jacopo owned at least one of these scarlet overgowns. In an inventory of his goods made after his death, the heirs listed Jacopo's "cioppa of red cloth with sleeves and lined," which describes precisely the overgown in the *Saint Jerome and a Penitent* and in the Misericordia altarpiece.[31]

But what was the occasion that the *Flagellation* memorialized? Several earlier writers have noted that the blond youth in the center of the group of three men appears otherworldly—Piero's means of indicating that he was dead. Many have noted that the barefoot stance of the youth approximates the appearance of Christ. Hence my suggestion is that Piero wished to communicate that the youth had been unjustly imprisoned and died so that his death as an innocent paralleled the death of Christ. A nineteenth-century observer recorded that the quote "CONVENERUNT IN UNUM" ("They came together") appeared on the painting or its frame. The quote is taken from Psalm II, verse 2, which in its complete form says "The kings of the earth stood up and the princes met together against the Lord and against his Christ." The princes (Herod and Pilate) had convened and had contributed to the death of Christ. In a parallel manner, princes had come together and had undertaken actions that led to the youth's death.

I am proposing that the blond youth in the *Flagellation* is Carlo, the son of Jacopo Anastagi. Carlo appears as the victim of two political miscalculations by his father, both related to the epic struggle between Sigismondo Malatesta in Rimini and Federico da Montefeltro in Urbino over control of the eastern part of central Italy. In the first, Carlo as the son of Sigismondo Malatesta's chief counselor Jacopo, married a young Montefeltro woman, Violante. In the second political miscalculation Jacopo sought an alternative to the rule of Rimini by Isotta and her son Sallustio in the absence of Sigismondo in 1465.

The marriage of Carlo di Jacopo Anastagi to Violante di Niccolò d'Antonio da Montefeltro involved political intrigue. On the surface this appears, and may have been, one of the many attempts to attenuate Malatesta–Montefeltro hostility through marriages of young members of the two princely houses or of their court. But this is uncertain because Violante's grandfather Antonio had been close to Oddantonio, the Duke of Urbino who was assassinated in 1444. Her father Niccolò participated in an abortive attempt to assassinate Federico in 1446, probably with the aid of Sigismondo Malatesta. In the later 1440s Niccolò and his son Antonio were in Rimini as guests of Sigismondo.[32] Thus we cannot say with assurance whether the Violante–Carlo marriage was arranged with Federico's approval or whether it was an attempt by the Malatesta to bring together the families of Jacopo and Niccolò d'Antonio da Montefeltro in an alliance against Federico.

Violante and Carlo were married by proxy in September 1460 in the castle of the noble Montedoglio family near Borgo. None of the immediate family members of the spouses was present. Piero's brother-in-law, Anastagio Anastagi, pronounced the vows for Carlo, and the Count of Montedoglio, Piernofro, took them for Violante with the Count as the guarantor of the dowry.[33] We know little about the spouses. Carlo was caught up in political machinations that led to his death. In 1465 Sigismondo Malatesta fought against Islamic forces in Greece as Venice's military commander. In his absence his wife Isotta and their son Sallustio ruled Rimini. Rumors swirled of Sigismondo's death in his military campaign and, according to Jacopo, of Isotta's infidelity. Isotta and her son Sallustio then arrested Jacopo and accused him of favoring Roberto, a son of Sigismondo by another woman, to succeed his father. Isotta and her son relied on Venetian support, but Florence, Milan, and the papacy at this time sought to contain Venetian control down the Adriatic. Jacopo favored an alliance with one or more of these states rather than Venice and it is this that probably led to his arrest.[34] Jacopo was incarcerated, tortured for a confession, and condemned to death. Despite appeals from Sansepolcro, Milan, and Florence, Isotta executed Jacopo in 1465 and arrested Carlo who later died in prison in 1467.[35]

With the death of her husband and father-in-law, Violante had only a distant cousin as a family protector in Rimini and Cesena, who was also named Violante. This Violante Montefeltro was half-sister of Federico and wife of Malatesta Novello. With the death of Malatesta Novello in late 1465, the older Violante chose or was forced to abandon her deceased husband's palazzo, liquidate her wealth in Cesena, and retire to a convent in Ferrara. Later documents indicate an accommodation between Federico and the family of the younger Violante (Carlo's wife), probably after the death of her father in the mid-1460s. Her two brothers became residents in the ducal palace in Urbino. I would suggest that the younger Violante returned to Urbino where, before she vanished from the historical record, she commissioned Piero to paint the *Flagellation* in honor of her deceased husband Carlo, an innocent victim of conniving princes.

In the *Flagellation* the "princes" would necessarily be Violante's father-in-law Jacopo on the right and (in the guise of the man on the left in the turban), one of the members of the Montefeltro entourage. A great deal has been made of the split beard of this man; some say he must be a Greek because Italians did not sport beards in the Quattrocento and others say he must be the Greek prelate Bessarion because he has a beard similar to one in a portrait of Bessarion. But to say that Italians did not possess beards does not mean that the occasional Italian did not choose to permit his facial hair to grow. In fact, one source of the generalization that Italian men did not wear beards comes from an Italian, the humanist Francesco Filelfo, who stated that other Italians looked at him with surprise because of his beard. Moreover, throughout his life Piero painted men with divided beards, perhaps because he had been struck by the pictorial effects of the split beard of the *Volto Santo* in his youth (see Illus. 14). For a few of the many examples of Piero's predilection to depict split beards, see Christ in *The Baptism of Christ*, John the Baptist in the Misericordia altarpiece, Saint Jerome in the Berlin painting of that saint, and the king Sigismundus in the Rimini fresco. Nothing definite can be made of the fact that the figure in the *Flagellation* has been given a split beard. In fact, a man closely involved with Federico da Montefeltro, Ottaviano Ubaldini della Carda (who will be discussed in Chapter 10), possessed a split beard. I would suggest that he is the most likely person to have participated with Jacopo Anastagi in arranging the marriage between Carlo Anastagi and Violante Montefeltro and thereby for political purposes contributed to Carlo's death.[36]

The most important distinguishing technical feature of the *Flagellation* is its powerful formal mathematical organization. As one might expect, there have been numerous discussions of Piero's perspective space in this painting. It has been shown that Piero used a basic geometrical module that was varied to represent the differing shapes in the painting's tiled floor. Piero built an incredibly deep perspective. Viewers are struck by these spatial qualities that have led some to see the painting as an exercise in perspective or a demonstration of Piero's abilities that would have been presented to a potential patron. This artwork is often seen as the most apt example of perspective in the Renaissance, rational in its organization of a complex set of spaces and shapes.

CHAPTER 10

Piero in Urbino in the Early 1470s

In the 1470s and 1480s Piero resided in Urbino on several occasions, the first some time in the period from November 1469 to June 1472. The details are unclear because of an absence of extensive documentation in exactly those years. In the period immediately after June 1472 Piero was often present in Borgo, so we know that his sojourn in Urbino in the early 1470s was limited to a couple of years. Urbino was important to Piero for several reasons. He found a major patron, Federico da Montefeltro, at a time when Federico was gaining renown as a professional military commander and as a patron of the arts and learning. He also provided Piero with an intellectually exciting court. Moreover, being in Urbino gave Piero access to Federico's large library, including mathematics texts important for Piero's own work in geometry.

How and when the two met, and why Federico commissioned Piero, can only be surmised. However, they almost certainly would have known of each other by reputation for many years. Piero was at this point nearing his sixtieth birthday (about ten years older than Federico) and had received renown as an artist. Moreover, as I suggested in the previous chapter, he had received the commission for *The Flagellation of Christ* from a Montefeltro family member.

Federico da Montefeltro

By the 1470s Federico da Montefeltro had achieved renown for his successes as a ruler of the most important territorial state in the eastern half of central Italy (the Marches) and as the most sought-after military commander in Italy.[1] Moreover, Federico's efforts to represent himself as a warrior patron of the arts had begun to win acceptance from Florence to Naples. His palace in the small town of Urbino had become the setting for the most important secular court in Quattrocento Italy, and, as the scene of later learned discussions in Baldassare Castiglione's *Book of the Courtier* (1508–28), it would become the model for monarchical courts in early modern western Europe.

Born in 1422, Federico was the illegitimate son of the successful *condottiere* and ruler of Urbino, Guidantonio da Montefeltro (1377–1443), who had Federico legitimized by Pope Martin V. Guidantonio made sure that his son would have the political education required of a ruler's son, sending him to the court of Gianfrancesco Gonzaga in Mantua. There he accompanied that ruler's sons to the school of the eminent humanist, Vittorino da Feltre, who introduced Federico to Petrarch's new curriculum based on ancient Latin texts of history and literature as well as to the traditional medieval curriculum of the liberal arts, especially mathematics and geometry. Federico also received military training under the *condottiere* Niccolò Piccinino, and at sixteen years of age began his campaigning in Lombardy in 1438, as well as occasionally aiding his father against Sigismondo Malatesta near Rimini.

When Federico's father died in 1443, the succession passed to his legitimate son Oddantonio, who while yet a teenager was accused of violent behavior toward his own people, including several sexual attacks on women in Urbino. But these criticisms of Oddantonio's behavior and character may have been invented or exaggerated to justify his assassination in his palace bed by a group of Urbino men in 1444. As fortune or prudential planning provided, by the morning after his half-brother's death, Federico was just outside Urbino. Upon entering, he successfully negotiated with the town elders for political power. Many, both then and now, have accused Federico of conspiring with friends in Urbino to murder his half-brother.[2] The evidence is not conclusive; in any event Federico seized the moment and ruled Urbino and its possessions, which he expanded threefold before his death in 1482.

Urbino and the Marches were under the nominal authority of the popes, who periodically negotiated with Count Federico over the terms of Montefeltro political control of the region. For the first two decades of his rule, Federico fought continuously with words and arms against Sigismondo Malatesta, likewise under the nominal authority of the popes, over who would dominate the eastern half of central Italy. As *condottieri*, the two also competed for the most lucrative and prestigious military contracts in Italy. Popes played one off against the other and against the other lords of the region to ensure that none of them attained hegemony. This changed in the early 1460s when Pope Pius II elevated Federico to an unprecedented dominance of the Marches that continued until his death.

The Marches was an agrarian region with no large city—other than Ancona—of merchants and artisans like those that elsewhere provided the socio-economic base for republics and humanism. Since the people of the Marches did not possess great wealth or the ability to pay substantial taxes, Federico followed the practices of his forebears, recruiting local men for military service and gaining contracts for himself as a mercenary captain from the leading states of Italy. At various times, Naples, Florence, Milan, and most often the papacy hired Federico as a military commander, so that toward the end of his career he had the highest income of any layman in Italy. Federico had to pay his soldiers and purchase the larger implements of war, but his income as a *condottiere* allowed him to govern the Marches with relatively low tax demands on his people.

He could afford to transform his family's small palace in Urbino into the grandest palace of any Italian lord and to support his library, scholars, and artists.

Federico's June 1468 commission to the architect Luciano Laurana from Dalmatia to expand his Urbino palace expresses his attitude toward all visual and constructive artists and artisans: "We judge to be worthy of honor and to be commended men ornamented with ingenuity and skill, and particularly those skills which have always been prized by both the ancients and the moderns, as has been the skill of architecture, founded upon the arts of arithmetic and geometry, which are the most certain, and which is an art requiring great knowledge and ingenuity and by me most esteemed and honored."[3] This quote, his later commission to Justus of Ghent to paint allegories of the seven liberal arts in his palace in Gubbio, and his hosting or rewarding scholars of the medieval liberal arts and Renaissance humanism, all suggest Federico's wide intellectual interests.

The Florentine humanists had taken from Aristotle the idea that the intense social interactions of a city were necessary to actuate full human potential. Although Urbino's population was only about six thousand, Federico created another form of social organization that mimicked the intensity of the interactions of a large city. His palace provided living quarters for several hundred people, from cooks, soldiers, and mule drivers to notaries, judges, artists, scientists, and courtiers. According to the idealized biography of Vespasiano da Bisticci, many parts of the palace including Federico's own throne room were available to the public. He described the ruler as open to the supplications of his people at almost every moment of his day. The Florentine humanists had also borrowed from Aristotle the idea that the fulfillment of human life required the political participation found only in a republic. Federico's palace was not a republic, but it did involve many men in the process of governing. He had brought the entire communal magistracies of Urbino and all the administration of the region into the palace. In recounting his residence there, Castiglione called it "a palace in the form of a city."

Federico da Montefeltro hosted scholars and artists in various media and placed some on a form of retainer so that they were resident in the palace for years. These artists and scholars embodied a combination of the artisan and the university cultures that we discussed as important in Piero's early formation. Federico's court provided a rich environment for someone like Piero who was open to the ideas and techniques of others. Even though he was in his early sixties, Piero was still absorbing and experimenting with painting techniques and ideas from artisan and scholarly cultures. The painters brought together by Federico contributed to these experiments, and the scholars whom Piero would have met there, or at least the books he would have read in Federico's library, would have contributed to Piero's treatise *On Perspective in Painting* and to his knowledge of the geometry of Archimedes that culminated in his decision to make his own copy of the *Opera* of the Greek geometrician.[4]

Many biographers of Piero assert that at various moments in his career he encountered Leon Battista Alberti, the leading humanist-artist of the Quattrocento, but there is no hard evidence for this view. Various writers have suggested that Piero encountered Alberti and gained essential knowledge from him in Florence in 1439, Ferrara in the 1440s, Rome and Rimini in the 1450s, and Urbino in the 1460s, before Alberti's death in 1472. If in fact the two did interact, it may have been in Urbino in the late 1460s or 1470–71. The fruit of the encounter, if it occurred, is unknown. Piero's treatise on perspective in painting, completed in the mid-1470s, shows only minimal influence of Alberti, although the idea of the treatise itself may have derived from the humanist's 1435 *On Painting* (*Della pittura*).[5]

Luciano Laurana remained as Federico's architect of his palace from at least 1468 to 1472, the earliest period of Piero's presence in Urbino. In the latter year the architect, painter, and writer Francesco di Giorgio Martini replaced Laurana. The painter Fra Carnevale, although not a member of court, lived in Urbino and many believe advised Federico in the 1470s. Fra Carnevale had been in Florence for several years in the mid-1440s, and he brought Florentine artisans, especially stoneworkers, to Urbino. He evolved a style of painting so similar to Piero's that in the nineteenth century two of Piero's later paintings in Urbino were attributed to him.

A permanent resident in the Urbino court was Federico's nephew Ottaviano (whom we encountered in Chapter 9), son of Federico's probable half-sister Aura and the condottiere Bernardino Ubaldini della Carda. The young Ottaviano had been sent to Milan in the 1430s and educated in the Visconti court by the humanist Guarino da Verona. At his father's death Ottaviano inherited several military squads but, being more interested in learning than the military life, handed them over to Federico. Ottaviano owned a painting by Van Eyck and was in contact with the painter Pisanello and the humanist Decembrio. He remained in the Visconti court until 1447 and, upon his return to Urbino, became Federico's faithful counselor, overseer of the state and court, and eventually regent for Federico's young son. Ottaviano was a practicing astrologer. Astrology possessed intellectual and academic respectability, and Federico's interest in it was expressed in patronage for the university professors of the subject, James of Spiers and Paul of Middelburg.

In this same period around 1470 Federico intensified his efforts to obtain manuscripts, and until the late 1470s he purchased most of these from the Florentine book dealer Vespasiano da Bisticci, who oversaw the copying of manuscripts on a wide variety of subjects. After Federico's involvement in the Pazzi Conspiracy in 1478, most of his texts were copied and decorated in a scriptorium in his palace by the best scribes and miniaturists of the period. The enmity between Federico and Lorenzo de' Medici that intensified around the moment of the conspiracy broke the commerce of manuscripts between Florence and Urbino. Among the artists and artisans of the palace there were scribes, decorators of the leather bindings of the manuscripts, and miniaturists brought from Mantua, Ferrara, and Rome. Federico's library eventually held texts in Italian, Latin, Greek, and Hebrew, covering almost every subject, especially Greek and Roman works but also works by Italian Renaissance humanists. Unlike many others of his generation, Federico collected texts in mathematics and related natural sciences.

We know Piero completed two paintings (the diptych in the Uffizi and the Brera altarpiece) and probably a third (the *Madonna and Child* in Senigallia) for Federico and was hosted in Urbino by Giovanni Santi (as mentioned earlier the father of Raphael), but there is no other documentary evidence of Piero in Federico's town. The occasional but recurring residences of Piero in Urbino and the dating of these paintings therefore have to be based on other types of reasoning.

Piero became familiar with the intensive court life in Federico's palace when he executed the commission for *The Flagellation of Christ* in either 1467–69 or 1470–72. I have introduced this chapter by suggesting that Piero was in Urbino in the period of late 1469–June 1472. Other documents confirm his absence from his home town in these years. First, the confraternity of the Misericordia, which had commissioned Piero in 1445 and would commission him again in 1477, had to seek a painter from Siena for a processional flag. In June 1470 they contracted with Matteo di Giovanni for such a flag, probably because Piero was unavailable and in Urbino. Second, in May 1470, when the patrons of the Sant'Agostino altarpiece in Borgo were prepared to make a payment for Piero's commission, he was not available and his brother Antonio, as his legal representative, accepted 50 florins in the painter's name.[6] Moreover, he witnessed only two documents on the same day (28 January 1470) in Sansepolcro during those years. Before the early 1460s and after 1472 he was often documented in his home town.

Given these facts, it is reasonable to assume that Piero was absent from Sansepolcro and spent a good part of 1470, 1471, and perhaps early 1472 in Urbino. It is only 27 miles from Sansepolcro to Urbino, although to complete the journey one has to climb over the mountains called the Alpe della Luna whose principal pass is just under one thousand meters. Despite this, it is apparent that Piero crossed this section of the Apennines several times in the last two decades of his life. A familiarity between Piero and the ruler of Urbino is suggested by a letter of Federico to the Florentine captain Francesco Lotto in Sansepolcro. Lotto had arrested one of Federico's soldiers named Corsetto Guelfo for robbery. In February 1471 Federico wrote to the captain that Guelfo should be freed and 36 large florins, apparently belonging to Guelfo, should be given to Piero's brother Marco, who would convey the florins to another man from Urbino. The episode demonstrates Federico's close familiarity with the Della Francesca family based, I would suggest, on Piero's presence in the Urbino court at that moment.[7]

The Uffizi Diptych of Federico da Montefeltro and Battista Sforza

Piero's earliest painting for the ruler of Urbino should be dated after the death of Federico's second wife Battista Sforza in 1472. Battista's father, Alessandro Sforza, was ruler of the Adriatic port city of Pesaro and had provided a Latin master for Battista in 1450 when she was three years of age. He had then sent her to the court of her uncle Francesco Sforza in Milan, where she received an excellent formal and informal court education. Returning to her father's court at age twelve, she delivered Latin orations to welcome visiting dignitaries. Married to Federico at fourteen, Battista brought light to his life in the decade of the 1460s, after the deaths of his first wife and their son Buonconte. Battista studied philosophy and theology with the humanist Martino Filetico and developed a specialized knowledge of Cicero's *Paradoxes of the Stoics*, in which Cicero demonstrated through rhetorical arguments how virtue, happiness, and honor are compatible. She defended the use of rhetoric from attacks that it could instigate evil by asserting the moral neutrality of the oratorical art. She gave birth to at least six daughters and finally a son in the year of her death. From 1460 to 1472, during her husband's frequent absences, Battista was virtual ruler of Urbino. We might note that the principal female attendant in Battista's entourage was Pantisilea Baglioni of Perugia, whom we encountered as the probable link between the Della Francesca and the Baglioni in the commission for Piero's polyptych of Sant'Antonio in Perugia.[8] Pantisilea may have also been instrumental in introducing Piero to the court in Urbino.

In early 1472 the Florentine government hired Federico to quell a revolt in Volterra, whose citizens had rebelled against Medici exploitation of their mines and against Florentine domination. Federico's troops broke the ramparts of Volterra and, in the worst scandal of his military career, the city was plundered. Perhaps as penitence, Federico refused to accept payment from Florence but did permit the city to give him a celebratory entry and a palace. Battista had given birth to their only son Guidobaldo in January and was on her deathbed in July when Federico returned from his service to Florence. Her death led to an outpouring of consolatory literature to the mourning Federico. It was in this context that he commissioned Piero to paint a small personal memorial to Battista and to their wedded life.

The diptych (Pl. IX) presents the portraits of Federico and Battista with a landscape background on the front side and on the reverse, chariots of triumph for each, with a landscape background and an inscription in the foreground (Illus. 19). The diptych is small (each portrait is 47 cm × 33 cm, or 18½ × 13 in) and was originally connected with a hinge that would permit the portraits to fold inward. The portraits have been seen as an early Italian adaptation of a Flemish style in which the subjects are set in a landscape background and are a pair, but Piero has also included elements from sculpted portraits found on ancient and contemporary medals and from Italian painted portraits.

Debate on the dating of the diptych has remained heated, but I am confident that Piero painted it soon after Battista's death.[9] Her whitened ghostly appearance suggests that she was deceased, though this whitened skin was also a feature of idealized feminine beauty in Quattrocento Italy. Battista is said to have prayed for a son while staying at Federico's palace in Gubbio and to have offered her life to the local Saint Ubaldo in exchange. And on her cart of triumph on the reverse of the portrait, Piero has painted one of the virtues, Modesty, dressed in Sforza blue (now debased to black) to mark the virtue as specific to Battista. The figure has a pelican in her lap, who picks at her own breast to feed her young. Pelicans were thought to have sacrificed themselves for their young and thus served as an analogue to Christ. Here the

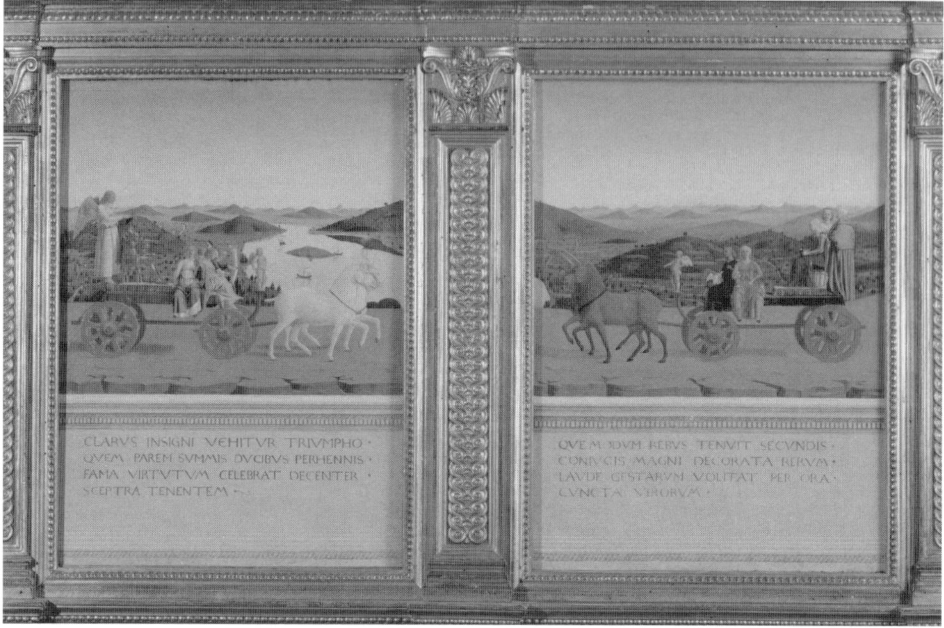

ILLUS. 19 Piero della Francesca, *Triumphs of Federico da Montefeltro and Battista Sforza* (diptych, reverse side), 47 × 33 cm each. Galleria degli Uffizi, Florence

pelican reminds viewers that Battista gave birth to a son and then died. Most importantly, Piero wrote the epithet under her *Triumph* in the past tense, whereas Federico's inscription is in the present tense. Moreover, Piero has painted a text with a classical idea first popularized by Petrarch, namely that humans have an earthly immortality through the memory of their virtues in the minds of future generations. The text for Battista reads: "She, who retained modesty in good fortune, adorned with the fame of her magnificent husband's deeds, now flies through all the mouths of men."[10] And when we understand the source and context of the latter part of the inscription, we see that it would be inappropriate for a living person. Piero or Federico's humanist adviser borrowed a passage from Cicero's *Tusculan Disputations* in which he quotes the first Roman poet Ennius: "Let no one honor me with tears or on my ashes weep. And why? I fly through the mouths of the living." Death has no warrant for Battista because her virtue of modesty and also her sharing of the deeds of Federico assure that her fame "flies through all the mouths of men." The first sentence of Piero's text derives from Petrarch's treatise on fortune and his notion that good as well as bad fortune required careful attention, lest one fall into destructive psychological states.

Hence Piero painted the portraits after July 1472 and their execution should be seen as part of an outpouring of consolatory sentiment for the widowed Federico. This presents a small problem. While Piero was most likely in Urbino from 1470 to early

1472, documents show him to have been almost continuously in Sansepolcro from June 1472 until February 1475, so he had returned to Borgo before Battista's death in July 1472. We can only surmise that Piero traveled to Urbino later in 1472 for a short period, during the mourning for Battista, at which time he received the commission and made drawings for the portraits. Others have already suggested that Piero did not necessarily execute the portraits in Urbino, and it does appear that he painted the diptych in Sansepolcro and delivered it to Urbino. Particular qualities of the portraits strengthen the hypothesis that Piero painted them outside of Urbino. The contour of Federico's head in the diptych and in the Brera altarpiece (to be discussed in Chapter 12) are almost identical, suggesting that the same drawing served as the base for the cartoons used in both (see Pl. IX; see Illus. 19, 23).[11] Most agree that Federico did not sit for his portrait. Many have noted that Piero's portrait of Battista is similar to a sculpture usually attributed to Francesco Laurana and that he and Piero may have drawn Battista's likeness from an extant death mask. In any event Piero's portrait of Battista is unusually generalized with few individualizing features beyond the high forehead and high cheekbones. But even these were features of idealized feminine beauty in the Quattrocento.

Piero used oil for both portraits. We have observed his increasing reliance on oil paints from the time of his portrait of Sigismondo Malatesta two decades earlier. This medium enabled Piero to depict many specific and identifying features of Federico, from his ruddy skin with its four warts and his sagging jowls to his hooked nose, which was the result of a sword stroke to its bridge in a tournament in 1451, when he also lost the sight of his right eye. However, this is nevertheless an idealized version of the man. As Joanna Woods-Marsden has well said, a commission to paint the portrait of a prince placed a naturalistic painter like Piero in a dilemma.[12] The painter would have been asked to represent the patron according to nature, but he could not include accurate details of the prince that would demean him or detract from his high estate or in any way lower him in the viewer's estimation. Other contemporary and more realistic depictions of Federico revealed unflattering details. In Justus of Ghent's portrait of the mid-1470s, for example, Federico appears with droopy eyes, pronounced jowls, wispy and thinning hair, and leathery skin, in what may have been an attempt to present him as reflective, but which verges on an image of a defeated, aged, ordinary man. Piero, instead, has presented Federico in the fullness of his powers with an upright body, resolute head and face, and with command over his territory shown behind him with its lake, cities, castles, and plain. Piero has produced an individual, identifiable prince; and this image becomes the norm for later depictions, but at the same time Federico is sufficiently idealized as the powerful yet prudential prince of political propaganda. Thus although the diptych originated from private mourning and from a desire for a vehicle of remembrance, it appears to have public purposes as well.

On the reverse side Piero painted *Triumphs* for the couple (see Illus. 19). The idea of the triumph derived from a Renaissance rethinking of the Roman practice of giving their victorious generals and emperors the occasion to parade their troops, captives, and booty in Rome. Petrarch reconceived the Roman military triumph as a poetic vehicle for celebrating abstract concepts, in particular the virtues. Miniaturists then took the motif for decorating manuscripts. Piero assigned specific virtues to the husband and wife. For Battista's *Triumph of Modesty*, Piero painted a chariot drawn by two unicorns, symbols of virginity and marriage. Battista sits with her eyes in a book, a pose of proper female modesty for which she had become famous in her lifetime. Two of the three Christian virtues sit on the front of the cart; as we have discussed, Charity or Modesty with the pelican and Faith with a chalice, the host, faithful dog, and Cross. Behind Battista there is the third Christian virtue, Hope, together with another unidentified female figure.

In Federico's *Triumph of Fame* Piero has painted Cupid guiding two horses that pull the prince's chariot. The four cardinal virtues ride at the front of the cart: Temperance, barely visible as the viewer sees only the back of her head, Fortitude holding a broken column, Prudence with her customary mirror, and Justice given emphasis as she faces the viewer with her scales and sword. Seated in his armor and with his scepter of command in his right hand pointed directly ahead, Federico receives the laurel crown from a female figure with wings representing Fame. The Duke's inscription reads: "This illustrious hero is celebrated for the fame of his *virtù*. Carried in glorious triumph and worthy of the scepter that he wields, he is equal to the greatest generals."[13] In this context the *virtù* of Federico must relate to the four cardinal virtues, but, as it is linked to military successes, it also suggests classical views of *virtù*, and presages the ideas of Niccolò Machiavelli in which calculation of the prince's self-interest is foremost. The concepts of fame and *virtù*, the quotes from Cicero and Ennius, the practice of inscriptions, and the lettering itself are all classical in inspiration. Together the two *Triumphs* integrate Christian and classical virtues, but Piero—or Federico in his instructions to the painter—clearly divided the virtues into male-classical and female-Christian categories.

Piero has painted a continuous landscape behind the heads of Federico and Battista and behind the carts of the *Triumphs*. He has the two portraits and the *Triumphs* set against distant landscapes. His combination of portraits with a landscape is the first in Italy, and the diptych presents an early Italian example of atmospheric perspective, lessening the intensity of tone and detail as the landscape and the sky converge on the horizon.[14] The far landscape itself is not as realistically drawn and painted as is the near landscape. The hills and mountains tend to be triangles with a minimum of individuation or detail. There are occasional castles, a lake, and a walled city, but no inhabitants. The landscape serves to frame the portraits, emphasizing especially Federico as sculptural and capacious in his abilities. The placement of the prince in the landscape commemorates Federico's rule and Battista's contributions. The painting celebrates Federico's abilities to command his realm, which Piero depicted as a unified territory in the portraits and in the *Triumphs*.

The diptych was at once a private statement of Federico's wish to memorialize his wife and their marriage as well as a statement of the ruler's relationship to his territory. As such, it is a subtle form of political propaganda. We may never know how Federico or his delegate instructed Piero, orally or in writing, or what the patron asked from

Piero. Did Federico or his delegate instruct Piero on the anticipated future location of the painting? The answer is probably yes, since it is double-sided. This would have informed Piero that the requested object would not hang on a wall. But its intended location remains a problem for us since it combines elements of the private and public. Keeping in mind that the diptych folded as a book with the *Triumphs* visible on the outside, I would suggest that Federico intended it for his "Studiolo" (study) in the Urbino Palace. It would not be unusual for important foreign dignitaries to be shown a prince's precious objects, jewels, medals, and books. Federico's Studiolo contained many such objects, including inlaid trompe l'oeil images of books, animals, cabinets, and musical instruments, as well as paintings of philosophers and humanists. The *Triumphs* would have at once impressed the viewer with Federico's knowledge of Roman practices and Petrarchan poetry, and, if the tablets were opened, the viewer would have seen the portraits as novel images combined with a ruler's territory and his memorial to the woman who died in sustaining his dynasty.[15]

CHAPTER 11

Piero in Sansepolcro, 1472–75

By the early summer of 1472 Piero had returned from Urbino to reside in Sansepolcro, where he remained until at least the early months of 1475. This three-year presence is one of the most fully documented periods of his life, especially following the recent discovery of several previously unknown documents. During these years Piero completed and delivered the Urbino diptych (as we saw in Chapter 10), obtained and completed an important commission for a fresco in the Badia di San Giovanni Evangelista in Sansepolcro, which has not survived, and also painted the extraordinary *Hercules* for his own home. In addition, Piero acted as the head of the Della Francesca family by overseeing the activities of his sister Vera and her daughter Cheopa and by becoming involved in several architectural or building projects, including that of the Della Francesca home.

In these three years Piero left many traces of his activities as both a principal and a witness in a variety of social and political contracts, often witnessing for people who are otherwise not known to be involved in Piero's life. The earliest of these contracts was recorded in June 1472 and establishes Piero's return to Borgo. In July of that same year, the conservators appointed Piero to a four-man committee to find and bring a medical doctor to the town.[1] This involved gathering names of prospective doctors and making inquiries as to their availability and interest. The committee members located master Niccolò Fontani and extended a year's contract to him to act as the town doctor.

In August 1472 Piero appeared as a witness in two notarial acts: the first records the establishment of a dowry with its schedule of payment; the second recognizes the right of the groom to sell land that had been included in the dowry. The notary recording the contracts was ser Francesco Pichi, whom we have encountered several times before, because his office was adjacent to the Della Francesca property on the Graziani Crossing in Sansepolcro. Lacking knowledge of any links between Piero and the families of the bride and groom, we can only assume that he was in his nearby family property and witnessed the acts as a convenience for the notary or the parties. Piero next appears as a witness in October 1472 in the office of the notary Leonardo Fedeli. Then in January 1473 two brothers exchanged property in Piero's presence. In an act in May 1473, recorded near the Della Francesca workshop on the Graziani Crossing, Piero and his brother Marco appointed their brother Antonio as a procurator to seek payment for their earlier sale of woad to ser Giusto di Giovanni from nearby Anghiari.[2] There are no specific contracts involving Piero in the remainder of 1473, but it is probably in this period that he received the commission to paint a fresco in the chapel of the Glorious Virgin in the Badia of San Giovanni Evangelista. In documents of September and November the abbot Girolamo and a confraternity, both patrons of the chapel, record the allocation of more than half of the funds necessary for the eventual payments to Piero. The act of November 1473 reads: "the commission of the lord abbot to maestro Pietro di Benedetto di Pietro painter for the pictures of the said chapel and for part of his salary."[3] By late 1473 Piero possessed the commission and his initial payment and soon thereafter began the process of painting the fresco in the Badia of Sansepolcro.

The Fresco of the Glorious Virgin of the Badia

As we have seen in earlier chapters, the confraternities of Sansepolcro were powerful voluntary associations of lay men and occasionally women organized for charity and Christian worship. In 1481–82 Piero would himself head Borgo's most important confraternity, that called the Fraternity of San Bartolomeo. The Fraternity provided services beyond charity that resemble modern state functions, among them keeping statistics of deaths, warning of possible bubonic plagues, and overseeing orphans. The confraternity of the Glorious Virgin, or the Madonna della Badia, had been formed in the fourteenth century and was a relatively small confraternity of men and women organized for the veneration of a wooden polychromed statue of the *Madonna and Child*, which had been sculpted in 1199 (Bode Museum Berlin). This confraternity specialized in *laude*, which were praises sung to the Madonna and Christ. The group also buried deceased members in their common sepulcher. The confraternal members congregated monthly, or even more often, at a chapel to the left of the Badia's high altar to sing their devotional songs.[4]

The Carsidoni family held rights to the sacred space of the chapel used by the confraternity. The family was one of the five or six most eminent of Borgo; their men had earlier been merchants, but by the mid-Quattrocento at least two practiced law.[5] In 1473 Piero's brother Marco married Panta, daughter of the deceased lawyer Cristoforo Carsidoni, after Marco's first wife Giovanna Anastagi died. Panta brought a 200-florin dowry. This amount and the status of the Carsidoni family demonstrate that the Della Francesca family had entered the elite of the town.[6] The Carsidoni already had shared the chapel with the confraternity prior to 1442, the year in which they confirmed its access to the chapel for their devotions, including prayers for the living and the dead.

It was at this time that the confraternity commissioned a local metalworker to construct an iron lattice grill to define their sacred space near the high altar.[7] In the 1450s the confraternity sought to raise 100 florins in support of a crusade. They anticipated that in return for their gift they would receive an indulgence from the Pope for their chapel and that this would encourage devotion and donations from members and visiting non-members. This campaign finally bore fruit at the time of Piero's commission. Like most monastic churches, the Badia had a rood screen that bisected the nave horizontally and served as a barrier to keep lay people, especially women, from approaching the high altar area in certain liturgical moments. But members of the confraternity, both men and women, possessed the right to congregate and pray in the sacred sector of their chapel near the high altar. The confraternity put the chapel to good use; in addition to singing *laude* and providing Masses for the dead, members daily said prayers in front of the wooden sculpture. The addition of a fresco on the wall behind this already ancient *Madonna and Child* sculpture would have enhanced the beauty of the chapel and emphasized the confraternity's dedication to the veneration of the Madonna.[8]

It was a member of the Carsidoni family, not the confraternity, who initiated the process of commissioning Piero to paint an undefined iconographic subject for the chapel of the Glorious Virgin Mary, although the abbot Girolamo eventually contributed to Piero's remuneration as well. Contessina Carsidoni provided much of the funding for Piero's painting, though the payments themselves were channeled through the confraternities of the Madonna and San Bartolomeo. Contessina Carsidoni was the widow of another Carsidoni lawyer, Lodovico, who had died in 1440, leaving a typical medieval library that included law books, Roman history (Valerius Maximus' *Memorable Deeds and Sayings*), an untitled work by Dante, and Ovid's *On the Art of Love*.[9] The children of Lodovico and Contessina were already deceased when the widow wrote her will in 1468. Her son Piersacchone died intestate, but he had left an oral request that 50 florins be conveyed "for a painting and ornamentation of the chapel of the Most Glorious Virgin of the Abbey."[10] The commission was given to Piero, but the written commission itself does not exist, and nowhere in the payment documents is there a discussion of the type of painting Piero was asked to paint. We assume it was a fresco because if a wooden panel painting were being commissioned and executed, there would have been a recurring mention of an altarpiece and most probably a carpenter. Moreover, as the art historian Machtelt Israëls has noted, until almost 1500, chapels in Sansepolcro—excepting high altar chapels—were decorated with statues and frescoes, not with paintings on wooden altarpieces.[11]

Given that the Badia chapel was dedicated to the Virgin and that the *Madonna and Child* statue would be in front of Piero's fresco, it is probable that the fresco depicted some event from Mary's life. We can speculate that the subject was the *Coronation of the Virgin*, and this is supported by the fact that the coronation would be an even more appropriate subject after the confraternity had commissioned an iron crown plated with silver and jewels from the goldsmith Angelo Antonello in the mid-1460s.[12]

The confraternity performed a ritual crowning of the Virgin as part of an Easter Saturday ceremony, when the confraternal members also dressed the wooden sculpture of Mary as part of the celebration of her Son's resurrection. In an inventory of the Badia of the 1490s, two crowns of the Madonna and two of the Child are listed, both probably deriving from the confraternity's Easter weekend ritual.[13] In paintings the coronation often was depicted as occurring in heaven with Christ performing the act, so we may imagine this representation in the chapel. Further support for the supposition that the lost work was a coronation is that in the decade before Piero's commission the confraternity had begun to add the adjective "immaculate" to the Virgin's name.[14] This would be part of the late Quattrocento process of enhancing Mary's place by asserting her freedom from the taint of original sin and thus making her even more worthy of a coronation in heaven.

Payments for this fresco demonstrate that Piero was occupied with the project for most of 1474. On 15 February he witnessed an unrelated contract in which the notary recorded the painter's presence on the "balcony" of the Badia, probably near the high altar and the confraternity's chapel.[15] Piero's presence there suggests that he had already begun the project. On 12 April the scribe of the Fraternity of San Bartolomeo wrote "we have promised him [Piero] for the priors of the confraternity of the Madonna della Badia for the bequest of madonna Contessina, that is, for the remainder of the bequest for painting the said Cappella della Madonna, 200 lire."[16] The Fraternity appears in this series of transactions because it was the primary beneficiary of Contessina Carsidoni, and it allocated her funds to Piero for the confraternity of the Madonna della Badia. The Fraternity often served as the universal or principal heir and doled out money to subsidiary heirs according to the dispositions in the deceased's testament. This transaction shows that Piero had already received a portion of his salary for the commission and probably had already begun painting. It also suggests, as will be confirmed below, that Piero received a large payment and that therefore the painting itself must have been large.

Piero received payments from the Fraternity's officials, beginning in May 1474 when it paid him slightly over 37 lire, followed by another payment to him of 20 lire on an unspecified day. On 22 July Piero's brothers Marco and Antonio received 26 lire and change on Piero's behalf. Finally on 22 November Piero accepted just over 116 lire, which completed the amount stated on 12 April 1474 of 200 lire (with the small change). The bequest of Piersacchone, however, was for 50 florins, or 250 lire. To complicate matters further, Piero accepted a quittance on 1 February 1475, in which he stated that he was fully paid, and the confraternity of Madonna della Badia agreed that Piero had fulfilled his commission. However, the stated amount that Piero received was 590 lire (118 florins), well beyond the 250 lire of Piersacchone's bequest or the 200 lire in the recorded payments. It appears that Contessina Carsidoni or the Fraternity of San Bartolomeo, or perhaps the confraternity of the Madonna della Badia, augmented Piersacchone's bequest and the abbot Girolamo's promise of 94 lire, to reach this considerably higher total of 590 lire. Piero's fresco near the high altar of the most important ecclesiastical site of the town would have been one of the few major paintings he executed in the last two decades of his life. It is strange that beyond these documents the fresco has received no notice in Sansepolcro or elsewhere. In fact, it entirely slips from historical comment until the twentieth century.

Piero as Builder

One of the questions raised about Piero's later life is whether he became a designer of buildings.[17] The contention that he served Federico da Montefeltro as an architect of the Urbino palace has been rejected by almost all researchers, even though the palace features architectural elements similar to those in Piero's paintings. There is no specific building that Piero can be shown to have designed, but his activities in his home town suggest that he had an interest in the process of building.

We have already seen that Piero retreated to Bastia in the upper Tiber valley in 1468 to escape the plague. While there he would have been present and probably active in the reconstruction of the villa that the Della Francesca family part-owned with the Antignalla and Baglioni families (see above, Chapter 9). In the previous year the Della Francesca brothers had been rebuilding the Villa Bastia so extensively that their co-owners from Perugia threatened legal action to halt the changes. Piero's brother Marco then agreed to halt construction in common areas, although continuing construction in the areas owned by the Della Francesca themselves. From a later document, we know that the Della Francesca family did in fact proceed with their building work in the Villa Bastia, though we cannot be precise about the role that Piero played in this.[18]

Vasari informs us that Piero "left substantial possessions in Borgo, with some houses that he had built himself, which were in part burned and destroyed in the factional strife in 1536." This remark has led to a discussion of what elements of Piero's designs have survived in the existing Della Francesca family house, today known as the Casa di Piero (Illus. 20 and 21). The Della Francesca family had occupied this house on the corner of via delle Giunte and via Borgo Nuovo since at least 1350. By the 1460s the family was composed of two married brothers and their children and Piero, with a total of eighteen or twenty members by the 1480s.[19] It should not then be surprising that the brothers sought to increase their living space. Their traditional house was enlarged in 1465 when the priest Luca Manaria, claiming to be related to the Della Francesca family, bequeathed to Piero and his brothers his house that abutted the Della Francesca family home. Just before Piero's death, the Della Francesca family divided their property, which had previously been held in common. In this division there appear many citations of an "old" and a "new" house, the latter referring clearly to the appended structure added in 1465 and perhaps other new additions to the family's traditional site.[20] The interest in architecture that Piero displayed in his paintings may well then have been expressed in designs for parts of the Della Francesca residences in both Bastia and Borgo, but as yet no one has successfully attributed any specific contributions to him.

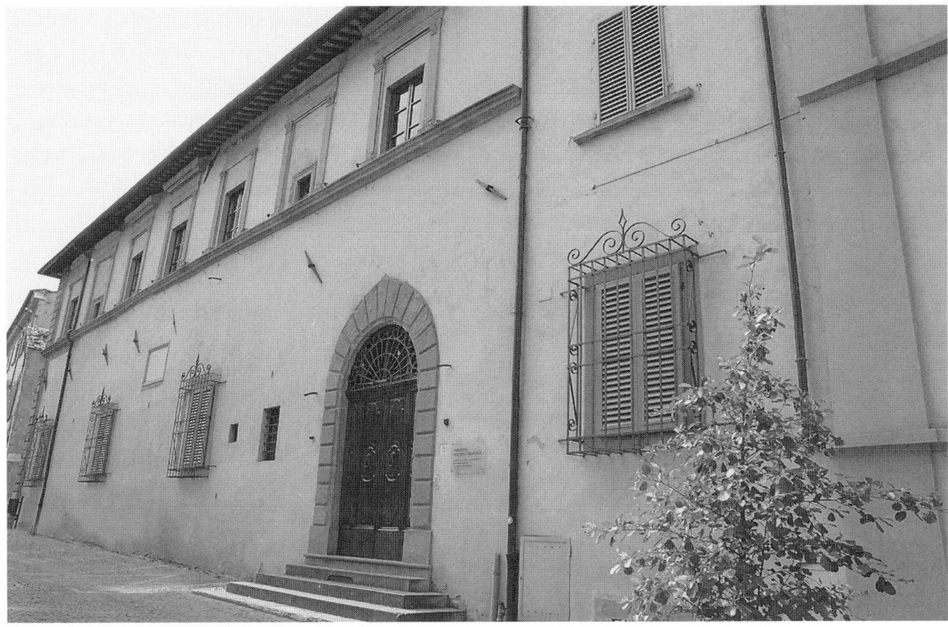

ILLUS. 20 Casa di Piero, Sansepolcro

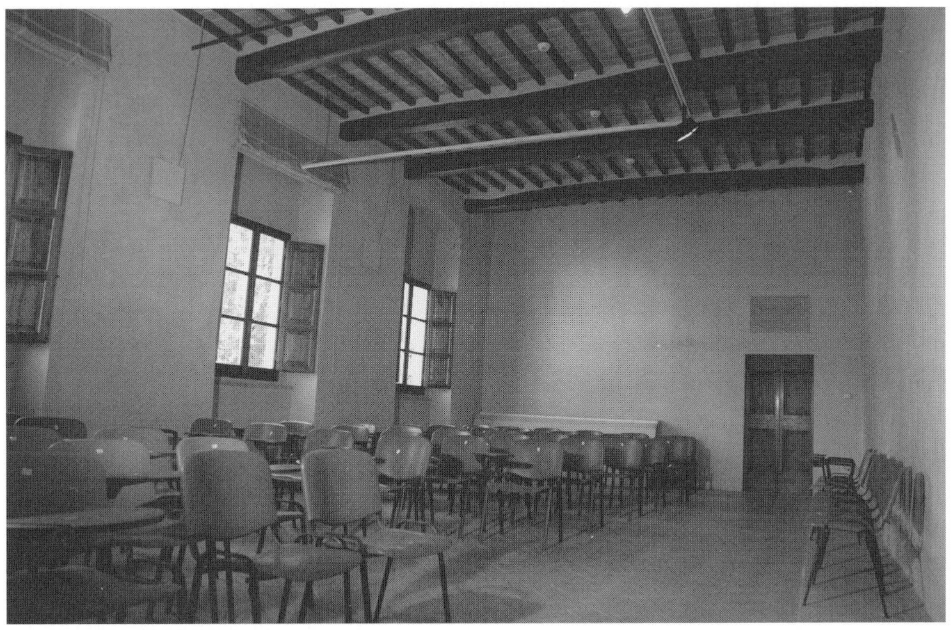

ILLUS. 21 Casa di Piero, Room of *Hercules*, Sansepolcro (facing the eastern wall)

On 20 February 1474 Piero was nominated to be "supervisor of the walls of the residence" of the conservators.[21] This is not the traditional office of supervisor of the city's fortifications, but a new and possibly temporary appointment specifically for the residence (communal palace). The conservators proposed Piero's name to the twelve good men, who approved his appointment by a vote of eleven to one. Piero's nomination found more opposition in the council of sixty, where he received eleven negative votes, but he nevertheless gained the position with forty-three affirmative votes. We do not know the reasoning behind these eleven negative votes. Piero never gained the highest political office as a conservator, particularly of an executive or leadership nature. He would have been expected to complete the term of office as supervisor of the walls of the residence at the end of October 1474, and indeed documents show his presence in Sansepolcro into 1475.

Construction of the "new residence of the conservators" had begun in the late 1450s, as we have seen. Another phase of construction occurred in 1474, concurrently with Piero's appointment as one of the supervisors of the walls of the residence. He took office on 20 February, and in early April the town officials appointed the stonemason (later called architect) Nardo di Pippo to build a brick support wall (*stola*) in the basement of the conservators' residence under Piero's *Resurrection of Christ*. Piero would have conceived, or helped to conceive, the project. In this construction Piero must have worked closely with Nardo, with whom he had cooperated in the church of Sant'Agostino in the 1460s when Piero painted his large polyptych there and Nardo refashioned the church's apse. In 1474 Nardo reconstructed the lower spaces in the residence called the "sala grande di socto" to facilitate the storage of military arms, and he also constructed a wall in "the great auditorium," in which Piero's fresco was located.[22] As one of the supervisors of the walls of the residence, Piero would have been involved in the planning of these works.

Behind the "great auditorium" and Piero's *Resurrection* was another part of the building that by the sixteenth century had become associated with the conservators—and it can be suggested that Piero was involved with the construction of this new space as well.[23] I would propose that in 1474 Piero and his fellow supervisors, with the architect/stonemason Nardo, reconstructed the large space behind Piero's painting as the living quarters of the conservators. In 1467 the four conservators, including the nominal head of government, the standard bearer of justice, had been given the privilege by the Florentine government of eating and sleeping in the residence for the three months of their office.[24] This would naturally have required extensive redesigning of a space in the residence and would explain, as the mere construction of a wall in the cellar would not, the special appointment of the "supervisors of the walls of the residence."

Hercules

Piero only ever painted one large work on a classical subject: the standing *Hercules* (Illus. 22) that he frescoed in the Della Francesca home on the second floor (*piano*

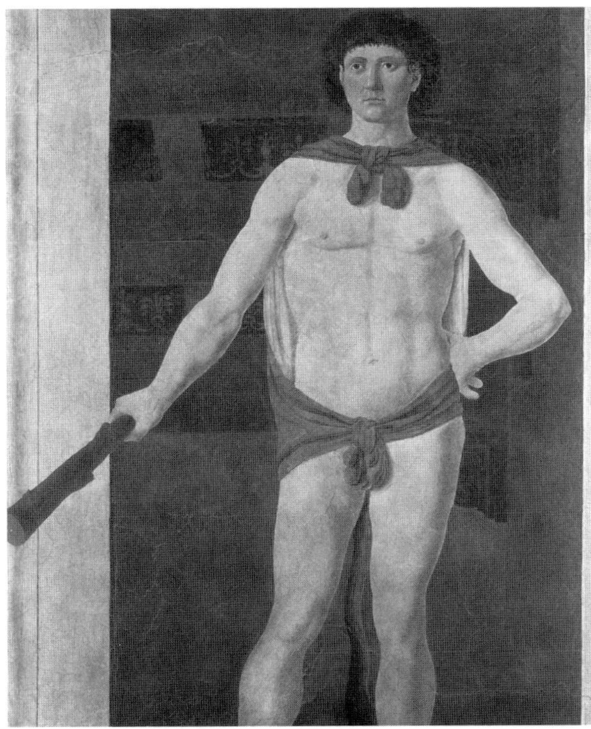

ILLUS. 22 Piero della Francesca, *Hercules*, 151 × 126 cm. Isabella Stewart Gardner Museum, Boston

nobile) of today's Casa di Piero (see Illus. 20 and 21).[25] The *Hercules* lacks any Quattrocento documentation and has been minimally discussed by scholars. This fresco has unusual aspects that make it difficult to date and place in the painter's development, but I have included it here and dated it in the late 1460s or 1473–75 due to the probable building activity in the Della Francesca home after the 1465 gift of the nearby house of Luca Manaria. The fresco is now 151 centimeters (59½ in) high, but the figure has had the lower part of his legs and feet removed, probably when a door was constructed under it. *Hercules* would have originally been life-size (approximately 180 cm, or 70⅞ in high, per Piero's original conception) and the figure was placed quite high on the wall, so that the viewing point is from below. Despite Vasari's account of a fire and destruction of the "houses" that Piero built and the later addition of a door, the room containing this fresco appears as it was in Piero's time. The *Hercules* was located on the right-hand side of the eastern wall and looks to his right into the middle of the room.

No one noted in print the painting's existence until around 1860 when an Italian senator named Collachioni discovered it in the Casa di Piero under a cover of plaster. Collachioni dismounted the fresco and took it to his villa in the countryside around 1880, where it remained for almost two decades before it was returned to Sansepolcro, either to the Casa di Piero or to another nearby Collachioni palace. Toward 1900 the nephew of the deceased Collachioni had the art dealer Elia Volpe prepare it for sale. An early photo of the painting shows substantial damage above and to the left of Hercules' head. Before Piero's *Hercules* was sold to the American art collector and philanthropist Isabella Stewart Gardner in 1903 or 1904, Volpe made a fresco copy of the image and placed it on the wall where it is said Piero's image had been mounted previously in the Collachioni Palace.

In the fresco itself, the marvelous image of the youthful and idealized Hercules stands with his wooden club and with the customary monumental calm of Piero's figures. Compared to other representations of Hercules in the Renaissance, Piero's figure is not particularly muscular and definitely not active. Piero slightly separates the hero from his background: a painted wall of finished stone blocks, some of which have ceramic rust-color bas-relief forms. These brown blocks and rust-colored ceramics, in addition to Hercules' hair and his garment, endow the whole fresco with a prominent monochromatic coloring. The most astonishing spatial feature is Hercules' foreshortened right arm and the club that extend out toward the viewer as if beyond the picture plane and nearly outside the fresco's side columns. In this period, only Andrea Mantegna's *Dead Christ* (Pinacoteca di Brera, Milan) compares to it in its perspectival virtuosity; interestingly enough, Mantegna too painted this image in his own home and for his own purposes, not those of a patron.[26]

Piero's *Hercules* is presented in what is known as a *contrapposto* stance taken from classical culture, with his now missing left foot engaged and carrying the hero's weight. Piero has moderated the effect of the stance by diminishing any suggestion of dynamic or overt movement. It seems that while he did not want to present us with a static frontal representation of a hero who was known above all for his dynamic physical deeds, nevertheless at the same time he refused to animate Hercules as a typical muscular protagonist. The body of the hero has a certain tenseness derived from these two opposed purposes.

For Renaissance painters and sculptors Hercules epitomized the active life, the involvement in which at times bordered on a frenzy that overcame even this most powerful of ancient heroes. Here, Hercules is clad in his traditional lion's skin lined with a light-colored cloth. The painter emphasizes his hero's union with the lion by having its skin tied at Hercules' neck and its paws at his genitals. The union is further suggested by the lion's long tail between Hercules' legs. Piero presents Hercules as calm and rational, possessing the power to control or conquer both the animal and his own ferocious nature. In this, Piero was in accord with Renaissance humanists who intellectualized Hercules as a hero precisely because through his rational powers he could tame his emotionally violent nature.

Why did Piero choose to paint Hercules in his house rather than another classical hero or a Christian saint? He could have chosen his patron saint Saint Peter, but with his usual attribute of keys this saint would have emphasized the formal Church hierarchy. On the other hand, there were plenty of other more personal options open to him from the panoply of Christian saints who would have been appropriate. For instance, for penitence or learning he might have chosen Saint Jerome, or Saint Luke, known as a painter and patron of painters' guilds. Neither did Piero opt for any other from a range of popular religious images of the Quattrocento: a Madonna and Child, for example, or another depiction of Christ's Flagellation, or Christ's head with its halo of thorns. Instead, Piero chose to represent Hercules, the epitome of masculine physical struggle in the Renaissance, and usually presented nude (or nearly so, as in Piero's representation). By choosing to depict the hero at rest before or after one of his twelve labors, Piero has chosen a more calm and reflective Hercules, one who was also known for his struggles to control his own emotional nature. Did Piero see in the classical figure an analogue to his own emotional make-up? Did he see himself in his life and art as expending great energy in a struggle to control the nature that he represented in such vivid detail under a structured three-dimensional vision?

Marco, Piero, and their Sister Vera

In Renaissance patriarchic families with undivided property the eldest brother guided the formal legal acts of family members after the death of the father. In 1464, with the death of Benedetto, Marco had adopted this role, even though Piero was older. Marco appears in countless notarial documents as the active brother, selling and buying property, accepting and giving dowries, receiving and giving payments, in his name and in the name of his brothers Piero and Antonio. Marco assumed the role of his older brother because Piero was frequently absent from Sansepolcro and because Marco was deeply experienced in commercial, family, and legal affairs.

An example of Marco's leadership of the Della Francesca can be seen in his handling of his sister Vera's affairs in 1466. Vera had married Giovanni Onofro Nardi in 1437, and, discounting a ten-year period when her father had paid her dowry, she had disappeared from the historical record and any documented relationships with her natal family for several decades.[27] In September 1466 Vera recorded an act similar to a last will in which she elected burial in the sepulcher of the Third-Order Franciscans in the church of San Francesco and made several bequests to ecclesiastical groups. Though married and doubtless living in her family home, Vera entered the Third-Order Franciscans.[28] Her decision may be related to an illness from which she was suffering at that time. A month after she associated herself with the Third Order, the town doctor Domenico d'Arezzo brought Vera's husband and Marco della Francesca to civil court for failure to pay him for "expenses" for Vera. In Italian marriages, responsibility for the well-being of the bride shifted to the groom's family. It is not clear, then, why the Della Francesca family should have been co-responsible for Vera's medical expenses, or why the father or brothers of Giovanni Onofro did not assist him. The social status and wealth of the Della Francesca and authority of Marco apparently overwhelmed patriarchic customs. The doctor also sought payment for medical care administered to, or medicine for, "maestro Piero." We have surmised earlier that Piero suffered from the plague in October 1466. Both he and Vera recovered, and Piero had returned to Arezzo by December. Marco ended the dispute by conveying cloth, or proving he had already given the cloth, to the doctor.[29]

By 1474 authority within the Della Francesca family had begun to shift from Marco to Piero, although it was only after 1480 that Piero definitely claimed his role as the dominant male in the family. We have a preview of this in 1474 in his involvement in the life of Vera. She reappears in extant documents in October of that year when she and her daughter Cheopa made Vera's husband their *procurator* (legal representative). Although the procuration document is incomplete, its purpose becomes clear in subsequent documents. Cheopa's husband Andrea Bartolomeo had just died; in his last will he had made his wife and her parents, Vera and Giovanni, the tutors of his and Cheopa's sons Piero and Giovanbattista. The three adults appeared before the Florentine captain Bartolomeo Popoleschi and his judge to have their tutorship formally recognized and to present an inventory of the patrimony of the deceased Andrea. Piero entered these legal proceedings as the responsible male representative of the Della Francesca family. He served as the legal guarantor for the tutors, thereby assuring communal authorities that if the tutors should fail to fulfill their roles as protectors of the two minors, Piero would be liable for any financial failures or any malfeasance.[30]

Piero's assumption of this responsibility, however, was soon followed by another absence from Sansepolcro. After accepting his final payments for the Madonna della Badia in February 1475, Piero apparently departed from Sansepolcro and is not documented as present there again until February 1477.

CHAPTER 12

Piero in Urbino, 1475–77

We have recounted Piero's presence in Sansepolcro from June 1472 to February 1475, but in the following two years he is not once noted in the town. This period 1475–77 would have been ample time for Piero to plan and to paint the large altarpiece of the *Madonna and Child with Saints and Angels*, known as the Brera altarpiece because of its location in the Pinacoteca di Brera in Milan (Illus. 23).

Madonna and Child with Saints and Angels

In the altarpiece Piero painted a group of six saints and four angels in a semicircle around the Virgin and Child with a kneeling Federico da Montefeltro in the foreground.[1] In the late 1460s in the Sant'Agostino and Sant'Antonio altarpieces Piero had attempted to minimize the patrons' preferences for placing saints in separate compartments by integrating the saints on continuous floors, a marble parapet running behind the saints in the first and a damask cloth behind the saints in the second. For the Brera altarpiece in the next decade, Piero chose, or Federico requested, the integration of all the personages in one group, in a sacred conversation (*sacra conversazione*).

While most historians now agree that Federico da Montefeltro commissioned the Brera altarpiece, some hold that it was executed in the 1460s or from 1472 to 1474. The newly discovered Borgo documents from 1472 to 1475 definitely exclude that latter possibility. And it is unlikely that Piero painted the altarpiece prior to the death of Federico's wife Battista Sforza in 1472 because, had she been alive, Federico would have required Piero to include her as a co-donor. The reason that some argue that the painting had to have been completed by 1474 is that Federico is depicted without any symbols of the honorary orders of knighthood—discussed below—that he received in that year. But this view is based on a misunderstanding of the purpose of the altarpiece. Piero had the task of representing Federico as a devoted warrior servant of Mary,

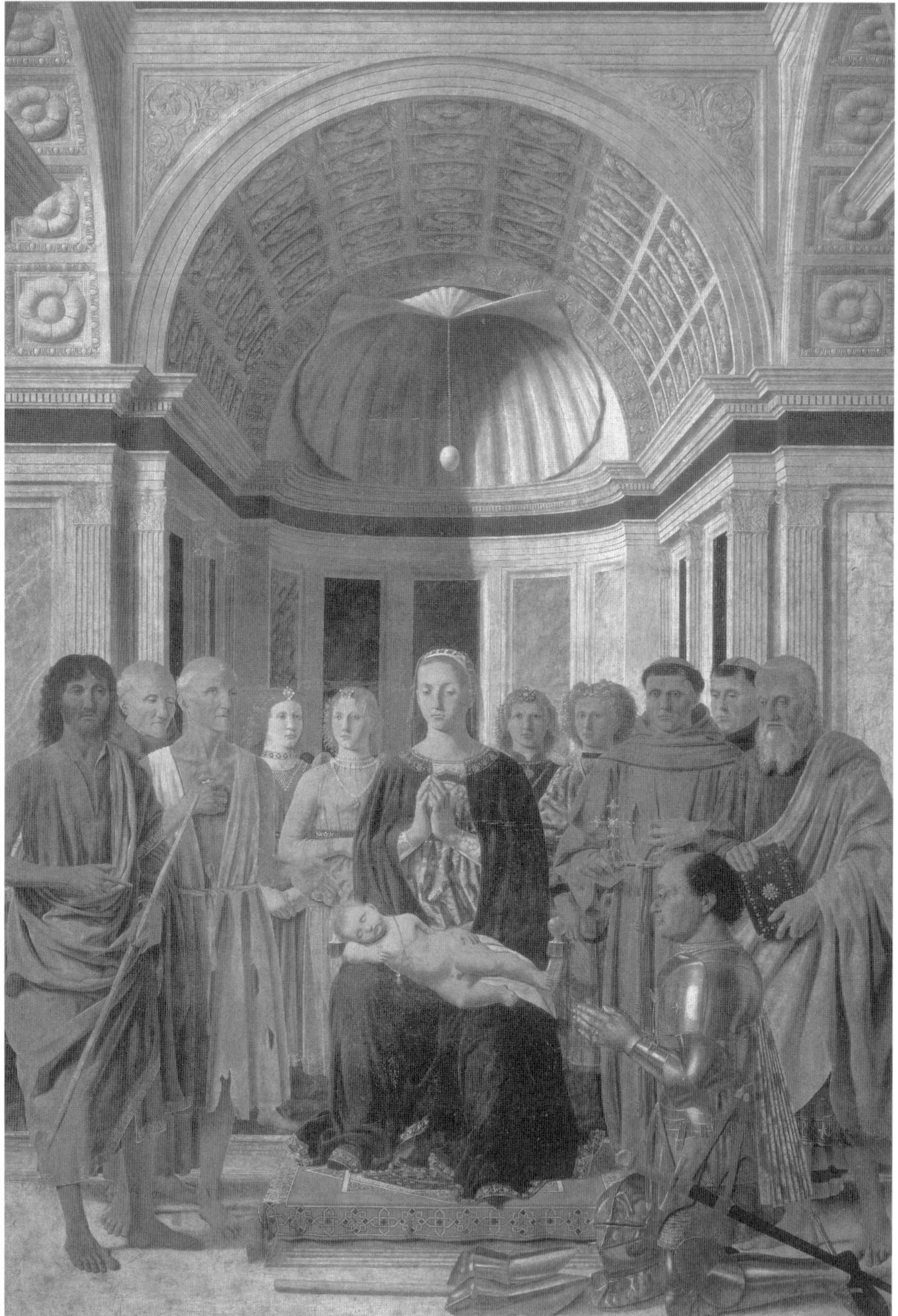

ILLUS. 23 Piero della Francesca, *Madonna and Child with Saints and Angels*, 2.48 × 1.7 m. Pinacoteca di Brera, Milan

and thereby of the Church. Symbols of his membership in feudal orders or as a duke would have weakened his humble, kneeling pledge of fidelity.[2] Moreover, it is generally accepted that the Spanish painter Pedro Berruguete made significant additions to Piero's altarpiece prior to 1482 by repainting, for some inexplicable reason, Federico's hands and adding at least one ring. Had Piero painted before 1474 and Federico later wanted symbols of his honors included in the altarpiece, he could have asked the Spanish painter to add them after Piero had completed the altarpiece.[3] No such insignia were added. Hence, the lack of indication of his feudal honors should not be used in dating the altarpiece.

In the mid-1470s Federico's court became an even more active center of artistic activity. It was around this time that the Flemish painter Justus of Ghent finished the large painting for the high altar of the oratory of the confraternity of Corpus Domini in Urbino, a commission that was probably offered to Piero in 1469. Justus and his assistants also executed other paintings in Federico's Studiolo in Urbino. One of his assistants was Pedro Berruguete, who painted a portrait of Federico and his son around 1476 and Federico's hands on Piero's Brera altarpiece. Although born in Spain, Berruguete had apprenticed or previously painted in Flanders. Both he and Justus, therefore, brought knowledge of specific paintings and practices of the Flemish painters to Federico's court.

In the mid-1470s Federico was in his late fifties with four decades of military campaigning behind him. He was a widower and vowed to remain one, since he had a male heir to perpetuate the Montefeltro dynasty. Federico probably intended the Brera altarpiece to be part of his tomb chapel, a memorial to himself, and an affirmation of his dynasty. However, Piero completed the altarpiece and Federico died prior to the construction of his mausoleum church of San Bernardino just outside Urbino. Piero's altarpiece and Federico's body were not moved to the church until the mid-sixteenth century, so there are questions of where the altarpiece and body were in the interim. These we shall leave for future scholars to resolve and instead discuss the relationship between Piero's intricate architectural setting of the altarpiece and the interior architecture of San Bernardino. The resemblances between the two suggest that dialogue occurred between Piero and Federico or between Piero and the architect of the church of San Bernardino. It is intriguing to note that the architect of San Bernardino was Francesco di Giorgio Martini, a painter, engineer, and writer of treatises with illustrative drawings, who, like Piero, was largely self-taught. Francesco arrived in Urbino in 1477; hence, given the similarities between Piero's painted architecture and Francesco's architecture in the church, he and Piero either discussed the architecture or Francesco imitated Piero's fictive architecture in the altarpiece.

At this point, Federico had many reasons to see his legacy and future fame tied to the papacy and the Catholic Church. He had earlier served as papal military commander, but from 1472 until 1474 Federico lacked a contract with any Italian state and remained in Urbino, tending to his government and constructing his palace. The college of cardinals in Rome resented him because he had earlier defeated a papal army in Rimini.

Federico had sought to restore good relations by supporting Pope Sixtus IV from the moment of his election in 1471. All this came to fruition in the summer of 1474, when Federico's alliance with Sixtus, despite the initial opposition from the cardinals, led to several extraordinary honors for him. First, King Edward IV of England, under pressure from the Pope, invested Federico with membership in the Order of the Garter, England's highest honor. King Ferdinand of Naples awarded Federico with membership in the Royal Order of Ermine. Sixtus made Federico Gonfaloniere of the Church and General of the Holy League. Even more treasured by Federico was the title of Duke granted to him by Sixtus. For thirty years Federico had had to deal with the fact that Pope Eugenius IV (*d.* 1447) had made Federico's unaccomplished teenage half-brother, Oddantonio, a Duke, while Federico until 1474 had to be content with his lesser title of Count despite his great service to the papacy. Also in this year Sixtus and the college of cardinals approved a marriage between Federico's daughter Giovanna and Sixtus' nephew Giovanni della Rovere.

By 1474 Federico could well see himself as defender of the Church and see part of his earthly legacy as derived from this role. His relationship to the Church also provided him with a propaganda tool. He was not just a warrior on contract; he could claim that his position elevated him above other mercenary commanders and lords of small states. Federico commissioned Piero to represent this idea of the warrior prince devoted to the Church in the altarpiece that was to be placed in Federico's mausoleum.

Piero's *Madonna and Child with Saints and Angels* was not the first altarpiece with its personages placed in a *sacra conversazione.* This and the altarpiece's large rectangular format (2.48 × 1.7 m) were common in Italian paintings of the late Quattrocento and perfect for someone like Piero so interested in organizing images in a large space. Note that the altarpiece contains neither pinnacles, predella, nor internal Gothic framing. Piero does not squeeze this or that saint into a separate space or compartment; here all those represented could interact in a dialogue. He has created a specific set of interactions. Federico kneels before the Virgin with his hands joined in a traditional donor pose, but he does not look toward the Madonna. Rather, he stares horizontally straight across the picture plane to an empty space in front of Battista Sforza's patron saint John the Baptist, where the co-donor spouse would usually be placed. This novel means of suggesting, but not representing, the presence of Federico's deceased wife informs us that Federico wanted the altar to memorialize Battista and the Montefeltro dynasty. Battista's absence may also be a means to represent the reality that she would not be buried with Federico in his mausoleum; she had chosen to be buried in another Franciscan church. Many of the saints and at least three of the angels stare out at the viewer, especially John the Baptist who, as was customary, invites the viewer into the dialogue with his eyes and points toward the Child with his finger.

The saints as a group are an unusual assortment. Saint Francis (third saint on the right) and Saint Bernardino (second saint's head on the left) would be appropriate in any Franciscan church, and the two Saint Johns (the Baptist as the first saint on the left and the Evangelist as the first on the right) were often found in altarpieces of the Madonna and Child. But Piero also includes Saint Jerome (second full-length saint on the left) and Saint Peter Martyr, a Dominican (second saint's head on the right). One might say that Jerome together with Francis and Bernardino convey a theme of renunciation or penitence, but Peter Martyr was more an inquisitor and defender of the Church. I am convinced by Marilyn Lavin's interpretation that Federico intended the altarpiece to memorialize the Duke as the defender of the Church by emphasizing his fidelity. The saints are summoned into the altarpiece to share in support of the Church, represented by Mary.[4]

While *The Flagellation of Christ* was Piero's monument to perspective, the Brera altarpiece is a virtuoso example of Piero's command of all his earlier techniques. Light defines and emphasizes the surfaces, which are differentiated to achieve Piero's three-dimensional bodies. Once again he has employed his now well-practiced method of placing cartoons with perforated lines on the painting surface and pouncing chalk through the holes, thereby leaving an outline for his painting (see Chapter 4, p. 60). And Piero continues the practice he had started in the 1450s of using both oil and tempera paints. His use of the two media enabled him to illuminate the surfaces of objects, whether in light or in shadow. Piero's rendering of metal is so shiny and luminescent that it acts as a mirror. The blues and browns of the marble and the precision of stone panels and gold tones on the barrel vault and architrave celebrate the presence of light. The distribution of light is accurate, derived from the right and creating powerful shadows. Whereas a glance at the altarpiece might lead one to say that the Madonna and other personages are located under the vault of the presbytery, in fact Piero has placed the semicircle of personages in front of the arch of the barrel vault. He has the orthogonals converging just above the left side of the Madonna's lips. Piero has integrated the figures of Duke Federico and the Madonna into the fictive architecture of a church. In this way the painter represents the military commander pledging his fidelity to Mary in a sacred setting.

The Senigallia *Madonna and Child*

Piero's second painting of this period is the *Madonna and Child* from the Adriatic city of Senigallia, approximately 50 miles east of Urbino. The painting has risen in art historians' evaluations ever since it was cleaned and restored to reveal much of its previously hidden beauty (Pl. X). It was first noted in the church of Santa Maria della Grazia just outside Senigallia, but this church was constructed at about the time of Piero's death so certainly it was not the image's original intended site. In addition, the fact that Piero placed the *Madonna and Child* in a domestic setting suggests that its placement in this church occurred much later. The painting's early life remains a mystery: there are no documents relating to it prior to 1822, when one of its discoverers noted it as "so beautiful, so true, so studied that one is not able to desire more."[5]

In spite of its lack of documentation before the early nineteenth century, the *Madonna and Child* has been linked to the Montefeltro. As discussed above, in 1474 Pope Sixtus IV and Federico had arranged the marriage of Giovanna, Federico's daughter, and Giovanni della Rovere, the Pope's nephew. This alliance brought Federico his title of Duke, and Federico ceded Senigallia to Giovanni della Rovere, who thereafter ruled the town. The political arrangements were made when Giovanna was fourteen years of age, so the marriage ceremonies only followed in 1478. The painting has been linked to this political alliance and Giovanna's transfer to Senigallia with the date of commission and painting placed variously between the dates of the alliance and the marriage. Because Piero was in Sansepolcro from 1472 to early 1475 and from 1477 to the summer of 1481, we can state with a high degree of certainty that Piero painted the Senigallia *Madonna* in the years 1475–76.[6] These dates would strengthen the frequent suggestion that Federico commissioned the painting as a gift to the couple. In addition, another link between the young couple and the painting has been suggested. The angel in blue-gray on the left is much more masculine in appearance than Piero's traditional asexual angels, whereas the angel on the right is more feminine. This has led to the claim that the two angels represent the groom and bride of 1478.

The image itself is relatively small at 61 by 53.5 centimeters (24 × 25/21 in), and for the only time in his career Piero experimented here with walnut as the surface of the painting; on this he placed a subtle preparatory layer, apparently thinking that the walnut was so strong and smooth it did not require an elaborate preparation. Overall the experiment proved to be successful as the painting has suffered little evident damage beyond some fading from the oil-based pigments. It has often been noted that Piero painted the Senigallia *Madonna and Child* with an oil medium (as well as tempera), supposedly showing the Flemish influence, but as we have seen he had already employed oil as early as 1451 for specific purposes. His use of more oil here, as well as his experiments with light, certainly show that Piero was aware of Flemish innovations. He integrated these northern influences into his specific style and for his own customary and experimental purposes without committing to Flemish surface accuracy or a landscape crowded with animals and objects. The oil medium permitted him to highlight the pearls of the angel on the right, the folds of the velvet of the baby's cloth, the transparency of the Virgin's veil on her forehead, and the fold of the Virgin's headpiece whose ends hang curled in space, and of course enabled Piero to depict the rays of light coming through the window, illuminating the dust in the air.

Critics have seen theological meanings in the Senigallia *Madonna and Child*, probably more than in Piero's earlier treatments of the subject. The domestic setting, white rose, and the light penetrating the window have led to numerous speculations. Although the art historian Millard Meiss did not discuss Piero's painting in particular, nevertheless he showed that even prior to the fifteenth century, painters understood the analogy between light penetrating a glass without any damage and the Son of God entering Mary without any compromising of her virginity. This was often represented in paintings, especially in Flanders. Saint Bernard of Clairvaux wrote: "Just as the brilliance of the sun fills and penetrates a glass window without damaging it, and pierces its solid form with imperceptible subtlety, neither hurting it when entering nor destroying it when emerging: thus the word of God, the splendor of the Father, entered the virgin chamber and then came forth from the closed womb."[7] Piero heightened the emphasis on Mary's purity with the symbol of a white rose including traces of red towards its base. According to Saint Bridget's vision of the Nativity, Christ informed her: "Mary was a rose, white for maidenhood, red for love; white in body, red in soul; white in her seeking after virtue."[8] Piero has placed the Virgin standing in a domestic setting, thereby removing her customary throne and, by inference, removing her from Paradise. The absence of gold enforces this idea that Piero had no intention of representing the Madonna in her traditional setting out of this world.

J. V. Field, a specialist on Piero's mathematical achievements, sees little mathematics in the overall spatial arrangements in this painting, although she grants that Piero perhaps used mathematical plotting in the small room on the left of the painting and in the depiction of the shelving.[9] In fact, she sees a disjuncture between the figures in the foreground and the objects in the back. Piero has moved the Madonna and the Child to the foreground. The right hand of the Madonna squeezes the right foot of Christ which is close to the viewer. Placement of these elements would be inappropriate for altarpieces intended for churches where the viewer could be expected to be a great distance away from an altarpiece. This placement of figures, and the intimate size of the picture, strengthen the argument that the Senigallia image was intended for a domestic setting.

The painting has Piero's sense of illusionistic three-dimensional arrangements. One art historian has written of a "dialectical rapport" between the figures and the architecture and between the light and shadow in the painting. And in her work on the painting J. V. Field has further identified a dislocation between foreground and background. The art conservator Maurizio Saracini asserts that "the architectural structure had been designed with a brush after the figures had been completed, in that the structure does not appear under them."[10] This was uncharacteristic of Piero, who often first painted the background even if foreground figures later covered part of the background painted surface, for example as discussed above in the *Saint Michael* of the Sant'Agostino altarpiece, where he first painted the jaw of the dragon but then painted it over with Michael's sword (see Illus. 18).

The Treatise *On Perspective in Painting*

As we shall see, it was around this time that Piero most probably started work on his *De prospectiva pingendi* (*On Perspective in Painting*). This work provides a perfect example of Piero's intermediate position between the artisans and the university elite that we discussed earlier, combining as it does elements from both cultures. Unlike his earlier *Treatise on Abaco*, where he follows the outline of earlier *abaco* textbooks, in *On Perspective* Piero created a new form of treatise combining elements from the *abaco* treatises with elements from medieval Latin treatises on optics and Greek geometrical works. He may have taken the idea of writing on perspective from seeing or hearing about Leon Battista Alberti's *On Painting* (*Della pittura*, 1435), in which the humanist discussed the most advanced methods for painting, and especially perspective, that derived from the ground-breaking discoveries of Brunelleschi and Florentine painters of the early Quattrocento. Despite Alberti's familiarity with the workshops of these artists, he wrote for a learned audience, and his distance from an artisan culture is clearly evident in his choice not to include diagrams. Piero may have seen Alberti's *On Painting*, although apparently few copies of the vernacular version circulated in the fifteenth century; moreover, *On Perspective* shows little evidence of familiarity with Alberti's treatise.[11]

Piero, however, accepted one part of Alberti's program completely. Alberti had seen the task of painting as forging a necessary unity between the viewer and the viewed. Alberti and Piero shared the idea that a system of perspective placed the viewer at a precise distance from and orientation to the picture plane. The resulting painting, the size and placement of objects in the picture, for example, would be determined by this preliminary decision. Alberti and Piero believed that sight should be understood as rays that traveled between the eye and the edges of objects in the world. Likewise a painter should determine the sizes of objects in a painting by the measurement of their distance from an eye (or the painter) set before the painting. The sizes of the objects (relative to one another) and the space they occupied were fixed in proportion to their distance from the eye. With a measurement of this distance, the exact sizes of objects could be represented.

One of the fundamental differences between a university and an artisan culture is that in mathematical treatises the scholar employed verbal constructions and no drawn diagrams, whereas the artisan employed numbers and relied upon the sort of drawn diagrams that were eschewed by the university scholar as his ultimate proofs. So, for instance, Alberti and the ancient Greek geometricians made verbal arguments without expressing their concepts and arguments in numbers or in diagrams. Rather they dealt in magnitudes and in finding similarities or convergences that could be expressed in words. Greek geometricians may have made their own drawings at the moment they constructed their propositions, but their readers were first to understand the geometrical proofs in the mind and then, if so inclined, make their own drawings. Piero, on the other hand, derived his first mathematics from *abaco* manuscripts where geometrical drawings were plentiful and where problems were conceived arithmetically, that is in numbers, and frequently the equations were separated from words and repeated in their own space. As a painter Piero had prodigious abilities of visual conception. It is only a slight exaggeration to say that he thought visually and would represent ideas first in paintings or geometrical designs and later in verbal form in his treatises. This emphasis on visual representation as a tool of preparation and a means of proof are the most powerful examples of Piero's retention of practices from the artisan world in which he had early been formed.

Due to the popularity and rationality of Euclid's treatises on geometry and optics, his way of demonstrating his ideas became the norm for those who wrote on these and related mathematical subjects in university circles. In Piero's proofs in his *Treatise on Abaco*, and, as we shall see in the discussion in his *Little Book on the Five Regular Bodies*, Piero relied on arithmetical proofs, quantities expressed in numerical form; in *On Perspective*, however, he employs the usual Greek means of establishing proofs through verbal constructions, to which he added designs. Although Piero later came in contact with the Greek procedures in reading the works of Archimedes, he undoubtedly first became familiar with them in Euclid's treatises on geometry and optics.

The Composition of *On Perspective in Painting*

We can determine that Piero composed *On Perspective* during the 1470s. As we have seen in his *Treatise on Abaco*, Piero knew Euclid's *Elements* well. Again Piero quotes directly from this classic of Greek geometry in *On Perspective*—so directly that he must still have held the same manuscript in his hand.[12] In *On Perspective* he consulted a second treatise by Euclid, the *Optics*, which he cites by an unusual title, *On the Diversity of Sight* (*De aspectuum diversitate*). This informs us that Piero drew from a manuscript derived from an Arabic version of Euclid's *Optics*. The manuscript now in the Vatican Library (Urb. Lat. 1329) is one of two extant Quattrocento manuscripts with the title *On the Diversity of Sight*. Piero surely consulted this manuscript because it was commissioned by Francesco del Borgo in Rome in 1458.[13] At some point the manuscript came into Federico's library in Urbino, where it would remain until the library was requisitioned by the papacy and returned to Rome in 1657. What is not clear is how and when the manuscript entered Federico's library, some time between 1458 and 1487–88, when it was recorded in an inventory in Urbino. There are three possible explanations: (1) the beautiful manuscript was prepared as a presentation copy and immediately afterwards papal authorities sent it to Federico as a gift. I find this improbable as the then Pope, Calixtus III, did not usually present other leaders with manuscripts as a tactic of foreign policy and Federico had not yet begun his aggressive campaign to form a library; (2) at the death of Francesco del Borgo in 1468, when an inventory of his possessions recorded approximately twenty manuscripts, Vatican authorities or a merchant acquired his possessions and sent this manuscript to Federico in Urbino; or (3) at Francesco's death his possessions were sent back to Sansepolcro and either his brother Pellegrino or Piero sent or carried the manuscript to Urbino for Federico's library.[14] Explanations two and three remain possible, with the former more likely. Hence we shall assume Piero possessed the optics manuscript in Urbino during the 1470s because it was continually available to him in Federico's library.

Watermarks served to date Piero's *Treatise on Abaco* to the mid-1460s. It is agreed that Piero published *On Perspective* after the *Treatise*, and it is certain that Piero finished the treatise on perspective prior to writing his *Little Book on the Five Regular Bodies*, because he mentions his treatise on perspective in the *Little Book*, dated by nearly all scholars to the 1480s. However, the dating of *On Perspective* is complicated by two factors. First, at least several of the perspectival drawings in the work had been used in earlier paintings, particularly in the Arezzo fresco cycle, the *Resurrection* and the *Flagellation*,[15] thereby suggesting that Piero had drawings available for his treatise a decade or two prior to the writing of *On Perspective*. Because we know that Piero was meticulous in the preparation of his paintings, we may assume the same for the composition and writing of his treatises, especially since Piero prepared numerous detailed and precise geometrical and perspectival drawings in the treatises. Second, the dating of his completion of the work is complicated by the fact that Piero produced at least four extant manuscripts of *On Perspective*, two in the vernacular (Parma, Reggio Emilia) and two in Latin (Bordeaux, Milan), all to be discussed in Chapter 13. His use of the treatise's drawings in earlier paintings and the production of several copies suggest that its writing and publishing required an extended period of years.

We can assume that Piero first composed a working copy in Italian. I have placed my discussion of Piero's *On Perspective* in this chapter because it is most probable that Piero consulted the Vatican manuscript of Euclid's *Optics* in Federico's library and composed most of the treatise in Urbino in 1475–77. Hence, Piero composed the working copy, unfortunately non-existing, in this period. On his return to Sansepolcro later in 1477 Piero continued to labor on the treatise by producing at least four copies of it.

The Contents of *On Perspective in Painting*

Piero began *On Perspective* with an explanation of the organization of the treatise. Here we can follow him as he divides and subdivides his contents and procedures into their component parts. He is extremely precise in conceiving the overall structure of the material of the treatise, dividing it into three books. Book I deals with plane geometry, defining the basic components of geometry and discussing the nature of sight. In Book II Piero addresses problems in solid geometry, demonstrating how to diminish proportionally various forms of the cube. Book III begins with a defense of perspective and the introduction of a new method of constructing the measurements necessary for complex three-dimensional forms, such as when painting a head or other structures of many surfaces. Most of Book III consists of complex instructions on how to diminish (*degradere*) these bodies in perfect perspective (Illus. 24).[16]

At the beginning of Book I Piero divides painting into three parts and defines each: drawing (*disegno*) denotes the outlines of objects and their surfaces; proportion (*commensuratio*) is these outlines and surfaces placed proportionally in their places; and coloring (*colorare*) is placing colors on objects as they vary in light. Piero informs his reader that the treatise will concentrate on *commensuratio*, which he equates with perspective. As we have discussed earlier, proportion is what interests Piero most of all. He divides proportion into five parts: the eye, the form of the object seen, the distance

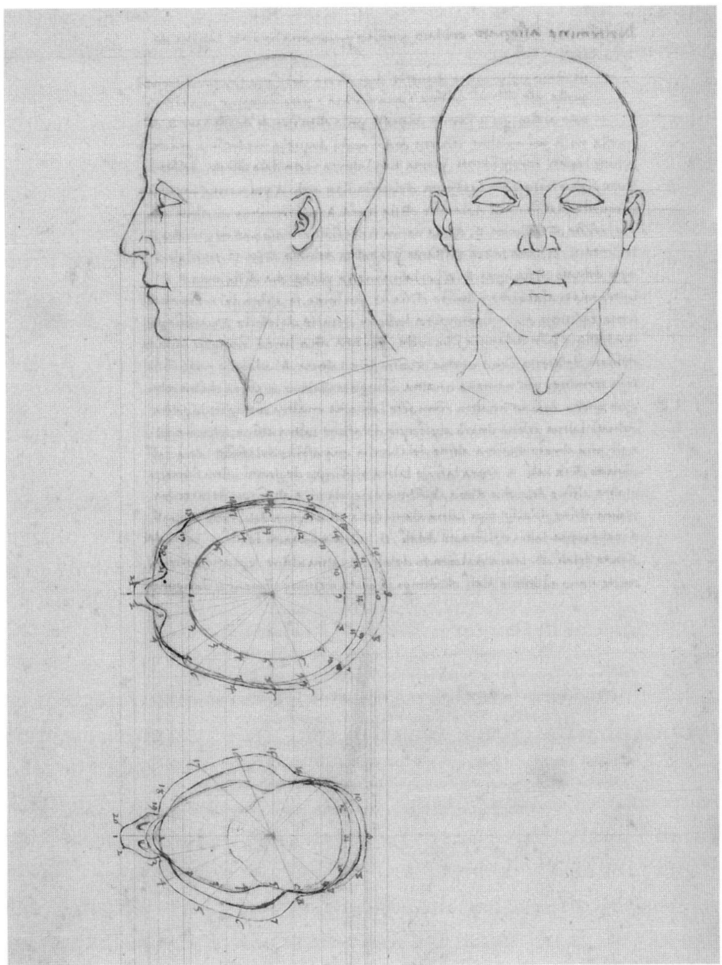

ILLUS. 24 Piero della Francesca, *De prospectiva pingendi*, cod. 1576, fol. 59v, Biblioteca Palatina, Parma

from the eye to that object, the lines or rays that go from the extremities of the object to the eye, and the plane that is between the eye and the surface where one draws or paints the object proportionally to the distance from the eye.

Medieval professors named the science of sight *perspectiva* and distinguished between *perspectiva communis* and *perspectiva artificialis*, with the first denoting the analysis of sight and the second the practical perspective of painters. Piero created a new genre of analysis by using the first for the purposes of the second. He anchors his analysis in the physical make-up of the eye, rather than starting with the practices or purposes of painting. Piero begins with an examination of the nature of the eye, its physical capacities and operations, and then how the eye sees objects based on an angle of vision defined by the extremities of the objects and their distance from the eye. In this discussion Piero demonstrates his knowledge of *perspectiva communis*, derived from Latin treatises on optics that were produced in universities. In these treatises medieval authors dealt with the problem of whether rays originate from the eye itself, or whether alternatively rays from the object initiate the act of seeing. Ptolemy and Euclid and their followers had held that sight originates in the eye, which emits rays that strike the objects of the external world (extramission theory). When Piero uses geometrical arguments he adheres to the later theory, known as intromission theory, a more modern position that began to be emphasized with the Islamic writer Al Hazen (*d. c.*1040), who believed that visual rays emanate from the external world and enter the eye. However, when Piero makes arguments based on the physiology of the eye, he reverts to the extramission theory.[17]

For instance, note the expression of the extramission theory in this quotation:

> [The] eye I say is spherical (*tondo*), and from the intersection of two little nerves which cross one another the power of sight comes to the centre of the glacial humor (*umore cristallino*), and from that the rays set out and extend in straight lines, passing through one quarter of the circle of the eye; so that this part subtends a right angle at the center...[18]

Piero holds that the maximum angle of human vision is ninety degrees because rays emanating from within the eye are limited by the form of the pupil. He appears to have taken these ideas from the medieval Latin textbook on optics, the thirteenth-century *Perspectiva communis* of John Pecham, which was available in Federico's library in Urbino (Vatican Library, Urb. Lat. 1374). But the idea of the angle of vision is taken from Euclid and profoundly defines Piero's concept of perspective.

Piero discusses how the eye and the edges of an object form a triangle; his discussion of perspective for two-dimensional and three-dimensional objects follows from the construction of this visual triangle (Fig. 12.1). There then follow twenty-nine propositions in Book I dealing with ever more complex shapes and their positioning. For example, in Proposition IV, he posits that if you have two objects equal in their bases, the one that is closer to the viewer will distend a larger angle and appear larger to the eye. J. V. Field has shown that Piero added a new theorem to Euclidean geometry in Proposition VIII. Here Piero constructs a line BC, divided into five equal parts. If one draws a line behind and parallel (HI) to the original and then draws lines from the marked intervals on BC to a point of their convergence (the vanishing point), the line segments on HI will be proportional to line segments on BC. Moreover, the triangles formed by the segments of the original line BC to the converging point and the triangles formed by the segments of parallel line HI will also be in proportion (Fig. 12.2).[19]

In Propositions XII and XIII Piero enters into the world of the painter when he introduces a filter or screen (between the eye and the object to be represented), which we would nowadays call the picture plane (Fig. 12.1). He recognizes that the placement

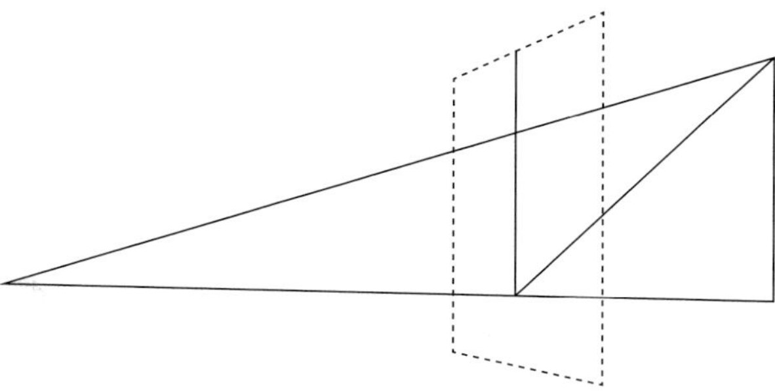

FIGURE 12.1 Piero della Francesca, *De prospectiva pingendi*, Book I, Proposition VIII, adapted from Reggio Emilia, Biblioteca A. Panizzi, cod. Reggiano A 41/2, fol. 4v

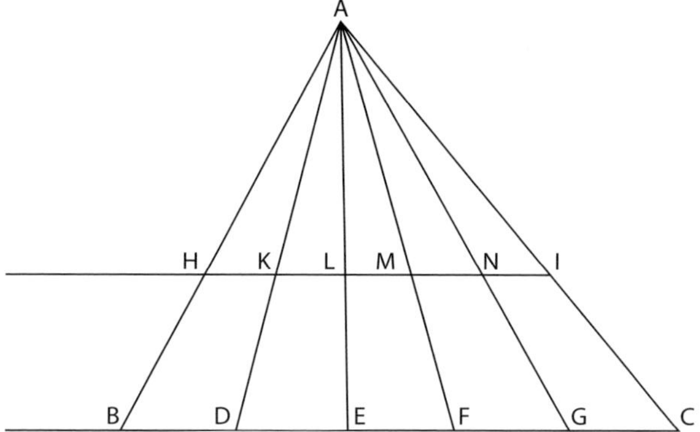

FIGURE 12.2 Piero della Francesca, *De prospectiva pingendi*, Book I, Proposition XII, adaptated from Parma, Biblioteca Palatina, cod. 1576, fol. 6r

of the eye in his construction is of great significance and that it is the basis for his discussions of perspective. The eye can be placed high or low, near or far, or right or left from the picture plane according to what "the painting requires." Piero introduces the term *degradere*, which is repeated in various contexts to denote the reduction of the size of objects within a geometrical or painting context. In Proposition XIV he uses the principle of proportionality established in Proposition XII, showing that if one begins with a straight line with equal segments (in effect on the picture plane) and draws several lines parallel, equidistant from each other, and behind it, lines drawn from the edges of line segments of the original straight line to a point of convergence would diminish segments of the parallel lines proportionally. These lines from the picture plane to the point of convergence are called orthogonals. Piero has an exact method for diminishing the size of objects in proportion to their distance from the picture plane. In the remainder of Book I, he demonstrates how to diminish various different shapes, from geometrical shapes to an eight-faced building.

Book II of *On Perspective* tackles the foreshortening of cubic, round, and quadratic shapes, all possessing "three dimensions: length, width, and height . . . Some are cubic, tetragonal (quadrilateral) which do not have equal sides, some are round, some are lateral, some are lateral pyramids and some have many and diverse sides, as one sees in natural and accidental things."[20] These geometrical forms require more complex constructions, but Piero employs the same methods and the propositions established in Book I. He shows how to foreshorten such complex objects as a six-sided well-head sitting on two hexagonal foundations, columns of sixteen faces, a large house with door and numerous windows, and a cross vault placed on four walls.

Book III has a long discursive introduction that might well serve as an introduction to the whole treatise:

> Many painters blame perspective because they do not understand the force of lines and of angles, which are produced from it, [and] by which proportionally every contour and line is described. Hence, it seems I must show how this science is necessary for painting. I say that perspective in its own name expresses how to deal with objects seen from a distance represented within certain given planes, proportionally according to the extent of the distance, without which it is impossible to degrade accurately. Because painting is nothing other than demonstrations of surfaces and of shapes degraded or enlarged on the picture plane placed so that the true things seen by the eye under diverse angles are represented on the said picture plane. And the intellect is not able to judge by itself their measure, that is what is near and what is in the distance. And moreover one part of every object is always nearer than the other to the eye and the nearer represents itself always under a greater angle than the more distanced one on the picture plane. Therefore, I say perspective is necessary, which discerns all the objects proportionately as a true science, degrading and increasing every object through the force of lines.[21]

We find here Piero's belief that painting could become a true science only through the use of perspective. The greatest achievement of painting is its representation on a two-dimensional picture plane of the illusion of three-dimensional objects placed in perspective, diminishing in size the greater the distance from the viewer. Piero is explicit here that the intellect cannot achieve this on its own, meaning that the mind cannot in itself replicate what the eye sees without "the force of lines," without working out graphically the lines that determine the exact "degrading" of objects in a geometrically determined space.

The assumptions in the quotation are also important. Piero makes a distinction between what the intellect understands abstractly and what the hand and geometry make evident in a graphic demonstration. Here we see the double preparation of Piero, his artisan training and his study of Greek geometry. The mind may understand perspective but that is not sufficient for its representation of reality; this requires a graphic representation. In a real sense, the artisan proves himself in a product of his hand. Most significantly for us, this superiority of the hand in representing what one sees is what makes Piero a painter from nature. He not only represented accurately the objects that present themselves as surfaces and edges to the eye, but also the underlying spatial relationships of those objects. As many have observed since the Italian art historian Roberto Longhi made this central to his interpretation, Piero is a painter of space as much as objects and humans.

The ancient painters who acquired "eternal fame" from their paintings, according to Piero, were experts in perspective. Piero took his list of ancient artists from the Roman writer on architecture, Vitruvius, although we cannot necessarily conclude from this that Piero had consulted Vitruvius directly because the same list of painters had also been cited by others. Piero continues by asserting that he wrote this book on the perspective that pertains to painting because he "is zealous for the glory of art and of this age." In naming the ancient painters and admitting that he aspires to gain fame analogous to theirs, Piero expresses sentiments taken from the rhetorical-literary humanism of Petrarch and his followers, a form of humanism in which he showed interest on only one other occasion: in the preface of his *Little Book on the Five Regular Bodies*, where he rehearses a similar, though not identical, list of ancient painters who did or did not achieve fame depending on their patrons.

Piero concludes his prologue by announcing that in this third book he will treat the foreshortening of more difficult bodies having irregular surfaces. This required a second method of presenting his perspective, due to the difficulties of drawing these complex objects. J. V. Field has named this "ray tracing," or a "rectangular coordinate system," for which Piero recommends that the student place at a predetermined viewing distance a point A which represents the eye of the viewer. The student was to place a needle or nail attached to a silk thread or horsehair at A and to construct a line from A to M in which M, the "vanishing point" as we would call it, is found in the middle of the picture plane. The main purpose of the nail and horsehair, however, was to note the precise measurements of the drawn object on "rulers" (drawn lines on which one enters the measurements), which were outside the object on the two sides and under the drawing.[22] These "rulers" could be, Piero said, thin sheets of wood for the sides and paper for the base, but they are represented as lines in his drawings. By swinging the thread or horsehair from point A and passing over the drawing and noting its proper "degrading" on the rulers on the base and sides, the dimensions of the object could then be drawn. If the line were curved, the painter would need to make many such measurements (Illus. 25).

By recommending the placement of these numeric coordinates on the side and bottom, Piero has proposed a plan and elevation approach with numbers that concur with the measurements of the objects to be drawn. This is most fully exemplified in the representation of human heads (see Illus. 24). As Piero had demonstrated in Book I (with plane objects like a square) and in Book II (with cubic objects), so too in Book III he would begin with a two-dimensional drawing of the head and show in arduous detail how its features were degraded (diminished) to achieve an illusionistic three-dimensional head. And not just for a head in profile, which is simply his starting point.

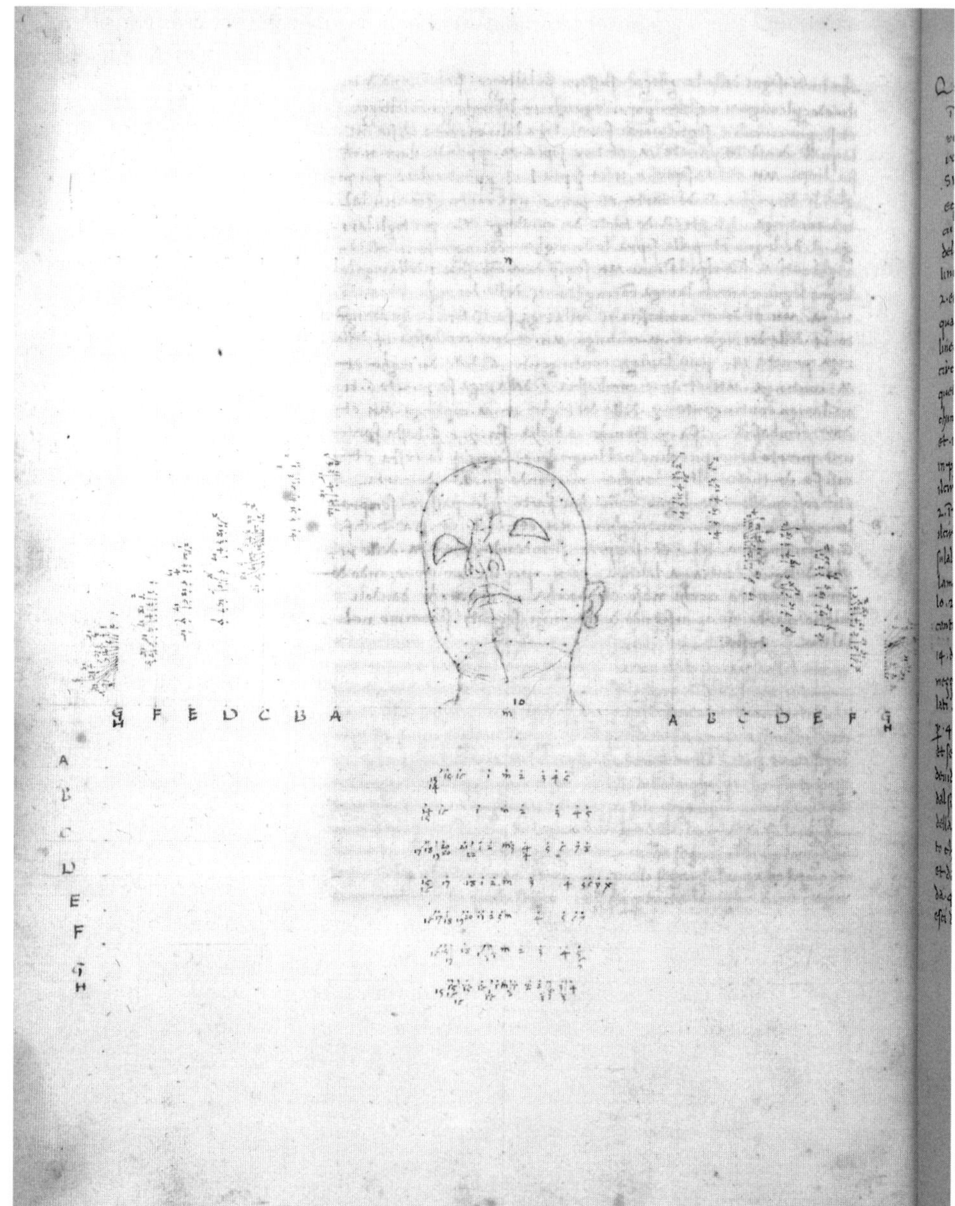

ILLUS. 25 Piero della Francesca, *De prospectiva pingendi*, Reggio Emilia, Biblioteca A. Panizzi, cod. Reggiano A 41/2, fol. 91v

After this, Piero goes on to instruct his reader on the methods for foreshortening heads from various angles: to show them full face, with head inclining, tipped to the side, and a number of other views of the cranium.

The Audience for the Treatise

For whom did Piero write the treatise? Despite the discursive introductions to its three books, the overwhelming content of the work is made up of detailed and laborious instructions on methods for drawing foreshortened objects. The instructor does not speak to an equal; rather, he addresses his listener in the familiar *tu* and frequently in the imperative. In the instructions for drawing the various inclinations of the head this can go on for pages.[23] A few of the many lines instructing the apprentice to foreshorten a head in profile presents a sense of Piero's rhetoric:

> Design a head with one eye, that is from the side with that profile that you intend to degrade and with that you make another [drawing of a head] from the front with two eyes of the same size and all the corresponding parts. First, draw a straight line from the top of the head in profile connecting it to the summit of the head with two eyes; and then draw another between that and the summit of the frontal view head which is line A; then lead another to the top of the frontal, which is line B, and draw one between the frontal [head] and the nose passing by the eye, which is line to C and [draw] a line the other passing by the hump of the nose, which is D; draw the other at the foot of the nose which is line E . . .[24]

And the above is only a small portion of the instructions for designing a foreshortened head. This is not a discourse written for a humanist whose criterion would first of all be eloquence. The purpose here is not persuasion but instruction in a technique. Piero intended this material for a practicing painter or perhaps a mature apprentice. It is apparent that there is a lack of consistency between the prefaces of the three books, with their discussions of the general propositions, and the lengthy technical discussions of how to draw lines and construct diagrams that follow on from them. Could apprentices in painters' workshops understand the general propositions from the Greek and medieval university traditions to be found in the prefaces, and on the other hand would anyone other than the apprentices or painters follow the lengthy instructions on how to construct the myriad of diagrams to be found in the material that follows? As it happens, the only known Renaissance readers of the treatise were mathematicians such as Luca Pacioli and sixteenth-century theorists of painting.

It has been said that the way in which the treatise is put together, with a rational sequence of propositions, each building on the one before, suggests that Piero conceived it as an "intellectually substantial" and important contribution to the medieval scientific optical tradition.[25] One thing we can say for certain is that it attempts to bridge the Quattrocento chasm between the Latin elite and the vernacular artisans. To locate *On Perspective* in this intermediate territory suggests either that Piero may not have thought a great deal about his audience or else that he misjudged the treatise's readability. All this may help explain why the treatise had only a limited circulation.

The Relationship of the Treatise to Piero's Paintings

Fifteenth-century painters customarily retained collections of their drawings, many of which they had used in one or more projects, while apprentices studied and copied their masters' drawings. Not one sheet of this kind of drawing by Piero is known to have survived, but there are many drawings in his treatises. Piero's *On Perspective* and his paintings have a complicated interactive relationship. The theory and drawings in the treatise contributed to Piero's ability to construct convincing paintings in perspective, but the converse is true as well. His experience as a painter contributed to the theory. Art historians have noted a close relationship between several diagrams in *On Perspective* and figures in Piero's paintings. Several of the objects found in paintings that match or nearly match drawings in the treatise derive from paintings finished before the treatise. And there is no close match between treatise drawings and paintings later than the treatise. This conforms to a general apparent weakening of Piero's passion for complex and thorough-going perspective paintings after *The Flagellation of Christ* and other paintings of the 1460s and the mid-1470s. Not that Piero ever abandoned his commitment to proportion and perspective; rather, his systematic application of perspective peaked in the 1460s and mid-1470s, and then diminished thereafter. Having mastered and internalized the techniques of rational construction of space and "degraded" figures, he may have, as Vasari said about Michelangelo, "held his compasses, that is to say his judgment, in his eyes and not his hands," and therefore could construct a convincing perspective freehand.

The most obvious example of matching a figure in a painting with a drawing in *On Perspective* is the inclining head of the second soldier from the left in *The Resurrection of Christ* (see Pl. VII) and the tilted head in Book III, Proposition VIII of *On Perspective* (see Illus. 25). Several heads in the scene of *Sheba Before the Wood* in the Arezzo frescoes (see Illus. 6) derive from a cartoon that was constructed from the heads in Proposition VIII. Moreover, a number of architectural structures in Piero's paintings appear again in the treatise; for example, the palace or town house on the extreme right of *The Flagellation of Christ* (see Pl. VIII) may have been taken from the diagram in the treatise in Book II, Proposition IX. Even if the treatise drawing is not identical to the building in the painting, the methods of constructing both were the same.[26]

In his late paintings Piero apparently ignored his categorical statement in *On Perspective* that the intellect was not sufficient to draw a painting in perspective; rather a graphic preparation of orthogonals was necessary. Piero never abandoned perspective, but he increasingly emphasized other means to achieve perspectival constructions.

CHAPTER 13

The Persuasiveness of Paternal Authority, 1477–81

Piero returned to Sansepolcro in the days or months prior to May 1477, when he was around sixty-five years of age. He remained in his home town for the following four years, where he put into practice his father's values. He painted less, privately assisted his fellow citizens and family, and devoted more time to public service. Also in this period, he recopied and illustrated his treatise on perspective and completed his own manuscript copy of the geometry of Archimedes.

We know of two paintings that Piero executed in the years 1477 to 1481, though one of these has been destroyed. The confraternity of Santa Maria della Misericordia commissioned Piero to paint a figure on a wall, and he began the project in the spring of 1477. The fresco has been lost and so too has the painting's subject. We are left only with a record of payments and the knowledge that the project kept Piero in Borgo for most of 1477.[1] Piero also very probably painted the Williamstown *Madonna and Child with Four Angels* in this period; the dating is based on its similarity to the Senigallia *Madonna and Child* (discussed in Chapter 12). The later Williamstown *Madonna and Child* and the Senigallia *Madonna and Child* exhibit elements of Piero's third painting phase.

The Lost Misericordia Fresco

In May 1477 the scribe of the Misericordia confraternity recorded an agreement between Piero and the confraternity, in which the painter agreed to paint "a figure" on the wall that connected the confraternal church and hospital. The location of the fifteenth-century church is not securely established and the hospital has been restructured, so there is little hope that the fresco can be recovered. Nonetheless, it is clear that the confraternity commissioned a fresco since, according to the confraternal scribe, a single figure was to be on a wall and the painter received lime mortar (*calcina*) from the confraternity to this end, doubtless for making the plaster base of the fresco. The "figure" that the document recalls could conceivably have been the confraternal patron, the Virgin Mary. However, this is unlikely as Piero's earlier altarpiece with its image of the Madonna was nearby, and there was also a processional flag featuring Mary at this time in a lateral chapel of the church, painted by the Siena-based artist Matteo di Giovanni.[2] Given this, I would suggest a crucifixion as the subject of Piero's mural here, since it would have been the most fitting subject for the patients in the hospital.

The confraternity promised Piero 87.5 lire for his fee, a modest sum for an established painter. Either Piero agreed to this amount as a gift or as a form of charity, or the confraternity could afford only a relatively small or simple image. As we saw in Chapter 11, only a few years earlier in 1474 Piero had painted a fresco in the Badia of Sansepolcro and eventually received a total of nearly 600 lire for his skill and labor. In May 1477 Piero acknowledged receiving 14.5 lire and a small amount for lime mortar from the confraternity. We know nothing more of Piero's labor in the Misericordia property until 31 December, when confraternal officials gave him a series of payments. First, the confraternal banker conveyed nearly 5 lire to Piero, and then the merchant Nardo di Gherardo bought woad from the confraternity and conveyed its sale price of 34 lire (plus change) to him. The prior of the confraternity and Piero then agreed that the confraternity remained indebted to Piero for nearly 30 lire (though the records suggest 34 lire). On this last day of December a local priest, Pietro Bofolci, "gave Piero his final compensation" from money returned to the confraternity that they had loaned to the town of Sansepolcro for the purchase of bread. It would seem then that the confraternity had to stretch its limited resources in order to pay Piero even this relatively small sum.

We saw in the last chapter how Piero prepared the Senigallia *Madonna and Child* for a domestic setting. The selection of a painting's setting has always been seen as the patrons' choice. Doubtless this is true, but it is also interesting to note that all of Piero's late extant paintings possess a familial setting: the Senigallia *Madonna*, the Williamstown *Madonna and Child with Four Angels*, and the *Nativity* (to be discussed in Chapter 14), which presents the mother, father, and child of the Holy Family (and which remained in the Della Francesca home into the modern period). The subjects of these paintings and their domestic settings perhaps suggest a convergence with Piero's more settled, family-centered lifestyle at this time. But whatever the ultimate underlying reason, the central fact remains that by the late 1470s Piero was accepting commissions for paintings with domestic settings or iconography related to the family and no longer (excepting the Misericordia fresco) painted in communal or ecclesiastical settings. Perhaps this was simply a matter of what patrons were asking for at this stage in his career. However, if this is so, then what the patrons were asking for seems to have been very much consonant with Piero's interests at this time: once he accepted these commissions, he very definitely painted with a set of private rather than public purposes in mind.[3]

The Williamstown *Madonna and Child with Four Angels*

Piero's *Madonna and Child with Four Angels* (Illus. 26) is also called the Williamstown *Madonna* because it is now in Williamstown, Massachusetts (Clark Art Institute). Most art historians attribute the Williamstown *Madonna* to Piero; the reservations of a few critics suggest that the painting does not exhibit the characteristics of the painter's classic style, most evident in his second phase. For example, J. V. Field doubts that Piero painted or completed this altarpiece in part because of its faulty perspective.[4] Here Piero's substantial participation in the conception and execution of the painting will be assumed because the painting's fictive architecture and other elements of its style and techniques are similar to those found in other of his paintings.

Piero has placed a classical white marble frieze or architrave above and behind the figures in the Williamstown altarpiece, with a strip of ceiling visible above. This frieze

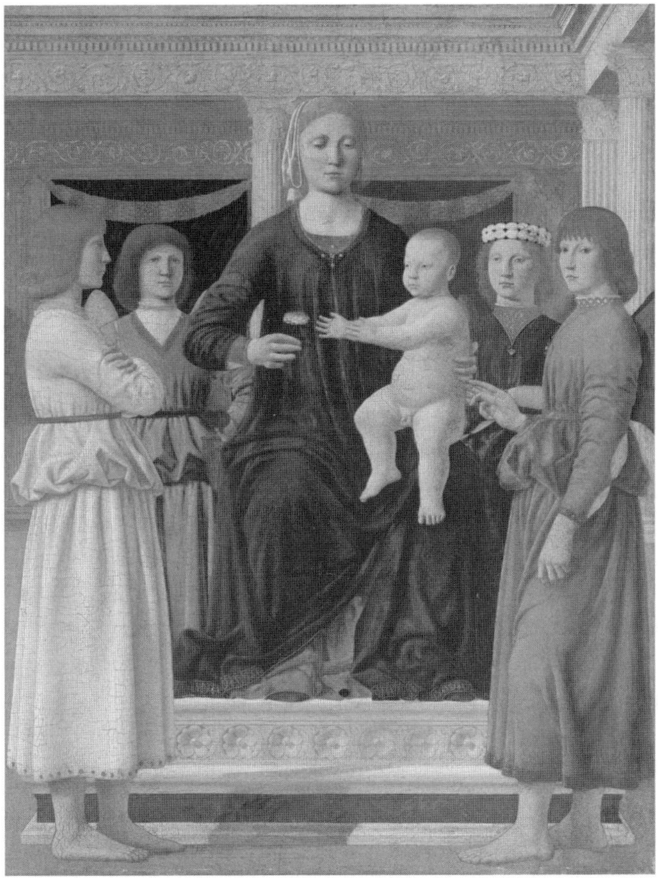

ILLUS. 26 Piero della Francesca, Williamstown *Madonna and Child with Four Angels*, 108 × 78 cm. Sterling and Francine Clark Art Institute, Williamstown, Massachusetts

continues in an angle toward the viewer on the right side. One fluted column with a Corinthian capital supports the long portion of the frieze behind the Madonna, with two columns supporting the frieze on the short right side. The frieze and its columns are not visible on the left of the painting. Behind and beneath the higher frieze Piero has designed a second darker frieze or architrave that sits on two fluted square columns or pilasters with simple capitals (a post-and-lintel construction?). The left column or pilaster of darker marble serves as the left border of the painting because the first frieze has neither a column nor a pilaster on that side. The lower frieze or architrave appears to continue to the right, leading the viewer to think that there is space beyond. These architectural contrivances are not in themselves symmetrically balanced, something that is highly unusual in Piero's art.

Piero has constructed a space or a room between the two friezes or architraves, but no one occupies that area—the Madonna, Child, and angels are all in front of the first frieze and its white marble center column. The Madonna is a massive figure and apparently sits on a stool, which is located on a raised platform. The lack of a throne suggests the Virgin occupies a domestic space rather than a room in Paradise. She and the stool are placed on a double plinth, one slim and the other larger with a frieze of roses. Two of the angels stand on the floor before the platform and the other two behind the platform. Why all this elaborate architecture? Piero appears to be playing with these elements that lend an obvious classical setting to the painting. The columns and friezes appear to have been planned as part of a room with specific architectural elements. This is reminiscent of Piero's *Hercules* (prepared for the Della Francesca house), in which he painted a portion of a ceiling that imitated the ceiling of the room where the work was found; in doing so he integrated the painting into the structure of the room.

Because the painting was eventually owned by the Gherardi family of Sansepolcro, and because the Gherardi came to hold patronage rights to the chapel of San Leonardo, it has been suggested that the family commissioned Piero to paint the *Williamstown Madonna and Child* for this chapel in the cloisters of the Badia of Sansepolcro.[5] The chapel was a privileged place of burial for the Camaldolese monks, and some Borgo families, including the Della Francesca and Piero himself, chose to be buried there. It was believed that this was the site of the original oratory established by the legendary founders of Sansepolcro, Egidio (or Giglio) and Arcano. However, it is almost certain that Piero's painting was not commissioned for this chapel. The subject of a Madonna and Child is not particularly appropriate for a sepulcher chapel. Second, there is no evidence that the Gherardi family had patronage rights to the chapel in Piero's lifetime. Most importantly, the chapel's dedication was not in any way connected to the Virgin Mary. Its full dedication was described in 1474 as the "Chapel of San Leonardo, called the Monagato [alternately Monacato], said chapel of San Giglio and San Arcano, our founders and protectors."[6] Within a century of Piero's death the Gherardi family or ecclesiastical officials commissioned the local artist Cherubino Alberti to paint a *Crucifixion* for the altar of the chapel, which as one might expect included depictions of

San Leonardo and one of Sansepolcro's pilgrim founders, specifically Arcano. Inasmuch as the chapel was dedicated to the three saints in the fifteenth and sixteenth centuries, one might expect that Piero would have also included at least one of them in any altarpiece for the chapel. He obviously did not. Thus we return to the judgment that the Williamstown *Madonna* was intended, given its complex architecture, for a domestic rather than an ecclesiastical setting. It is generally agreed that it remained in Sansepolcro until it was sold in the nineteenth century[7].

In the painting itself, Piero has used a variety of materials in the surface preparation and in the binder for the paints. Here again he demonstrates an eclectic approach along with a willingness to apply various materials for specific purposes. For example, Piero reverts to a practice seen in his earliest paintings (*The Baptism of Christ*, for instance) of employing the traditional *terraverde* (green earth) for some flesh tones, but he also employs a gray preparation in other areas for these same tones (as in the Senigallia *Madonna*) The various binders that he chose for his pigments reflect Piero's specific purposes in each case. For most of the cloth and architectural elements, for example, he employed the traditional tempera to bind and carry the pigments, whereas in more detailed and important areas such as faces he used an oil medium.[8]

As in the Senigallia painting, so here with the Williamstown example, the Madonna is brought forward with the two angels on either side even closer to the viewer. The location of the figures, including the Madonna, in relationship to the architecture again results in a sense of disjuncture between the two elements. This suggests that Piero may have intended the viewer to be placed on a level beneath the painting, which would lessen the visual disjuncture. If so, this would strengthen the interpretation that the painting was intended for a domestic setting, where family members would adore the Madonna and offer prayers while on their knees. In a public chapel worshipers would more often be seated or standing before the altarpiece in a liturgical service led by a priest.

Piero's Scriptorium and the Four Copies of *On Perspective in Painting*

In Chapter 12 I suggested that Piero prepared a working copy of his *On Perspective in Painting* in Urbino. During the years that followed, from 1477 to 1481, he supervised the production of the content and the physical layout of four more copies of this treatise in Sansepolcro. This required a significant personal and financial commitment on his part and illustrates the importance the treatise must have had for him. Only one of the extant manuscripts is completely in Piero's hand, but he intervened with emendations to two other manuscripts to clarify the text and in addition drew the intricate designs for two of the manuscripts. To perform this labor, Piero must have put together a scriptorium (a room or workshop with the necessary space and tools for the production of manuscripts). He supervised at least two scribes. For the translation of the treatise, according to the mathematician Luca Pacioli, Piero employed "the famous orator, poet, rhetorician, that Greek and Latin Master Matteo, his assiduous associate and countryman, who translated the text into the most ornate Latin tongue, word for word with an exquisite vocabulary."[9] This florid description permits us to identify Piero's translator as master Matteo di ser Paolo d'Anghiari, who instituted a private school of grammar and who was frequently appointed master of the communal grammar school in Borgo between the 1450s and the 1480s. The translation of the technical terms from optics, geometry, and painting from Italian into Latin required close collaboration between author and translator, which may explain why Pacioli called Piero's translator an "assiduous associate."[10]

From watermarks and the identity of the translator, we can confidently conclude that Piero established his scriptorium in Borgo for the preparation of his manuscripts of *On Perspective* and also for his copy of the works of Archimedes. In addition, as we shall see in Chapter 14, in the 1480s two manuscripts of Piero's *Little Book on the Five Regular Bodies* were produced in the Borgo scriptorium. Piero participated in the preparation of at least four manuscripts of his treatise on perspective, two in the Italian vernacular and two (perhaps three) in Latin, all with the Latin title *De prospectiva pingendi*.[11] There is no evidence that the original *volgare* working copy has survived. The two extant versions in the Italian dialect of Sansepolcro are today in Parma and Reggio Emilia. The manuscripts in Latin translation are in Bordeaux and Milan, and perhaps Piero saw the copy now in London.[12]

The Parma manuscript is a complete autograph (see Illus. 24), meaning Piero copied the text from the earlier working copy and drew the 128 figures to illustrate his text. He added some corrections in the margin and left space for ornamental letters. In his final preparation of the manuscript Piero was content with some lacunae or loose connections in the interface of the text and the constructions of the figures. He apparently was less concerned with consistency between the verbal propositions and the drawings than with presenting an "elegant graphic presentation."[13] Piero probably prepared this manuscript as a gift to someone who would appreciate the manuscript's overall beauty.

In his construction of the 142 figures in the Reggio Emilia manuscript Piero followed more closely his written propositions when he came to draw the designs, and was careful to provide a more complete set of designs than in the Parma manuscript. The text of this manuscript was written by an unknown scribe, although Piero copied two folios (66v–67r) and made corrections and additions to the text.

Turning to the manuscripts in Latin, the one from Bordeaux appears to be prepared directly from the early working copy, rather than from either of the two extant manuscripts in Italian. The Bordeaux example has interventions by Piero, who made corrections and additions in Latin to the text, and possibly also made the drawings. The person who wrote the Latin text is not known. Luca Pacioli informs us that Piero's friend master Matteo translated *On Perspective in Painting* into Latin for Piero, so it seems plausible to suggest that his translation copy is the Bordeaux manuscript.

The Milan Latin text was copied from the Bordeaux predecessor with Piero's additions and corrections, but in organization it follows the Reggio Emilia manuscript. This is probably because the same scribe copied both the Milan and Reggio Emilia manuscripts. Though the London example appears to be contemporary with Piero, he made no specific interventions in this particular manuscript.

It is not clear why Piero chose to prepare at least four copies of the treatise. Perhaps the Parma and Milan manuscripts were intended as presentation copies, for they have decorated capitals and some marginal decoration. In the dedication of his *Little Book on the Five Regular Bodies* to Duke Guidobaldo da Montefeltro (Federico's son), Piero asked the Duke to place this work among the volumes in the Urbino library "near another little work of ours, a *Perspective*, which we brought forth in earlier years."[14] Thus at some point between his composition of *On Perspective* and Federico's death in 1482, Piero must have presented him with a copy of the treatise, perhaps the vernacular Parma or the Latin Milan manuscript. As is usual with Piero, there is another mystery. Subsequent inventories of the Urbino library, including one as early as 1487–88, failed to list Piero's perspective treatise, although Luca Pacioli, who visited Urbino and Guidobaldo just after that date, asserted that Piero's treatise was in the library.[15] But Piero's perspective manuscript never has been listed in the library at Urbino, and it did not appear in the Vatican Library in 1657, when the Urbino collection was appropriated by the papacy.

These manuscripts throw an interesting light on the degree of Piero's knowledge of and familiarity with Latin, as well as on the type of Italian *volgare* that he employed in his writing and probably used in his everyday speech. The evidence of the manuscripts demonstrates clearly that he read and understood Latin, although the constructions in the translated Latin treatise are not elaborate paragraphs with a complexity of style and grammar. In his additions and corrections in the two Latin copies Piero demonstrated both his comprehension of the Latin translation and that he could also compose sentences, although there is no extant lengthy Latin construction of a paragraph or anything longer than that. His written Italian vernacular, on the other hand, was a combination of the Tuscan dialect and the specific upper Tiber valley dialect of Borgo (which incorporates influences from Umbria and the Marches). In his paintings Piero occasionally used Latin majuscule lettering, which reveals humanistic influence. In the manuscripts Piero's writing technique (notably his use of lowercase letters) shows elements of a humanistic style mixed with a style more like that of merchants and government offices. Taken as a whole, these elements of his general skills suggest an autodidact, a person who had appropriated elements of the elite scribal culture on his own without extensive formal education and especially university preparation.

An examination of the watermarks in the paper of these manuscripts aids in establishing the period when Piero finished composing them. Not one of these manuscripts carries a date, but the Parma and Reggio Emilia manuscripts of the treatise have unusual watermarks that permit us to date their production to the years 1477 to 1479. The Parma manuscript has a watermark of a balance within a quatrefoil with scales or balances (weighing device) of triangular weights. This watermark was not found in Italy until the 1470s.[16] Moreover, watermarks similar in size to those of the balance in the Parma manuscript only appeared in the paper of several notaries of Sansepolcro in 1477 and thereafter. The Reggio Emilia manuscript of *On Perspective* also has an unusual watermark, a Gothic R in a circle, which likewise was not found in Italy until the 1470s. To be more specific, watermarks similar to the R in a circle in the Reggio Emilia manuscript do not appear elsewhere (other than in the town of Fabriano in 1475–76) until the many examples in the paper of notaries of Sansepolcro in the years 1476–79. Certainly paper with the R in a circle and the balance within a quatrefoil was available after 1479, but we know that Piero had sent a copy of the treatise to Federico da Montefeltro prior to the latter's death in 1482. Piero was resident in Borgo from late March 1477 through to April 1481; as a consequence we can safely say that he worked on and supervised the production of at least two of the manuscript versions in Sansepolcro in this period.

Piero and Archimedes

It is fitting that Piero with his finely tuned intellect can be shown to have appreciated one of the greatest minds in Western civilization, that of the Greek geometrician Archimedes (*d.* 212 BCE). Piero cited several propositions of Archimedes in his *Treatise on Abaco*, although for this treatise he did not consult the works of the Greek directly; rather, he took his knowledge of Archimedes from one or more medieval commentators. In his third treatise, the *Little Book*, Piero cited directly from the writings of Archimedes. We now know that not only did Piero consult a manuscript of the Greek geometrician's works, but in fact he copied the *Opera* of Archimedes in his own hand and thus had a manuscript of the works for his own library and consultation.[17]

We saw in Chapter 6 how Pope Nicholas V had sponsored the revival of Greek science by commissioning translations and, in particular, had supported the humanist scholar Jacopo da San Cassiano in translating Archimedes. After the Pope's death, Francesco del Borgo commissioned copies of three Greek mathematical treatises in Latin, the *Elements* and *Optics* of Euclid and the *Opera* of Archimedes. Just what happened immediately to these three manuscripts on Francesco's death remains unknown. Two of the three eventually turned up in Federico da Montefeltro's Urbino library, but when and how they arrived there remains a mystery.

There are only five extant Quattrocento manuscripts of the Latin translation of Archimedes by Jacopo da San Cassiano. Three of them are of interest to us because they are related to Francesco del Borgo and Piero:[18] Paris, Bibliothèque Nationale de France, Nouv. Acquis. Lat. 1538 (no. 1); Biblioteca Apostolica Vaticana, Urb. Lat. 261 (no. 2); and Florence, Biblioteca Riccardiana, Lat. 106 (no. 3).[19]

Piero at one time or another held each of the three manuscripts in his hands. As we saw in Chapter 6, Francesco del Borgo had possession of Jacopo da San Cassiano's original translation (no. 1), from which he commissioned a copy in 1457–58, which was later in Urbino until it was sent to the Vatican Library in 1657 (no. 2). These two texts were likely among the approximately twenty books in Francesco's library at his death. How the two Archimedes copies made it into Piero's hands is an intriguing question and is analogous to the problem of explaining how Francesco del Borgo's copy of Euclid's *Optics* came to end up in the Urbino library (as discussed in the preceding chapter).

Piero himself copied the written text of Archimedes' *Opera* and approximately two hundred geometrical figures in what today is manuscript Lat. 106 in the Riccardiana Library in Florence (Illus. 27).[20] This manuscript is beautiful in its regular organization and its geometrical figures, but it is not a copy to be presented as a gift as it lacks significant decoration. It has elementary decorated letters at the beginning of paragraphs with only slightly more decoration of the letters that begin each of Archimedes' treatises. Piero prepared the manuscript for his own uses and consultation.[21] Scholars had earlier speculated, and it has since been convincingly demonstrated, that Piero copied the text of Archimedes' treatises from the Urbino manuscript (no. 2 above). Piero also copied many of the geometrical drawings with some corrections from the Urbino manuscript, but this manuscript lacks the geometrical figures for the section entitled 'The Quadrature of the Parabola.' Why this is so is unknown, but it does raise the following question: where did Piero obtain the geometrical figures that he copied into his Riccardiana manuscript for 'The Quadrature of the Parabola'? This question has been answered by the Italian scholars Paolo D'Alessandro and Pier Daniele Napolitani who, in an example of superb philological and geometrical sleuthing, have worked out the relationships between the three Archimedes manuscripts.[22] Piero, they conclude, took the geometrical drawings for the 'Quadrature' section from the Paris manuscript (no. 1 above) and the text of this and all the other sections and other geometrical drawings from the Urbino manuscript of Archimedes (no. 2).

When did Piero do this and how did he come across these manuscripts? One reconstruction would point to the years 1458–59, when Piero is known to have been in Rome. According to this argument, Francesco del Borgo could easily have made both the Paris and Urbino manuscripts of Archimedes available to Piero in this period. By the time he returned to Sansepolcro and perhaps Arezzo in 1459, Piero would—in this reconstruction—have had his copy of the Riccardiana Archimedes (no. 3) in his hands, where it remained for the rest of his life.

However, there are two reasons why this is implausible, in fact near impossible, that Piero could have copied Archimedes this early in his life. First, Piero shows only indirect knowledge of the *Opera* of Archimedes in his *Treatise on Abaco*, which as we have seen could not have been written before the mid-1460s and certainly not prior to 1457–58, the period when the Urbino Archimedes (no. 2) was created. If Piero possessed his own copy of the Archimedes manuscript when he wrote the *Treatise on Abaco*, he would surely not have cited from someone else's comments on Archimedes but would have consulted his personal copy and quoted directly from it. Second, when Piero began copying the

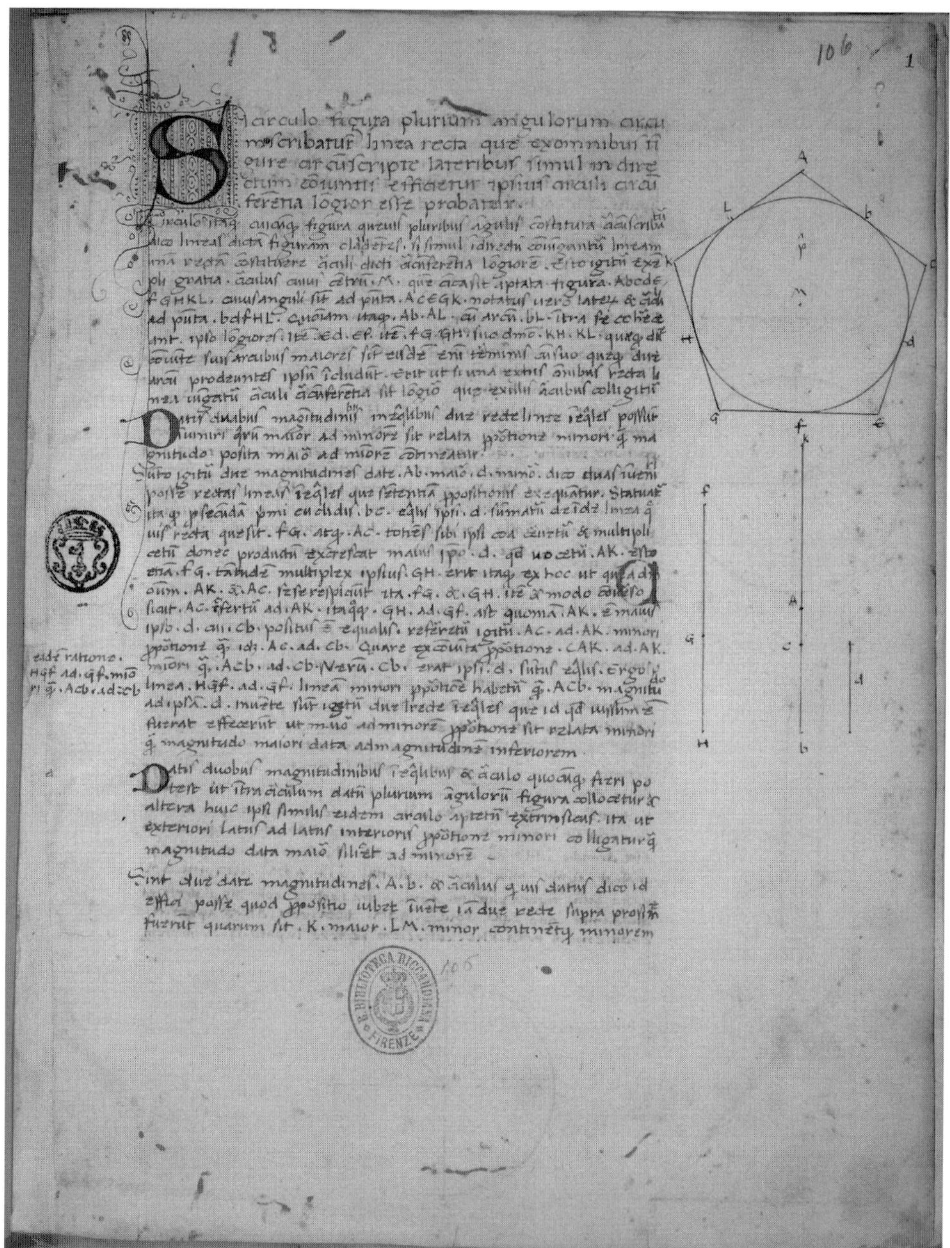

ILLUS. 27 Archimedes, *Opera*, Lat. 106, fol. 1r, Biblioteca Riccardiana, Florence

manuscript of Archimedes, he wrote on paper that featured two watermarks that did not exist in 1458–59. One of these was the *balestra* in a circle, which, as we have seen in the discussion of Piero's *abaco* treatise above, simply did not exist before the 1460s.

This is also true for the second watermark of the paper used by Piero for the first sixty or so folios of his Archimedes manuscript. Piero copied most of the Archimedean *Opera* on paper with the watermark of an eagle in a circle. This watermark was even more uncommon than the *balestra* in a circle and only appears, and even then rarely, in the 1470s, although tellingly the Sansepolcro notary Francesco Pichi used paper with a watermark of an eagle in a circle, similar to Piero's, in 1476. All in all, the watermark evidence clearly establishes that Piero could not have copied the Riccardiana manuscript of Archimedes in 1458–59 in Rome.

So, given the evidence, the best dates for Piero's initial copying of the Archimedes manuscript are the years immediately before 1476 in Urbino and then finishing in Sansepolcro between 1477 and 1481. Further suggestive of this conclusion is the fact that, by 1476 and before his return to Sansepolcro the following year, Piero had completed the composition of *On Perspective in Painting*—a work in which, interestingly enough, he did *not* mention Archimedes at all. In the 1480s, however, when he wrote his *Little Book on the Five Regular Bodies*, Piero made frequent references to specific Archimedean propositions.[23]

Where he copied the Archimedes manuscript cannot be definitively resolved, though I believe that he labored on it in both Urbino and Sansepolcro.[24] The most persuasive argument that Piero copied at least part of the manuscript in Urbino is that his basic source for Archimedes, the Vatican manuscript (no. 2), ended up in Federico da Montefeltro's library. Moreover, the eagle watermark found in the paper of this manuscript was a frequently repeated emblem of the Duke (who is known to have granted monopolies to the local papermakers in the nearby town of Fermignano and purchased paper from them for his chancellery). However, no paper bearing the watermark of the eagle in a circle has been found from Quattrocento Urbino. Since there is no evidence that the Paris manuscript (no. 1) was ever in Urbino for Piero to consult when drawing the geometrical figures that are lacking in the Urbino version of the manuscript, it is nearly certain Piero copied these geometric designs in Sansepolcro.

Supporting the conclusion that Piero copied the geometrical designs in Sansepolcro are the following facts. First, Piero can be documented in Sansepolcro in the years 1477 to 1481, the most likely years for this copying. Second, given the proud declaration on its first folio by an unknown writer that Francesco del Borgo participated in the creation of the Paris manuscript (no. 1), it is perfectly plausible that this manuscript ended up in Sansepolcro around this time. In this reconstruction Francesco del Borgo's heirs in Sansepolcro would have obtained the Paris manuscript (no. 1) in his patrimony after his death in 1468. Piero would then have had it available in Sansepolcro for copying the designs of the 'Quadrature of the Parabola' section of Archimedes' works into his Riccardiana Lat. 106 (no. 3; Illus. 28).

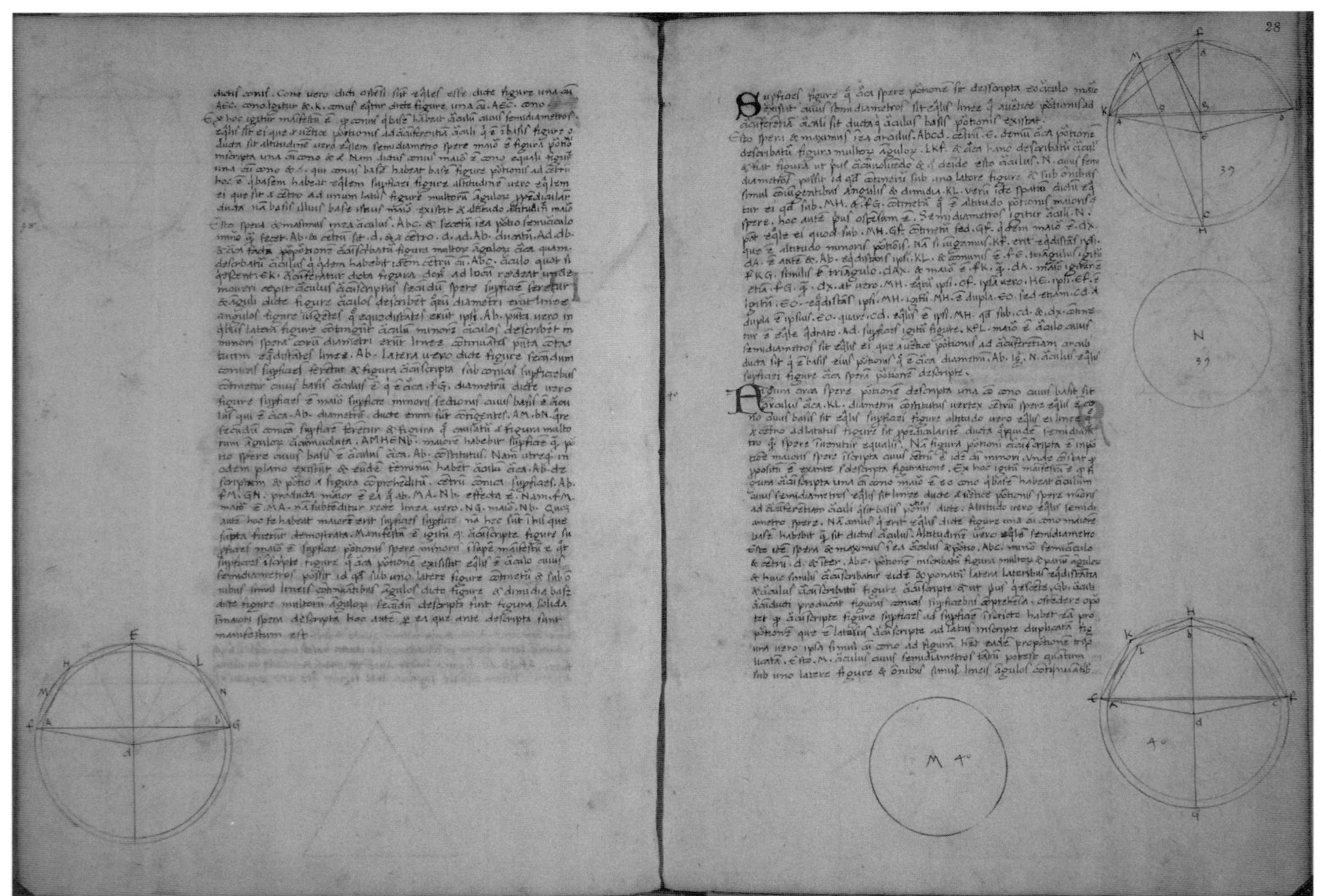

ILLUS. 28 Archimedes, *Opera*, Lat. 106, fols. 27v–28r (formerly 17v–18r), Biblioteca Riccardiana, Florence

By studying Archimedes in the original, Piero discovered a new set of problems that he would not have found in his perusal of Euclid and of the medieval commentators on Archimedes. This new set of problems revolved around the relationship of solid rectangular figures to solid circular and conic figures. Archimedes differed from Euclid in that he tackled problems relating to spirals, although both used formulas for measuring solid shapes to discover the different features of cylinders. One might argue that Archimedes moved Piero away from the simpler question of the proportional relationships of quadratic shapes to the more complex study of curved geometrical figures. It has been pointed out that Piero mentioned Archimedes on eight occasions in his *Little Book* and that: "All these instances have to do with either the circle or the sphere" (including surface and volume of spherical segments).[25] Ultimately, Piero's copying of Archimedes is less significant in the history of painting than in the history of mathematics, especially since the copying occurred late in his life and after he had painted his masterpieces (we will look further at the importance of Archimedes in Piero's *Little Book* in Chapter 14).

Piero's Political Activities

It is only in the period from 1477 to 1481 that documentation of all of Borgo's communal office-holders has survived. In these documents Piero is noted as having been selected for three different offices and serving as a *fidejussor* (a guarantor) for others in public offices. However, Piero was never selected for the town's highest office as a conservator. His father had served as a conservator.[26] In Piero's case his name may have been placed only in bags for lesser offices that required a minimum of political experience.

In this period Piero's highest office was as a member of the council of sixty. The reader will recall from Chapter 2 that the painter had been placed in the 300-member council of the people in 1442 and maintained that membership until his death. The council's chief purpose was to define the political class of the town and to provide the members of the councils of the twelve and the sixty. In this period names for Piero's group (*cedula*) of twenty men were extracted from the bags to serve in the council of sixty beginning on 1 July 1477 and again two years later, in each instance for four months. In this and on other occasions when he was selected to the council, Piero may or may not have attended its meetings.[27]

Piero was selected for lesser offices in this period as well. In 1477 he was chosen as one of the four "supervisors of the residence," the same position he had held in 1474.[28] His office as supervisor would have lasted the customary electoral year from November 1477 to the end of October 1478. There are, however, no known discussions of construction or repairs during this period in which Piero might have been involved.

In October 1480 Piero was given another position that put his mathematical abilities to use, when his name was drawn from the bag for the "accountants of the commune of Borgo." He and his three fellow committee members were entrusted with the responsibility of overseeing the accounts of the town treasurer in the period from November 1480 through October 1481.[29] The four accountants were to examine the accounts in the large "Red Book" and usually signed their approval of the calculations of the treasurer. Having written a textbook on the *abaco* that dealt with mathematics, Piero would have been well versed in performing this internal audit for his town, although neither he nor the other authors of the *abaco* tradition gave instruction in accounting.

Piero also participated in the political affairs of Sansepolcro on a more voluntary basis, attesting to his interest in the well-being of his town. The town's constitution specified that the highest executive and financial offices required their holders to present a list of men (*fidejussores*) who would guarantee the office-holders' honesty and stand surety for losses of communal funds. In most cases, family members and friends volunteered their services. Beyond demonstrating Piero's concern for his native town, his service in this capacity demonstrated the artist's standing in the community and his social ties and loyalty to his family. For instance, on 1 March 1477 Piero guaranteed the performance as a conservator of Francesco di Gasparre dei Rigi. Francesco had married Piero's sister Angela in 1450, and Piero here served his brother-in-law as *fidejussor*.[30] On 1 September 1478 Piero's name is listed among those who chose to be guarantors for Giovanbattista di maestro Michelangelo Palamidessi as he began to serve as one of the conservators in October 1478. The Palamidessi were wealthy members of the spice merchants guild in Sansepolcro, and Giovanbattista's father Michelangelo was the most important lay humanist in the town. Master Michelangelo's rich library remained in the hands of Giovanbattista until his death in 1487. Piero's assistance to the Palamidessi family in 1478 suggests that he and Michelangelo were friends with common intellectual interests; master Michelangelo appeared as a witness for the Della Francesca and the Graziani in 1461 in the two families' division of the house on the Graziani Crossing, and later Piero appeared as a witness to a testament with Michelangelo in 1462.[31]

On 1 January 1480 Piero served as guarantor for the notary ser Niccolò di Bartolomeo di ser Mario of the Fedeli family, whose members acted as notaries for approximately three hundred years in Borgo. Piero and his family had frequently used the services of ser Niccolò's grandfather, ser Mario, and Niccolò's uncle, ser Leonardo, and after their deaths the Della Francesca family often employed ser Niccolò to write their contracts.[32]

Piero returned to closer family ties when on 1 March 1481 he permitted his name to be recorded as *fidejussor* for his nephew Gasparre di Francesco dei Rigi, son of his sister Angela. On that occasion this relatively young man had been selected as conservator.[33] Still within the network of family relations was Piero's standing as guarantor for the doctor of law Anastasio d'Antonio degli Anastagi on 1 May 1481, who was selected as one of the conservators. Piero's brother Marco had married Giovanna, Anastasio's sister, in 1446, thereby establishing the link between the Della Francesca and Anastagi families. Moreover, Giovanna and Anastasio's father Antonio had been chosen by the

Florentine humanist Giannozzo Manetti to serve as his judge when Manetti was the Florentine captain in Pistoia in 1446. One of Antonio's orations exhibits humanistic aspirations, and it was recorded alongside other examples of humanistic literature as a model oration for judges in Tuscany.[34] It should not go unnoticed that among the others serving as *fidejussor* for Anastasio besides Piero were those who made up the circle of intellectuals in Sansepolcro, including the masters of grammar Francesco dei Rigi and Matteo di ser Paolo d'Anghiari, the latter of whom we have already encountered as Piero's translator of *On Perspective in Painting*.

Soon after 25 June 1480, Piero served as *fidejussor* for this same Matteo di ser Paolo, when he gained the town's highest honor of the office of standard bearer of justice.[35] Piero chose to support him as guarantor; they both served together as *fidejussores* for Anastasio Anastagi; Matteo had been present in the Della Francesca house as witness to the marriage of Piero's niece Romana later in 1480; they were both present as witnesses for a contract of August 1486. The combination of these activities demonstrates two friends serving each other through their mutual and reciprocal exchanges of service and honor.[36]

In all these exchanges it is possible to observe the parameters of Piero's family loyalties and more importantly the group of men with whom he shared like interests in his last two decades. This suggests that, even though—or perhaps because—Sansepolcro was a relatively small provincial center, it had a small but tight-knit group of humanists and scholars, which included Piero.

But Piero's most important public office in Sansepolcro occurred in the last year of his intense four-year period of political-social involvement in the town, as a prior of the Fraternity of San Bartolomeo. The many communal responsibilities of this Fraternity had resulted in its becoming a quasi-communal magistracy.[37] Inasmuch as the Fraternity never congregated and possessed few if any members, its leaders, called priors, constituted the Fraternity from at least the middle of the fifteenth century. Thus the priors could not be chosen by and from members; rather, they were chosen by lot for one year by the commune. In 1480 four names were extracted from the bags and two died soon after the priors took office on 24 July. In August the conservators and the council of twelve met and selected Piero as one of the substitutes, and on the 31st of that month he accepted and swore to undertake the obligations of a prior. The taking of an oath was not a usual part of the procedure for priors to take office; the communal officials' intention here probably was to commit Piero to reside in Borgo for the remainder of the one-year term.[38]

Piero proved to be an active prior of the Fraternity and kept his promise to remain in Sansepolcro through July of 1481. He served alongside a member of the Palamidessi family and Angelo d'Anechino dei Roberti, a local wool merchant. In the thirteen acts and contracts that we know of relating to these priors, Piero was absent for only one of them, on 23 October 1480, although he had participated in an earlier land sale as a prior a few days earlier, on 16 October.[39] Most of these acts were property sales and rents, but on 13 December 1480 the four priors assembled with Amata, widow of the doctor of law Jacopo Anastagi, to choose a chaplain to be rector of a recently constructed chapel dedicated to the Virgin, located just outside the walls.[40]

In this same period Piero and his fellow priors oversaw one of the Fraternity's traditional annual charities. For two centuries the priors had distributed cloth to the poor of the town at the onset of winter. On 8 December 1480, at the command of the "honorable" priors, the priest of the Fraternity distributed approximately 69 *braccia* (around 140 square feet) of cloth to twenty-three different individuals. This distribution was consistent with the amount of wool given as charity in these years, but considerably less than the 240 *braccia* distributed at mid-century and the 400–600 *braccia* distributed yearly around 1400.[41]

Another example of Piero and his fellow priors serving the people of Sansepolcro involved the priors in a disputed bequest. Niccolò di Guido Pichi had endowed a chapel in the Badia of Sansepolcro, but after his death his liquid resources were not sufficient to build it. As executors of Niccolò's will, the priors of the Fraternity had to gain a favorable ruling from the Florentine government to sell some of Niccolò's land in order to carry out his plan to build the chapel. On 24 May 1481 Niccolò's heir, Angelo Pichi, made the priors, including Piero, his legal representatives to sell sufficient land to complete payment for the chapel. On 21 July 1481 Angelo conceded 150 lire to Piero and the other priors, a sum that was then conveyed to the stonemason master Antonio di Domenico da Cortona, to pay for the stones and for his labor on the chapel.[42] Piero as one of the priors involved in the construction of the Pichi chapel surely played an important role in granting the commission to the stonemason to execute this work.

In conclusion, Piero demonstrated faithful service in carrying out his duties as prior. He remained in Sansepolcro for the period August 1480 to July 1481 and dutifully exercised his office by being present on nearly every one of the numerous occasions when the priors acted. Moreover, in this period he also acted as *fidejussor* for the standard bearer of justice and (with another prior) acted as a witness to a contract.[43] Piero's office of prior apparently increased his dedication, or at least his availability, to his fellow citizens.

Family Service

In this period when he was settled in Sansepolcro, Piero also participated in the activities of his siblings' families. In contrast to his lack of involvement in the 1440s, 1450s, and 1460s, Piero formally aided and supported his brothers and sisters and their many children from the 1470s onwards, and increasingly in the 1480s. His assistance to them was most intense in the 1480s and only abated as he approached death.

As we have seen in Chapter 12, Piero helped his sister Vera and his niece, her daughter Cheopa, by agreeing to guarantee their supervision as tutors of the lives and property of Cheopa's minor children in 1474. And, as we have seen in this chapter, Piero assisted his sister Angela's family on two occasions in this period serving as guarantor for her husband Francesco dei Rigi in 1477 and for their son Gasparre in 1481, when each was elected to be a conservator, on these two occasions nicely combining his family loyalties with the wider political-social world of the town of Sansepolcro.

In December of 1480 Piero led the Della Francesca family into a marriage arrangement with the Pichi family, one of the two or three most important families in Sansepolcro during the fifteenth century. Piero and the other male Della Francesca agreed to give the large dowry (for Sansepolcro) of 350 florins for Romana, daughter of Piero's brother Antonio, in her marriage to Paolo Pichi.[44] Then on 15 July 1481 Piero went with his brothers Marco and Antonio, Marco's son Francesco, and at least three other men from Sansepolcro to Montevarchi in the Arno valley (29 miles distant). In the church of San Lorenzo there, Piero, his brothers, and Francesco accepted a dowry from Gasparre di ser Giovanni from Montevarchi for the marriage of his daughter Laudomia to Piero's nephew Francesco. The amount of the dowry totaled 500 florins, certainly the largest dowry paid or received by the Della Francesca in the Quattrocento, and consisted of a credit in the Florentine government dowry fund of 350 florins in addition to some property. The value of the latter was to be determined by two men from Sansepolcro, Agnilo di Jacopo del Gaio and Niccoloso d'Andrea dei Rigi. In this document as in those for Romana, Piero's name preceded that of Marco, Marco's son, and Antonio, indicating that Piero was the oldest of the brothers and took the chief place of honor and responsibility for the agreement in accepting the dowry and the terms of that agreement. Another consequence of Piero accepting the dowry was that he was responsible for its return should his nephew predecease Laudomia, which did in fact occur, although after Piero's death.[45]

So, from 1477 to the summer of 1481 Piero participated in a wide range of communal and family activities requiring his almost constant residence in Sansepolcro. These activities amply demonstrate that his fellow citizens and family members held Piero in high esteem, although the town's political elite apparently did not hold him in sufficient esteem to offer him the town's highest political office. The question of course remains as to whether Piero personally aspired to any of these political offices, or whether he was merely following the path of convention in accepting these obligations. It is perhaps hard to imagine Piero the artist and intellectual, committed to the pursuit of ever more complex geometrical problems, finding anything more than passing satisfaction in the fulfillment of such social and family roles.

CHAPTER 14

Piero in the Last Decade of His Life

As we saw in the previous chapter, from 1477 to at least the summer of 1481 Piero participated in a wide range of communal and family activities that required his residence in Sansepolcro. On 22 April 1482, however, he appeared in the coastal town of Rimini (in the Romagna region of Italy, just over 100 kilometers north-east of his home town), and rented part of a house there for a year (see Map 1). Was he escaping his bourgeois life in his native town and wishing to extract himself from what he may have felt to have been burdensome relationships and obligations? Did he have fond memories of his year in Rimini back in 1451, when he had painted for Sigismondo Malatesta, and did he wish to reinvigorate himself in a seaside town as he approached seventy years of age? Or was his decision to reside in Rimini the result of a commission? The 1482 document describes the space that Piero rented: a room and anteroom above the owner's residence, although Piero also possessed rights to a well, entrance, courtyard, and the use of storage space for wood and wine.[1] There is not any mention of a workshop that would indicate Piero possessed space for painting. The one hint of a commission in Rimini is the name of "master Gabriele di Stefano painter" as a witness to the contract. The identity of this painter Gabriele is unknown, and the notary simply indicated Rimini as the painter's native city. The contract was drawn up in the house of the nobleman Raniere Migliorati, whose family members played important roles in the local Malatesta court.[2]

Piero's presence in Rimini was the beginning of an extended period into the mid-1480s in which he was absent from Sansepolcro. After 24 July 1481 and his term as a prior of the Fraternity of San Bartolomeo had ended, Piero did not leave a documentary trace of himself in Borgo or anywhere else (other than the rental contract) until September 1484. During this period there were certainly occasions when, given his practices in the period 1477–81 and the late 1480s, one might expect that he would have aided his family and thereby appear in documents. For example, on 19 March 1482 his niece Albera, daughter of his sister Angela and Francesco dei Rigi, renounced rights to certain unnamed properties in favor of her brothers. This type of renunciation required the presence of several people, including the maternal side of the family. Inasmuch as Piero had served as *fidejussor* for Albera's father and her brother in 1477 and 1481, one might expect, had he been present in Sansepolcro, that he would have served his niece as well. Instead his brother Marco stood as the Della Francesca representative.[3]

I can only suggest that Piero chose Rimini as his residence for at least one year because he believed he required uninterrupted time to undertake or complete the composition of his third treatise, *The Little Book on the Five Regular Bodies.* If so, his choice to write the treatise in Rimini suggests that Piero brought his manuscripts of Euclid's *Elements* and Archimedes' *Opera* with him, inasmuch as he cites these works so precisely in the *Little Book* that he would have had them to hand while writing it. Although there is no specific documentary evidence until 1484, given his earlier commissions in Urbino and the library there, I would suggest that Piero sojourned in the Montefeltro court for part of the period 1482 to 1484, in part because the other books were available in the Montefeltro library. The court in Federico's palace at Urbino after his death in 1482 continued to be a site of great intellectual activity. Painters, miniaturists, scribes, and scientists worked there. Given that Duke Guidobaldo was ten years of age when he succeeded his father, supervision of the court fell to the regent Ottaviano Ubaldini. Piero's relations with him are unknown; if Piero had spent any time in Urbino in the 1480s, relations with the regent would have been important for the painter.

The Little Book on the Five Regular Bodies

Piero opened his *Little Book* with a letter of dedication to the young Duke of Urbino, Guidobaldo da Montefeltro (Illus. 29). This letter may be the most personal of Piero's writings, although it is true that the ideas expressed were commonplaces in the Quattrocento. Guidobaldo's father Federico had died in September 1482, and thus the letter followed that date, and probably by a good number of months or years, because Piero did not express any consolatory sentiments. Most researchers assume that the treatise was composed after 1482 because of this letter and because Piero writes that "it [his mind] is now out of use and almost consumed by age" and he sends "this little work in this last mathematical exercise of my old age which I brought forward lest the mind should become torpid by inaction."[4] This assumption that the treatise was written after 1482 has to be tempered by the fact that the dedicatory letter was written after the text was completed. The letter was written in a hand different from Piero's and from that in the text; moreover, the writer of the dedicatory letter composed in a more elegant and literary Latin style than the writer-translator of the text. This suggests that Piero first created the manuscript in cooperation with the translator and then drew the geometrical figures and made corrections and additions to the Latin text. Piero appears then to have removed the final blank folio of the manuscript and attached it at the front of the manuscript (thereby changing the original numbering), and got another person to

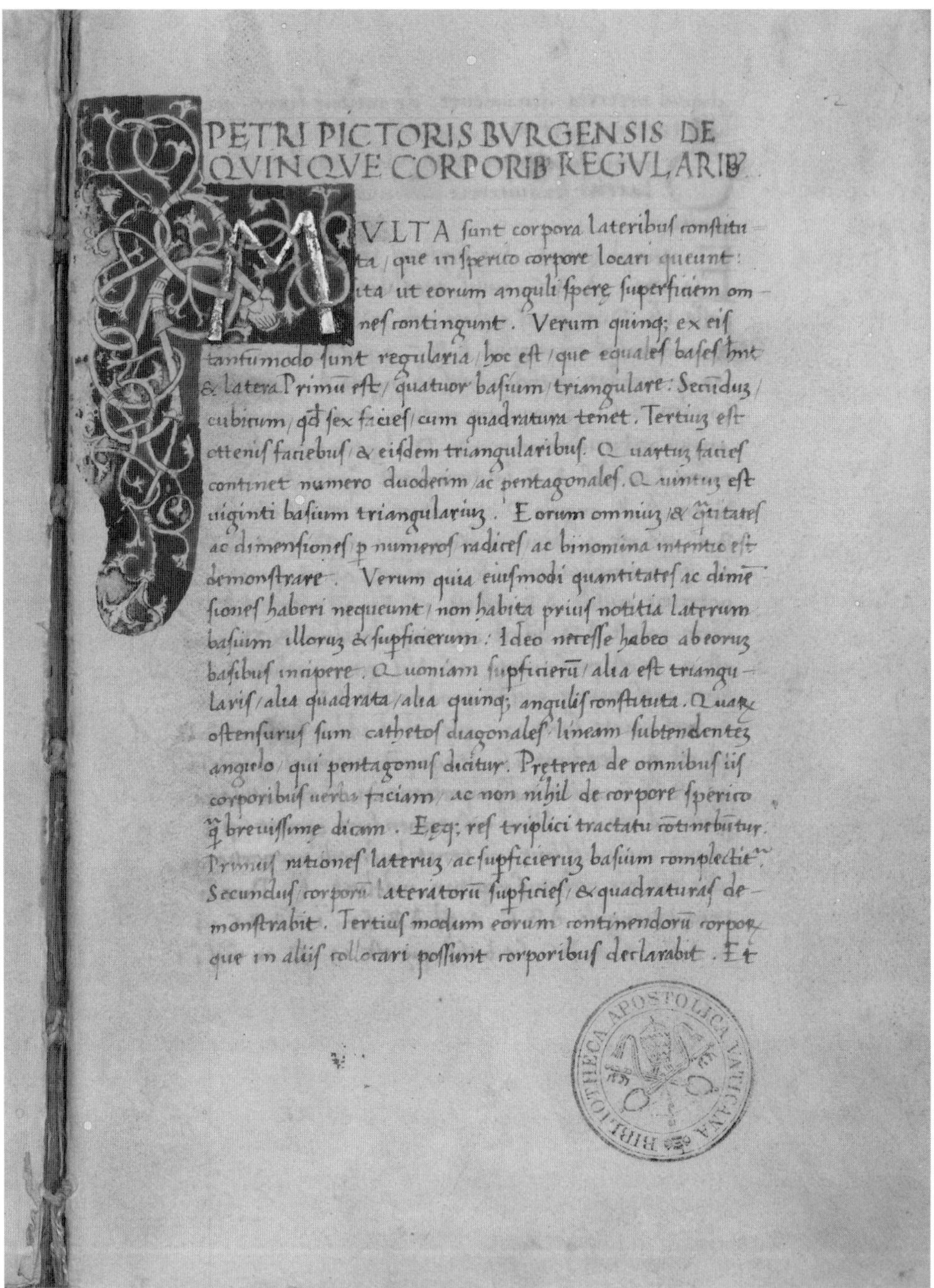

PETRI PICTORIS BVRGENSIS DE
QVINQVE CORPORIB REGVLARIB

MVLTA sunt corpora lateribus constituta, que in sperico corpore locari queunt: ita ut eorum anguli spere superficiem omnes contingunt. Verum quinque ex eis tantummodo sunt regularia, hoc est, que equales bases habent & latera. Primum est, quatuor basium triangulare: Secundum cubicum, quod sex facies cum quadratum tenet. Tertium est octenis faciebus & eisdem triangularibus. Quartum facies continet numero duodecim ac pentagonales. Quintum est uiginti basium triangularium. Eorum omnium & quantitates ac dimensiones per numeros radices ac binomina intentio est demonstrare. Verum quia eiusmodi quantitates ac dimensiones haberi nequeunt, non habita prius notitia laterum basium illorum & superficierum: Ideo necesse habeo ab eorum basibus incipere. Quoniam superficierum alia est triangularis, alia quadrata, alia quinque angulis constituta. Quare ostensurus sum cathetos diagonales lineam subtendentem angulo qui pentagonus dicitur. Preterea de omnibus iis corporibus uerba faciam, ac non nihil de corpore sperico quam breuissime dicam. Eaque res triplici tractatu continebitur. Primus rationes laterum ac superficierum basium complectitur. Secundus corporum lateratorum superficies & quadraturas demonstrabit. Tertius modum eorum continendorum corporum que in aliis collocari possunt corporibus declarabit. Et

ILLUS. 29 Piero della Francesca, *Libellus de quinque corporibus regularibus*, Urb. Lat. 632, fol. 2r, Biblioteca Apostolica Vaticana, Vatican City write or translate the letter to Guidobaldo. It is possible the treatise was written over an extended period prior to 1482, and that Federico da Montefeltro's death in that year then triggered the writing of the dedicatory letter in which Piero quickly reaffirmed his willingness to serve the Montefeltro.[5] According to this reconstruction Piero would have delivered the manuscript soon after the death of Federico. At this point in time there is not sufficient evidence to conclude whether the manuscript was completed prior to 1482 and then delivered to Urbino late in that year or whether Piero simply wrote the treatise in the years after 1482. In any event the *Little Book* is his final treatise and written in his "old age."

In the letter to Guidobaldo, Piero identified two groups of artists in the ancient world. One, led by Policretus, Phidias, and Apelles, had gained fame through the eminence of their patrons, while another group, who were equal in skill and diligence, had not succeeded in inscribing their names on posterity's memory because their patrons were less eminent. Piero then drew an analogy between the famous group and himself by saying that his "works and pictures have taken all they have of luster from the highest and most glittering star and greatest luminary of our time, that of your father [Duke Federico], the best of men." One wonders whether Piero thought of himself when he wrote that the second group suffered their diminished fame in part because they had spent "time with humbler people." He did write that only his association with Federico da Montefeltro could gain him any "luster," any fame that would result in earthly immortality.

It is well established that Piero or his translator took these names and the linkage of fame and patron from the Roman writer Vitruvius' *On Architecture.* The wording is so similar that Piero probably wanted the reader to recognize his familiarity with the classical source.[6] We possess only the Latin version and not Piero's vernacular text so we cannot be sure whether Piero or his translator first appropriated the citation, but we should recall that Piero made an analogous comment in *On Perspective in Painting* in Italian and thus prior to the Latin translation of that treatise. This suggests that Piero held these ideas as his own. In the perspective treatise Piero lists many of the same painters who had gained "eternal fame" from their perspectival paintings and states that he was "zealous" for the fame that would derive from his painting. In the *Little Book* Piero characterized Policretus and his group as achieving "nobility through art." Here in his declining years our painter appears to have recognized that his constant striving with great intelligence and diligence may not have been sufficient to gain him fame, that fortune and his modest circumstances may have obscured his achievements. If he did harbor such doubts, they proved to be prophetic, as his fame waned for four hundred years after his death.

Piero closed the letter expressing what appears to be genuine affection for the young Duke Guidobaldo, who would have been a pre-teenager when Piero dedicated his *Little Book* to him. The painter offered his treatise as "a monument and reminder of me," a portion of "my old affection and perpetual service." This suggests an earlier familiarity with the child when Piero was in Urbino executing the commissions for the young Duke's father Federico in the 1470s.

The *Little Book*, Piero informed Guidobaldo, deals with concepts that Euclid and other geometricians had studied but that in his treatise are "newly expressed in arithmetical terms." Here Piero demonstrates that he understands he is creating a novel mathematical method that combines the prose propositions and procedures of the elite Latin culture of the university with the *abaco* tradition. In the treatise Piero appropriated difficult geometrical propositions, seeking to demonstrate congruencies and similarities, which Euclid and Archimedes had expressed in words. Piero instead presented his proofs in numerical form, "in arithmetical terms," thereby founding a whole new genre of mathematical literature that integrated the *abaco* vernacular tradition of arithmetic computations with the Latin and university tradition of Greek geometry.

Piero stated there would be three parts to his *Little Book*, but in fact there are four.[7] He presented 140 problems and 174 geometrical diagrams. Of the problems, eighty-eight were already present in his *Treatise on Abaco*; most of these were placed in the first two parts of the *Little Book*. The presentation of the problems in the later work is much clearer and more concise than in the *Treatise on Abaco*. This may be due in part to the Latin of Piero's translator, but it also reflects Piero's firmer grasp of the mathematics. In any event, the *Little Book* is the fruit of his long-term fascination with and study of mathematics and geometry.

In the first part of the *Little Book* Piero presented elementary problems in plane geometry, starting with the triangle and then proceeding to ever more complex polygons: squares, pentagons, hexagons, and finally circles. In the second part of this work Piero introduced solid geometry by discussing the five regular or Platonic bodies that are featured in the title of his *Little Book* (see Fig. 6.1). These regular bodies, each with equal angles and equal sides that are identically organized at the vertices, were discussed in Piero's earlier *Treatise on Abaco*. The regular bodies are:

1. the six-sided cube, or hexahedron, with right angles and six square faces;
2. the dodecahedron, with twelve regular pentagons;

(then three polyhedra composed of equilateral triangles)

3. the tetrahedron, or pyramid with four faces;
4. the octahedron, with eight faces; and
5. the icosahedron, composed of twenty faces.

Piero discussed these as enclosed within a sphere, in which case each of the vertices of the regular bodies would touch the sphere; for many of the problems, Piero used the radius of the circles to aid him in finding the length of the sides of the regular bodies.

In the third part of the *Little Book* Piero introduced materials in the first thirteen problems that had not been considered in the *Treatise on Abaco* and that represented a more difficult level of geometry. The problems are more complex, primarily dealing with the placement of one regular body in another, with the two sharing a common side, or a vertex of one dividing the side of another. In this third part he cited Book XV of Euclid's *Elements* on twelve occasions in his first thirteen problems, following, more or less, the order of this source.[8] The first three problems deal with placing an octahedron in a tetrahedron, a tetrahedron in a cube, and an octahedron in a cube, followed by the many polyhedra with more sides, and finishing with the complex construction of a dodecahedron in an icosahedron.

Piero entitled the fourth part of the *Little Book* "On the Irregular Bodies." The reader will recall that Piero had taken from Euclid the five regular or Platonic bodies. Here Piero discusses five of the more complex and relatively unknown Archimedean thirteen "irregular" bodies, each a polyhedron composed of two or three equilateral and equiangular polygons. These thirteen are "irregular" only because they are composed of more than one type of regular polygon. In each irregular body the faces are arranged identically around every vertex. In the *Treatise on Abaco* Piero had discussed two of the thirteen irregular bodies. In one of these discussions, he took a regular tetrahedron and cut off the vertices in the middle of the sides and ended up with an irregular body called a "truncated tetrahedron" with four equilateral triangles and four equilateral hexagons. In the second, he constructed a "truncated cube" by cutting the vertices of the cube one-third down the sides, thereby producing an irregular body of six pentagons and eight equilateral triangles.

In the *Little Book* Piero analyzed four more of Archimedes' thirteen irregular polyhedra, in addition to revisiting his discussion of the truncated tetrahedron. He repeated this discussion of the truncated tetrahedron because he apparently wanted an example of an irregular polyhedron derived from each of the five Platonic regular bodies. In constructing three of the irregular bodies Piero used the same method of truncation by snipping the vertices one-third or half of the way down the sides of the regular bodies and then drawing lines as the planes between the points of truncation. A second construction from the cube and one from the dodecahedron required a more complex method for determining the points of truncation on the sides. Piero's instructions for the dodecahedron show his customary style and his mode of reasoning:

> Given a solid of 32 bases that consists of 20 equilateral triangular bases and 12 equilateral decagons and all of whose angles touch the concave surface of the sphere in which it is contained. Let us investigate the diameter of the sphere, the sides, the surface, and volume [of the solid].
>
> And . . . this solid is produced from a regular solid containing 12 pentagons bases [a dodecahedron] by cutting off its 20 angles, thus producing 20 [equilateral] triangular surfaces, with 12 regular decagonal bases of equal sides remaining . . . [To construct the body] we ought to divide BC [which is the side of one of the pentagonal faces of the regular dodecahedron] so that the middle part is the side of the regular decagon inscribed in the pentagonal base. And so I draw a circle whose diameter is 8 and radius is 4. 4 is also the side of the hexagon [inscribed in the same circle]. And by Book XIII, proposition 8 [9 in most editions of the *Elements*] Euclid for dividing the side of the hexagon according to an extreme and mean ratio, the larger segment [resulting from that division] is the side of a decagon inscribed in the same circle [and is also the side of the decagon to be inscribed in the pentagon] . . .[9]

Piero went on to determine the surface and volume of the sphere, which inscribed the truncated dodecahedron. To find the points of the truncation he employed the "divine proportion," here using Euclid's term of "extreme and mean ratio." In the *Little Book* (in addition to the truncated tetrahedron and truncated dodecahedron), Piero formed the following Archimedean polyhedra:

1. The irregular body of six regular squares and eight regular hexagons constructed by truncating a regular octahedron.
2. The irregular body cuboctahedron constructed by taking a cube and cutting its vertices, which yielded eight equilateral triangles and six regular octagons.
3. The irregular icosahedron constructed by truncating the icosahedron yielding twenty hexagons and twelve regular pentagons.

The construction of these irregular bodies required excellent geometrical knowledge and considerable skill in playing with formulas and listing a lengthy series of steps. In his two mathematical treatises Piero assembled a total of six of the thirteen Archimedean bodies.

In the fourth treatise of the *Little Book* Piero presented material that had only one ancient precedent; moreover, no known medieval author had shown knowledge of how to construct the Archimedean irregular polyhedra. Archimedes' text on the irregular bodies had long been lost by the Middle Ages, and in fact we know that Archimedes discovered the irregular bodies from the testimony of only one ancient source. Writing in the fourth century BCE, the Greek mathematician Pappus attributed the thirteen irregular bodies to Archimedes and specified the type and number of regular polygons in each of them. Even more rare are descriptions of the tortuous methods of constructing these bodies. In fact, in the ancient world only one anonymous commentator explained Archimedes' construction methods, and then only for four of the irregular bodies. No one can explain how Piero obtained his knowledge of the Archimedean solids and how to construct six of them. In his detailed research on Archimedes in the Middle Ages the historian of science Marshall Clagett confessed to being "profoundly puzzled" by Piero's knowledge and could not explain how Piero knew how to construct the irregular bodies because Pappus' treatise is not known to have been available or known in the Quattrocento. And it was in Greek. Even more "puzzling" is the prospect that Piero learned either from a lost unknown source or through his own ingenuity how to construct two irregular bodies, on whose construction even Pappus' commentary had given no instruction.[10]

Another mystery in the fourth part of Piero's *Little Book* involves his construction of two circular columns or cylinders that intersect at right angles. In Problem 10 he asked what would be the volume of the area that the two cylinders share. The solving of this problem required approximately two pages of explanation and proofs. By doing this, Piero had constructed a famous problem in the history of mathematics without, apparently, knowing that he had done so. In Archimedes' most acclaimed treatise *On the Method* he states proudly that he had sent this same problem to his friend Eratosthenes whom he challenged to supply the proofs. This Archimedean treatise had disappeared in the early Middle Ages and was rediscovered in 1906 only to be lost again until just recently, when it was recovered in a palimpsest. Hence Piero could not have known of the problem directly from Archimedes, and the painter does not mention the Greek geometrician here. It is possible that Piero had heard of the crossing cylinder problem, but not its solution, from some obscure commentary on a Greek treatise. More likely he had constructed the problem from his familiarity with crossing vaults in the architecture of his day, especially since he had discussed and had drawn crossing vaults in his *On Perspective in Painting* as an architectural element to be placed in perspective. His knowledge of the problem and its solution most certainly derived from his own visual acumen and his recognition that it involved a complicated geometrical problem, just as Archimedes had done.[11]

In the last decade of his life Piero had become one of the leading geometricians in Italy. Vasari had an appreciation of his mathematical achievements, writing that Piero was "a rare master of the difficulties of drawing regular bodies, as well as of arithmetic and geometry."

In September 1484 Piero can once again be located in his home town and may have remained there to his death in 1492, although he is not documented again in Borgo until 1486. His whereabouts in 1485 are unknown. His return in 1484 led to contacts with master Matteo di ser Paolo, the Latin translator of *On Perspective in Painting* and probably the *Little Book*. Master Matteo lived into the late 1480s and can be placed together with Piero in 1486, when the two appeared as witnesses in a notarial document.[12] As discussed above, Piero retained control of his treatise. This is evident in his additions and corrections to the Latin translation. It is difficult for us to appreciate the challenge of taking Greek words and geometric concepts and finding Italian words to render their precise meanings (or at least to approximate them), and then repeating the process in the translation into Latin. This would require Piero and the translator to work together closely over an extended period of time. For this treatise Piero chose, for the first time, the more expensive vellum rather than paper, so, despite the fact that the dedicatory letter to Guidobaldo was added after the treatise was completely translated and copied, he doubtless always intended the manuscript to be a presentation copy.

The Nativity of Christ

In early 1500 the doctor of law Bartolomeo, son of Piero's brother Antonio, inventoried the goods of his deceased cousin Francesco di Marco in the Della Francesca home and described seeing in the room of Francesco's widow Laudomia "a panel painting (*tabula*) with the *Nativity* of our Lord in the hand of master Petro."[13] In the year after Francesco's death in 1494, Laudomia had decided to remarry, and Sebastiano, Francesco's brother, was occupying the room when the inventory was taken.[14] Thus we can securely say that *The Nativity of Christ* today in London's National Gallery maintained an honored place in the Della Francesca home after Piero's death—indeed, it remained with the family's descendants until it was placed on the art market in the nineteenth century.[15]

As we saw in Chapter 13, in 1481 Piero led the Della Francesca family to the town of Montevarchi in the Arno valley to accept Laudomia and her dowry of 500 florins in her marriage to Francesco. One theory is that Piero painted *The Nativity* as a wedding gift for Laudomia and Francesco, which is plausible, although there is no other link between the painting and Laudomia other than that it was in a room she occupied before leaving the Della Francesca family. If this had been a wedding gift, it would place the date of painting in 1481. We do not know which room Laudomia and presumably Francesco occupied prior to Piero's and Francesco's deaths or whether the painting accompanied Laudomia as she moved from room to room. Another theory is that Piero painted *The Nativity* for himself, which is again plausible, yet in the 1500 inventory the painting is not listed in Piero's room but in that of Laudomia and later her brother-in-law Sebastiano's room. The large panel painting may have been moved, but the fact that the 1500 inventory mentions it as being in the room of Laudomia (absent for five years by that date) suggests that it remained in the same room.

The painting is large and almost square. There is disagreement as to whether Piero left the painting incomplete, or whether it suffered damage, or both, but certainly today the painting is worn thin or has no paint in certain sections (Illus. 30). *The Nativity of Christ* was a familiar iconographic topic, and in painting it Piero adopted several elements that were being developed by other painters after 1460. They all took parts of the iconography from Saint Bridget of Sweden, who, in the fourteenth century, had a vision of a blond and naked baby Jesus on the ground and a light-haired Mary in adoration immediately after the painless birth. Piero has placed the baby on a part of the Madonna's cloak; she adores the child in her now light blue dress with her richer-colored blue cloak wrapped around her waist and twisted to accommodate the child. Saint Bridget had envisioned the Christ Child emanating light, but this is not evident today in Piero's rendering, although the Child's naked body is white and light in tone. The major source of light comes from the upper left. Other details from Saint Bridget include the singing angels, but Piero excludes her vision of the presence of God the Father.

Many of these elements that originated in Saint Bridget's vision were first represented in paintings in Flanders, and most researchers emphasize the powerful Flemish influence on Piero's *Nativity.* These influences are seen in the kneeling Madonna with hands joined, the shed structure behind the adoration drama, and the blondness of the Mother and Jesus. The art historian Marilyn Lavin has emphasized that Piero's painting had many elements similar to those of other paintings roughly contemporary with Piero. His borrowings raise the question posed by several writers as to whether this suggests Piero's loss of his powerful capacity to conceive and represent innovatively traditional iconographic subjects. Does the increasing Flemish influence and apparently waning power of innovation constitute a substantial change in Piero and his style? Had Piero's

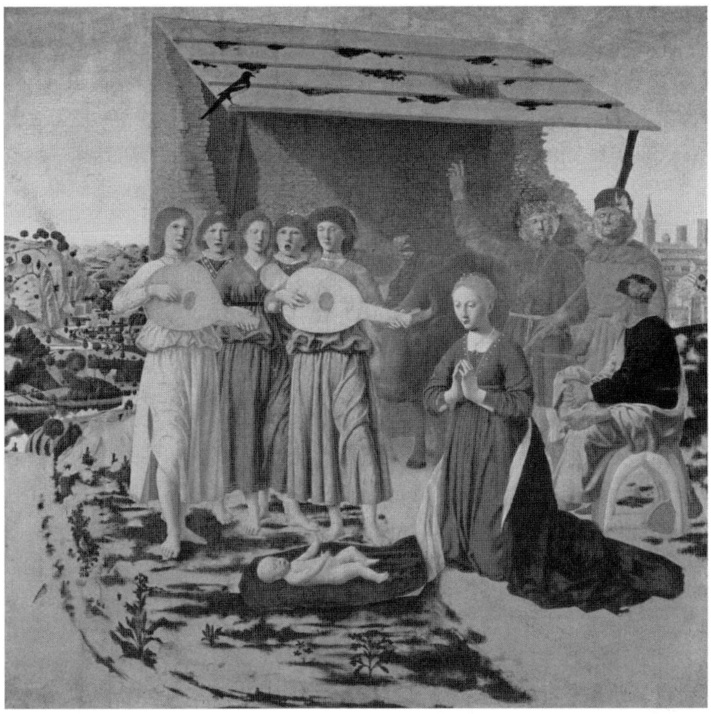

ILLUS. 30 Piero della Francesca, *The Nativity of Christ*, 124.5 × 123 cm. National Gallery, London

sojourns in Sansepolcro and the changing demands of patrons had an effect upon his style? We should keep in mind that by the mid-1480s Piero had entered his eighth decade and may simply have been more intrigued by geometric propositions than by painting traditional religious paintings at this stage of his life. Researchers have often commented on the particular religious quality in the *Nativity*, one of them remarking on the painting's "intense emotion ... with a sentiment of religiosity and a profound mysticism," and another on the painting's "heartfelt reverence for simple faith."[16]

Marilyn Lavin is one of the few scholars to have written extensively on the *Nativity*.[17] She speaks of Piero's celebration of his birthplace and family, most evident in the familiar scene of the winding river on the left that was also represented in *The Baptism of Christ* (see Pl. I) and the two early paintings of Saint Jerome (see Pl. II, Illus. 3). The river recalls both the River Tiber and the River Afra, the latter spiraling down from the Alpe della Luna and joining the Tiber just east of the town. On the right side Piero has painted a memory of the streets and roofs of Borgo, probably looking down via delle Guinte from the east (see Map 2). He has also introduced a prominent role for Joseph at the moment of Christ's birth. In her vision Saint Bridget had succeeded in diminishing Joseph's role by emphasizing the presence of God the Father with a burning candle, while Joseph's was extinguished. Piero instead has placed Joseph on the right of the painting and placed him on a saddle, thereby evoking a remembrance of his own father and his metier as an artisan and merchant of leather, including saddles.

Lavin goes further and sees the painting as a personal affirmation of Sansepolcro. The figures possess a simple rural ruggedness; Piero decided to minimize the elegance in the figures, despite endowing his shepherds, usually portrayed as rough countrymen, with a solid monumental presence and with hats that might better have been found on the Magi. Joseph sits on the saddle barefooted with his hands clasped but not in adoration as he gazes at the braying mule. On the ruined shed Piero has painted a magpie, whose descendants command the countryside of Borgo to this day. The stolid cow, mule, shed, saddle, shepherds, and the country setting all serve to suggest that Piero wished to use rural Sansepolcro as a means of representing Bethlehem.

In this painting Piero apparently never intended to provide an overall perspectival organization of his subject as he had done in *The Flagellation of Christ* (see Pl. VIII). There are certainly elements that suggest depth, for example, the faint atmospheric perspective and the distant river scene on the left. The viewer senses rational organization and there may be several vanishing points, but there are no orthogonals that order all the parts of the painting and lead to one vanishing point.

Piero in his Final Years

In the last six years of his life Piero returned to his home-town lifestyle of 1477 to 1481, witnessing notarial contracts and assisting his family in Borgo. However, he apparently did not hold public offices in his latter years; perhaps communal officials spared him responsibilities uncongenial to his age, although his contemporaries sought his judgment and presence on various problems.

Piero served a friend as a witness on 5 August 1486. He and the translator of *On Perspective in Painting*, master Matteo di ser Paolo, went into a shop on the Piazza Comunale of Sansepolcro and witnessed an act for Paolo Genari, who was a kinsman of Matteo. Piero's assistance to this member of his intellectual circle was the final in a series of links between the two before Matteo's death the following year.[18] Piero also appeared as a witness in June 1488, when Blasio di Lazzaro di Orlandino d'Arezzo, a skinner, received some pelts from two butchers of Sansepolcro.[19] More significant was Piero's decision to serve the family of the deceased Jacopo Anastagi, who had commissioned his *Saint Jerome and a Penitent* and aided Piero by introducing him to the court of Rimini and probably to Sigismondo Malatesta himself in 1451. On 29 December 1488, at the age of approximately seventy-six, Piero went to the spice shop of Meo Pichi and witnessed for Jacopo's widow, Amata.[20]

Piero remained active serving as a mediator or evaluator of artistic and construction projects. The assignment of judging the quality of such work presumes that Piero was not incapacitated in any fundamental way. On two occasions, May 1488 and July 1489, he made evaluations of work that required the use of his eyes, proving he retained his sight until just before his death in 1492. For the first of these occasions Niccolò di Gasparre, who had been a builder in Sansepolcro for decades as his father had before him, selected Piero and another man to evaluate construction in the Franciscan convent of San Leo della Strada.[21]

In 1489 Piero and the builder Nardo di Pippo, whom we encountered with Piero in the church of Sant'Agostino and in the conservator's residence, evaluated the work of the stonemason master Antonio da Cortona (whom we also met earlier as the builder of the Pichi chapel in the Badia of Sansepolcro).[22] Master Antonio had on this occasion constructed another chapel commissioned for the confraternity of Santa Maria delle Laude in the church of Sant'Agostino. Piero and Nardo estimated the value of work in the chapel, which resulted in Antonio receiving 6 lire for his final payment.[23]

Piero was again active in support of his family in this period. Most of his activity at this time was focused on providing for the future generations of the Della Francesca family. The first record we have of Piero doing something in this period, however, is related to an artistic commission or commissions in Arezzo. In October 1486 Piero with his brothers Marco and Antonio appointed Bernardo d'Andrea dei Grifoni from Arezzo and Lodovico d'Antonio della Francesca as their representatives to pursue payments "for a picture or pictures made by said master Piero from many persons in Arezzo as well as in whatever else location."[24] It has been suggested that these payments were for Piero's labor in the Cappella Maggiore in San Francesco in Arezzo for the Bacci family. They may have been, but the document could also refer to paintings in the Cathedral of Arezzo (Saint Mary Magdalene) and in the surrounding Aretine countryside. In appointing Bernardo dei Grifoni, Piero and his brothers chose a member of an old and respected family of Arezzo, but there is no indication whether the procurators succeeded in securing payments for Piero's labor.

In 1487 Piero, Antonio, and the sons of the now deceased Marco appointed another procurator. The Della Francesca men chose the notary ser Niccolò Fedeli (for whom Piero had served as *fidejussor* in 1480) as their representative in all causes against the "brave man" Alessandro Inghirami. The nature of the conflict with this former military commander of Florence is not mentioned here, but a subsequent act of 23 August 1488 suggests it related to the villa in Bastia that was jointly owned by the Della Francesca, Inghirami, and Baglioni families, together with another Perugia family. The 1488 notarial act describes a division of the villa between the families with "the outstanding man Master Piero" agreeing to the division on behalf of the Della Francesca.[25]

In August 1487 Piero participated in a legal act for his sister Angelica and her daughter Bartolomea. Angela's husband Francesco dei Rigi had died, and the widow wanted to assure the orderly descent of his property to their sons. Piero's niece was in the 15 percent of young women of Sansepolcro who formally renounced their rights to their father's patrimony in exchange for their dowries. Bartolomea passed her claims to her brothers Gasparre and Giovanni, who in exchange promised their sister her dowry and her right to return, if widowed, to her natal family's home. Several persons had to be present in cases such as this in order to approve a young woman—often a teenager—renouncing her rights. In this case, the witnesses included the town judge, priors of the Fraternity, members of the deceased father's family, and a member of the mother's family, the last of whom was represented by Piero.[26]

Piero's interest in organizing the future of the children of his siblings is also apparent in his arrangement for the dowry and wedding of his niece Contessina, daughter of Marco. Before his death Marco had contacted marriage brokers, and on 23 January 1487 he and the prospective groom recorded the terms of the dowry in the presence of the marriage brokers Emilio Pichi and Agnilo del Gaio.[27] Marco promised his daughter in marriage to master Michele d'Antonio Zanzani with a dowry of 300 florins, subject to the agreement that at the "petition and will" of Michele, Marco would give the groom 100 florins, with the remainder paid within four years. Three days later Piero entered the negotiations and represented the Della Francesca. He and master Michele made another agreement in which, with the future groom writing its particulars, they agreed to establish a union of the two families. Piero was present for this agreement of 26 January 1488, but he did not sign it at this time. Instead the apparent family friend or marriage broker Agnilo del Gaio signed for the Della Francesca family.

After the death of his brother Marco on 22 June 1487, Piero took leadership of the marriage arrangements for Contessina. He accepted the earlier 26 January 1487 contract, writing in his own hand that "on December 27, 1487, I, master Pietro Franceschi painter, am content in what is recorded in that agreement."[28] In April and again in May 1488 Piero conveyed unspecified amounts of the dowry to master Michele, totaling the initial payment of 100 florins. Piero's participation indicates his interest in the future generation, even though Contessina was hereby entering another patrilineal group.

These and other marriages of the Della Francesca family demonstrate that Piero and his brothers had succeeded in elevating the family into the merchant and professional elite of Sansepolcro and the surrounding region. Marco had begun this phase of social elevation by marrying a daughter of the Carsidoni family in 1472–73, and his daughter Contessina married a doctor in 1488. Moreover, the children of Antonio succeeded in ascending to a higher social class than those of Piero's generation. In 1480 Antonio's daughter Romana had entered into one of the wealthiest and most prestigious families of Sansepolcro, when she married Paolo Pichi. In 1493 the son of Antonio, the doctor Bartolomeo, married Caterina, daughter of the Count of Montedoglio, the head of the most powerful noble family of the upper Tiber valley.[29]

Professional and noble fathers chose Della Francesca children as spouses for their children because they perceived the family as essentially equal to theirs and that its status conferred honor on their families. Contemporaries may have regarded the Della Francesca as among the town's elite families, but probably not as a result of Piero's successes. His achievements in Urbino may have elevated his renown, but this promised meager tangible benefits for future generations. It was Marco's successes as a merchant, banker, and political man of influence and Antonio's international merchant activities, together with the resulting wealth from each, that really laid the basis for the family's reputation.

In November 1488 Piero, as head of the family, received from an otherwise unknown man named Neri Tondoli a final notification that Piero and the Della Francesca had completed the terms of an unknown contract.[30] On one occasion in 1490 and three instances in January 1491 Piero served as a witness for men and families who attempted to end their conflicts through legal acts of pacification. In each instance there was no known earlier relationship with Piero or the Della Francesca. The men promised to resolve their strife in formal legal contracts and to live in peace. In the earliest of these instances, Piero traveled to nearby San Giustino to serve as a witness for two families. One of the other witnesses was Alexandro d'Alexandro Uguccioni, a powerful representative of the Guelf Party in Florence, and the peace was accomplished under the auspices of the captain of Sansepolcro and Vitellozo Vitelli, then ruler of Città di Castello.[31] Perhaps Piero was serving one of the contracting families or was an acquaintance of one of these men of political authority in Florence or Città di Castello. In the three instances in January 1491 Piero appeared as a witness in the agreements to end the conflicts between the Toscani and Lamubori families and within the Nomi family (all from Sansepolcro).[32]

Piero appears in another document at this time, the origins of which remain a mystery. In March 1491 a certain Polidoro d'Angelo d'Antonello purchased a house from the five sons of Bartolo Lasciagire. The Lasciagire owed Piero della Francesca 56 lire. As part payment for the house, Polidoro repaid the debt to Piero.[33] We do not know how the Lasciagire had incurred this debt, but if it had been the result of a property sale by Piero, the document would have mentioned Piero's brothers or their sons, as their property was held in common. This makes it more plausible that the debt resulted from Piero's specific service or commission of a painting.

Piero's Preparation for Death

The death of Marco on 22 June 1487 prompted Piero to prepare for his own death and afterlife. Within two weeks of that event the painter drew up notes for his last will and testament (Illus. 31). These notes are not the last extant example of Piero's writing, but they demonstrate his fine hand and suggest that in 1487 his reputed sight problem was not far advanced. The notes indicate his specific choices, which his notary would place within a conventional testament template. Piero wrote his notes in Italian and in his own hand with still well-formed letters. The notes read in the form that Piero composed them:

> My burial I want that it is in the Badia in our [Della Francesca] tomb.
> I leave [bequeath] to the opera of the Badia ten lire
> I leave to the Body of Christ ten lire
> And to the Madonna della Badia ten lire
> And ten lire to the Madonna della Reghia

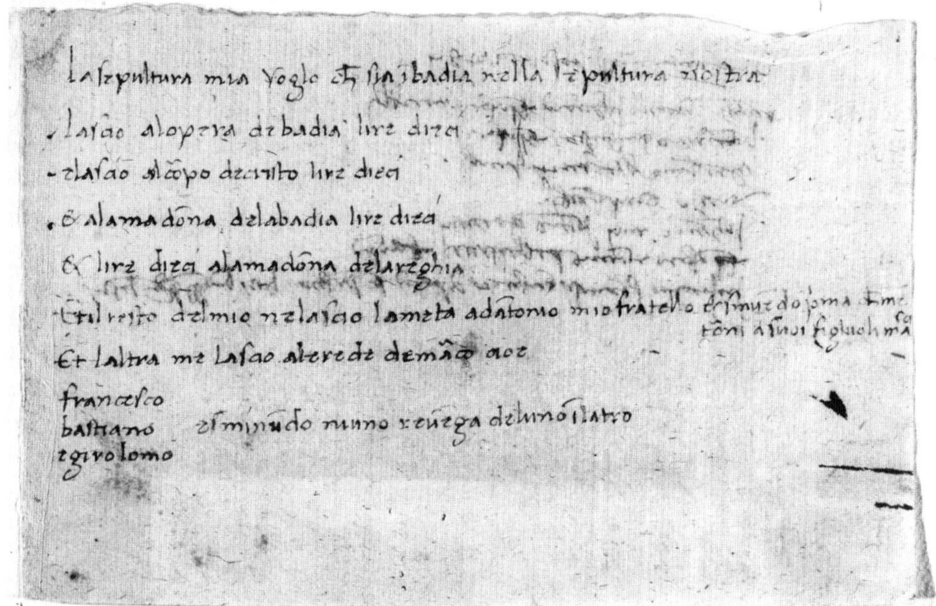

ILLUS. 31 Piero della Francesca, Preparatory Notes for his Testament, Archivio di Stato, Florence, Serie degli autografi, Box 301, Armadio 6

> And the remainder of mine I leave half to Antonio my brother and Antonio dying before me to his male children
> And my other [half] I leave to the heirs of Marco, that is,
> Francesco, Bastiano, e Girolamo, and one dying, receives from the one the other [others].[34]

From these notes, the notary Leonardo Fedeli drew up Piero's last will and testament and read it in the notary's office in the presence of the legally required seven witnesses, none of whom was especially important or a known friend.[35] Piero's testament of July 1487 can be characterized as entirely customary and similar to that of his brother Marco and most other males of their generation. To Piero's choices for his burial and patrimony the notary added the traditional legal formulas for other elements in Piero's testament. The notary first attested to Piero's health of mind and body and his intention to dispose of his goods. As was customary in the testaments of Sansepolcro, the notary then attended to Piero's spiritual well-being by recommending his soul to "his most high Redeemer." The notary also recorded Piero's request of burial in the Badia of San Giovanni Evangelista in the tomb of his predecessors. We know from the notary's version of the testament that Piero chose burial in the Della Francesca tomb in the chapel of San Leonardo, also called the Monacato, in the Badia cloisters. Piero provided for his soul by making four pious bequests for ecclesiastical entities. In the first the notary added to Piero's words that the payments were for "the love of God and for his soul." Piero bequeathed 10 lire for his burial site, which could be seen as a counter-gift for the Badia's provision of the site and presumably Masses at his funeral. His pious gifts focused on the Badia with two other bequests of 10 lire for its Corpus Christi celebrations (a feast celebrating the Holy Eucharist) and for the chapel of the Glorious Virgin Mary. In the latter bequest Piero honored and supported the chapel for which he had painted the lost fresco in 1474. In the remaining pious bequest Piero chose to grant 10 lire to the chapel of Santa Maria della Reghia, which was outside the walls of the town, along a channel of the River Afra.[36]

After 1300 an increasing number of Italian merchants, artisans, and their wives had begun to write testaments, as a means of taking wealth from their patrimony for specific and largely pious purposes that, lacking a testament, would pass seamlessly to their family heirs. Piero chose not to give much of his patrimony to charitable or other purposes; for example, he did not endow a large expensive funeral chapel, nor enlarge the dowries of his nieces, nor sustain an individual cleric or clerical group with property for annual death Masses or prayers. Instead, his wealth passed to his closest male family members, his brother Antonio and the sons of his deceased brother Marco, all of whom Piero designated as his universal heirs. Thus they inherited all of Piero's property and legal rights and were legally responsible for paying the 40 lire for the pious bequests. This too was customary in Sansepolcro and much of Italy—that unmarried males would seek to perpetuate the family's name and fortunes, which meant where possible favoring their male rather than their female relatives. Despite the emphasis I have placed on Piero's assistance to female members of his family, when the critical issue of descent of property arose, he accepted and perpetuated dominant patriarchic values. The same was true in 1487, when he witnessed and oversaw his niece Bartolomea's renunciation of her claims to her inheritance in favor of her brothers and in exchange for her dowry.

Until the year of Piero's death, he and his brothers Antonio and Marco (and with the latter's death, his sons) chose to keep their property undivided. From 1464 Piero and his brothers were legally in a *fraterna*, in which their wealth was held in common with income pooled and expenses shared. For most of the last thirty years of his life, except for Piero's sojourns in Arezzo, Rimini and Urbino, and Antonio's merchant travels, the three brothers lived together in the family house on the corner of via delle Giunte and via Borgo Nuovo. But the death of Marco in 1487, the fact that Marco and Antonio had many children, along with the anticipated death of Piero, led the Della Francesca family in February 1492 to divide their property in two parts, one half for Piero and Antonio and the other half for Piero and the sons of Marco.[37] Thus with Piero's death the formerly common property would be divided neatly into the two branches of the Della Francesca family.

The division of the property required the listing of all the extensive wealth of the Della Francesca by a notary. As with his testament, so too with the division of property, Piero wrote at least one note of instruction for the notary. On a small piece of paper he recorded the more complex obligations of the Della Francesca regarding the dowry of Mathia, daughter of Antonio, debts owed to the town government, and cash held by

Antonio. This previously unknown scrap of paper is important because it is dated 30 January 1492, five days before the notary wrote the family's inventory. Piero's formation of letters and words on this piece of paper remains as regular and well-constructed as his 1487 notes for his testament.[38] This is interesting because Vasari said that Piero "became blind through an attack of catarrh at the age of sixty, and lived in that condition to the eighty-sixth year of his life." If we bring together Piero's death in 1492 with Vasari's estimates, then Piero would have become blind in the mid-1460s. All we can conclude is that Vasari had made a gross error about when exactly Piero lost his sight, although it does seem that he did eventually become blind because a man from Sansepolcro recalled in the mid-1550s that he as a boy led the blind Piero around Borgo by the hand.[39] So, unless the witness had read Vasari and wished to share in Piero's biography, we can be confident that at a certain point Piero did indeed eventually lose his sight. However, this must have occurred just prior to his death because in 1487 he wrote notes for his testament in a perfect hand. In 1487–88 he wrote his agreements to the dowry of Contessina also in a fine hand. Until early 1491, he witnessed documents, and blind men were not eligible to be witnesses. Finally, as just noted, a mere eight months before his death Piero wrote coherently and in his customary fashion. Hence, Piero's blindness, which we grant may have been progressive, seems only to have become serious in the last months of his life.

We complete this extensive examination of documents late in Piero's life with the short recording of his death in the "Libro de' morti" maintained by the priors of the Fraternity: "maestro Piero di Benedetto de Francesschi pictore famoso a dì 12 [ottobre 1492] a Badia."[40] It is interesting that despite the significance of Piero in Renaissance painting and geometry and the scribe's note of Piero being "famoso," his funeral did not lead the town government or the confraternities to contribute large candles, or indeed many candles, in his memory. It is also indicative that Piero's death entry was written in the same size as most others. In an entry for a member of the elite, by contrast, the name of the deceased was sometimes commemorated by some unusual and evident notation. For example, Marieta, wife of the local noble Conte Cattani—both otherwise unknown in history—was remembered in large and capital letters and with more candles.[41] Such distinctions probably would have made little difference to Piero, who never appears to have been overly concerned with ceremonial or social identity.

We know little about Piero's intellectual and artistic activities from the later 1480s until his death in 1492. After he completed *The Little Book on the Five Regular Bodies*, did he continue his studies of geometry? After he completed the *Nativity*, did he continue to paint for himself and his family? A later inventory mentions a *Madonna* in the family house. It is difficult to imagine that he allowed his perennially hyperactive mind to atrophy; we know that he wished to ward off "torpor" with his late geometric studies. Certainly we have seen he maintained an active social life and assisted his family and others. But in 1492 he was approaching eighty years of age and, on account of his deteriorating eyesight, probably seeing less and less of the world that he had come to know so intimately through his careful observation and had depicted so brilliantly in his painting.

Conclusion

It is my hope that having reached the end of this book, readers will have acquired a richer, more complete, and more accurate picture of Piero della Francesca's evolution as a man, a painter, and a geometrician. At the very least, by making use of all the newly available documents, I hope to have arrived at a more precise dating of Piero's paintings and treatises.

Using these documents and other sources of evidence, I have been able to identify three stages of Piero's painting career (subject to further consideration and adjustment should other documents come to light). In the first stage, through to the early 1450s, his paintings are marked by a strong sense of proportion but lack elaborate systems of perspective, and he is only beginning to use cartoons and pouncing. In the second stage, after he completed the right lunette in Arezzo around 1453, his human figures are less demonstrative, more monumental, and more sculptural. To this second stage belong Piero's "classic" schemes of perspective and his abundant use of cartoons, most evident in *The Flagellation of Christ* (*c*.1470). In the third stage, comprising the last fifteen years of his life, Piero's powerful organizational skills in painting are expressed without any obvious aid of a perspective system. In this stage he appears to shift his powers of concentration to geometry and to his writing. For whatever reasons—his interest in geometry, his age, or the lack of patrons with major commissions—in this final stage Piero undertook few and less ambitious commissions, or painted for his family.

In this book I have attempted to place Piero in his historical context as a means of understanding him and his accomplishments in painting and geometry, and I trust that my presentation of these contexts has led to a fuller portrait of both the man and his intentions. One thing that I hope has definitely emerged from this approach is the importance of the local society and people of Sansepolcro. For, as we have seen, Piero's cohort, especially Francesco del Borgo and the early associate and relation through marriage Jacopo Anastagi, played a fundamental role in his artistic and geometrical achievements. Moreover, Piero's education in the mixed merchant-artisan culture of Sansepolcro remained a vital element in his painting and writings until his death, influencing the language he used in his vernacular treatises, and evident in the deep respect that he retained throughout his life for the beautiful products from the hands of artisans, whether clothing, leather book bindings, gems, or veils.

Unfortunately, all the available research and documents still cannot demonstrate that Piero was an intimate of the intellectual elite of the Italian Renaissance; it would have enlarged my conception of the artist had I been able to show him conversing with Brunelleschi, Alberti, or Cardinal Bessarion. Piero definitely borrowed the concepts of linear perspective from Brunelleschi and the idea of writing a book on painting from Alberti, but it stops at that. There is no evidence of personal interaction with them, and there are few convergences of time and place in which Piero and his reputed interlocutors could have met. He did learn from the writings of others, specifically the mathematicians Fibonacci, Euclid, and Archimedes. In terms of painting, Piero borrowed practices from other painters to which he added his own visual skills. Several scholars have mentioned that he thought more in images or geometrical designs than in words, but this idea remains to be explored further. In the abstract world of geometry Piero found a welcome second home where he could employ his visual perspicuity. He possessed an extraordinary ability to integrate his reading of *abaco* and Greek texts with a capacity to see and construct visual representations of complex geometrical problems. In this sense his painting and his geometrical treatises are the products of the same visual acumen.

I have also alluded to Piero's defining and strained relationship with his father. This tension derived from Benedetto's desire for the economic and social success of his family, and his disappointment in his firstborn's choice of a career as painter with its socially mediocre status and meager financial returns. Piero did indeed choose a life work that was regarded as a "hand craft" and thus socially inferior, but he always attempted to elevate his artisan craftsmanship by intellectualizing it. He may be said to have transformed his father's drive for a higher social status into a quest for more prestigious intellectual activities, those most often performed by sons of the elite who possessed university learning and degrees.

Throughout his painting career Piero endeavored to represent human subjects with dignity. No one, servant or prince, is diminished or demeaned. The best examples of this are the dwarf in the *Visit of Sheba to Solomon* and the workman in the *Burial of the Wood*, both from the fresco cycle in San Francesco in Arezzo. The workman is painted with as much dignity as the surrounding royal personages. The defeated pagan Chosroes, on his knees before his execution, similarly retains his dignity (the *Death of Chosroes*). And not only all individuals are given worthiness and power; Piero represents all human activities as noble and significant. At the same time, he presents his figures naturalistically and also manages to accommodate the Christian teaching of God's creation and the theology of salvation.

One of my themes has been Piero's union of *abaco* mathematics used in commerce with his understanding of Greek geometry. His mind worked in terms of geometrical forms, and he saw basic structures of the natural world in arithmetical or numeric terms. This "mathematization" of nature is of course basic to modern science. It is a long way from Piero in the fifteenth century to modern science, but it is significant that he had prepared for this numerical conceptualization of the basic structures of nature.[1]

Another of Piero's qualities, and one of his most significant and enduring contributions to the history of art, is his powerful sense of proportion and the importance he attached to it. Linear perspective is rightly associated with Piero, but that significant achievement of the Renaissance is fundamentally nothing more than the diminishing of pictorial space proportional to its distance from the viewer. Luca Pacioli, the first scholar who systematically studied (as well as plagiarized) Piero's treatises, summarized this nicely when speaking about *On Perspective in Painting*: "In this work of every ten words, nine of them translate into proportion."[2]

Piero's Christianity was at best conventional, which is evident in his last will and testament. His paintings are based on Christian history, theology, and iconography, which he presents with great respect, although abstracted and yet presented as a drama involving humans. He does not sentimentalize Christian theology or its historical personages; rather, he elevates them by presenting them in a geometrically defined space, monumentalizing their bodies and endowing them with gravitas. The viewer senses an emotional distance from Piero's paintings of Christian subjects (but one could also say this about all his paintings). He chose never to impart to saints any quality or attribute representing penitence that required depicting them with an emaciated or weakened body. This is especially noteworthy in his *Saint Mary Magdalene* (see Illus. 15). Other artists of the Renaissance, Donatello for example, represented her as emotionally wrought, with a tortured body weakened by earlier sinful indulgences. Piero's Christian subject matter, in contrast, as seen in this *Magdalene* or in his figures in *The Death of Adam* (see Illus. 7), portrayed humans participating at an elevated level with the Divine to gain eternal life, not in the sullied state of sin or its resulting human infirmities.

Piero introduced into his painting and treatises a distinct form of humanism. He had little interest in Petrarchan literary humanism or in civic humanism. His writings demonstrate no evidence of the study of rhetorical theory or grammatical practice that characterized so much humanist writing. That said, he did appropriate one important idea from literary humanism: that achievement in the arts could lead to the artist's immortality through remembrance by subsequent generations. In both *On Perspective in Painting* and *The Little Book on the Five Regular Bodies* Piero discusses his desire to acquire fame through his art. He also shared with the literary humanists an admiration for ancient authors, although his authors were Greek geometricians and he studied them for their geometrical formulas and procedures. Where a literary humanist might study Cicero in order to imitate his Latin style or cite the feats of Julius Caesar to stimulate heroic behavior, Piero on the other hand studied Euclid and Archimedes partly to master their propositions, but more importantly to understand their complex procedure of establishing proofs and their concern with congruence and the similarity of abstract forms. Many Renaissance painters depicted Greek and Roman literary and historical texts in their art. In no extant painting of Piero's did he locate one of these ancient narrative texts and then attempt to transform the words into images. However, in his treatises he illustrates complex geometrical propositions derived from Greek mathematical texts and represents these geometrical figures as proofs that were superior to the original purely verbal arguments to be found in the original texts.

Euclid's ideas and procedures pervaded Piero's thought and writings for at least the last three decades of his life. It is therefore intriguing that he ignored a key idea attributed to Euclid in the *Elements*. Piero discussed the five Platonic or regular bodies at great length in his *Treatise on Abaco* and his *Little Book*. In much of his discussion he followed Euclid's formulations carefully and noted precisely where he found the propositions in the Greek's text. Integral to Piero's copy of the *Elements* was the linkage of the five regular bodies to Plato, who saw them as the metaphysical elements of the universe, underlying visual reality. This form of mystical materialism apparently did not appeal to Piero, despite its presence in Book XV of the *Elements* from which the painter otherwise appropriated so much.

Piero's quest to find and record the representation of proportion in the world along with his full discussion of the five regular bodies did not lead him to link this fundamental understanding of the natural and historical world to wider philosophical, religious, or metaphysical discussions. Luca Pacioli took Piero's analysis of the mathematical basis of reality back to Plato's linkage of the five regular bodies to the four basic elements of being and the universe, and then (Pacioli was a Franciscan friar) proceeded to link this all back to Christian theology.[3] It is notable that Piero himself refused to make any such conjectures that would have gone beyond his empirical understanding of the natural world, with the exception of that which is visible in his art: the mathematical structures intrinsic to the natural world.

As we have seen, Piero likewise minimized the significance of the "divine proportion" or "Golden Section." Others, Pacioli for example, celebrated the particular beauty found in the ratio between a line or a rectangle divided at a point where the larger part is to the smaller part as the whole is to the larger part. For this ratio Piero appropriated from Euclid the less mystical name of "extreme and mean ratio". Piero made use of the ratio in his constructions, but he went no further. He made no elaborate claims for its beauty or even its usefulness. For him, geometric shapes, formulas, and proportions were all part of a vast system that could be visualized, measured with numbers, and manipulated in myriad configurations. He clearly found great satisfaction in the pure world of geometrical shapes, propositions, and mathematical numbers. However, there is no evidence that for him these geometrical or numeric worlds possessed some underlying religious or philosophical meaning.

There exists an art industry that ascribes mystical or symbolic intentions to Piero. According to these conjectures, the artist hides his most firmly held beliefs beneath the surface of his paintings, which can only be understood through discovering their hidden signs and geometrical designs. These signs apparently reveal that Piero was a member of some secret society, perhaps the Masonic Lodge, or a follower of the Templars. These myths and stories might be fascinating, but they are completely unsubstantiated by what the remaining documents and works of art tell us about Piero. The real Piero was from early on committed to researching the *historical* and the *natural* world—and it is this, and this only, that pervades his painting. He uses his naturalism to signal religious symbols and meaning (as his patrons would have demanded and his public expected), but his representations always remain at the natural level, with no need or inclination to distort the natural to reveal more mystical truths. Truth is discovered or represented in the world as it presents itself to the eye. It was not only for the purposes of his painting that Piero studied and wrote on optics; he researched how the eye came to comprehend the objects and humans of the natural world.

Piero did not write a book of poetry as Michelangelo did; nor have his notebooks survived as have Leonardo's; nor did he write an autobiography as did Cellini; nor are there accounts of his anger at a patron as with Donatello; nor accounts of his passionate love for a woman as with Fra Filippo Lippi. However, it may well be that the documents we do have tell us all we really need to know about Piero the person, a man who was fundamentally absorbed in his craft and his research into the underlying proportions of the natural world and how to represent them. What we do know of his personal life is that Piero addressed his craft and intellectual interests with total commitment and involvement, leaving little time for developing personal relationships, in marriage for example, beyond his family circle. Piero was an intellectual in that he wanted a secure rationalized base for his painting; he was not content with painting beautifully and profitably, for he wanted to understand the process that made images appear as if from the natural world, thereby leading him to research the nature of the eye, light rays, and recurring geometrical shapes. This interest, we might even say compulsion, may even have led him late in life to forgo profitable commissions, or at least to paint less, and to concentrate on his purely intellectual interest in geometry. If so, then this would have been an entirely appropriate development for a man who, as we have seen, was always much more than one of the greatest visual artists of the Renaissance.

NOTES

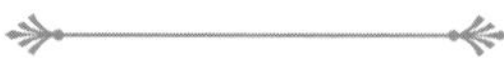

Prologue

1. I am convinced that if Piero were in his home town for months and years, he would have left evidence of his presence, and if absent, there would be no documents. My confidence in this approach is bolstered by the reality that Sansepolcro probably has more extant documents per capita than any other urban center of the Renaissance. Several hundred books of fifteenth-century contracts survive; these yield a continuous account of the cultural, social, and economic life of the town. Readers will want to make their own assessment of my method on the basis of the particulars of each occasion and whether in the end it leads to a more coherent and convincing narrative of Piero's life and work.
2. No one previously has laid out three phases in Piero's development, but see the following studies for indications of elements of this evolution: Gilbert 1968; Paolucci 1989, 73–77; Christiansen 1993, 117–24; Field (2005, 9, 97–119) has a list of paintings that, with one exception, fall within my first phase.
3. Banker 2013a.

Chapter 1

1. For this and subsequent discussions of Sansepolcro, Fanfani 1984; Banker 1988; Banker 2003, 12–56.
2. For the following, Banker 2003, 134–45.
3. Banker 2003, 145–58.
4. Banker 2003, 57–92; Sansepolcro's grammar school was similar to the one in nearby Arezzo discussed by Black 1996.
5. Banker 2003, 159–209, here and for the following discussion.
6. Dabell 1984a, 74–75, 85–86; Banker 2013a, 23, docs. XXXII, XXXIII. It is more likely that Piero performed these two projects, rather than his brothers, because Francesco was already a monk and Piero's two younger brothers were training to be merchants and are never said to have done any manual labor or painting.
7. Banker 2013a, 23–24, doc. XXXIV; Banker 1990, 245–47.
8. For these documents, Banker, 2013a, 28–29, 35–36, docs. XL, L; Banker 2003, 194–201.
9. Longhi 2002, 175.
10. De Marchi 2008a, 99–106.
11. Banker 2003, 192–94; 225–45; Baxandall 2003, 130–31.
12. Banker 2003, 85–89.

13. Banker 2003, 225–36, 253–56.
14. For the following, Banker 2003, 236–45.
15. Banker 2013a, 24–25, doc. XXXV.
16. For the documents involving Piero, Banker 2013, 27–28, 29, 30–31, docs. XXXIX, XLII, XLIV. For the document of Benedetto, ASF, NA 19308, unfol., 28 May 1437.
17. Banker 2013a, 31, doc. XLV.
18. Bellosi 1992, 17–54.
19. Lightbown 1992, 104.
20. Shearman 1995, 213–21; Kemp 1996, 40–44.
21. Field 2005, 97–98.

Chapter 2

1. For the following discussion and the accounts in the chapel of Sant'Egidio, Battisti 1992, II, 608–09, doc. XVIII; Banker 2003, 213–15, 245; Banker 2013a, 37, doc. LIII.
2. On this transformation of the visual culture of the West and a comparison with that of Islam, Belting 2011.
3. My view of Piero in Florence has been particularly influenced by Bellosi (1992, 17–54) and Bertelli (1992, 8–12).
4. See the discussions in the volume *Pittura di luce*, ed. Bellosi 1990.
5. Boschetto 2000, 96.
6. Field 1997c, 61–88.
7. Mazzalupi 2006, 37; De Marchi and Mazzalupi 2008, 64–66; for the document, Franceschini 1995, 608, II, 1, app. 9, and Banker 2013a, 37–39, doc. LIV.
8. Mazzalupi, 2006, 37; Camaiti 2007, 25–26. Another document (Di Lorenzo 2004, 291–92, 294) records the presence of a "Piero di Benedetto" in Florence on 12 April 1442. This also was within an artistic setting as it involved this "Piero" conveying 2 lire to the painter Filippo Lippi for his *Incoronazione della Vergine* in the church of Sant'Agostino. Here there are three elements that would tie this "Piero" to our painter: the names "Piero" and "Benedetto" and the artistic setting. We should remember though, this person conveying the 2 lire was not necessarily a painter and is not named a master, and the lack of a mention of the home town implies he was from Florence. He may have been a shop boy or assistant or performing some other tasks in the church; he was not necessarily in the workshop of the artist. It is less likely that the individual in the Florence document is Piero della Francesca than the Petro in the document of Modena.
9. ASCS, Ser. II, reg. 2, fols. 94r, 144r; Degli Azzi 1914, 107.
10. Dabell 1984b, 361–71.
11. ASCS, Ser. II, reg. 2, fol. 40, 22 July 1442; Banker 2004, 253–54; Banker 2013a, 39, doc. LVI.
12. ASF, NA 7026, fol. 51v; Banker 2013a, 40, doc. LVIII.
13. Banker 2013a, 39–40, doc. LVII.
14. For the document, Banker 2013a, 40–41, doc. LIX.
15. ASF, NA 7027, fol. 9r; Banker 2013a, 41–42, doc. LX.
16. Banker 2003, 147, n. 53.
17. Bertelli 2007, 31–32.

18. Bertelli 2007, 34–36; Pacioli 1509, Prima pars, capitolo 19, fol. 33, left side.
19. On Leonello's court, Baxandall 1963, 304–26.
20. Bertelli 2007, 34–39, though many earlier writers had made a similar argument.
21. Pacioli 1509, "Dedication of the treatise on architecture," fol. 23, left side.
22. For this discussion of Piero in Ancona and the document of 1450, Mazzalupi 2006, 37–54; idem, 2008, 224–45, 346–47; Banker 2013a, 51–54, doc. LXIX.
23. Field 2005, 79.
24. The humanistic hand was introduced in the fifteenth century as a replacement for the Gothic hand, which was characterized by highly decorative serifs, slanted letters, and irregular spacing. The humanists sought to imitate the classical Roman hand (although in fact the letters were largely derived from Carolingian manuscripts), aided by inscriptions from Roman antiquities. The letters of the humanistic hand were simplified with the elimination of serifs or other decorative elements. They were presented in a square format with equal space for each letter. The staffs of most letters were perpendicular to the writing line.
25. Calvesi 1998, 193; Bertelli 2001, 258; idem 2007, 32.
26. Bertelli 2001, 258.
27. For the following, see Mazzalupi 2006, 37–54, idem, 2008, 227–30.

Chapter 3

1. Banker 2013a, 44–47, docs. LXII, LXIII, LXIV.
2. Banker 1993b, 163–91; Banker 1995b, 20–31; Banker 2003, 89–92, 152–54; Martelli 2012, 45–71. Thirty years later Jacopo was still identified as "outstanding and most famous" in ASF, NA 7000, filza 1483, no. 3.
3. ASF, NA 14044, unfol., 7 January 1432; ASF, NA 19306, unfol., 22 April 1435.
4. Broglio Tartaglia 1982, 184. For the Malatesta court, Jones 1974, 176–239; Soranzo 1911, 25–27.
5. This chapter deals with three men with similar names: Sigismondo, ruler of Rimini; Sigismund, German king and Holy Roman Emperor (1433–37); Saint Sigismundus, the sixth-century king of the Burgundians, who was instrumental in converting his people to orthodox Christianity.
6. Jones 1974, 176–78.
7. Pasini 1992, 14–15; Paolucci 2001, 41–48; Hope, 1992, 51–154, esp. on the late role of Alberti in Rimini.
8. Woods-Marsden 1989, 132.
9. Poesch 1962, 116–18.
10. Woods-Marsden 1989, 132.
11. Broglio Tartaglia 1982, 184.
12. Mitchell 1978, 82.
13. Woods-Marsden 2002, 94–95.
14. Banker 1993b, 165.
15. Broglio Tartaglia 1982, 184.
16. Delucca 2008, 15, n. 8.
17. ASF, NA 7054, filza 1450–1459, no. 3.
18. Lightbown 1992, 86; Turchini 1986, 168.

19. Paolucci 1989, 30.
20. Bertelli (1992, 182) and Battisti (1992, I, 294) for the identification of the town as Borgo. See Andreini (2009, 25–27) for his identification of the castle as the now destroyed Castello di Montedoglio, once near Borgo.
21. Some writers assert that a man named Girolamo Amadi was the patron of the panel, because under the penitent's elegant red cloak someone has written "Hier. Amadi Aug F." The scrawling of the name Girolamo Amadi asserts "I am the owner." Had he in fact been the original patron, Amadi's name would have been on the frame or included with Piero's inscription; hence, it would have been unnecessary for him to repeat his claim to be the patron or owner on the painted surface. Piero wrote his inscription in quasi-humanistic capitals. Whoever added the Amadi name inscribed uppercase letters, but they are slightly cursive. The writings do not match and are definitely from different centuries. So the Amadi name is probably that of a later owner, not that of the patron; see Bertelli and Paolucci 2007, 196–99. Roberto Longhi argued most strongly for a Venetian provenance and patron for the *Saint Jerome* painting, in part to substantiate his view that Piero visited Venice and influenced subsequent painting there. But other than the fact that the panel's earliest known location is Venice in the nineteenth century, there is no reason to assume that the panel was executed there or for a Venetian. Longhi 1914; Longhi 2002, 86–87, 101.
22. ASCS, Ser. XXXII, reg. 177, fols. 28r–33v; see also Mazzalupi 2012, 102–06, docs. 43, 44, 46.
23. Bridgeman (2002, 79–80) demonstrates this position and disposes of suggestions that the strip had other significances.
24. It was not uncommon for someone to endow a chapel or painting in honor of a saint other than his or her namesake. For example, in 1482 Jacopo Mercati endowed a chapel in the Badia of Borgo in honor of San Giuliano; see Mazzalupi 2012, 116, doc. 67; Banker 2013b, 72–73.
25. ASF, NA 7054, filza 1450–1459, no. 9, and for a redaction in Latin, see ASF, NA 7034, fol. 40v; Banker 2013a, 59–61, doc. LXXV; Mazzalupi 2012, 100–01, doc. 4.
26. On the chapel of Jacopo, see Martelli 2012, 45–71; Mazzalupi 2012, 100–06, Appendix I, docs. 40–47; Banker 2013a, 61–62, doc. LXXIV.
27. Hope 1992, 97–101.
28. Iannucci 2001, 82–88.
29. For Jacopo's palace, ASF, NA 16725, fols. 75v–76r; Banker 1993b, 172; Martelli 2012, 53.
30. ASF, NA 16725, fol. 111v, 20 August 1460.
31. Hope (1992, 93–96) remains the best guide to the construction of the Tempio and Alberti's participation.
32. Pasini 1992, 109–10.
33. Lollini 2001, 57–61.
34. For the following, Banker 1993b, 163–91.
35. Laclotte 1984, 84; Paolucci 2001, 41–48. Although some have denied that Piero painted the image of Sigismondo in the Louvre or suggested that he passed the commission to an assistant, most Piero scholars today attribute the work to him.
36. Bertelli 2001, 24.
37. Laclotte 1984, 97–99 and esp. 98, n. 37.
38. Woods-Marsden 2002, 94–95.
39. Laclotte 1984, 87, n. 25; Woods-Marsden 2002, 95.

40. Bellucci and Frosinini 1997, 167–87; Bertelli 2001, 24.
41. Laclotte 1984, 81–87.
42. Pasini 1992, 79–80.
43. Département des Arts Graphiques, Musée du Louvre, Paris, inv. 2479.
44. For my discussion of the two traditions, Lavin 1974, 345–74.
45. Laclotte 1984, 84; Paolucci (2001, 45) has emphasized the ceremonial nature, the "courtly formality," of the relationship between Sigismondo and his patron.
46. Pasini 1992, 38ff.
47. Paolucci 2001, 43.
48. Woods-Marsden 1987, 209–16.
49. Paolucci 2001, 46.

Chapter 4

1. The best English introductions to the Legend are Borsook 1980, 91–102; Wood 2002, 51–65: Lavin 2002, 114–84.
2. Borsook 1980, 92; Wood 2002, 52–56.
3. For this discussion of San Francesco, the Bacci, and the commissioning of Piero, Centauro 1990, 94, doc. 21; Centauro et al. 2000, esp. 49–96 and docs. 201–52.
4. Centauro 1990, 33.
5. Hypotheses that either Piero's father knew the Bacci or that Giovanni Bacci governed the commission are unlikely; Centauro et al. 2000, 211, doc. 0004 and their discussion, 55–56; Ginzburg 1981, 27–51. Piero's maternal uncle Nardo di Renzo da Monterchi was an employee of the Bacci and may have suggested his nephew for the commission; Centauro et al., 215–16, 219, and docs. 0010, 0011, 0019. On this Nardo, Banker 2003, 128–34.
6. Borsook 1980, 92–93; Banker 2013a, 103–05, doc. CXXVII and below Chapter 8.
7. Piero was in or around Arezzo in the year 1464 and later, but few if any scholars today would have Piero painting in the Cappella Maggiore that late.
8. Lightbown 1995, 11–19; Pinelli 2002, 7–30; Angelini 2011b, 15–27.
9. Longhi 2002, 162.
10. Bertelli 1992, 22–26, 79–114, 81 for changes in Piero's style, 186–91; Bertelli 2001, 18–19; Borsook 1980, 92–93. For different evaluations of the evolution cf. Gilbert 1968, 19–26; Battisti 1992, I, 100; Calvesi 1998, 40–50.
11. Lightbown 1992, 83; Lightbown 1995, 11–19; Pinelli 2002, 8–9; Longhi 2002, 57, 121–22; Lavin 2002, 115, 181–82; Paolucci 1989, 53–55.
12. Pinelli 2002, 7–30; Pinelli examined an earlier article by Bellosi (1987, 15–35), in which the latter art historian had concluded that the paintings by Giovanni di Piamonte in the church conclusively proved that Piero had finished the Arezzo cycle by 1459–60.
13. This error of dating the Pichi's recall to 1455 derives from the mistaken assumption that Sansepolcro adopted the Florentine calendar in 1441; Beck (1978, 53) introduced this error into Piero studies; Banker (2004, 255) for the 25 December date as the beginning of the year in Sansepolcro.
14. See the essays in Israëls 2009, I.

15. Banker 1991, 11–58; Banker 2009b, II, 568–72, docs. IX, X, XV, XXIV; Cobianchi 2009, I, 107–19.
16. I do not accept the notion that Piero's Arezzo frescoes are saturated with propaganda deriving from the papacy to promote a Christian crusade against Islam. Kenneth Clark introduced many English speakers to Piero and to this interpretation (1981, 38–39). The idea that Piero's murals in Arezzo are best understood as part of the campaign led by Cardinal Bessarion and Pope Pius II to liberate the Holy Land has been most vigorously argued by the cultural historian Carlo Ginzburg (2000) and repeated by the Byzantine expert Sylvia Ronchey (2006). The interpretation fails on several grounds, but primarily because the iconography of Piero's frescoes was chosen before the fall of Constantinople (Istanbul today) in 1453 and well before Pope Pius II (1458) began his frenzied campaign to organize a crusade; and secondly because the interpretation requires that Piero would have painted most of the fresco cycle after mid-1459, but we now know that the painter could not have been in Arezzo for any extended period in the early 1460s. Also, Ginzburg has retracted key parts of his interpretation; Ginzburg 2000, Appendix II, 116–28.
17. Borsook 1980, 93, 95.
18. Wood 2002, 51–56.
19. I have followed Lavin in my discussion, including her organization of the sequence of the scenes. Lavin 1994, 15–17; Lavin 2001, 27–37. The latter contains a summary of Lavin's more detailed study entitled *The Place of Narrative: Mural Painting in Italian Churches, 431–1600* (1990).
20. Gilbert 1968, 77–78.
21. Borsook 1980, 91, 95.
22. Lavin 1994, 16; cf. Maetzke 1998, 100–01.
23. Bridgeman 2002, 78–79.
24. The positions of the stars in the fifteenth century are derived from computer projections; for this discussion, Valerio 2007, 81–85.
25. Gaddi did paint an emperor in a dream, but he mistakenly made the later Byzantine emperor Heraclius the subject. In the *Golden Legend* Jacobus Voragine recounted that before a battle on the Danube river, Constantine received a message from an angel holding a bright cross with gold lettering stating that in this sign he would triumph, and in fact the next morning his army was victorious. In his *Dream of Constantine* Piero has corrected Agnolo Gaddi's erroneous identification of the emperor and the *Golden Legend*'s erroneous location of the battle.
26. Maetzke 1998, 127.
27. Lightbown 1992, 162.
28. Cappel 1996, 143–57.
29. Lazzeri 1989, 259.
30. Borsook 1980, 95–97; Centauro 1990 for my discussion of Piero's techniques.
31. I am in agreement with Field (2005, 183) that Piero never established a large workshop.
32. Lightbown 1992, 140; Bertelli 1992, 89.
33. Bertelli 1992, 84–85; Longhi 2002, 162.
34. Lightbown 1992, 162.
35. Smith 1995, 223–53.
36. Lavin 2001, 35.
37. Longhi 2002, 158–59.

Chapter 5

1. Field 2005, 83–88.
2. For the following, Banker 1988, 145–73, esp. 150–51, 170–72.
3. Gore 2010, 51–52.
4. For the earliest notices of the Misericordia confraternity, Banker 1988, 150–51, 244, n. 49; Banker 2010a, 19–21, docs. 1–10; Banker 2013a, 3–4, 6, 8–9, docs. V, VII, X, XIII, XIV–XVI. Some (for example, Ahl 2002, 18) confuse an earlier "Casa di Misericordia" in a different area of Borgo with the later Misericordia. For the document of 1428, Lightbown 1992, 30, 285, n. 8. Some have suggested (Ahl 2002, 25) that, rather than a banner, a statue of Mary decorated the high altar in this early period. One does not exclude the use of the other.
5. Banker 1988, 150, 263, nn. 14, 21; ASCS, AM 24, fol. 57r–v.
6. For the foregoing, ASCS, AM 24, fols. 57r–166v.
7. Banker 2010a, 23, doc. 15, and Banker 2013a, 39, doc. LV for Marco della Francesca.
8. ASCS, AM 24, fol. 96r.
9. Banker 2010a, 19, docs. 1–4; Banker 2013a, 3–4, 6, 8–9, docs. V, VII, X, XIV–XVI.
10. Di Lorenzo 2010, 85–97.
11. Banker 2010a, 20, 22–23, docs. 9, 13; Banker 2013a, 14, 26, docs. XXII, XXXVII.
12. Banker 2010a, 21–22, docs. 11, 12; Banker 2013a, 17–18, 19–20, docs. XXVI, XXIX; Dabell 1984a, 81–82; on the lateral piers, Gardner von Teuffel 1979, 21–65.
13. Banker 2010a, 23, doc. 17; Banker 2013a, 40–41, doc. LIX, and for a slightly different English translation, Baxandall 1974, 20.
14. The contractual requirement to follow this model in width and specifically to provide the altarpiece with "legs," and thereby lateral piers, rules out the possibility that the confraternity originally commissioned a triptych from Piero with the two outer saints on the main register added only after 1450, when one of these, San Bernardino of Siena, was made a saint.
15. ASCS, AM 24, fols. 57r–166v.
16. For the account of the indulgence, Banker 2010a, 25–26, doc. 22; Banker 2013a, 76–79, doc. XC; for Malatesta Cattani, Scapecchi 1984, 210–13; Israëls, 2010, 102.
17. Israëls 2010, 99–116; for processional flags, Marshall 1994, 506–25.
18. See the insightful discussion of Lightbown 1992, 43–44.
19. ASCS, AM, *Libro grosso*, fol. 1r.
20. The increasing prominence of the image of the Holy Sepulcher and of the town's legendary founders, Arcano and Egidio, diminished the town's emphasis on Saint John the Evangelist, but the saint remained frequently present in religious images and written sources; Gardner von Teuffel 1999, 163–208.
21. Polcri (1996b, 106–17) interpreted the appearance of Saint John the Baptist as a nod to the patron saint of Florence because that city had taken political authority over Sansepolcro in 1441. Perhaps, but this saint often appeared on altarpieces in Sansepolcro before that date.
22. Salmi 1942, 26–44; Banker 1995a, 27 and docs. 7, 30; Banker 2010a, 26, doc. 23; Banker 2013a, 68, 80, docs. LXXXIV, XCIII.
23. On the interpretation of the order of the panels of the predella, Castelli and Gori 2010, 157–61; Israëls 2010, 104–12; Israëls 2013, 46–67.

24. Israëls 2010, 104–12, esp. for the importance of the Passion in interpreting the altarpiece. As we have seen in Chapter 4, Marilyn Lavin has shown that there were a variety of ways of organizing narratives in the Middle Ages and Renaissance.
25. Banker 2010a, 24, docs. 19, 20; Banker 2013a, 54–55, 62–63, docs. LXX, LXXVIII.
26. Ibid.
27. Some hold that Piero was in Borgo for a presentation of arms for the commune in 1453, but that opinion derives from a misreading of the documents; Banker 2004, 254–55.
28. For these payments and this discussion of them, Banker 1995a, 21–35.
29. Banker 2013a, 66–67, doc. LXXX.
30. Dabell 1993, 76–77; Banker 2013a, 68, doc. LXXXIII.
31. It may be that the Pichi never completely paid the bequests of 110 florins to Piero or the confraternity; thus the Pichi obligation remained only Urbano di Meo Pichi's 60 florins. The Pichi are recorded as paying just under that amount.
32. Bellucci and Frosinini 2010, 189–202; Cavagli 2010, 203–18.
33. Cavagli 2010, 204–05; Bellucci and Frosinini 1999, 89–93.
34. Cavagli 2010, 209–12.
35. Cavagli 2010, 206–07.

Chapter 6

1. Giusti 1996, 319–29. Florence possessed excellent schools of *abaco*, and Piero could have begun his study there in 1439 through conversations and texts, but Giusti judges that no Florentine master, other than Paolo Gerardi, was especially influential in Piero's *Treatise*.
2. Black 1996, 110–11, 123–24, 159–61; for specific masters of *abaco*, see 494–98, 504–05, 508–11, 525, 612–13, and for Piero da Montepulciano, 512–13ff, docs. 537–39, doc. 550, 521–22, 569.
3. Napolitani 2007, 27–46.
4. Folkerts 1996, 293–312; for the *Elements* I have drawn from the excellent website, http://alepho.clarku.edu/~djoyce/java/elements/elements.html.
5. For Francesco del Borgo, Frommel 1983, 108–54; Frommel 1984, 129–38; Frommel 2006, 79–313; Banker 1992a, 54–56.
6. Bertelli (1992, 21, 35–36), Lightbown (1992, 179), and Pinelli (2002, 16–18) have noted Francesco del Borgo's importance in Piero's life.
7. Banker 2003, 89–92, 112.
8. Polcri 2007, 244–50.
9. For this discussion of Francesco del Borgo's architecture, see n. 5 above. The degree of Alberti's involvement in the urban renewal of Rome has been hotly debated; see the excellent summary of the debate, Grafton 2000, 302–15.
10. Vatican City, ASV, Cam. Ap., Intr. et Ex., 426.
11. Francesco's humanistic hand is very different from the handwriting attributed to him by Frommel (1983, 122, Illus. 15) in ASR, Camerale I, 1503. In the latter, for an account book of expenses Francesco apparently employed a notarial hand, while in the Vatican City, ASV, Cam. Ap., Intr. et Ex., 426, Francesco used a more elegant hand and writes the income and expenses in complete sentences. On the humanistic script, Wardrop 1963, 1–18. For Piero's handwriting in his paintings, Lightbown 1992, 32, 49–50, 76, 81, 88.

12. Frommel 1984, 134.
13. Both manuscripts have shields at the bottom of the first folio, where one would expect the owner to place his family arms, but the shields themselves are in fact blank. This suggests that Francesco may have intended the manuscripts as gifts.
14. Grafton 2000, 246–48; Maddalo 1990, 191–99.
15. Clagett 1978, 3, III, 321; see the forthcoming study by Pier Daniele Napolitani and Paolo D'Alessandro.
16. Bibliothèque Nationale, Paris, Nouv. Acquis. Lat. 1538. Jacopo's hand has been identified in this manuscript by Paolo D'Alessandro. On the research of Napolitani and D'Alessandro, compare with the forthcoming book by Stefano Pagliaroli, *Iacopo Cassiano e l'Arenario di Archimede*.
17. BAV, Vat. Urb. Lat., 261. fol. 130v: "Finis librorum Archimedis quos transcribi iussit Dominus Franciscus Burgensis semper Deo laus."
18. BAV, Vat. Urb. Lat., 261, fol. 115v.
19. ASR, Rome, Collegio Not. Cap., 1913, fol. 1r–v; Spotti Tantillo 1975, 86ff.
20. Bibliothèque Nationale, Paris, Nouv. Acquis. Lat., 1538, fol. 1r; Clagett 1978, 3, III, 323–24, 331; Frommel 1984, 134.
21. Paolo D'Alessandro first noted this in his paper "Il Tetragonis parabolae" given in the conference "Archimede e le sue fortune," 24 June 2008, in Syracuse.
22. ASV, Cam. Ap., Intr. et Ex., 442, fol. 123v; Banker 2013a, 68–69, doc. LXXXV.
23. For the original Italian of Vasari, see Battisti 1992, II, 640–43; for the death of Romana, Banker 2013a, 73, doc. LXXXVII.
24. Banker 2013a, 68–69, doc. LXXXV.
25. Lightbown 1995, 11–12.
26. Giusti 1996, 319–29. On the use of several mathematical sources, see Clagett 1978, 3, III, 385.
27. Gamba and Montebelli 1996, 266.
28. For the dating of the 1450s, Battisti 1992, I, 216; Daly Davis 1977, 16, n. 49. Neither Battisti nor Daly Davis offers evidence to indicate why they hold that Piero wrote the book in the 1450s. Andrea Di Lorenzo has suggested a date in the 1460s for Piero's finishing of the *Treatise* on the basis of the probable dating of a miniature on fol. 3r; see Di Lorenzo 2010, 90, 94–95, nn. 55–57. A date in the 1480s for Piero's completion of the work has been suggested by Lightbown 1992, 280.
29. For the following, see Banker 2013c.
30. Briquet 2000, rpt. edn.; Picard, http://www.piccard-online.de/struktur.php; Zonghi 1953, rpt. edn.
31. It is obvious that Piero could have purchased and then held the paper for years or purchased the paper later because paper with the work's watermarks continued to be produced after its initial appearance. However, paper was expensive, and Piero's manuscripts demonstrate he used and exhausted his supply of paper of one watermark (with one exception) before introducing paper with another mark.
32. See n. 1 above.
33. Giusti, 1996, 319–29.
34. There is an Italian National Committee in the process of publishing Piero's works in critical editions. Their edition of the *Treatise* was to be published in 2010; unfortunately, its publication was delayed until 2012 after this book was completed. Both it and the editors' analyses would have been valuable for my study.

35. For my reading of the *Treatise*, see the edition of Arrighi 1970, here fol. 3r (39). The quote was translated by Daly Davis 1977, 21.
36. See the excellent study of the Pichi, Di Lorenzo 2010, 85–97, and esp. on the *Treatise*, 90, 94–95, nn. 54–57.
37. Besomi 2002, 140–41. The following discussion of the *Treatise* is informed esp. by my reading of Clagett 1978, 3, III, 384–89; Daly Davis 1977, 25–41; Field 1997a, 62–75; Field 2005, 119–24.
38. Piero, *Treatise*, fols. 3r–15v, in Arrighi 1970, 40–62; Daly Davis 1978, 25–41; Field 1997a, 64; Field 2005, 17–18.
39. For the foregoing, Piero *Treatise*, fols. 16r–23v (fol. 17r for the problem) in Arrighi 1970, 62–75; Field 2005, 23, Appendix I, 325–28.
40. Piero, *Treatise*, fol. 24r, in Arrighi 1970, 75.
41. Daly Davis 1978, 24–27; Piero, *Treatise*, fols. 24r–79v, in Arrighi 1970, 75–169.
42. Daly Davis 1978, 27–41; Field 2005, 24–31.
43. Piero, *Treatise*, fols. 80r–104v, in Arrighi 1970, 169–224.
44. Piero, *Treatise*, fols. 80r–104v for polygons and 105r–120r for polyhedra, esp. for the regular and irregular bodies (Arrighi 1970, 169–256).
45. My discussion and the quote are taken from Field 1997a, 68–75, and Field 1997b, 241–53.
46. Clagett 1978, 3, III, 399.
47. Piero, *Treatise*, fol. 110r, in Arrighi 1970, 235.
48. For a parallel discussion of the following, Field 2005, 6–7.
49. Piero accepted from medieval tradition and probably from the title on the manuscript that Euclid wrote Books XIV and XV. We know today that Euclid did not.
50. Field 1997a, 64.

Chapter 7

1. Battisti 1992, II, 617–18, docs. CXI–CXIV.
2. Examples of rent payments for workshops, Banker 2013a, 51, 98–99, docs. LXVIII, CXIX. The commercial activities of Marco and Antonio required other sites out of the center of the town where raw materials could be stored and turned to finished goods. In 1462 Marco purchased for the family "a storeroom for woad in Borgo in the parish of San Giovanni Battista"; ASF, NA 7040, fol. 128r.
3. For the following, Banker 1999, 147–62; for the documents, Banker 2013a, 73–76, docs. LXXXVIII, LXXXIX.
4. For his protocols, see ASF, NA 16725–16742.
5. Banker 2013a, 79, 81–82, docs. XCI, XCV.
6. For these documents, Banker 2013a, 87–89, docs. CIV–CVI.
7. Banker 2013a, 89–90, doc. CVII; Mazzalupi 2012, 106, doc. 47.
8. For this discussion, Giorni n.d., 3–14 and esp. 35–40 for docs. XI, XIV, XV, XVIII, XXX; Benigni 2009, 7–20.
9. For the following, Banker 2003, 129–34; Banker 2013a, 10–13, doc. XIX.
10. Centauro et al. 2000, 216, doc. 0011.
11. Franchi et al. 1989, 367–79.
12. ASF, NA 16740, filza 1441–1493, no. 19, 30 January 1467.

13. Banker 2013a, 82, doc. XCVII.
14. For this discussion, ASCS, Ser. II, reg. 5, fols. 5r–6v; Banker 2013a, 82, doc. XCVI; Gasparotto 2000, 15–22.
15. See the essays by Israëls 2013, 47–67; Silver 2013b, 26–45; Banker 2013b, 69–81; Guazzini and Squillantini 2013, 129–33.
16. Others date the *Saint Julian* to the early 1450s, most recently Dabell 2011, 124–26; the hypothesis that Giglio Cresci commissioned the *Saint Julian* would favor this earlier date for Piero's painting, perhaps just after his residence in Rimini. I wish to thank Guazzini and Squillantini (2013, 129–33) for their design of the church of Sant'Agostino and conversations on the Cresci chapel.
17. Banker 2013a, 55, doc. LXXI. For the Augustinians' acceptance of the bequest for the chapel, ASF, NA 7033, fols. 1r–3r, 84r–v. It should be noted that Giglio did not commission the chapel or the fresco in the name of his patron saint. This was not all that unusual; see Banker 2013b, 72–73.
18. Franklin 1999, 473–75; Banker 2013a, 202–04, doc. CCLIX; Guazzini and Squillantini 2013, 129–33.
19. Salmi 1955, 230–36; Franklin 1999, 473–75; Casciu 2000, 23–37; Dabell 2011, 124–26.
20. ASCS, Ser. II, reg. 2, fols. 94r, 144r; Battisti 1992, II, 482–83.
21. ASF, NA 7049, unfol., 8 June 1457: "Actum in nova residentia magnificorum conservatorum." Verrazzani 2009, 9; Degli Azzi 1914, 178–79; Battisti 1992, II, 483.
22. This drawing, attributed to Remigio Cantagallina, is preserved in the Pinacoteca di Brera, Milan.
23. Battisti 1992, II, 482–83; Salmi, 1975, 276–78, and Fig. 15 (284) for an image of the large door leading into the assembly hall with three coats of arms, including one of the Lorini family. See also Borri Cristelli 1989, 13–15; Verrazzani 2009, 10.
24. Banker 2013a, 108–09, doc. CXXXI.
25. ASCS, Ser. II, reg. 4, fol. 40r–v, 28 February 1460. Borri Cristelli (1989, 20 and n. 26, 31–32) writes that the "official of Danno Dato" (the judge of civil disputes) sent profits from fines to the conservators, who, at least later, paid for expenses and construction in the residence.
26. Some have said that the image has been moved from its original setting, but this has been proved improbable by technical analyses of the wall and the fresco. After the fresco had been painted, this and the adjacent room were vaulted. According to Salmi (1975, 267–75), this occurred around 1470; Battisti 1992, II, 479–80; Borri Cristelli 1989, 13–27.
27. See the analogous comments of Silver (2013b, 26–45) for both the panel painting and the *Volto Santo*.
28. See the essays in Maetzke 1994, esp. that of Schleicher, 60–66.
29. The Pantocrator Christ usually blesses with his right hand while the left holds a book; the gesture and the book are missing in the Sansepolcro *Volto Santo*.
30. See the scintillating essay of Baxandall 2003, 117–61, esp. 125–26.
31. Longhi 2002, 58; Clark 1951, 40; Maetzke 1998, 249.
32. For the Bellini, see the Gemäldegalerie, Berlin; for the Michelangelo, see the British Museum, London.
33. I owe many of my comments here to the discussions of the *giornata di studio* entitled "Indagini conoscitive sull'affresco della *Resurrezione* di Piero della Francesca," 28 February 2011, Museo Civico, Sansepolcro.
34. Gardner von Teuffel 1999, 163–208.

Chapter 8

1. Banker 2013a, 102–03, doc. CXXVI.
2. For the following, Franklin 1991, 193–94; Franklin 1995, 747–50; for the commission document, Banker 2013a, 94–95, doc. CXIV.
3. See the discussion and references of Caracciolo 2012, 54–56; Henry 2009, 28–30.
4. Franklin 1991, 193; Caracciolo, 2012, 54–55, 299.
5. Banker 2013a, 94–95, doc. CXIV.
6. Dabell 2008, 129. Banker 2013a, 101–02, doc. CXXV.
7. Banker 2013a, 102–03, doc. CXXVI.
8. ASCS, Ser. XXXII, reg. 144bis, "Libro de' morti dell'anno 1460 fino all'anno 1519," fols. 16r–30v.
9. Banker 2013a, 103–05, doc. CXXVII.
10. This is the wording of the contract. This confraternity of Arezzo named itself the Annunziata (Annunciated), thereby celebrating the Madonna to whom the angel had already announced her role in bringing the Divine to this world. Fifteenth-century painters differentiated various mental states of Mary in the process of the Annunciation; Baxandall 1974, 49–56.
11. Banker 2013a, 106, 109, docs. CXXVIII, CXXXII.
12. For the following, Lightbown 1992, 183–85.
13. Banker 2013a, 109–10, doc. CXXXIII.

Chapter 9

1. For this discussion of the altarpiece, Lightbown 1992, 218–27, and the essays in Garibaldi 1993.
2. For the following, Balzani 1993, 45–56, and the bibliography cited there.
3. Mancini 1993, 65–72.
4. Banker 2013a, 93–94, doc. CXIII; ASF, NA 16731, fol. 162v; Balzani 1993, 46–47, 51. We should note here that in the 1460s this Pantisilea was in the court of Federico da Montefeltro as an attendant to Battista Sforza.
5. For the documents of the Baglioni–Della Francesca relationship, cf. n. 4 above and Banker 2013a, 187–89, doc CCXLIII
6. Lightbown 1992, 220.
7. For this discussion and the following on technical means employed by Piero, see the essays in Garibaldi 1993, esp. the discussion by Fusetti and Virilli, 137–51.
8. The Augustinians had founded the church in the thirteenth century and had remained there until the mid-1550s, when nuns under the rule of Saint Clare replaced them, forcing them to dismantle Piero's high altar polyptych. The church was desacralized in the eighteenth century and only recently has been restored to a fine Baroque setting; Czortek 2010, 15–66; Banker 2013b, 69–81; Guazzini and Squillantini 2013, 129–33.
9. For this and subsequent documents on Sant'Agostino and its altarpiece, Banker 1987, 645–51; Banker 1996a, 101–04; Polcri 1996a, 73–100, 143–51; Banker 2013a, 42–44, 48–51, docs. LXI, LXVII.
10. For this series of documents, Banker 2001, 210–18; Banker 2009b, II, 568–70, 574, docs. IX, X, XV, XXXIII; Banker 2013a, 15–16, 55–56, docs. XXIV (1426), LXXII.

11. For gesso preparation and carbon black, Bellucci and Frosinini 1998, 89–93; 2009, I, 383–84. Piero may have had to remove old layers of gesso, as the preparation may have so hardened that it would not receive paint, though there is no evidence of old layers having been removed; Bellucci and Frosinini 2009, I, 361–62, n. 3.
12. For the altarpiece, see the essays and documents in Di Lorenzo 1996a, esp. Di Lorenzo 1996b, 13–43; Israëls 2013, 47–67.
13. For a reasoned suggestion that the central panel displayed a *Coronation of the Virgin*, see Israëls 2009, I, 250.
14. Banker 2013a, 63–66, doc. LXXIX.
15. Glasser 1997, App. A, 279–88; Banker 2013a, 111–13, doc. CXXXVII; Di Lorenzo 1996b, 37.
16. Banker 2013a, 66–67, docs. LXXX, LXXXI.
17. Banker 2013b, 69–81; Banker 2013a, 111–14, 128–29, docs. CXXXVII, CXXXVIII, CLIV.
18. Meiss 1941, 53–68, for the following discussion.
19. On the Augustinians and their church, Czortek 2009, 15–66; for Blessed Angelo, Pallone 2009, 89–114.
20. Lavin 2002, 211, 214.
21. See a photomontage and discussion of the altarpiece in Guazzini and Squillantini 2013, 129–33; Di Lorenzo 1996b, 44–46.
22. For the following, Di Lorenzo 1996b, 28–31.
23. Lavin 1995, 14.
24. Banker 2013a, 110–11, doc. CXXXV.
25. Banker 2013a, 111, doc. CXXXVI.
26. The bibliography on the *Flagellation* is immense. Among the many recent attempts to explain the genesis and meaning of the painting, Roeck 2007; Ronchey 2006. The best discussions of the problems surrounding the interpretation of the image are those of Ginzburg 2000, 48–59, and Londei 1991, 29–34.
27. On formal relationships I have followed Lavin. Her discussion of earlier depictions of the *Flagellation* is also excellent; Lavin 1972; Lavin 2002, 80–112.
28. My discussion of the clothing of this and the other figures is informed by the research of Bridgeman 1992, 218–25, and Bridgeman 2002, 76–90.
29. Bridgeman 1992, 219.
30. ASF, NA 19282, fols. 1r–2r, 26 December 1412.
31. ASF, NA 7053, filza 1460–1469, no. 12. "Unam cioppam panni rosadi cum manichis ad mantellum foderatum." On Jacopo, see also Martelli 2012, 45–71.
32. Roeck 2007, 60–63.
33. Banker 2013a, 79–80, doc. XCII.
34. Soranzo 1911, 243ff.
35. Banker 1993b, 163–91; for the death of Carlo Anastagi, ASF, NA 7050. fol. 170v.
36. Lavin (2002, 107–11) has already suggested that the man with the split beard represents Ottaviano Ubaldini.

Chapter 10

1. For Urbino and Federico, Vespasiano 1963, 84–114; Daffra 2007, 53–67; Cerboni Baiardi et al. 1986; Bonvini Mazzanti 2008, 13–19; and the other essays in Peruzzi 2008.

2. For the most persuasive arguments by a modern historian who sees Federico as guilty, Roeck 2007, 11–38.
3. Morolli 1996, 323.
4. I employ the term *Opera* ("works") to designate the then known works of Archimedes. We know that the Greek geometrician had written other treatises that were rediscovered in the twentieth century.
5. Field 1997c, 61–88.
6. Banker 1987, 648–49; Banker 1995a, 27–28, 32, doc. 14; Banker 2013a, 113–14, doc. CXXXVIII. Piero apparently returned to Sansepolcro during the winter of 1470–71; Banker 2013a, 116–17, docs. CXLI, CXLII.
7. Banker 2013a, 115, 117–18, docs. CXL, CXLIII.
8. Peruzzi 1986, I, 243, n. 53. See this essay for an excellent analysis of the court of Federico, 225–96.
9. Angelini 2011a, 59–72; for the following, Gilbert 1968, 29–32 and 91–104, nn. 43–52.
10. I have taken this translation and the following discussion from Zöllner 2005, 23–40.
11. Bellucci and Frosinini 1997, 167–71.
12. Woods-Marsden 1987, 209–16; Woods-Marsden 2002, 91–114.
13. I have taken this translation and much of this discussion from Woods-Marsden 2002, 96, 108–10.
14. Lavin 2002, 258–60.
15. Woods-Marsden 2002, 112–14.

Chapter 11

1. Banker 2013a, 118–19, docs. CXLV, CXLVI.
2. Banker 2013a, 120–22, 122–24, docs. CXLVII–CL, CLII; Centauro et al. 2000, 247–49, doc. 0138 for 5 May 1473.
3. Banker 2013a, 127–30, docs. CLIII, CLV.
4. Banker 1988, 113–14; Banker 2003, 38–39; Gardner von Teuffel 1999, 172.
5. Fanfani 1984, 11–86.
6. Banker 2003, 151–55.
7. On the chapel's location and reconstructions, Mazzalupi 2012, 20–23, 97–99, docs. 34–36.
8. Around 1500 this confraternity divided into male and female sections or became exclusively female; Franklin 1998, 47.
9. ASF, NA 19282, fol. 183r.
10. ASF, NA 7001, fol. 85r–86r, "pro pictura et ornamento capelle gloriosissime Virginis Marie de Abbatia." Banker 2013a, 127–8, doc. CLIII.
11. Israëls 2013, 47–67.
12. Alternately, the subject of the painting might have been an *Assumption of the Virgin*. On this chapel, Mazzalupi 2012, 20–23.
13. ASF, NA 7003, filza "1490–93," fol. [1r].
14. In 1465 the confraterity commissioned a "coronam argentiam con ymagini immaculate verginis Dei genetricis Marie de Abbatie"; Mazzalupi 2012, 106, doc. 47.
15. Banker 2013a, 131, doc. CLVII. The other witness was "Lactantio de Arminio," and one wonders whether this is the later Venetian painter. For the traditional place of confraternal worship on the "balcony," ASF, NA 7032, fol. 164v, 24 December 1451.

16. Banker 2013a, 131–32, doc. CLIX. For the remainder of the payments and the quittance document, Banker 2013a, 132–33, 135–36, docs. CLX, CLXI, CLXV.
17. Salmi 1975, 267–75.
18. Banker 2013a, 108, doc. CXXX.
19. Banker 2013a, 1–2, doc. I; Lavin 2006, Ch. III, "Piero della Francesca and the Joyful Self."
20. Banker 2013a, 98, 196–201, docs. CXVIII, CCLVI. For hypotheses of Piero's designs in the Della Francesca house, Salmi 1975, 276–96.
21. Banker 2013a, 131, doc. CLVIII. Battisti (1992, II, 619, doc. CXXX) titles this an office of "fortifications of the city"; the document expressly states an office for the "walls of the residence."
22. Battisti 1992, II, 619–20, doc. CXXXV.
23. Verrazani 2009, 9–10.
24. ASF, *Balie*, 30, fols. 82v–84v, 31 December 1466; ASF, NA 7043, fol. 88r.
25. Gilbert 2002, 107–16; Simons 2008, 632–64. Piero also painted other elements from classical culture, the pagan god on a column in the *Flagellation of Christ* for example, but they are defined and neutralized by the Christian context. The reverse side of the small Uffizi diptych also has classical references. See the collected sources on the *Hercules*, Manescalchi 2011.
26. See the comments of Lavin 2006, Ch. III.
27. Banker 2003, 154–55.
28. Banker 2013a, 100–01, docs. CXXIII, CXXIV.
29. Banker 2013a, 102–03, doc. CXXVI.
30. Banker 2013a, 133–35, docs. CLXII, CLXIII.

Chapter 12

1. Trevisani 1997, 31–83.
2. On the theme of fidelity, Lavin 1969, 367–71. There were Quattrocento examples of other altarpieces in which princes are depicted as donors without the presence of their living wives, but to use these as evidence that Battista was intentionally and similarly omitted, one would have to demonstrate that the donors and their wives shared the affection and joint rule of Federico and Battista. I find the idea that Piero painted the altarpiece in the mid-1460s unlikely, as he was frequently occupied in Sansepolcro, Arezzo, and Perugia in the period 1464 to 1468.
3. Bertelli 1992, 132. For technical questions about the Brera altarpiece and its relationship to the Urbino diptych, see the fundamental article of Bellucci and Frosinini 1997, 167–87.
4. Lavin 1969, 367–71.
5. Barucca 2007, 232–34, for an excellent introduction to the painting; Garibaldi 2011, 127–28.
6. It is possible that Piero could have left Borgo for a few months in 1479 or that while renting a house in Rimini in 1482, or soon thereafter, he traveled down the Adriatic coast to Senigallia (about 48 miles) at the request of the young couple. However, if the painting is related to Federico, the dates of 1475–77 are almost certain because Piero was otherwise in Borgo from 1472 to just before Federico's death in 1482.
7. For this discussion and its translation, Meiss 1945, 175–81 (176).

8. Saint Bridget took the quote from Saint Bernard of Clairvaux.
9. Field 2005, 115, 119.
10. Garibaldi 2011, 127, citing the conservator Saracini; Battisti 1972, I, 376–77.
11. Alberti also produced a manuscript of *On Painting* in Latin, now known to have been written in 1436. On Alberti's familiarity with Florentine culture, Boschetto 2000; for an excellent comparison of the two treatises, Field 1997c, 61–88.
12. Folkerts (1996, 293–312) for this discussion of Piero and his knowledge of Euclid's two treatises.
13. Of course, Piero might have consulted the other extant or another now lost Quatttrocento copy of the work, but since Urb. Lat. 1329 was copied under the aegis of Francesco del Borgo and later appears in the library of Federico da Montefeltro, it is reasonable to assume that Piero consulted it. Argante Ciocci has informed me that he has located a second manuscript of *On the Diversity of Sight* from the fifteenth century: Milan, Biblioteca Ambrosiana, P. 81 sup.
14. Banker 2005, 165–69.
15. Clergeau 1996, 65–76; Lavin 2002, 219–28.
16. Here as elsewhere I have taken Piero's discussion from the facsimile edition of the Parma MS. of *On Perspective*; Piero della Francesca 1992, fol. 1v.
17. Belle 2007, 94–102.
18. Piero 1992, fol. 16v; translation of Field 1986, 81; Field believes Piero held to the extramission theory.
19. Field 2005, 138–40, 353–54.
20. Piero 1992, fol. 17v.
21. Piero 1992, fol. 32r.
22. Field 1997a, 102–13.
23. Field 1997a, 64.
24. Piero 1992, fol. 59r.
25. Field 2005, 173.
26. For matching images in Piero's treatise and his paintings, see above n. 15.

Chapter 13

1. Banker 2013a, 138, doc. CLXVIII.
2. Banker 2013a, 114–15, doc. CXXXIX; Banker 1995a, 27–8, 32. Matteo di Giovanni, though born in Sansepolcro, won acclaim in his adopted home of Siena. In 1470 he returned to Borgo and painted a processional flag for the Misericordia confraternity.
3. Battisti (1992, II, 557) suggested that the Williamstown *Madonna and Child with Four Angels* was painted by Piero for the chapel of the Pichi in the Badia of Sansepolcro. There are existing documents on the chapel, but these are concerned with its cost and payments to the stonecutter Antonio da Cortona, who constructed it. As one of the priors of the Fraternity of San Bartolomeo, Piero was involved in disentangling financial problems for the Pichi chapel, but in several documents on that chapel there is no mention of a painting or fresco in the chapel and nothing about Piero providing a painting there. He may have offered advice; Di Lorenzo 2012, 85–97; Mazzalupi 2012, 112–16, docs. 56–65, 68.
4. Field 2005, 255–60.

5. See the discussion of Bellucci et al. 2005, 271–77, and Mazzalupi 2012, 39–40.
6. Archivio storico di Stato, Arezzo, Catasto di San Sepolcro, "Chiese e forestieri, 1474," reg. 68, fol. 124r. This register from the 1470s reads "Cappella di S. Lionardo chiamato el Monagato dicta capella di S. Giglio et Arcano, nostri primi autori et protectori."
7. This does not exclude the possibility that the Gherardi family were the patrons of the Williamstown altarpiece for their substantial home. A sixteenth-century member of this family, Cristofano Gherardi called Il Doceno, was an accomplished painter who assisted Vasari and also has been taken to be an informant for Vasari's biographies of painters from Sansepolcro. However, Vasari does not mention this painting among Piero's works; Lightbown 1992, 270–73. On the recent history of the altarpiece, Dabell 2009, 67–71.
8. Bellucci et al. 2005, 274–76.
9. Pacioli 1494, Tractatus I, Dist. 6, fol. 68v. Born in Sansepolcro around 1446, Pacioli became the leading Italian disseminator of mathematical knowledge by the 1490s. Often wrongly assumed to be trained by Piero, Pacioli instead was trained in Venice. He started as a teacher of *abaco* and, by consulting the texts of Euclid and Piero (whom he frequently plagiarized), became a teacher in universities and courts, including the Milanese court of Ludovico Sforza where be befriended Leonardo da Vinci. See Ciocci 2003 and 2009; Ulivi 2009.
10. Banker 1992b, 331–40.
11. For the following discussion, Derenzini 1995, 29–55; Besomi 2009, 105–06.
12. The fifteenth-century manuscripts of Piero's *On Perspective*: Parma, Biblioteca Palatina, cod. 1576; Reggio Emilia, Biblioteca A. Panizzi (Municipale), cod. Reggiano A 41/2; Bordeaux, Bibliothèque Municipale, cod. 616; Milan, Biblioteca Ambrosiana, cod. S. P. 6 bis; and London, British Library, MS. Add. 10366.
13. Besomi 2009, 106.
14. See the translation in Field 2005, Appendix 7, 350–51.
15. Luca Pacioli 1494, fol. 2r; Banker 2012, 7–13.
16. For the evidence of the conclusions presented here on the watermarks, see Banker 2013c, 117–32.
17. Banker 2005, 165–69. I am using the word *Opera* to indicate the then known works of Archimedes. We now know other works that have survived in a manuscript that was not available in the Quattrocento. For the judgment of Piero's borrowing from medieval commentators and Archimedes, see Marshall Clagett's classic research on Archimedes in the Middle Ages and Renaissance (1978, 3, III, 383–415).
18. The other two MSS. from the Quattrocento are in a different MS. tradition: Venice, Biblioteca Marciana, f. a. 327; Nuremberg, Stadtbibliothek, Cent. V. 15.
19. For these manuscripts, Clagett 1978, 3, III, 328–31.
20. Banker 2005, 165–69; Piero assigned the copying of Book II of Archimedes' *De Sphaera et Cilindro* (fols. 20–28) to an unknown scribe.
21. Lazzi 2007, 65–69.
22. For this and the discussion of the Archimedes' MSS. and geometrical figures, see the forthcoming book by Pier Daniele Napolitani and Paolo D'Alessandro. I have been assured by historians of mathematics that Piero could not have drawn the geometrical figures without earlier examples.
23. It is not plausible that Piero used either the Urbino or Paris MS. when he cited Archimedes in his *Little Book* rather than consulting his own Riccardiana MS., or that he created this

latter MS. after having written the *Little Book*. For more complete evidence on the watermarks of Piero's Archimedes manuscript, see Banker 2009a, 73–84.

24. Ciocci 2012, 43–64.
25. Folkerts 1996, 306–07.
26. For Benedetto, ASF, NA 19303 in June 1444.
27. Banker 2013a, 138, 140, docs. CLXVIII, CLXIX.
28. Banker 2013a, 139, doc. CLXX. Battisti notes this document but asserts that it recorded Piero's re-election as a "consigliere"; Battisti 1992, II, 620, doc. CXLVI.
29. Banker 2013a, 142, doc. CLXXIX; ASF, *Statuti Comunità autonome e soggette*, reg. 795, unfol., Ch. XIV.
30. Banker 2013a, 137, doc. CLXVII.
31. Banker 2013a, 140, doc. CLXXII. For the death of Giovanbattista and the listing of his books by his heirs, ASF, NA 16739, no. 55, and for a Latin copy NA 16740, no. 120. Also, on 1 September 1478 Piero stood as *fidejussor* for an unknown office taken by Lucantonio di Bardo dei Paci, but Piero's relationship to this man remains unknown; ASCS, Ser. III, reg. 1, *Tratte*, 19r–v.
32. Banker 2013a, 140, doc. CLXXIV. Ser Niccolò's protocols are numbered NA 7151–NA 7159 in the ASF. For one of many examples of the Della Francesca family employing ser Niccolò, see ASF, NA 7159, filza 1479–1490, no. 3. It should be clear, however, that the Della Francesca employed several notaries.
33. Banker 2013a, 155, doc. CCI.
34. Banker 2013a, 156, doc. CCVI. For Antonio Anastagi as chancellor of San Sepolcro, see Degli Azzi 1914, 117, and for fragments of his chancellor activity in 1458–59, ASCS, Ser. II, reg. 4. Antonio's surviving notarial activity is limited to one protocol, ASF, NA 4115; Banker 2003, 152–53.
35. Banker 2013a, 141, doc. CLXXVI. For a fuller account of this master Matteo, Banker 1992b, 331–40.
36. Banker 2013a, 147, doc. CLXXXVI for the wedding of Romana.
37. Banker 1988, 38–109.
38. Banker 2013a, 141–42, doc. CLXXVIII. ASCS, Ser. II, reg. 1, fol. 30v for the appointment of a substitute prior with no formal oath.
39. Banker 2013a, 143–44, docs. CLXXX (16 October), CLXXXI (23 October).
40. Banker 2013a, 148 doc. CLXXXVIII; for typical rents and sales by the priors; Banker 2013a, 143, 144, docs. CLXXX, CLXXXII.
41. Banker 2013a, 148, doc. CLXXXVII. ASCS, Ser. XXXII, reg. 169, unfol., 8 December 1480; Banker 1988, 100–01.
42. For the letter from Florence, ASF, *Signoria, Carteggi: Missive*, seconda cancelleria 10, fol. 42; for the priors' acts with the Pichi, ASF, NA 12220, fol. 182r. Banker 2013a, 156–57, doc. CCVII. For this chapel and stonemason, Di Lorenzo 2012, 74–83, and Mazzalupi 2012, 112–15, docs. 57–65.
43. Banker 2013a, 150, 156, docs. CXCII (9 January 1481) and CCVI (1 May 1481). Battisti (1992, II, 622–63) cited documents that purportedly show that Piero was also a prior in 1481–82 and 1482–83, but he has misread and misdated the following: docs. CLXXXVII, CLXXXVIII, CXC, CXCIII, and CC.
44. Banker 2013a, 145–47, docs. CLXXXIV–CLXXXVI.
45. Banker 2013a, 159–62, docs. CCXI–CCXIII.

Chapter 14

1. Banker 2013a, 169–70, doc. CCXXVI.
2. A Lodovico Migliorati was a counselor of Pandolfo di Roberto Malatesta and a doctor of law and had an imposing library; Campana 1952, 13–14.
3. Banker 2013a, 182–83, doc. CCXXXVIII. The act of renunciation is not fully written out but has the witnesses and the title in the margin that reads: "Renunciation and donation of the children of Francesco di Gasparre dei Rigi."
4. For the letter I have taken the translation of Field (2005, Appendix 7, 350–51) with some slight changes.
5. Grayson, Dalai Emiliani, and Maccagni, "Introduction," in Piero della Francesca 1995, I, XXII–XXVI.
6. Field (2005, Appendix 7, 351–52) presents Vitruvius' passage and Piero's Latin analogue.
7. For this discussion of the *Little Book*, I am indebted to historians of mathematics, esp. Daly Davis 1977, 44–63; Clagett 1978, 3, III, 390–415; Field 1997b, 241–53, 278–85; Field 2005, 124–26.
8. As mentioned above, Books XIV and XV of the *Elements* were mistakenly attributed to Euclid in the Middles Ages and Renaissance.
9. For the translation and interpolations, Clagett 1978, 3, III, 401–02.
10. Clagett 1978, 3, III, 405–07.
11. Clagett, 1978, 3, III, 407–15; Gamba, Montebelli, Piccinetti 2006, 49–59.
12. Banker 2013a, 170–72, docs. CCXXVIII, CCXXX.
13. Banker 2013a, 202, doc. CCLVIII. In 1514 the Della Francesca family contested the ownership of Piero's patrimony and among three paintings in their possession mentioned a "persepio," by which they refer to *The Nativity*: see Banker 2013a, 204–05, doc. CCLXI.
14. ASF, NA 7155, fols. 32r–33r, 12 February 1495.
15. Lavin 2006, Ch. 3.
16. Lavin 2006, Ch. 3; Maetzke 1998, 284.
17. Lavin 1995, 127–42; Lavin 2002, 298–312; Lavin 2006, Ch. 3.
18. Banker 2013a, 172, doc. CCXXX. And for his death date, see Banker 1992b, 332, and ASCS, Ser. XXXII, reg. 144bis, "Libro de' morti dell'anno 1460 fino all'anno 1519," fol. 101v.
19. Banker 2013a, 187, doc. CCXLII.
20. Banker 2013a, 190–91, doc. CCXLV.
21. Banker 2013a, 187, doc. CCXLI. For earlier Della Francesca involvement in the convent's construction, ASF, NA 7044, fols. 95r–96v, 23 January 1468; ASF, NA 16733, fol. 164r, 13 June 1472.
22. Banker 2013a, 191, doc. CCXLVI.
23. Di Lorenzo 2012, 76–79.
24. Banker 2013a, 172–77, doc. CCXXXI.
25. Banker 2013a, 182, doc. CCXXXVII.
26. Banker 2013a, 182–83, doc. CCXXXVIII.
27. Banker 2013a, 183–87, docs. CCXXXIX and CCXL. For two other documents of the marriage on 16 February 1487 and 29 September 1487 (10 florins), see ASF, NA 6995, unfol.
28. Banker 2013a, 183–86, doc. CCXXXIX.
29. Banker 2013a, 145–47, doc. CLXXXIV, CLXXXV. Battisti 1992, II, 627–28, doc. CCXXIX.
30. Banker 2013a, 190, doc. CCXLIV.
31. Banker 2013a, 191–92, doc. CCXLVII

32. Banker 2013a, 193–94, docs. CCL, CCLII, CCLIII.
33. Banker 2013a, 194–95, doc. CCLIV
34. Banker 2013a, 180, doc. CCXXXV.
35. Banker 2013a, 180–81, doc. CCXXXVI.
36. I had earlier suggested that Jacopo Anastagi had commissioned this chapel, in addition to his chapel in the Badia, in part because Jacopo's wife Amata had the legal right together with the Fraternity and another confraternity to appoint the chapel's chaplain. Perhaps Jacopo or Amata commissioned this chapel of Santa Maria della Reghia or Amata gave land for the chapel. For a full account of Jacopo's chapel, Martelli 2012, 45–71.
37. Banker 2013a, 196–201, doc. CCLVI; see below n. 38 for Piero's copying of some elements of the division.
38. Banker 2013a, 195, doc. CCLV.
39. Battista 1992, II, 642.
40. Banker 2013a, 201, doc. CCLVII.
41. ASCS, Ser. XXXII, reg. 144bis, "Libro de' morti dell'anno 1460 fino all' anno 1519," fol. 116r.

Conclusion

1. For this concept of "mathematization" in Luca Pacioli, Ciocci 2003.
2. Pacioli 1494, Tractatus I, Dist. 6, fol. 68v: "Ne la quale opera, de le diece parole, le nove recercano la proportione."
3. See now the fundamental study of Pacioli, Ciocci 2003.

SELECTED BIBLIOGRAPHY

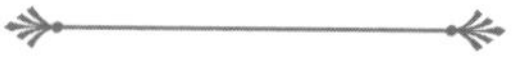

I. Printed Editions of the Works of Piero della Francesca

De prospectiva pingendi, ed. C. Winterberg (Strasburg, 1899).

De prospectiva pingendi, ed. G. Nicco Fasola, 2 vols. (Florence, 1942), republished in 1984 with comments of Eugenio Battisti and F. Ghione.

De prospectiva pingendi, photographic facsimile of Parma manuscript 1576. Bibliographic note by Jane Andrews Aiken, Liana de Girolami Cheney, and Leonardo Farinelli (New York and Williamstown, 1992).

De prospectiva pingendi, De la Perspective en peinture: Ms Parmensus 1576, trans. Jean-Pierre Le Goff, preface by Hubert Damisch (Paris, 1998).

De prospectiva pingendi, facsimile edn., Massimo Mussini and Luigi Grasselli, facsimile of Reggio Emilio Codex, Aboca Ed. (Sansepolcro, 2008).

Libellus de quinque corporibus regularibus, ed. G. Mancini, "L'opera *De corporibus regularibus*, di Pietro Franceschi detto della Francesca usurpata da fra Luca Pacioli," *Memorie della R. Accademia dei Lincei, Classe di scienze morali, storiche e filologiche*, Ser. V, XIV (7), 1915 (Rome, 1916), 441–580.

Libellus de quinque corporibus regularibus, facsimile edn. of Biblioteca Apostolica Vaticana, Urb. Lat. 632, in addition, vol. 1, *Edizione critica del testo*, and vol. 2, *Edizione critica dei disegni*, Scientific Commission, Cecil Grayson, Marisa Dalai Emiliani, Carlo Maccagni, et al. (Florence, 1995).

Trattato d'abaco. Dal codice Ashburnhamiano 280*(359*–291*) della Biblioteca Medicea Laurenziana di Firenze*, ed. and intro. Gino Arrighi (Pisa, 1970).

Trattato d'abaco, anastatic edn. of Biblioteca Medicea Laurenziana, Codex Ashburnham 359*, in addition, vol. 1, *Testo e note*, and vol. 2., *Disegni,* Edizione Nazionale degli scritti di Piero della Francesca, Scientific Commission, Marisa Dalai Emiliani, Ottavio Besomi, Carlo Maccagni, et al. (Rome, 2012).

(Piero's copy of the *Opera* of Archimedes) *L'Archimede di Piero. Contributi di presentazione alla realizzazione facsimilare del Riccardiano* 106, 2 vols., eds. Roberto Manescalchi and Matteo Martelli (Sansepolcro, 2007).

II. Books and Articles Cited in the Text

(*Gli*) *Agostiniani a Sansepolcro e il Beato Angelo Scarpetti* (Tolentino, 2009).

Aguzzoli, M., ed., *La vita e il mondo di Leon Battista Alberti*, 2 vols. (Città di Castello, 2008).

Ahl, Diane Cole, "The Misericordia Altarpiece: Reflections on Spiritual and Visual Culture in Sansepolcro," in Wood, ed., 2002, *The Cambridge Guide to Piero della Francesca*, 14–29.

Andreini, Luigi, *Piero and His City*, tr. Maureen Banker (Sansepolcro, 2009).

Angelini, Alessandro, "Per la cronologia del dittico dei Montefeltro di Piero della Francesca," *Prospectiva*, 141–42 (2011a), 59–72.

Angelini, Alessandro,"Piero della Francesca e la pittura di luce a Roma da Niccolò V a Pio II," *Predella, rivista semestrale di arti visive*, 30 (2011b), 15–27.

Archimides, *Opera omnia cum commentrariis*, 3 vols., ed. Johan L. Heilberg (Leipzig, 1910–15).

Balzani, Serena, "Il monastero e il politico: Dati d'archivio e memorie," in Garibaldi, ed., 1993, *Piero della Francesca: Il polittico di Sant'Antonio*, 45–56.

Banker, James R., "Piero della Francesca's S. Agostino Altarpiece: Some New Documents," *The Burlington Magazine*, 129 (1987), 645–51.

Banker, James R., *Death in the Community: Memorialization and Confraternities in an Italian Commune in the Late Middle Ages* (Athens, GA, 1988).

Banker, James R., "Un documento inedito sull'attività di Piero della Francesca per la chiesa di S. Francesco in Borgo San Sepolcro," *Rivista d'arte*, Ser. 4, VI (1990), 245–47.

Banker, James R., "The Program for the Sassetta Altarpiece in the Church of San Francesco in Borgo San Sepolcro," *I Tatti Studies*, 4 (1991), 11–58.

Banker, James R., "Piero della Francesca, il fratello Don Francesco di Benedetto e Francesco dal Borgo," *Prospectiva*, 68 (1992a), 54–56.

Banker, James R., "Piero della Francesca's Friend and Translator: Maestro Matteo di ser Paolo d'Anghiari," *Rivista d'arte* (1992b, 1993), Ser. 4, VIII, 331–40.

Banker, James R., "Piero della Francesca as Assistant to Antonio d'Anghiari in the 1430s: Some Unpublished Documents," *The Burlington Magazine*, 135 (1993a), 16–21.

Banker, James R., "A Legal and Humanistic Library in Borgo San Sepolcro in the Middle of the Fifteenth Century," *Rinascimento*, 33 (1993b), 163–91.

Banker, James R., "The Altarpiece of the Confraternity of Santa Maria della Misericordia in Borgo Sansepolcro," in Lavin, ed., 1995a, *Piero della Francesca and His Legacy*, 21–35.

Banker, James R., "Soluzione di uno degli enigmi della *Flagellazione* di Piero della Francesca," in Uguccioni, ed., 1995b, *Incontri sulla biografia di Piero della Francesca*, 20–31.

Banker, James R., "Un documento inedito sul polittico di Sant'Agostino," in Di Lorenzo, ed., 1996a, *Il polittico Agostiniano di Piero della Francesca*, 101–04.

Banker, James R., "Piero della Francesca: Gli anni giovanili e l'inizio della sua carriera," in Cieri Via, ed., 1996b, *Città e corte nell'Italia di Piero della Francesca*, 40–46.

Banker, James R., "The Second 'Casa di Piero della Francesca' and Hypotheses on Piero's Studio: His Role as a Builder in Borgo San Sepolcro," in Osti, ed., 1999, *Mosaics of Friendship*, 147–62.

Banker, James R., "Piero della Francesca, the Carpentered Altarpiece of San Francesco, His Sant'Agostino Polyptych, and Quattrocento High Altarpieces in Borgo San Sepolcro," *Arte cristiana*, 89 (2001), 210–18.

Banker, James R., *The Culture of San Sepolcro during the Youth of Piero della Francesca* (Ann Arbor, MI, 2003).

Banker, James R., "Contributi alla cronologia della vita e delle opere di Piero della Francesca," *Arte cristiana*, 92 (2004), 248–58.

Banker, James R., "A Manuscript of the Works of Archimedes in the Hand of Piero della Francesca," *The Burlington Magazine*, 147 (2005), 165–69.

Banker, James R., "Piero della Francesca e il manoscritto 106 sulle opere di Archimede," in Manescalchi and Martelli, eds., 2007a, *L'Archimede di Piero*, 1–12, 56–64.

Banker, James R., "Piero e i suoi libri a Sansepolcro," in Bertelli and Paolucci, eds., 2007b, *Piero della Francesca e le corti italiane*, 7–11.

Banker, James R., "Un manoscritto finora sconosciuto dell''Opera' di Archimede di mano di Piero della Francesca e la rinascita della scienza greca a Roma," *1492. Rivista della Fondazione Piero della Francesca*, Anno I, nos. 1–2 (2008), 15–23.

Banker, James R., "The Watermarks of the Manuscripts of Archimedes in the Quattrocento: Dating Piero della Francesca's Riccardiana Lat. 106," *1492. Rivista della Fondazione Piero della Francesca*, Anno II, no. 2 (2009a), 73–84.

Banker, James R., "Appendix of Documents Relating to the High Altarpiece, the High Altar, and the Tomb of the Blessed Ranieri in the Church of San Francesco in Borgo San Sepolcro," in Israëls, ed., 2009, *Sassetta: The Borgo San Sepolcro Altarpiece*, II, 566–83.

Banker, James R., "Documenti relativi alla Compagnia di Santa Maria della Misericordia e alla tavola di Piero della Francesca," in Betti, Frosinini, and Refice, eds., 2010a, *Ripensando Piero della Francesca: Il polittico della Misericordia*, 15–30.

Banker, James R., "La vita culturale a Sansepolcro nel Quattrocento," in Czortek, ed., 2010b, *La nostra storia: Lezioni sulla storia di Sansepolcro*, 331–53.

Banker, James R., "The Mystery of Piero della Francesca's Presumed Urbino Manuscript of *De prospectiva pingendi*," *1492. Rivista della Fondazione Piero della Francesca*, Anno IV, nos. 1–2 (2011)/ Anno V, nos. 1–2 (2012), 2012, 7–13.

Banker, James R., *Documenti fondamentali per la conoscenza della vita e dell'arte di Piero della Francesca*, in Collana, Fonti 3, Istituzione Culturale Biblioteca Museo Archivi storici, Città di Sansepolcro (Selci-Lama, 2013a).

Banker, James R., "Piero della Francesca: The Commission and Completion of the Sant'Agostino Altarpiece," in Silver, ed., 2013b, *Piero della Francesca in America*, 68–81.

Banker, James R., "Dating Piero della Francesca's Treatises *Trattato d'abaco* and *De prospectiva pingendi*: Research on the Watermarks of the Painter's Manuscripts," *Pagine Altotiberine*, 50 (2013c), 117–32.

Banker, James R., and Lowe, Kate J., "Female Voice, Male Authority: A Nun's Narrative of the Regularization of a Female Franciscan House in Borgo San Sepolcro in 1500," *The Sixteenth Century Journal*, 40 (2009), 651–77.

Barucca, Gabriele, Catalog entry in Bertelli and Paolucci, eds., 2007, *Piero della Francesca e le corti italiane*, 232–34.

Battisti, Eugenio, *Piero della Francesca*, 2 vols. (Milan, 1971); new edn., Marisa Dalai Emiliani, ed., 2 vols. (Milan, 1992).

Battisti, Eugenio, "Alcuni accenni al dibattito pierfrancescano in corso," in *Convegno internazionale sulla "Madonna del Parto" di Piero della Francesca* (Città di Castello, 1982), 189–91.

Baxandall, Michael, "A Dialogue on Art from the Court of Leonello d'Este: Angelo Decembrio's *De Politia Litteraria*, Pars LXVIII," *Journal of the Warburg and Courtauld Institutes*, 26 (1963), 304–26.

Baxandall, Michael, *Painting and Experience in Renaissance Italy*, ppb. edn. (New York, 1974).

Baxandall, Michael, *Words into Pictures* (New Haven, CT, 2003).

Beck, James, "Una data per Piero della Francesca," *Prospettiva*, 25 (1978), 53.

Beck, James, "Piero della Francesca. Un 'peregrinaggio' storico-artistico," in Centauro, Settesoldi, and Beck, eds., 2000, *Piero della Francesca: Committenza e pittura nella chiesa di S. Francesco ad Arezzo.*

Belle, Riccardo, "Piero della Francesca e i manoscritti scientifici: il caso dell'ottica," in Manescalchi and Martelli, eds., 2007, *L'Archimede di Piero*, II, 94–102.

Bellosi, Luciano, "Giovanni di Piamonte e gli affreschi di Piero ad Arezzo," *Prospettiva*, 50 (1987), 15–35.

Bellosi, Luciano, "Sulla formazione fiorentino di Piero della Francesca," in Bellosi, ed., 1992, *Una scuola per Piero. Luce, colore, perspectiva nella formazione fiorentino di Piero della Francesca*, 17–54.

Bellosi, Luciano, ed., *Pittura di luce: Giovanni di Francesco e l'arte fiorentina di metà Quattrocento*, exh. cat. (Milan, 1990).

Bellosi, Luciano, ed., *Una scuola per Piero. Luce, colore, perspectiva nella formazione fiorentino di Piero della Francesca* (Venice, 1992).

Bellucci, Roberto, and Frosinini, Cecilia, "Ipotesi sul metodo di restituzione dei disegni preparatori di Piero della Francesca: il caso dei ritratti di Federico da Montefeltro," in Daffra and Trevisani, eds., 1997, *La pala di San Bernardino*, 167–87.

Bellucci, Roberto, and Frosinini, Cecilia, "Piero della Francesca's Process: Panel Painting Technique," in Roy and Smith, eds., 1998, *Painting Techniques: History, Materials and Studio Practice*, 89–93.

Bellucci, Roberto, and Frosinini, Cecilia, "La pianificazione dell'opera e il disegno preparatorio nel polittico della Misericordia," in Betti, Frosinini, and Refice, eds., 2010, *Ripensando Piero della Francesca: Il polittico della Misericordia*, 189–202.

Bellucci, Roberto, et al., "Piero della Francesca: *Madonna and Child Attended by Angels*," Catalog entry in Christiansen, ed., 2005, *From Filippo Lippi to Piero della Francesca*, 271–77.

Belting, Hans, *Florence and Baghdad: Renaissance Art and Arab Science*, trans. Deborah Lucas Schneider (Cambridge and London, 2011).

Benati, Daniele, Natale, Mauro, and Paolucci, Antonio, eds., *Melozzo da Forlì: L'umana bellezza tra Piero della Francesca e Raffaello* (Milan, 2011).

Benigni, Paola, "Su alcuni documenti 'perduti' relativi alla *Madonna del Parto*," *1492. Rivista della Fondazione Piero della Francesca*, Anno II, no. 2 (2009), 7–20.

Bensi, Paolo, "Il ruolo di Piero della Francesca nello sviluppo della tecnica pittorica del Quattrocento," in Dalai Emiliani and Curzi, eds., 1996, *Piero della Francesca tra arte e scienza*, 167–81.

Bertelli, Carlo, *Piero della Francesca: La forza divina della pittura* (Milan, 1991).

Bertelli, Carlo, *Piero della Francesca*, trans. Edward Farrelly (New Haven, CT, and London, 1992).

Bertelli, Carlo, "Piero e la storia," in Maetzke and Bertelli, eds., 2001, *Piero della Francesca. La Leggenda della Vera Croce in San Francesco ad Arezzo*, 11–25.

Bertelli, Carlo, "Piero da Perugia a Urbino," in Bertelli and Paolucci, eds., 2007, *Piero della Francesca e le corti italiane* (Milan, 2007), 29–46.

Bertelli, Carlo, and Paolucci, Antonio, eds., *Piero della Francesca e le corti italiane* (Milan, 2007).

Berti, Luciano, ed., *Nel raggio di Piero: La pittura nell'Italia centrale nell'età di Piero della Francesca* (Venice, 1992).

Bertolini, Lucia, "Sulla precedenza della redazione volgare del *De pictura* di Leon Battista Alberti," in Santagata and Stussi, eds., 2000, *Studi per Umberto Carpi*, 181–210.

Bertolini, Lucia, "Come 'pubblicava' l'Alberti: ipotesi preliminari," in Zaccarello and Tomasin, eds., 2004, *Storia della lingua e filologia*, 219–40.

Besomi, Ottavio, "Edizione Nazionale degli scritti di Piero della Francesca: Criteri di studio per il *Trattato d'abaco* e *De prospectiva pingendi*," *Scholion*, 1 (2002), 140–43.

Besomi, Ottavio, "I lavori in corso per l'edizione del *De prospectiva pingendi*," *1492. Rivista della Fondazione Piero della Francesca*, Anno II, no. 2 (2009), 105–06.

Besomi, Ottavio, and Sorci, Alessandra, "Edizione Nazionale degli scritti di Piero della Francesca: Criteri di studio per il *Trattato d'abaco* e *De prospectiva pingendi*," *Scholion*, 3 (2004), 150–59.

Betti, Mariangela, Frosinini, Cecilia, and Refice, Paola, eds., *Ripensando Piero della Francesca: Il polittico della Misericordia di San Sepolcro, storia, studi e indagini tecnico-scientifiche* (Florence, 2010 [2012]).

Black, Robert, "Humanism and Education in Renaissance Arezzo," *I Tatti Studies*, 2 (1987), 173–237.

Black, Robert, *Studio e scuola in Arezzo durante il medioevo e il rinascimento* (Arezzo, 1996).

Bonvini Mazzanti, Marinella, "Politica e cultura," in Peruzzi, ed., 2008, *Ornatissimo Codice*, 13–19.

Borri Cristelli, L., "Il Palazzo della Residenza e la *Resurrezione* di Piero della Francesca," in *Ricerche su Piero*, 1989, 7–33.

Borsook, Eve, *The Mural Painters of Tuscany from Cimabue to Andrea del Sarto*, 2nd edn. rev. and enlarged (Oxford 1980).

Boschetto, Luca, *Leon Battista Alberti e Firenze: Biografia, storia, letteratura* (Florence, 2000).

Boskovits, Miklos, "Il San Nicola da Tolentino di Piero della Francesca restaurato," *Arte cristiana*, 81 (1995), 227–30.

Bridgeman, Jane, "'Belle considerazioni': Dress in the Works of Piero della Francesca," *Apollo*, 136 (1992), 218–25.

Bridgeman, Jane, "'Troppo belli e troppo eccellenti': Observations on Dress in the work of Piero della Francesca," in Wood, ed., 2002, *The Cambridge Companion to Piero della Francesca*, 76–90.

Briquet, Charles Moïse, *Les Filigranes: Dictionnaire historique des marques du papier dès leur apparition vers 1282 jusqu'en 1600* (Paris, 1907), rpt. edn., 4 vols. (Mansfield Center, CT, 2000).

Broglio Tartaglia, Gaspare, *Cronaca Malatestiana del secolo XV (dalla Cronaca universale)*, ed. Antonio G. Luciani (Rimini, 1982).

Buonocore, Marco, ed., *Vedere I classici: L'illustrazione libraria dei testi antichi dall'età romana al tardo medioevo* (Rome, 1996).

Burke, Peter, *The Italian Renaissance: Culture and Society in Italy*, rev. ppb. edn. (Princeton, NJ, 1987).

Calvesi, Maurizio, *Piero della Francesca* (Milan, 1998).

Calzona, A., "Leon Battista Alberti e l'architettura: un rapporto complesso," in Aguzzoli, ed., 2008, *La vita e il mondo di Leon Battista Alberti*, II, 471–515.

Camaiti, Cristina, "Donatello e Michele da Firenze nel *fonte* del Duomo di Arezzo," *Bollettino d'informazione Brigata aretina degli amici dei monumenti*, 41 (2007), 17–32.

Campana, Augusto, "Due note su Roberto Campana," *Studi Riminesi e bibliografici in onore di Carlo Lucchesi, Società di Studi Romagnoli* (Faenza, 1952), 13–14.

Cappel, Carmen Bambach, "Piero della Francesca, the Study of Perspective and the Development of the Cartoon in the Quattrocento," in Dalai Emiliani and Curzi, eds., 1996, *Piero della Francesca tra arte e scienza*, 143–66.

Caracciolo, Raffaele, "'Molto nella sua giovinezza si sforzò d'imitare il maestrro': Signorelli e Piero della Francesca," in De Chirico et al., eds., 2012, *Luca Signorelli*, 49–57.

Carminati, Marco, *Piero della Francesca* (Milan, 2003).

Carter, B. A. R., "A Mathematical Interpretation of Piero della Francesca's *Baptism of Christ*," in Lavin, ed., 1981, *Piero della Francesca's "Baptism of Christ,"* 149–63.

Casciu, Stefano, ed., *L'"Ascensione" di Cristo del Perugino* (Milan, 1998).

Casciu, Stefano, ed., "L'*Ascensione di Cristo* di Pietro Perugino nella Cattedrale di San Sepolcro: certezze ed ipotesi per la storia del dipinto in margine al restauro," in Casciu, ed., 1998, *L'"Ascensione" di Cristo del Perugino*, 11–42.

Casciu, Stefano, ed., "Il restauro del San Ludovico di Tolosa," in Gasparotto, ed., 2000, *Il restauro del San Ludovico di Piero della Francesca*, 23–37.

Cavigli, Rossella, "Osservazioni sulla tecnica pittorica del *Polittico della Misericordia*," in Betti, Frosinini, and Refice, eds., 2010, *Ripensando Piero della Francesca*.

Centauro, Giuseppe, *Dipinti murali di Piero della Francesca. La basilica di S. Francesco ad Arezzo: Indagini su sette secoli* (Milan 1990).

Centauro, Giuseppe, Settesoldi, Enzo, and Beck, James, eds., *Piero della Francesca: Committenza e pittura nella chiesa di S. Francesco ad Arezzo (con nuovi documenti inediti)* (Poggibonsi, 2000).

Cerboni Baiardi, Giorgio, Chittolini, Giorgio, and Floriani, Piero, eds., *Federico di Montefeltro: Lo stato, le arti, la cultura*, 3 vols. (Tivoli, 1986).

Ceriana, Matteo, ed., *Fra Carnevale: Un artista rinascimentale da Filippo Lippi a Piero della Francesca*, exh. cat. (Milan, 2004).

Christiansen, Keith, "Alcune osservazioni critiche sulla pala di Perugia e sulla sua collocazione nella carriera di Piero della Francesca," in Garibaldi, ed., 1993, *Piero della Francesca: Il polittico di Sant'Antonio*, 117–24.

Christiansen, Keith, ed., *From Filippo Lippi to Piero della Francesca: Fra Carnevale and the Making of a Renaissance Master*, exh. cat. (New York, 2005).

Christiansen, Keith, Kanter, Laurence, and Strehlke, Karl, eds., *Painting in Renaissance Siena, 1420–1500* (New York, 1988).

Cieri Via, Claudia, ed., *Città e corte nell'Italia di Piero della Francesca* (Venice, 1996).

Ciocci, Argante, *Luca Pacioli e la matematizzazione del sapere nel Rinascimento* (Bari, 2003).

Ciocci, Argante, *Luca Pacioli tra Piero della Francesca e Leonardo* (Perugia, 2009).

Ciocci, Argante, "L'Archimede latino di Jacopo da Cremona, Francesco dal Borgo e Piero della Francesca," *1492. Rivista della Fondazione Piero della Francesca*, Anno IV, nos. 1–2 (2011) / Anno V, nos. 1–2 (2012), 2012, 43–64.

Clagett, Marshall, *Archimedes in the Middle Ages*, 3 vols., esp. *The Fate of the Medieval Archimedes, 1300–1565*, vol. 3, *The Medieval Archimedes in the Renaissance, 1450–1565*, pt. III (Philadephia, PA, 1978).

Clark, Kenneth, *Piero della Francesca* (London, 1951), 2nd edn. (Ithaca, NY, 1981).

Clergeau, Marie Françoise, "Du *De prospectiva pingendi* à la peinture de Piero: quel lien?," in Dalai Emiliani and Curzi, eds., 1996, *Piero della Francesca tra arte e scienza*, 65–76.

Clough, Cecil H., "Federigo da Montefeltro's Patronage of the Arts, 1468–1482," *Journal of the Warburg and Courtauld Institutes*, 36 (1973), 129–44.

Cobianchi, Roberto, "Franciscan Legislation, Patronage Practice, and New Iconography in Sassetta's Commission at Borgo San Sepolcro," in Israëls, ed., 2009, *Sassetta: The Borgo San Sepolcro Altarpiece*, I, 107–19.

Cooper, Donal, "Franciscan Choir Enclosures and the Function of Double-Sided Altarpieces in Pre-Tridentine Umbria," *Journal of the Warburg and Courtauld Institutes*, 64 (2001), 1–54.

Cooper, Donal, and Banker, James R., "The Church of San Francesco in Borgo San Sepolcro in the Late Middle Ages and Renaissance," in Israëls, ed., 2009, *Sassetta: The Borgo San Sepolcro Altarpiece*, I, 53–105.

Corazzini (di Bulciano), Francesco, *Appunti storici e filologici su la Valle Tiberina Superiore*, rpt. (Città di Castello, 1994).

Czortek, Andrea, "I frati eremiti di Sant'Agostino a Sansepolcro nei secoli XIII e XIV," in *Gli Agostiniani a Sansepolcro e il Beato Angelo Scarpetta*, 2009, 15–66.

Czortek, Andrea, ed., *La nostra storia: Lezioni sulla storia di sansepolcro (novembre/dicembre 2009–aprile/maggio 2010)*, I, *Antichità e Medioevo* (Sansepolcro, 2010).

Dabell, Frank, "Antonio d'Anghiari e gli inizi di Piero della Francesca," *Paragone/Arte*, 417 (1984a), 73–94.

Dabell, Frank, "Un Senese a Sansepolcro: documenti per Pietro di Giovanni d'Ambrogio," *Riviste d'arte*, 24 (1984b), 361–71.

Dabell, Frank, "Domenico Veneziano in Arezzo and the Problem of Vasari's Painter Ancestor," *The Burlington Magazine*, 127 (1985), 29–32.

Dabell, Frank, "New Documents for the History of the Compagnia della SS. Trinità in Arezzo," *Arte cristiana*, 79 (1991), 412–17.

Dabell, Frank, "Piero della Francesca e la committenza francescana: appunti per un'indagine," in Garibaldi, ed., 1993, *Piero della Francesca: Il polittico di Sant'Antonio*, 73–78.

Dabell, Frank, "Piero della Francesca e i pittori prospettici," in Fornasari, Gentilini, and Giannotti, eds., 2008, *Arte in terra d'Arezzo: Il Quattrocento*, 107–29.

Dabell, Frank, "Florence, 1837: A Note on the Provenance of the Williamstown Madonna by Piero della Francesca," *1492. Rivista della Fondazione Piero della Francesca*, Anno II, no. 2 (2009), 67–71.

Dabell, Frank, "Piero della Francesca, San Giuliano," Catalog entry in Benati, Natale, and Paolucci, eds., 2011, *Melozzo da Forlì: L'umana bellezza tra Piero della Francesca e Raffaello*, 124–26.

Daffra, Emanuela, "Urbino e Piero della Francesca," in Bertelli and Paolucci, eds., 2007, *Piero della Francesca e le corti italiane*, 53–67.

Daffra, Emanuela, and Trevisani, Filippo, eds., *La pala di San Bernardino di Piero della Francesca: Nuovi studi oltre il restauro* (Florence 1997).

Dalai Emiliani, Marisa, and Curzi, Valter, eds., *Piero della Francesca tra arte e scienza* (Venice 1996).

Daly Davis, Margaret, *Piero della Francesca's Mathematical Treatises: The "Trattato d'abaco" and "Libellus de quinque corporibus regularibus"* (Ravenna, 1977).

De Chirico, Fabio, et al., eds., *Luca Signorelli* (Milan, 2012).

Degli Azzi, Giustiniano, "Inventario degli archivi di S. Sepolcro," *Gli archivi della Storia d'Italia*, 2nd ser., 4 (Rocca S. Cassiano, 1914).

Delucca, Oreste, *I poderi della Ghirlandetta a Rimini dai Malatesta ai fratelli Davide e Luigi Fabbri* (Rimini, 2008).

De Marchi, Andrea, "Identità di Giuliano Amadei miniatore," *Bollettino d'arte*, 93–94 (1995), 119–58.

De Marchi, Andrea, "Antonio di Anghiari e gli inizi di Piero," in Fornasari, Gentilini, and Giannotti, eds., 2008a, *Arte in terra d'Arezzo: Il Quattrocento*, 99–106.

De Marchi, Andrea, "Ancona, porta della cultura adriatica. Una linea pittorica, da Andrea de' Bruni a Nicola di maestro Antonio," in De Marchi and Mazzalupi, eds., 2008b, *Pittori ad Ancona nel Quattrocento*, 16–95.

De Marchi, Andrea, and Mazzalupi, Matteo, eds., *Pittori ad Ancona nel Quattrocento* (Milan, 2008).

De Marchi, Andrea, and Valazzi, M. R., eds., *Il Rinascimento a Urbino. Fra' Carnevale e gli artisti del Palazzo di Federico* (Milan 2005).

Derenzini, Giovanna, "Note autografe di Piero della Francesca nel codice 616 della Bibliothèque Muncipale di Bordeaux. Per la storia testuale del *De prospectiva pingendi*," *Filologia antica e moderna*, 9 (1995), 29–55.

Derenzini, Giovanna, "Considerazioni preliminari sul codice Vaticano Urbinate Latino 632, unico testimone del *Libellus* di Piero della Francesca," in Dalai Emiliani and Curzi, eds., 1996, *Piero della Francesca tra arte e scienza*, 269–76.

Di Lorenzo, Andrea, ed., *Il polittico Agostiniano di Piero della Francesca*, exh. cat., Museo Poldi Pezzoli (Turin, 1996a).

Di Lorenzo, Andrea, ed., "Il polittico Agostiniano di Piero della Francesca: dispersione, collezionismo, restauri, ricostruzione," in Di Lorenzo, ed., 1996b, *Il polittico Agostiniano di Piero della Francesca*, 13–43.

Di Lorenzo, Andrea, ed., "Registo fiorentino," in Ceriana, ed., 2004, *Fra Carnevale: Un artista rinascimentale da Filippo Lippi a Piero della Francesca*, 290–303.

Di Lorenzo, Andrea, ed., "I Pichi di Sansepolcro e le loro commissioni artistiche nel Quattrocento," in Betti, Frosinini, and Refice, eds., 2010, *Ripensando Piero della Francesca*, 85–97.

Di Lorenzo, Andrea, ed., "La Cappella Pichi, la Fraternita di San Bartolomeo e Piero della Francesca," in Di Lorenzo, Martelli, and Mazzalupi, 2012, *La Badia di Sansepolcro nel Quattrocento*, 73–86.

Di Lorenzo, Andrea, ed., Martelli, Cecilia, and Mazzalupi, Matteo, *La Badia di Sansepolcro nel Quattrocento* (Selci-Lama, 2012).

Donati, Angela, "Il recupero dell'antichità classica," in *Il potere, le arti, la guerra* 2001, 39–40.

Fanfani, Amintore, *Un mercante del Trecento*, rpt. edn. (Città di Castello, 1984).

Field, J. V., "Piero della Francesca's Treatment of Edge Distortion," *Journal of the Warburg and Courtauld Institutes*, 49 (1986), 66–90.

Field, J. V., *The Invention of Infinity: Mathematics and Art in the Renaissance* (Oxford, 1997a).

Field, J. V., "Rediscovering the Archimedean Polyhedra," *Archive for the History of Exact Sciences*, 50, nos. 3–4 (1997b), 241–89.

Field, J. V., "Alberti, the Abacus and Piero della Francesca's Proof of Perspective," *Renaissance Studies*, 11 (1997c), 61–88.

Field, J. V., *Piero della Francesca: A Mathematician's Art* (London and New Haven, CT, 2005).

Folkerts, Menso, "Piero della Francesca and Euclid," in Dalai Emiliani and Curzi, eds., 1996, *Piero della Francesca tra arte e scienza*, 293–312.

Fornasari, Liletta, Gentilini, Giancarlo, and Giannotti, Alessandra, eds., *Arte in terra d'Arezzo: Il Quattrocento* (Firenze, 2008).

Franceschini, Adriano, *Artisti a Ferrara in età umanistica e rinascimentale. Testimonianze archivistiche*, II, 1 (Ferrara, 1995).

Franchi, Roberto, et al., "Stato di conservazione e tecnica di esecuzione," in *Un progetto per Piero della Francesca*, 1989, 367–79.

Franklin, David, "An Unrecorded Commission for Piero della Francesca in Arezzo," *The Burlington Magazine*, 133 (1991), 193–94.

Franklin, David, "A Gonfalone Banner by Giorgio Vasari Reassembled," *The Burlington Magazine*, 137 (1995), 747–50.

Franklin, David, "Il patrocinio della palla del Perugino per l'altar maggiore dell'Abbazia di Sansepolcro," in Casciu, ed., 1998, *L'"Ascensione di Cristo" del Perugino*, 43–51.

Franklin, David, "Piero della Francesca's *St Julian* at Sansepolcro," *The Burlington Magazine*, 141 (1999), 473–75.

Frommel, Christoph L., "Francesco del Borgo: Architekt Pius' II. und Pauls II.," *Römisches Jahrbuch für Kunstgeschichte*, 20 (1983), 108–54; 21 (1984), 129–38.

Frommel, Christoph L., *Architettura e committenza da Alberti a Bramante* (Città di Castello, 2006).

Fusetti, Sergio, and Paolo Virilli, "Il restauro," in Garibaldi, ed., 1993, *Piero della Francesca: Il polittico di Sant'Antonio*, 137–51.

Gamba, Enrico, "Matematica e prospettiva in Leon Battista Alberti e in Piero della Francesca," in *Il potere, le arti, la guerra*, 2001, 76–81.

Gamba, Enrico, and Montebelli, Vico, "La geometria nel *Trattato d'abaco* e nel *Libellus de quinque corporibus regularibus* di Piero della Francesca: raffronto critico," in Dalai Emiliana and Curzi, eds., 1996, *Piero della Francesca tra arte e scienza*, 253–68.

Gamba, Enrico, Montebelli, Vico, and Picccinetti, P., "La matematica di Piero della Francesca," *Lettera matematica PRISTEM*, 59 (2006), 49–59.

Gardner von Teuffel, Christa, "The Buttressed Altarpiece: A Forgotten Aspect of Tuscan Fourteenth-Century Altar Design," *Jahrbuch der Berliner Museen*, 21 (1979), 21–65.

Gardner von Teuffel, Christa, "Niccolò di Segna, Sassetta, Piero della Francesca and Perugino: Cult and Continuity at Sansepolcro," *Städel Jahrbuch*, 17 (1999), 163–208.

Garibaldi, Vittoria, ed., *Piero della Francesca: Il polittico di Sant'Antonio* (Perugia, 1993).

Garibaldi, Vittoria, ed., "Piero della Francesca, *San Giuliano*," Catalog entry in Benati, Natale, and Paolucci, eds., 2011, *Melozzo da Forlì: L'umana bellezza tra Piero della Francesca e Raffaello*, 127–28.

Gasparotto, Davide, ed., *Il restauro del San Ludovico di Piero della Francesca* (Lama, 2000).

Gasparotto, Davide, ed., "Il San Ludovico di Tolosa del Museo Civico di Sansepolcro: qualche considerazione sulla vicenda storica e critica," in Gasparatto, ed., 2000, *Il restauro di San Ludovico di Piero della Francesca*, 15–22.

Gherardi Dragomanni, Francesco, *Vita di Piero della Francesca pittore del Borgo San Sepolcro scritta da Giorgio Vasari Aretino, dedicate a Giuseppe Franceschi Marini in occasione del suo matrimonio da Margherita vedova Pichi* (Florence, 1835).

Gilbert, Creighton, *Change in Piero della Francesca* (Locust Valley, NY, 1968).

Gilbert, Creighton, "The *Hercules* in Piero's House," *Artibus et historiae*, 23, no. 45 (2002), 107–16.

Ginzburg, Carlo, *Indagini su Piero* (Turin, 1981), trans. M. Ryle and K. Soper as *The Enigma of Piero* (London, 1985); rev. edn. with appendices (London and New York, 2000).

Giorni, Bruno, *La Madonna del Parto di Piero di Piero della Francesca e la chiesa di Momentana* (Sansepolcro, n.d.)

Giusti, Enrico, "L'algebra nel *Trattato d'abaco* di Piero della Francesca: osservazioni e congetture," *Bollettino di storia delle scienze matematiche*, 11, no. 2 (1991), 55–83.

Giusti, Enrico, "Fonti medievali dell'*Algebra* di Piero della Francesca," in Dalai Emiliani and Curzi, eds., 1996, *Piero della Francesca tra arte e scienza*, 313–29.

Glasser, Hannelore, *Artists' Contracts of the Early Renaissance* (New York and London, 1977).

Gore, Andrea, "La chiesa e l'oratorio dell'ospedale della Misericordia: due ambienti per il polittico di Piero della Francesca," in Betti, Frosinini, and Refice, eds., 2010, *Ripensando Piero della Francesca*, 43–53.

Grafton, Anthony, *Leon Battista Alberti: Master Builder of the Italian Renaissance* (New York, 2000).

Graziani, Anton Maria, *De Scriptis invita Minerva*, 2 vols. (Florence, 1746).

Grendler, Paul, "What Piero Learned in School: Fifteenth-Century Vernacular Education," in Lavin, ed., 1995, *Piero della Francesca and His Legacy*, 161–74.

Guazzini, Giacomo, and Squillantini, Elena, "Appendix," in Silver, ed., 2013a, *Piero della Francesca in America*, 129–33.

Hendy, Philip, *Piero della Francesca and the Early Renaissance* (London and New York, 1968).

Henry, Tom, "One Picture, Ten Names, and a Proposal for the Early Career of Luca Signorelli," *1492. Rivista della Fondazione Piero della Francesca*, Anno II, no. 2 (2009), 21–40.

Hope, Charles, "The Early History of the Tempio Malatestiano," *Journal of the Warburg and Courtauld Institutes*, 55 (1992), 51–154.

Hope, Charles, and Taylor, P., "Piero's Flagellation and the Conventions of Painted Narrative," in Uguccioni, ed., 1995, *Incontri sulla biografia di Piero della Francesca*, 48–101.

Iannucci, Maria, "Il castello, a decoro della città," in *Il potere, le arti, la guerra*, 2001, 82–88.

Israëls, Machtelt, "Polyptychs without Paintings: Sassetta, Piero della Francesca, and the Rejection of Unpainted Altarpieces," in Israëls, ed., 2009, *Sassetta: The Borgo San Sepolcro Altarpiece*, 243–53.

Israëls, Machtelt, "Commissioni parallele e narrazioni insolite: Piero della Francesca e il Sassetta a Borgo SanSepolcro," in Betti, Frosinini, and Refice, eds., 2010, *Ripensando Piero della Francesca*, 99–116.

Israëls, Machtelt, "Piero della Francesca's Panel Paintings for Borgo San Sepolcro," in Silver, ed., 2013, *Piero della Francesca in America*, 2013, 46–67.

Israëls, Machtelt, ed., *Sassetta: The Borgo San Sepolcro Altarpiece*, 2 vols. (Cambridge, MA, 2009).

Jaitner-Hahner, Ursula, "Die öffentliche Schule in Città di Castello vom 14. Jahrhundert bis zur Ankunft der Jesuiten 1610," *Quellen und Forschungen aus italienischen Archiven und Bibliotheken*, 73 (1993), 170–302.

Jones, Philip, "The Vicariate of the Malatesta of Rimini," *English Historical Review*, 67 (1952), 321–51.

Jones, Philip, *The Malatesta of Rimini and the Papal State* (Cambridge, 1974).

Kemp, Martin, *The Science of Art: Optical Themes in Western Art from Brunelleschi to Seurat* (New Haven, CT, and London, 1990).

Kemp, Martin, "New Light on Old Theories: Piero's Studies of the Transmission of Light," in Dalai Emiliani and Curzi, eds., 1996, *Piero della Francesca tra arte e scienza*, 33–45.

Laclotte, Michel, "Il ritratto di Sigismondo Malatesta di Piero della Francesca," in Lavin, ed., 1984, *Piero della Francesca a Rimini: L'affresco nel Tempio Malatestiano*, 75–102.

Lattaioli, Paolo, "Storia e architettura del monastero di Sant'Antonio da Padova," in Garibaldi, ed., 1993, *Piero della Francesca: Il polittico di Sant'Antonio*, 57–64.

Lavin, Marilyn Aronberg, "Piero della Francesca's Montefeltro Altarpiece: A Pledge of Fidelity," *Art Bulletin*, 51 (1969), 367–71.

Lavin, Marilyn Aronberg, *Piero della Francesca: The Flagellation* (London, 1972).

Lavin, Marilyn Aronberg, "Piero della Francesca's Fresco of Sigismondo Pandolfo Malatesta Before St. Sigismund," *Art Bulletin*, 56 (1974), 345–74; rpt., trans., and with additional material in Lavin, ed., 1984, *Piero della Francesca a Rimini*, 3–74.

Lavin, Marilyn Aronberg, *Piero della Francesca's "Baptism of Christ"* (New Haven, CT, 1981).

Lavin, Marilyn Aronberg, *The Place of Narrative: Mural Painting in Italian Churches, 431–1600* (Chicago, IL, 1990).

Lavin, Marilyn Aronberg, *Piero della Francesca, San Francesco, Arezzo* (New York, 1994).

Lavin, Marilyn Aronberg, "Piero's Meditation on the *Nativity*," in Lavin, ed., 1995, *Piero della Francesca and His Legacy*, 127–42.

Lavin, Marilyn Aronberg, "Piero the Storyteller: Tradition and Innovation in the *Legend of the True Cross*," in Maetzke and Bertelli, eds., 2001, *Piero della Francesca: The Legend of the True Cross*, 27–37.

Lavin, Marilyn Aronberg, *Piero della Francesca* (London, 2002).

Lavin, Marilyn Aronberg, *Artists' Art in the Renaissance* (London, 2006).

Lavin, Marilyn Aronberg, ed., *Piero della Francesca a Rimini: L'affresco nel Tempio Malatestiano* (Bologna, 1984).

Lavin, Marilyn Aronberg, ed., *Piero della Francesca and His Legacy*, in the National Gallery of Art's series *Studies in the History of Art, Symposium Papers*, 28 (Hanover and London, 1995).

Lazzeri, Silvano, "Ricognizione visiva," in *Un progetto per Piero della Francesca*, 1989, 259–84.

Lazzi, Giovanna, "L'Archimede di Piero," in Manescalchi and Martelli, eds., 2007, *L'Archimede di Piero. Contributi di presentazione alla realizzazione facsimilare del Riccardiano 106*, 65–69.

Lightbown, Ronald, *Piero della Francesca* (London, 1992).

Lightbown, Ronald, "La vita e le opere di Piero della Francesca nel *Dizionario biografico*: problemi ancora aperti," in Uguccioni, ed., 1995, *Incontri sulla biografia di Piero della Francesca*, 11–19.

Lollini, Fabrizio, "La decorazione libraria per i Malatesta nel XV secolo: un panorama generale," in *Il potere, le arti, la guerra*, 2001, 49–61.

Londei, Enrico Ferninando, "La scena della *Flagellazione* di Piero della Francesca: la sua identificazione con un luogo di Urbino del Quattrocento," *Bollettino d'arte*, 65 (1991), 29–66.

Longhi, Roberto, "Piero dei Franceschi e lo sviluppo della pittura veneziana," *L'arte*, 17 (1914), 198–221, 241–56.

Longhi, Roberto, *Piero della Francesca* (Rome, 1927); republ. in Roberto Longhi, *Edizione delle opere complete di Roberto Longhi*, III (Florence, 1963).

Longhi, Roberto, *Piero della Francesca*, trans. with preface by David Tabbat (Riverdale-on-Hudson, 2002).

Luni, Mario, ed., *Castrum Firmignani: Castello del Ducato di Urbino* (Urbino, 1994).

Maccagni, Carlo, "Cultura e sapere dei tecnici nel Rinascimento," in Dalai Emiliani and Curzi, eds., 1996, *Piero della Francesca tra arte e scienza*, 279–92.

Maccagni, Carlo, "Cultura delle tecniche e delle macchine nel Quattrocento," in *Il potere, le arti, la guerra*, 2001, 76–81.

Maddalo, Silvia, *In Figura Romae: Immagini di Roma nel libro medioevale* (Rome, 1990).

Maetzke, Anna Maria, ed., *Il Volto Santo di Sansepolcro: Un grande capolavoro medievale rivelato dal restauro* (Milano 1994).

Maetzke, Anna Maria, ed., *Introduzione ai capolavori di Piero della Francesca* (Milan, 1998).

Maetzke, Anna Maria, ed., and Bertelli, Carlo, eds., *Piero della Francesca. La Leggenda della Vera Croce in San Francesco ad Arezzo* (Milan, 2001); Eng. trans. as *Piero della Francesca: The Legend of the True Cross* (Milan, 2001).

Mancini, Francesco Federico, "'Depingi ac fabricari fecerunt quandam tabulam . . .'. Un punto fermo per la cronologia del polittico di Perugia," in Garibaldi, ed., 1993, *Piero della Francesca: Il polittico di Sant'Antonio*, 65–72.

Mancini, Girolamo, "La madre di Piero della Francesca," *Bollettino d'arte*, 12 (1918), 61–63.

Manescalchi, Roberto, *L'Ercole di Piero tra mito e realtà* (Ancona, 2011).

Manescalchi, Roberto, and Martelli, Matteo, eds., *L'Archimede di Piero. Contributi di presentazione alla realizzazione facsimilare del Riccardiano* 106 (Sansepolcro, 2007).

Mariani, Franco, "La cartiera dei duchi d'Urbino a Fermignano (1408–1870)," in Luni, ed., 1994, *Castrum Firmignani: Castello del Ducato di Urbino*, 213–29.

Marshall, Louise, "Manipulating the Sacred: Image and Plague in Renaissance Italy," *Renaissance Quarterly*, 47 (1994), 485–532.

Martelli, Cecilia, "Bartolomeo della Gatta, Giuliano Amadei e Guglielmo Giraldi miniatori a Urbino: i 'Corali' quattrocenteschi del Duomo," *Prospectiva*, 110–11, 2003 (2004), 30–57.

Martelli, Cecilia, "Il cappella di Jacopo Anastagi e l'affresco di Bartolomeo della Gatta," in Di Lorenzo, Martelli, and Mazzalupi, 2012, *La Badia di Sansepolcro nel Quattrocento*, 45–71.

Mattesini, Enzo, "Autografia del quotidiano. Quattro scritte di Piero della Francesca," *Lingua e stile*, 46 (2011), 225–45.

Mazzalupi, Matteo, "'Uno se parte dal Borgo ...e va ad Ancona': Piero della Francesca nel 1450," *Nuovi studi. Rivista di arte antica e moderna*, 11, 2006 (2007), 37–54.

Mazzalupi, Matteo, "Ancona alla metà del Quattrocento: Piero della Francesca, Giorgio da Sebenico, Antonio da Firenze," in De Marchi and Mazzalupi, eds., 2008, *Pittori ad Ancona nel Quattrocento*, 224–49.

Mazzalupi, Matteo, "Altari, patronati, opere d'arte al tempo degli abati. Un saggio di topografia sacra," in Di Lorenzo, Martelli, and Mazzalupi, 2012, *La Badia di Sansepolcro nel Quattrocento*, 1–44.

Meiss, Millard, "A Documented Altarpiece by Piero della Francesca," *Art Bulletin*, 23 (1941), 53–68.

Meiss, Millard, "Light as Form and Symbol in some Fifteenth-Century Paintings," *Art Bulletin*, 27 (1945), 175–81.

Milanesi, Gaetano, ed., *Nuovi documenti per la storia dell'arte Toscana dal XII al XV secolo* (Firenze, 1901).

Mitchell, Charles, "Il Tempio Malatestiano," *Studi Malatestiani (Istituto storico italiano per il medio evo)* (1978), 71–103.

Morolli, Gabriele, "Federico da Montefeltro e Salomone. Alberti, Piero e l'ordine architettonico dei principi-costruttori ritrovato," in Cieri Via, ed., 1996, *Città e corte nell'Italia di Piero della Francesca*, 319–45.

Napolitani, Pier Daniele, "Piero e la tradizione del testo di Archimede nel Quattrocento," in Manescalchi and Martelli, eds., 2007, *L'Archimede di Piero*, II, 27–46.

Osti, Ornella F., ed., *Mosaics of Friendship: Studies in Art and History for Eve Borsook* (Florence, 1999).

Pacioli, Luca, *Summa de aritmetica, geometria, proportioni et proportionalità* (Venice, 1494).

Pacioli, Luca, *De divina proportione* (Venice 1509).

Pallone, Cecilia, "Il beato Agostiniano Angelo Scarpetti da Sansepolcro: vicenda biografica, culto e iconografia," in *Gli Agostiniani a Sansepolcro e il Beato Angelo Scarpetti*, 2009, 89–114.

Paolucci, Antonio, with appendix of Lenzini, Margherita Moriondo, *Piero della Francesca* (Florence, 1989).

Paolucci, Antonio, "Anno Domini 1450," in *Il potere, le arti, la guerra*, 2001, 41–48.

Pasini, Piergiorgio, *Piero e i Malatesta: L'attività di Piero della Francesca per le corti romagnole* (Milan, 1992).

Peruzzi, Marcella, ed., *Ornatissimo codice: La biblioteca di Federico di Montefeltro* (Milan, 2008).

Peruzzi, Piergiorgio, "Lavorare a corte: 'Ordini et officij'. Cortigiani e funzionari al servizio del Duca d'Urbino," in Cerboni Baiardi, Chittolini, and Floriani, eds., 1986, *Federico di Montefeltro: Lo stato*, 225–96.

Pinelli, Antonio, "Esercizi di metodo: Piero a Benozzo a Roma, tra cronologia relativa a cronologia assoluta," *Ricerche di storia dell'arte*, 76 (2002), 7–30.

Pizzorusso, Claudio, "Sul *Battesimo* di Piero della Francesca," *Artista*, 2 (1991), 122–33.

Poesch, Jessie, "Ennius and Basinio of Parma," *Journal of the Warburg and Courtauld Institutes*, 25 (1962), 116–18.

Polcri, Franco, "A proposito di Piero della Francesca e della sua famiglia: nuove fonti archivistiche a Sansepolcro," *Due ritrovamenti d'archivio a Sansepolcro* (Sansepolcro, 1990), 8–24, extracted from *Proposte e ricerche*, 21 (1988).

Polcri, Franco, "Gli Agostiniani e il polittico di Piero della Francesca. Documenti e committenza," in Di Lorenzo, ed., 1996a, *Il polittico Agostiniano di Piero della Francesca*, 73–100, 143–51.

Polcri, Franco, "Sansepolcro: la città in cui Piero della Francesca prepara il suo rapporto con le corti," in Cieri Via, ed., 1996b, *Città e corte nell'Italia di Piero della Francesca*, 97–117.

Polcri, Franco, "A proposito di Francesco del Borgo," in Bertelli and Paolucci, eds., 2007, *Piero della Francesca e le corti italiane*, 244–50.

(Il) Potere, le arti, la guerra: Lo splendore dei Malatesta (Milan, 2001).

(Un) Progetto per Piero della Francesca (Florence, 1989).

Ricerche su Piero, Dipartimento di Teoria e Documentazione delle Tradizioni Culturali, Facoltà di Magistero, Università degli Studi di Siena (Arezzo, 1989).

Roeck, Bernd, *Piero della Francesca e l'assassino* (Turin, 2007).

Ronchey, Silvia, *L'enigma di Piero: L'ultimo bizantino e la crociata fantasma nella rivelazione di un grande quadro* (Milan, 2006).

Rose, Paul Lawrence, *The Italian Renaissance of Mathematics: Studies on Humanists and Mathematicians from Petrarch to Galileo* (Geneva, 1975).

Rotondo, A., "Niccolò Tignosi da Foligno (polemiche aristoteliche di un maestro del Ficino)," *Rinascimento*, 9 (1958), 217–55.

Roy, Ashok, and Smith, Perry, eds., *Painting Techniques: History, Materials and Studio Practice* (London, 1998).

Salmi, Mario, "Piero della Francesca e G. Amedei," *Rivista d'arte*, 24 (1942), 26–44.

Salmi, Mario, "L'affresco di Sansepolcro," *Bollettino d'arte*, 40 (1955), 230–36.

Salmi, Mario, "La casa di Piero della Francesca," *Commentari*, 26 (1975), 267–75.

Salmi, Mario, "Perché 'Piero della Francesca'," *Commentari*, 27 (1976), 121–26.

Santagata, Marco, and Stussi, Alfredo, eds., *Studi per Umberto Carpi. Un saluto da allievi e colleghi pisani* (Pisa, 2000).

Scapecchi, Piero, "'Tu celebras burgi iam per oppida nomen': Appunti per Piero della Francesca," *Arte cristiana*, 72 (1984), 209–21.

Scharf, Gian Paolo G., *Borgo San Sepolcro a metà del Quattrocento: Istituzioni e società (1440–1460)* (Florence, 2003).

Schleicher, Barbara, "Il restauro: interventi, osservazioni tecniche, indagini scientifiche," in Maetzke, ed., 1994, *Il Volto Santo di Sansepolcro*, 60–66.

Sensi, Mario, "Niccolò Tignosi da Foligno: l'opera e il pensiero," *Annali della Facoltà di Lettere e Filosofia*, Università degli Studi di Perugia, 9 (1971–2), 359–495.

Shearman, John, "Reflection and Refraction," in Lavin, ed., 1995, *Piero della Francesca and His Legacy*, 213–21.

Silver, Nathaniel, ed., *Piero della Francesca in America: From Sansepolcro to the East Coast*, James Banker, Machtelt Israëls, Nathaniel Silver, with an Appendix by Giacomo Guazzini and Elena Squillantini (New York, 2013a).

Silver, Nathaniel, ed., "Piero 'in terra nostra': Image-Making for Borgo San Sepolcro," in Silver, ed., 2013, *Piero della Francesca in America*, 2013b, 26–45.

Simons, Patricia, "Hercules in Italian Renaissance Art: Masculine Labour and Homoerotic Libido," *Art History*, 31 (2008), 632–64.

Smith, Christine, "Piero's Painted Architecture," in Lavin, ed., 1995, *Piero della Francesca and His Legacy*, 223–53.

Soranzo, Giovanni, *Pio II e la politica italiana nella lotta contro i Malatesti, 1457–1463* (Padova, 1911).

Spotti Tantillo, A., "Inventari inediti di interesse librario, tratti da protocolli notarili romani (1468–1523)," *Archivio della Società Romana di Storia Patria*, 98 (1975), 77–94.

Studi Malatestiani in *Studi storici*, 110–11, Istituto storico italiano per il Medio Evo (Rome, 1978).

Tanner, Marie, "Concordia in Piero della Francesca's *Baptism of Christ*," *Art Quarterly*, 25 (1972), 3–19.

Tozzi, Ileana, "I gonfaloni perugini, testimonianza d'arte sacra e di devozione popolare," *Arte cristiana*, 90 (2002), 30–34.

Trevisani, Filippo, "Struttura e pittura: i maestri legnaiuoli grossi e Piero della Francesca per la carpenteria della pala di San Bernardino," in Daffra and Trevisani, eds., 1997, *La pala di San Bernardino di Piero della Francesca: Nuovi studi oltre il restauro*, 31–83.

Turchini, Angelo, "L'imperatore, il santo e il cavaliere: note su Sigismondo Pandolfo Malatesta e Piero della Francesca," *Arte cristiana*, 74 (1986), 165–80.

Turchini, Angelo, *Il Tempio Malatestiano, Sigismondo Pandolfo Malatesta e Leon Battista Alberti* (Cesena, 2000).

Uguccioni, Alessandra, ed., *Incontri sulla biografia di Piero della Francesca*, Istituto della Enciclopedia Italiana (Rome, 1995).

Ulivi, Elizabetta, "Documenti inediti su Luca Pacioli, Piero della Francesca e Leonardo da Vinci, con alcuni autografi," *Bollettino di storia delle scienze matematiche*, 29, (2009), 15–160.

Valerio, Vladimiro, "Piero e gli astri. Il primo cielo stellato nella pittura occidentale," in Bertelli and Paolucci, eds., 2007, *Piero della Francesca e le corti italiane*, 81–85.

Vasari, Giorgio, *Le vite de più eccellenti pittori, scultori ed architettori italiani*, in *Opere*, ed. Gaetano Milanesi (Florence, 1906).

Verrazzani, Enrico, *Il Museo Civico di Sansepolcro nel costume cittadino: Da piccola raccolta d'arte all'inaugurazione come istituzione comunale* (Florence, 2009).

Vespasiano da Bisticci, *Renaissance Princes, Popes & Prelates. The Vespasiano Memoirs: Lives of the Illustrious Men of the XVth Century*, intro. Myron Gilmore (New York, 1963).

Wardrop, James, *The Script of Humanism: Some Aspects of Humanistic Script* (New York, 1963).

Wittkower, Rudolf, and Carter, B. A. R., "The Perspective of Piero della Francesca's *Flagellation*," *Journal of the Warburg and Courtauld Institutes*, 16 (1953), 292–302.

Wood, Jeryldene M., ed., *The Cambridge Companion to Piero della Francesca* (New York, 2002).

Wood, Jeryldene M., ed., "Piero's *Legend of the True Cross* and the Friars of San Francesco," in Wood, ed., 2002, *The Cambridge Companion to Piero della Francesca*, 51–65.

Woods-Marsden, Joanna, "'Ritratto al naturale': Questions of Realism and Idealism in Early Renaissance Portraits," *Art Journal*, 46 (1987), 209–16.

Woods-Marsden, Joanna, "Images of Castles in the Renaissance: Symbols of Signoria / Symbols of Tyranny," *Art Journal*, 48 (1989), 130–37.

Woods-Marsden, Joanna, "Piero della Francesca's Ruler Portraits," in Wood, ed., 2002, *The Cambridge Companion to Piero della Francesca*, 91–114.

Zaccarello, Michelangelo, and Tomasin, Luigi, eds., *Storia della lingua e filologia. Per Alfredo Stussi nel suo sessantacinquesimo compleanno* (Florence, 2004).

Zippel, Giuseppe, "Piero della Francesca a Roma," *Rassegna d'arte*, 6 (1919), 81–94.

Zöllner, Frank, "The 'Motions of the Mind' in Renaissance Portraits: The Spiritual Dimension of Portraiture," *Zeitschrift für Kunstgeschichte*, 68 (2005), 23–40.

Zonghi, Aurelio, *Zonghi's Watermarks* (with Zonghi, Augusto, and Gasparinetti, A. F.), rpt. in *Monumenta Chartae Papyraceae Historiam Illustrantia*, III (Hilversum, 1953).

PICTURE ACKNOWLEDGEMENTS

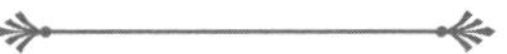

Alinari Archives, Florence: **15**, **23**; Serge Domingie/Alinari Archives, Florence: **II**; Mauro Magliani/Alinari Archives, Florence: **VIII**, **X**; Bencini Raffaello/Alinari Archives, Florence: **IX**, **19**; Seat Archive/Alinari Archives, Florence: **III**; Archivio di Stato, Florence, su Concessione del Ministero per i Beni e le Attività Culturali: **31**; The Art Archive: **18**; Biblioteca Apostolica Vaticana, Città di Vaticano: **29**; Biblioteca Medicea Laurenziana, Florence, su Concessione del Ministero dei Beni e delle Attività Culturali: **10**; Biblioteca Palatina, Parma, su concessione del Ministero per I Beni e le Attività Culturali: **24**; Biblioteca Panizzi, Reggio Emilia: **25**; Biblioteca Riccardiana, Florence, su Concessione del Ministero per I Beni e le Attività Culturali: **27**, **28**; The Bridgeman Art Library: **I**, **4**, **22**, **26**, **30**; Comune di Monterchi: **VI**; Fondazione Piero della Francesca, Sansepolcro: **20**, **21**; Museo Civico, Sansepolcro: **V**, **VII**, **1**, **2**, **9**, **11**, **12**, **13**; BPK/Scala, Florence: **3**; Scala, Florence: **8**; Nathaniel Silver: **17**; Alessandro Benci/ Soprintendenza Beni A.P.S.A.E. di Arezzo: **IV**, **5**, **6**, **7**, **14**; Sopritendenza BSAE dell'Umbria, Perugia: **16**.

INDEX OF LIFE, PAINTINGS, AND TREATISES

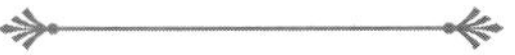

Life

abaco (commercial mathematics):
combination with Greek geometry 95, 174, 179–80, 216
its customary concentration on the practical 82
lack of systematic instruction 79
location of Piero's writing his treatise on *abaco* 79, 81, 88, 89–90
Piero as autodidact 79
Piero's combination with Greek geometry 79, 94, 202
Piero's knowledge of 79, 81, 82
role of Arezzo masters in Piero's knowledge of 79, 81
absences from Sansepolcro xxi, 130
in Arezzo 74, 75–6
in Rome 87
in Urbino 134–5, 146, 149, 162, 163, 199
long periods 20–1, 22–3, 74, 198–9
short periods 149
Amadi, Girolamo 221 n. 21
Ancona, Piero's presence 24–8
Antonio d'Anghiari, *see also* in General Index:
employer of Piero 1, 7–9
break with Piero 9
apprenticeship 1, 6, 7
Archimedes, *see also* General Index, Archimedes:
construction of the Archimedean bodies 203–4
irregular bodies 203–4
Piero's copy of his *Opera* 188–93
Piero's knowledge of 88
Piero's uniting vernacular and Latin culture 169, 180, 215
problem of intersecting cylinders 204–5
architectural activity, *see* builder
architecture, painted 42, 59, 62, 126, 183–4
artisan culture, *see also* in General Index:
Piero's familiarity with and appropriation from 203–5, 216
Piero's involvement with 1–2
Piero's lifelong respect for products of hands 9, 215
proximity to 9
assistant to Antonio d'Anghiari:
labor in chapel of Saint Lorenzo (Badia) 8
labor in chapel of Saint Michelangelo (Citerna) 8
labor in Sant'Agostino on image of the Madonna *Annunziata* 8
preparation of altarpiece for San Francesco 7–8
assistant to Domenico Veneziano 1
in Florence in chapel of Sant'Egidio 17–18
in Perugia 1, 17, 123
assistant to Michele da Firenze 20, 23
assistants to Piero 52, 61, 126, 127
association with elite families 23–4, 25–6
autodidact 79, 187

biographies of xx, xxiii
birthyear 1, 5
blindness 207, 211, 213–14
bodies, human
monumentality and dignity 216
volumetric treatment 15

builder:
  appointment by communal officials to supervise building 158, 193
  enlarging of *Casa di Piero* 156
  participation in the Della Francesca renovations in villa at Bastia 156

cartoons 102
  maximum use in second phase xxii, 42, 60, 215
  minimal use in the *Sant'Antonio* altarpiece 127
  practice of reusing and adjusting dimensions of the cartoon 39–40, 105, 149
  use in Brera altarpiece 167
  use in *Legend of the True Cross* 60
  use in *Madonna del Parto* 102
  use in Rimini paintings 29, 39–40, 42, 60, 61
  use in *Saint Augustine* altarpiece 134
  use in the *Flagellation*, 167
  use in the *Resurrecttion*, 112
childhood cohort 6, 29
cloth's treatment 13
Christianity
  expression in last will 211–13
  never expressed asceticism in human figures 217
  view of 217
chronology of xviii–xix
composition and organization of space, *see* spatial organization

documents xxi–xxiii
domestic settings of late paintings 182

early preparatory and painting projects:
  in San Francesco 7–8, 128
  labor in chapel of Saint Lorenzo (Badia) 8
  labor in chapel of Saint Michelangelo (Citerna) 8
  labor in Sant'Agostino, 8
  paints candles for a confraternity 7
  preparation of flags 7, 8–9
  status as an independent painter 7, 9
education in formal Latin 5–6; *see also* grammar school

family and social networks, 29–30
family, *see* Della Francesca family in General Index
Ferrara, possible presence in 20, 23–4
final years 208–14
  bequests for his soul 212–13
  burial in chapel of San Leonardo 212
  death 214
  division of family property earlier held in common 213–14
  last will and testament 212–13
  last will and testament as an expression of patriarchic values 213
  notes for last will 211–12
  notes of instruction for division of property 213–14
  presence in Sansepolcro 208
  question of declining creativity 206–7
  service to his family 209–11
  witnessing in acts of conflict resolution 211
formation in Sansepolcro 1–16
Flanders, *see* influences from, Flanders
Florence, *see* influences, from, Florence

gauging with the eye xxii, 180
Girolamo Amadi, *see* Amadi, Girolamo
Greek geometry, *see also* Archimedes, Euclid in General Index:
  combination with *abaco* tradition 95, 176–7, 202, 216
  lack of systematic or university preparation 79, 82
  love of abstract geometrical bodies 218
  possession and use of manuscripts of *Opera* of Archimedes 87
  possession and use of treatises of Euclid 81–2, 87, 94
  Rome as likely place of acquisition of knowledge of 79

handwriting of Piero 187
historical interest in xx–xxi
history
  conception of divine 44, 62–3, 111–13, 216, 217

conception of human 44, 62–3, 111–13, 216, 217
humanism:
admiration for Greek writers on geometry and optics 217
eschewing of mystical elements in nature 218
expression of idea that achievement in arts brings immortality 177, 201, 217
little interest in Petrarchian or civic humanism 217
research of the historical and natural 218–19

iconography:
aversion to paint figures as ascetic 34–5, 117, 131, 217
combination of two traditions 41–2, 71–72, 111
conception of human and divine history 44, 62–3, 111–13
domestic setting and subject of nearly all late paintings 182
no commissions for narrations of classic texts 217
representation of political ideas 29, 34, 42–3, 149, 150–1, 166–7
influences from:
Greece and Rome 46–7, 60–1, 62
Florence 9–10, 12–16, 17–20, 221 n. 8
Flanders 24, 28, 38–9, 168, 206
Siena 9–10
illness 115, 161–2

judge of artistic objects and construction 100, 208–9

Latin:
Piero as an autodidact 187
Piero's treatises in Latin 173, 186, 187, 188, 189, 199–205
reading of geometric texts in Latin 81
knowledge and use of 1, 5–6, 14–15, 81, 187, 205
uniting of Latin culture with vernacular *aboca* tradition 79
letter of xxii, 199, 201, 202
light in paintings 13
in *Baptism of Christ* 15–16
in Brera altarpiece 167
in *Legend of the True Cross* 57
in *Saint Jerome in the Desert* 26
in *Sant'Agostino* altarpiece 131
in *Sant'Antonio* altarpiece 127
in Senigallia *Madonna and Child* 168
rationalization of rays of 57

Malatesta court, *see also* Malatesta, Sigismondo in General Index:
presence in 34–43
departure from 43
Mary (the Virgin) 64–5
Masaccio
influence on 13, 14, 18–19
mathematics:
acquisition and sources of knowledge 10, 79, 82
lack of formal instruction 79
product of union of Greek geometry and *abaco* instruction 82, 176–7, 216
Vasari's comments 6
mathematization of nature 216
Modena, presence in 20

naturalism 27–8, 176–7
definition, 113, 219
derived from concentration on what the eye viewed 18, 19
in portraits 42, 149
observation of natural phenomenon 15
patrons' limits on 64, 77

Optics:
Euclid's treatise 15, 85, 87, 171, 172, 188, 189
Piero's use of the *Optics* 15, 87, 171, 172, 188, 189
orthogonals in treatises 175

paint mediums:
egg tempera xxii, 39, 61, 77, 134, 167, 185
oil xxii, 29, 38–9, 42, 77, 116, 127, 134, 149, 167, 168, 185

perspective, see also *De prospectiva pingendi* xxii
abandonment of strict use of systems of perspective in paintings 180, 208
defined as *commensuratio* 172
equated with proportion 15, 172, 216
graphic representation essential for perspective 176
importance in phases of development xxii
innovation of Florence 18–20
necessary for a "science" of painting 176
two systems of perspective in the *Resurrection* 108
use in achieving realistic atmospheric effects 150, 208
use in *Flagellation* 141
phases of artistic development:
characteristics of second phase 42, 44, 59, 60, 120
lessening of use of complex systems of perspective in later paintings 180
markers of first and second phases 39
third phase 181, 183
three phases xxii, 215, 220 n. 2
pigments, *see* paint mediums
political participation:
appearance as *fidejussor* for friends and family 193, 194–5
appointment as one of communal accountants 193–4
as one of the priors of the confraternity of San Bartolomeo 195–6
assessment of his attitude toward public service 197
communal appointment as one of two supervisors of building in conservators' palace 158, 193
communal appointment as one on a committee to find communal doctor 152
failure to gain highest communal office 158, 193
member of council of the people 21, 193
member of council of the twelve 104
oversight as prior of cloth gifts to poor 196
participation in council of sixty 21, 193
supervision of finances for construction of a chapel in the Badia 196
presence in Sansepolcro xxi, 88
for extended periods 76, 88, 96–119, 131, 152–62, 181–97, 205, 208–14
for short periods 21–2, 52, 75, 115, 128, 131, 134, 148–9
proportion:
assessment of its importance to Piero by Luca Pacioli 216
centrality of proportion to perspective 172, 216
importance to Piero xxii, 216
relation to perspective 15, 172

relationship to Cristoforo and Lorenzo Canozi da Lendinara 24
relationship to his family and its members, *see also* Della Francesca family in General Index:
assistance to family members 162, 196–7
assumption of leadership of Della Francesca family 197
exclusion from documents on family property until death of his father 97
his choice of painting métier 6, 98
supervision of dowering and marriage of his niece Romana 197
supervision of marriage of his nephew Francesco 197
to his father 1, 6, 97–8, 216
relationship to Leon Battista Alberti 19–20, 144–5, 170, 216
representation of the human beings 61, 216
Rimini:
commissions from Sigismondo Malatesta and Jacopo Anastagi 29–43
takes house in rent 198–9
Rome:
absorption of Ancient Rome's visual culture 46–7, 62
acquisition of a knowledge of Greek geometry there 82
conditions in 1450s 83

painting in the Vatican Palace 47, 50, 87–8
presence in Rome 44, 46, 47, 52, 62, 82, 86–8

sacred conversation (*sacra conversazione*) 124, 131, 163, 166
scriptorium 185–8
Siena, *see* influences from, Siena
signature of 26
spatial organization:
compositional abilities 15
importance to Piero xxii, 51
in Brera altarpiece 166
in *Legend of the True Cross* 44, 55, 60–2
in the *Baptism of Christ* 15
style, painting, *see also* phases of artistic development:
domestic setting and subject of nearly all late paintings 182
interpretive problems 13–16
supposed lack of change in xxi

techniques in painting, *see also* paint mediums; cartoons; light in paintings; spatial organization:
adjustments to achieve a sacred conversation 125
animal glue (*colla*) and oil as preparatory layer 77, 134
a secco additions 47, 60, 102, 112
borrowing from classical Rome 46–7, 60–2
continuous narrative 60–1
depictions that establish monumentality and gravity 102, 126
foreshortening 26, 160, 175, 177, 179
fresco 60
ground of marble dust, animal glue, and plaster 51, 55,
interest in panels' preparation 2, 27, 77, 134, 168
orthogonals xxii 133, 167
painting over a previously painted element 134, 169
placement of wet cloths on plaster 61
positioning of Madonna and Child close to picture plane 167, 169, 185
predella's order 124–5
preparation of altarpieces' wood with carbon black 77, 128, 134
presence of *spolveri* 60, 112, 134, 167
representation of trees and sky 47
scoring with a sharp instrument 39, 102, 107, 112, 127, 134
spacial adjustments to achieve a sacred conversation 125
thin space left unpainted along outline of figures 134
two systems of perspective in the *Resurrection* 108
unconventional narrative sequences 55, 73–4
use of *terra verde* xxii, 14, 185
use of gold leaf 64, 69
use of humanistic script 26, 29, 42, 85,105
use of ultramarine 68, 69, 112, 114, 116
wood preparation with chestnut and walnut for panel paintings 27 168

university attendance 1
university culture:
acquisition in Rome 79
union with vernacular culture 79, 82
vernacular culture, union with university-based culture 79, 82
vernacular, treatises in specific dialect of Sansepolcro 187
visual acuity xxii, 170, 216
of nature 14–15
in seeing water's reflection and refraction 14–15

witness in notarial contracts xxi, 12, 20, 21, 24, 34, 99, 100, 152–3, 155, 194, 195, 196, 205, 208, 210, 211, 214

Paintings

Baptism of Christ (Pl. I) xx, 2, 10, 10–16, 69
dating of 11, 21–2
importance of light 15–16
non-immediate initial payment 22

Baptism of Christ (cont.)
original location of 11
Piero's presence in area of church of San Giovanni Battista 12
place in Piero's development 13–14
preparation of wooden structure 12–13, 22
Battista Sforza:
Portrait, see Uffizi Diptych
Triumph, see Uffizi Diptych

Chapel of Cardinal D'Estouteville (Chapel of Saint Michael and Saint Peter); (Illus. 8) 51–2
dating the painting 52
geometric composition in the vaults 51
use of novel ground of plaster, glue, and marble dust 51

Federico da Montefeltro
Portrait, see Uffizi Diptych
Triumph, see Uffizi Diptych
Flagellation of Christ (Pl. VIII) 134–41
crimson strip of cloth on figure on extreme right 137–8
dating the painting 134, 146
figure on extreme right as Jacopo Anastagi 136–41
formal relationship of paintings two portions 135
interpretations 135–6
perspectival organization 141
use of geometrical module 141

Hercules (Illus. 22) 158–61
choice of this classical hero 160–1
dating of the fresco 159
location in Della Francesca home 159
physical and mental attributes 160
sole large painting with a classical subject 159, 234 n. 25
tension in figure from static and dynamic features 160

Legend of the True Cross (Pl. IV, Illus. 5–7) xx, xxii, 44–63
agreement on final payments 115
Annunciation to Constantine 57
Annunciation to Mary 57, 63
Burial of the Wood 56
change of painting style and technique 46, 47
choice of subjects 45, 53–4
Chosroes Executed Before his Throne 137
commission by Baccio Bacci 45
dating the painting 46, 52
Death of Adam 47, 56, 61, 63
Exaltation of the Cross 47
Invention of the Cross 58–9, 62
mistaken interpretation that the *Legend* is propaganda to promote a crusade 225 n. 16
narrative sequence 55–60
parallelisms 55
presence of Piero in Arezzo 76
presence of star constellations 57
Raising of Judas from the Well 58
Victory of Constantine 55, 57–8
Victory of Heraclius 59
Visit of Sheba to Solomon 47, 55, 56, 62, 137
lost and non-extant paintings
battle scenes in Ferrara 23–4
flags and insignia of Eugenius IV 8–9
fresco of *Incornation of the Virgin* in the Badia 153–6
image of Saint Vincent in church of San Bernardo, Arezzzo 117
image of San Donato in church of Santa Maria della Grazia, Arezzo 117
Madonna in the *Casa di Piero* 214
Misericordia fresco 181–2
night scene of Christ in the garden located in Sargiano, Arezzo 117, 119
painting in the Vatican Palace for Nicholas V 47, 50
painting in the Vatican Palace for Pius II, 87
probable painting in church of Santa Maria della Neve 76
processional banner for the confraternity of Holy Trinity 114–15
processional banner for the confraternity of the Annunziata 116–17, 231 n. 10

Madonna and Child with Saints and Angels (Brera altarpiece), (Illus. 23) 163–7
altarpiece expresses fidelity to Mary and the church 163, 165, 234 n. 2
dating the painting 163, 165
relationship of its depicted architecture and Urbino church of San Bernardino 165
virtuoso display of Piero's techniques 167
Madonna del Parto (Pl. VI) 101–2
as devotional image for women of Monterchi 101
grace and dignity of the *Madonna* 102
located originially in church of Santa Maria Momentana, Monterchi 101
mistaken idea of the image's association with a cemetery 101
rapidity of execution 102
use of *a secco* method on thin layer of plaster for more important areas 102
Misericordia altarpiece (Pl. V, Illus. 9) 64–78
commission contract 21–3, 68–9
creation of the sacred 65–7, 69, 71
iconography in the altarpiece 71–2, 76–7
liturgical purposes 69, 71, 73
Madonna della Misericordia 69–78
minimal Roman influence 64
pace of painting and payments 74–6, 100
papal indulgence 66, 67, 71
payments 22
placement in Piero's development 13
predella sequence and painter 73–4
presence of lateral piers 226 n. 14
role of the Pichi family 67–8, 68–9
slow pace of realization 68
Virgin as intercessor 72

Nativity of Christ (Illus. 30) 205–8
celebration of Sansepolcro 207–8
Flemish influence 206
influence of Saint Bridget's narration 206
lack of overall perspectival organization 208
presence and location in *Casa di Piero* 205–6

Portrait of Sigismondo Malatesta (Illus. 4) 38–40
cartoon in *Portrait* and *Sigismundus Before his Patron Saint Sisgimundus* 29, 39–40
role of Jacopo Anastagi 30, 34
use of oil 29, 38–9

Resurrection of Christ (Pl. VI) 107–13
attention to subsidiary details 112
Christ figure as human and divine 111–13
civic function of image 108, 113
combination of seated judge and triumphant warrior 111
dating of the painting 108
iconic or static qualities 110
image as triumph warrior and eternal judge 109
local precedents 109–10
location in hall where council of sixty convened 108, 230 n. 26
related to additions to the Residence of the conservators 107–9
treatment of beards 110
two systems of perspective 108

Sant'Agostino altarpiece (Illus. 17) 128–34
architectural setting 128
contract of commission 130
description of altarpiece 133
dismantlement and dispersal 129–30, 133
lost central panel 129, 133
oil and carbon black as preparatory layers 77, 232 n. 11
payments and pace of painting 75–6, 120, 130–1
purchase of wooden frame 128
sacred conversation 131
Saint John the Evangelist 132–3
Saint Michel (Illus. 18) 131–2
Saint Nicholas Tolentino 132

Sant'Antonio altarpiece (Illus.X 16) 120–7
Annunciation 121, 125, 126, 127
architectural setting and representation 124, 126
date of painting 123

Sant'Antonio (cont.)
debate on relationship of main tier and *Annunciation* 121, 126
Franciscan saints and emphasis 124–5
frequent use of incised lines as guides 127
Madonna and Child 125
main tier as a sacred conversation 125
minimal use of cartoons 127
oil as preparatory layer and paint medium 77, 127
Perugian communal contribution for altarpiece's expense 123
poverty of Franciscan saints deemphasized 126
Saint Jerome and a Penitent (Pl. II) 34–8
commission as means of introducing Piero to Sigismondo 30, 34
depiction of Sansepolcro 35
inscription 35
Jacopo Anastagi as depicted patron 30, 34, 136
painting's representation of scarlet cloth strip 36, 136
penitent's character 34–5, 136
Saint Jerome in the Desert (Illus. 3) 24–7
copy of 26–7
Ferretti patron 24–7
light in painting 26
representation of Jerome 26
Saint Julian (Illus. 12) 105–7
date of execution 44, 106, 230 n. 16
depicted as a knight 10
legend of the saint 106–7
saint's forlorn gaze 107
Saint Louis of Toulouse (Illus. 11) 102–5
dating and location of the painting 103, 104
grandeur of the saint 105
iconography 105
legend of the saint 104–5
role of Lodovico Acciaioli 103–4
Saint Mary Magdalene (Illus. 15) 117
fully sculpted youthful body 117
refused to portray as emaciated 117, 217
represented as myrrh-bearer 117
Senigallia *Madonna and Child* (Pl. X) 167–9
dating the painting 168, 234 n. 6
lack of overall perspectival organization 169
linkage to marriage between the Montefeltro and Della Rovere 168
preponderance of oil as paint medium 168
theological interpretations 168–9
Sigismondo Malatesta Before His Patron Saint Sigismundus (Pl. III) 40–3
cartoon in *Portrait* and *Sigismundus Before his Patron Saint Sisgimundus* 39–40
combination of religious and political traditions 41–2
role of Jacopo Anastagi 30, 34
use of humanistic script in inscription 42

Uffizi Diptych (Pl. IX, Illus. 19) 146–51
Battista Sforza, Portrait 147
Battista Sforza, Triumph 147–8, 149–50
consolatory inscription on Battista's *Triumph* 147–8
context and dating of the painting 146, 147
continuous landscape as background 150
dilemma of naturalistic portraits of rulers 149
Federico da Montefeltro, Portrait 147, 149
Federico da Montrfeltro, Triumph 147, 150
location 151
representation of Christian and Roman virtues 149–50

Williamstown *Madonna with Child and Four Angels* (Illus. 26) 183–5, 235 n. 3
domestic setting 184, 185
intricate classical architectural setting 183–4
stylistically similar to Senigallia *Mother and Child* 181

Writings

Archimedes, *Opera* (copy of):
dating the period and place of copying 189, 191
manuscripts that Piero copied from 189, 191
Piero borrowed most markedly from discussions of circles and spheres 192

Piero's copy of text and geometrical diagrams 189
watermarks demonstrate copy not made in Rome in 1450s 189, 191

De prospectiva pingendi 134, 169–80
audience 179–80
cites directly from Euclid's *Optics* and *Elements* 171
concentrates on perspective defined as *commensuratio* 172
construction of crossing cylinders or vaults 205
derives from painting experience 20
desire for fame that derives from perspective in painting 176, 201
discussion of eye and sight 172–4
expression of joining of artisan and university traditions 169, 170, 174
extended period of composition 79, 88, 172
four extant manuscripts of the treatise 172
importance of establishing viewer's position visa-a-via the image 170, 173–4, 175
importance of proportion 216
instructions for drawing heads 177, 179
joins abaco mathematics and Greek geometry 170
likely date of composition 88, 171–2, 187–8
necessity of drawing diagrams because intellect not sufficient 170, 174
new geometric theorem 174
outline of treatise 172
participation of Piero in the four copies of the treatise 185–7
perspective method for objects of irregular shapes 177, 179
presentation of a copy of the treatise to Federico da Montefeltro 187
proofs established by quantities expressed in numerical form 171
relationship to Alberti's *On Painting* 20, 170
"science" of perspective necessary for painting 176
similarity between diagrams in treatise and images in paintings 172, 180
translator into Latin of the treatise 186
use of both intromission and extramission theories of sight 174
visual triangle formed by the eye and the edges of painting 174
working copy 172, 185, 186

Libellus de quinque corporibus regularibus 199–205
affection for Guidobaldo 201
Archimedean bodies 203–4
assessment of his career 201
cites Archimedes directly from his *Opera* 188, 192
combines Greek prose geometry with *abaco* numerical arithmetic 202
comments on ancient artists, patrons, and fame 201
construction of Archimedean irregular bodies 203–4
dedicatory letter 199, 201
extreme and mean ratio 204
gift of treatise to Guidobaldo da Montefeltro 187
intended as presentation copy 205
likely date of composition 88, 199, 201
organization 202–3
Piero's notes and corrections in Latin 205
possible site for writing 199
problem of intersecting cylinders or vaults 204–5
regular bodies 202–3
relationship to *Trattato d'abaco* 202
style of writing 203

Trattato d'abaco 88–95, 134
abstract nature of approach 92
construction of Archimedean irregular bodies 92–4
discussion of geometry 92–5
extended period of composition 79, 88
extreme and mean ratio (divine proportion or Golden Section) 94
five regular bodies 92–3
geometrical drawings as proofs 94

Trattato d'abaco (*cont.*)
indirect knowledge of Archimedes from medieval sources 188, 189
likely date and place of composition 88–90, 228 nn. 28, 31
organization of the treatise 90
presence of Pichi coat of arms in manuscript 90
rule of double false position 91–2
rule of three 90–1
uncommon knowledge of geometry 94–5
union of university-based Greek and artisan-based commercial mathematics 79, 94
use of watermarks to date treatises' composition 89

GENERAL INDEX

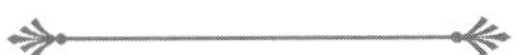

abaco (commercial arithmetic)
  arithmetic proofs establish by quantities expressed in numerical form 171
  emphasis on Arabic numbers 170
  emphasis on the practical 82
  lack of masters of *abaco* in Sansepolcro 6, 79
  no instruction in accounting 194
  proofs established with diagrams, 170
  schools of 6
  treatises 79
abbey of San Giovanni Evangelista, *see* Badia of Sansepolcro
abbey of San Giovanni Evangelista in Marzano 12
Acciauoli, Lodovico d'Adovardo 103–5
Afra River 207
Agnilo di Jacopo del Gaio 197, 210
Agnola, wife of Niccolò di Zengho 83
Agnolo Gaddi 54, 58, 225 n. 25
Agostino di Duccio 33, 40
agrimensores 10
Alberti, Leon Battista 24, 84
  drawing of Rome in his *Delineation of the City of Rome (Descriptio urbis Romae)* 85
  instruction on perspective 19–20
  participation in construction of the Tempio in Rimini 33
  possible influence on Piero 19–20, 144–5, 170, 216
  preference for sculptures rather than frescoes in churches 43
  presentation of his treatise *Ten Books on Architecture* to Pope Nicholas V 83
  treatise *On Painting* 19–20, 170, 216, 235 n. 11
Alessandro Sforza 146
Amadei, Giuliano 73
Anastagi, family, *see also* Anastagi, Jacopo di Jacopo:
  Amata, wife of Jacopo di Jacopo 195–6, 208
  Anastasio d'Antonio 35, 140, 194, 237 n. 34
  Antonio di Lorenzo 30
  Carlo di Jacopo di Jacopo di Paolo 134, 139–41
  Giovanna, wife of Marco della Francesca, wedding and death 30, 35, 153, 194
  Violante, wife of Carlo di Jacopo and daughter of Niccolò de Montefeltro 140–1
Anastagi, Jacopo di Jacopo 29–31
  adviser to Malatesta Novello (Domenico) Malatesta in Cesena 30, 139
  as patron of and penitent in *Saint Jerome and a Penitent* 30, 35–8, 136
  birth 139
  capolista in council of people in Sansepolcro 139
  circumstances of his death 139–40
  depiction in *Legend of the True Cross* 56–7, 137
  depiction in the *Flagellation* 134, 137–41
  depiction in the Misericordia altarpiece 72, 137
  education 29–30
  imitation of Malatesta in funeral chapel, library, palace 36–8
  importance in life of Piero 29, 30, 215
  member of Piero's youthful cohort 6
  painted by Piero in five instances 30, 136–41
  Piero's entrée to Malatesta court 29
  recommendation of Piero to Sigismondo Malatesta 30
  related to Piero by marriage 29, 30
  secretary and adviser of Sigismondo Malatesta 30, 139

Ancona 2, 24–8
Angela di Niccolò d'Aduiti Zenghi 83
Angelico, fra (Guido da Firenze) 83
Angelo (Blessed) 132
Angelo d'Antonello 100, 154
Angelo di Giovanni di Simone 128, 130, 131, 132
Angelo di Niccolò Zenghi (fra) 132, 133
Anghiari, 10
animal glue (*colla*) 77
Antignola, family (Perugia) 123, 124, 156
Antonio di Domenico da Cortona 196, 209, 235 n. 3
Antonio di Giovanni d'Anghieri 19
  art-historical assessement 9
  commission to paint San Francesco altarpiece 7–8, 10, 128
  painting in communal palace 19, 107
  paintings 9
  paints flags and insignia for Eugenius IV 8–9
  Piero's employer 1, 8
  separation from Piero 9
Antonio di Giovannozzo 36
apprentices and apprenticeship 9
Archimedes:
  access to his manuscripts 81
  manuscripts of his *Opera* in the Quattrocento 188
  translation of his *Opera* into Latin in Rome 85, 88, 188, 236 n. 22
Archimedean (irregular) bodies 93–4, 203–4
Arezzo 2, 44–5, 114–19
  abaco instruction and schools 79, 81
  likely place of composition of Piero's *Trattato d'abaco* 89–90
  subjection to Florence 44
Aristotle 144
artisans:
  and Piero 1, 9
  literacy 1
  nature of their knowledge 1–2
  preparation of painters 7
artisans' culture 1–2, 144
  abaco and vernacular 79
  emphasis on objects and drawn diagrams as proofs 95, 170
  emphasis on oral instruction and viewing 1–2
  proofs established by quantities expressed in numerical form 171
  relationship to Latin culture 179–80
  use of the vernacular 6, 95, 215
a secco frescoes, *see* techniques in Piero della Francesca Index
Augustinians 4, 130

Bacci family (Arezzo) 45, 53
  Angelo di Girolamo 115
  Baccio (Bartolomeo), commission of high altar chapel 45
  proximity to Franciscans 45
  payment to Bicci di Lorenzo for high altar chapel 45
Badia (monastery of Saint John the Evangelista) of Sansepolcro:
  abbots 3–4, 12, 66, 153, 154, 155
  chapels 8
  ecclesiastical authority 3
  internal architecture 154
  Piero's bequests for 213
Baglioni family (Perugia) 14, 123
  Andronica, daughter of Pandolfo 123, 124
  Angela, daughter of Galeotto Nelli 124
  Blannola, daugher of Galeotto 124
  Braccio 123
  Ilaria, daughter of Braccio 123, 124
  Pantisilea wife of Pandolfo 123, 124, 147
  property and political refuge in Bastia 123–4, 156
  relations with the Della Francesca 123–4
banners, processional 114–17
Bartholomeo di Giovannino d'Angelo 67, 68, 128
Bartolo Lasciagire 211
Basini, Basinio 33, 37
Bastia 115, 124, 209
  agreement on construction in family villa 209
  Baglioni property there 123
  building in the family villa 156
  Piero's presence in family villa 117, 119, 156

Battista Sforza, *see* Montefeltro (de) family
Battisti, Eugenio 235 n. 3
Battle of Milvian Bridge 57–8
Battle of Piombino 33
Beck, James 224 n. 13
Bellini, Giovanni 112
Belosi, Luciano 13–14, 224 n. 12
Benedetto d'Antonio Cereo (del Cereo) 2
Benedetto Sinigardi 53–4
Bernardo d'Andrea dei Griffoni d'Arezzo 209
Bernard of Clairvaux, Saint 168–9
Bertelli, Carlo xxiii, 24, 26, 62
Bessarion (cardinal) 85, 141
Bicci di Lorenzo:
  as assitant to Domenico Veneziano 18
  in Cappella Maggiore, San Francesco, Arezzo 45, 46, 53, 54
Binoche, Juliette xx
bishop of Città di Castello 3
Blasio di Lazzaro di Orlandino d'Arezzo 208
Bolfoci, Pietro 182
Bonaventure, Saint 53, 54
Borgo and Borgo San Sepolcro, *see* Sansepolcro
braccio (*braccia*) xvii
Bramante 47, 50
Bramantino 47, 50
Bridgeman, Jane 138
Bridget of Sweden, Saint 206, 207
Brunelleschi, Filippo 18–20, 170, 216
bubonic plague 115, 117, 153, 156

calendar of Sansepolcro 52, 224 n. 13
calzolai 4
Camaldolese order 3; *see also* Badia of Sansepolcro
Capolona 115
captains (Florentine), *see* Sansepolcro, government
carbon-black layer 77, 128, 134; *see also* techniques in Piero della Francesca Index
Carda, della, *see* Ottaviano Ubaldini
Carsidoni family 30, 153–4, 210
  Contessina, wife of Lodovico di Iubeleo 154, 155
  Lodovico 154
  Panta di Cristoforo, wife of Marco della Francesca 153, 210
  Piersacchone di Lodovico 154, 155
cartoons xxii
Cattani family 30, 98
  Conte 214
  Malatesta, cardinal of Camerino 6, 71
  Marieta, wife of Conte 214
Casa di Piero 156, 206
Cereo family (or del Cera), *see* Francesco del Borgo
Cesena 2
chapels:
  Cappella Maggiore (San Francesco, Arezzo) 44–61
  Chapel of Cardinal D'Estouteville (Saint Michael and Saint Peter) 51–2
  Glorious Virgin of the Badia 153–6, 213
  of Relics (Tempio, Rimini) 40, 41
  Saint Jerome (San Francesco delle Scale, Ancona) 27
  Saint Lorenzo (Badia) 8
  Saint Michelangelo (Citerna) 8
  San Leonardo (Badia cloisters) 184–5, 212
Cherubino Alberti 184–5
Chosroes 216
churches:
  San Bernardino (Urbino) 165
  San Francesco (Arezzo) 44–63
  San Francesco (Sansepolcro) 53
  San Giovanni Battista (San Giovanni d'Afra) 11, 12
  Sant'Agostino (Sansepolcro) 105–6, 231 n. 8
  Santa Maria del Carmine in Morocco (Val di Pesa) 52
  Santa Maria della Neve (Sansepolcro) 76
Cicero 147, 148
cioppa 136, 137, 138, 139
Citerna 8
Città di Castello 84
  abaco instruction 79
  bishops 3, 66
Clagett, Marshall 204
Clark, Kenneth 111
clergy 4

colors of paints, see pigments
confraternities 4, 64–5, 114–17, 153
confraternity of Corpus Domini (Urbino) 135, 165
confraternity (Fraternita) of San Bartolomeo
  its books of the dead 214
  payments to Piero for the *Coronation of the Virgin* fresco 155
  Piero as prior 153, 195–6
  priors selected by lot in communal selection 195
  responsibilities for the weak and poor 4, 153
confraternity of Santa Caterina d'Alexandria 21
confraternity of the Glorious Virgin (Madonna della Badia) 153–6
  devotions near the twelfth-century *Madonna and Child sculpture* and high altar of Badia 153, 154
  dressing of the *Madonna and Child* 155
  group singing of lauds 153
  papal indulgence 154
  payments to Piero for their fresco *Coronation of the Virgin* 153, 155–6
  sharing of their chapel with the Carsidoni family 153–4
confraternity of Santa Maria della Misericordia 21–2, 146; *see also* Paintings, *Misericordia* altarpiece in Piero della Francesca Index:
  agreement with Piero to paint a 'figure' 181–2
  burial of the dead 65, 66
  charitable acts 65, 66–7
  commission to Matteo di Giovanni for a banner 146, 182
  commission to Piero for altarpiece 64–78
  hospital 66–7
  iconography of Mary 65, 67
  papal indulgence 66, 67, 71
  participation in the sacred 65–7, 71
  participation of the Della Francesca family 66–7
  payments to Piero for altarpiece and 'figure' 74–6, 182
  processional banners 65, 71, 182
  site and layout of their church 65–6
confraternity of Santa Maria della Notte 7
confraternity of Santissima Trinità (Holy Trinity, Arezzo) 114–16
confraternity of the Annunziata (Arezzo) 46, 116–17, 119
Constantine 57–8
contracts 12
Corsetto Guelfo 146
Council of Lyon 54
cross 53–4
crusades 54

Dabell, Frank xxiii, 230, n. 16
D'Alessandro Paolo 189, 228 n. 16
Della Francesca, Antonio di Benedetto di Pietro 209
  as merchant 97, 98, 210
  as representative of Piero 76, 131, 146, 153, 155
  birth 5
  in a *fraternal* with brothers 213
  marriage of daughter into elite of Sansepolcro 210
  services to Baglioni 123, 124
Della Francesca, Benedetto di Pietro di Benedetto (father of Piero):
  active into his eighties 96–8
  as leather artisan and merchant 4–5
  as witness 12
  children 5
  marriage to Romana 5
  member of Misericordia confraternity 67
  persuasiveness of his values 181, 193–7
  political offices 10, 20–1
  reception of payments for Piero 8, 22, 74
  responsibility for Piero 8, 68, 69, 74, 75–6, 97
  sale of salt 10
  strained relationship with Piero 1, 6, 97–8, 216
  varied economic activities 4–5
Della Francesca, family 4, 211
  artisans and merchants of leather 1, 4
  assumption of family leadership by Piero 97, 162, 197, 210

division of a building with the Graziani 98–9
division of previously common property 213–14
home (*Casa di Piero*) 4, 156, 159
origin of family name 4
Marco as leader of family after the death of Benedetto 97, 99, 161
marriages into elite families of Sansepolcro 210
patriarchic nature of Della Francesca until death of Benedetto 97
Piero's last will as an expression of patriarchic values 213
successfull struggle into Sansepolcro's elite 153, 210
workshops 98–100, 229 n. 2
Della Francesco, Marco di Benedetto 153, 156, 209
acceptance of Piero's leadership of Della Francesca family 197
appearance before town judge for the family 115, 161–2
as leader of family after the death of Benedetto 97, 161–2
birth 5
daughter's marriage 210
death 210
in a *fraternal* with brothers 213
marriages into Anastagi and Carsidoni families 29, 30, 153, 194, 210
reception of payments for Piero 74, 75–6, 130, 131, 155
service as Piero's procurator 76
service to Federico da Montefeltro 146
services to the Baglioni 123, 124
socially, politically, and economically successful 97, 161, 210
spedaliere in confraternity of the Misericordia 66–7
Della Francesca, family members, *see also* Della Francesca, Antonio di Benedetto di Pietro; Della Francesca, Benedetto di Pietro di Benedetto; Della Francesca, Marco di Benedetto; Piero della Francesca Index:
Albera, daughter of Angela di Benedetto di Pietro 198–9
Angela di Benedetto di Pietro 5, 194, 196–7, 198–9, 209–10
Bartolomea, daughter of Angela di Benedetto di Pietro and wife of Francesco di Gasparre Rigi 209–10
Bartolomeo d'Antonio Benedetto 205
Cheopa, daughter of Veria di Benedetto di Pietro e Giovanni d'Onofrio Nardo and wife of Andrea Bartolomeo 152, 162, 196
Contessina di Marco di Benedetto and wife of Michele Zanzani 210
Francesca (Cecca), wife of Benedetto di Francesco and daughter of Lorenzo di Paolo di Giovanni (birth, fourteenth century) 67
Francesca, wife of Pietro di Benedetto di Francesco (fourteenth century) 4
Francesco di Benedetto di Pietro 5, 6
Francesco di Marco di Benedetto 197, 205, 206
Giovanna, wife of Marco di Benedetto, *see* Antonio di Lorenzo degli Anastagi
Giovanbattista, son of Andrea di Bartolomeo e Cheope, daughter of Veria di Benedetto di Pietro 162
Laudomia, wife of Francesco di Marco di Benedetto and daughter of Guasparre di ser Giovanni di Matteo di Paolo de Montevarchi 197, 205
Lodovico (Vicho) d'Antonio di Benedetto 209
Matia (Mathia) d'Antonio di Benedetto 213
Pietro di Benedetto di Francesco (fourteenth century) 4, 67
Piero, son of Andrea di Bartolomeo and Cheopa (daugter of Vera di Benedetto di Pietro) 162
Romana, wife of Benedetto di Pietro di Benedetto, daughter of Renzo di Carlo da Monterchi:
marriage to Benedettto di Pietro di Benedetto 5
children 5, 101–2

Della Francesca, family members (*cont.*)
death 76, 87, 96
hypothesis of the relationship of her death to the *Madonna del Parto* 101–2
Sebastiano (Bastiano) di Marco di Benedetto 205, 206
Vera, daughter of Benedetto di Pietro and wife of Giovanni Onofrio Nardo 5, 115, 161–2, 196
Della Rovere, Giovanni 166, 168
De Marchi, Andrea 9
De'Medici, Giovanni 40, 43
Decembrio, Angelo 23–4, 145
Di Lorenzo, Andrea, 221 n. 8, 228 n. 28
divine proportion 94, 204, 218; *see also* mean and extreme ratio
Domenico d'Arezzo 115, 161
Domenico Veneziano 23
and Piero's early style 13, 14
Piero's employer 1, 17–18, 19, 20, 123
commission in Perugia 14, 123
Donatello 13, 14, 18, 19, 105, 217, 219
dowries 5, 30

Elements of Geometry, *see* Euclid
Elizabeth of Hungary, Saint 124–5
Eliot, T. S. xx
emancipation 97
Ennius 148, 150
Eratosthenes 204–5
Este family 20
Borso 23
Ercole I 24
Ginerva, daughter of Niccolò Este and wife of Sigismondo Malatesta 32
Leonello 23, 32
Niccolò 32
Euclid 57
discussion of five regular bodies 93, 203, 217
discussion of the extreme and mean ratio 94, 204, 217, 218
Elements of Geometry 10, 15, 85, 171, 202
emphasis on proportion xxii, 15
importance to Piero 174, 216, 218
known by university-educated 10, 82
medieval notion that Euclid wrote Books XIV and XV of the *Elements* 229, n. 49
Optics 15, 85, 171, 235 n. 13
Piero's possession and use of the *Elements* 81, 82, 87, 94, 171, 202, 218
theoretical-deductive method 81–2, 171, 217
translation of his *Elements* and *Optics* in Rome, 85–6
verbal proofs based on magnitudes, similarity, and proportionality 81
Eugenius IV 2–3, 8, 71, 83
extramission theory of sight 174
extreme and mean ratio 94, 203, 204, 218

Falcigiano, 9
family, Tuscan naming practices 5
feast days 53, 54, 67, 72
Fedeli, family 194
Leonardo di ser Mario 194, 212
Mario di ser Matteo 194
Niccolò di ser Bartolomeo 194, 209
Federico da Montefeltro, *see* Montefeltro (de), Federico
Fermignano 191
Ferrara 23–4
Ferretti family (Ancona) 24–8
Giovanni 25
Girolamo d'Antonio as patron of Piero's *Saint Jerome in the Desert* 27
Simona, daughter of Filitiano Vannutii and wife of conte Giovanni 24, 27
Fibonacci (Leonardo Pisano) 81, 92, 93, 94, 216
Field, J. V. xxiii
Piero's geometry 174
Piero's instructions for drawing complex shapes 177
Piero's language in treatises 95
Piero's perspective 15, 183
Piero's spatial organization 15, 169
Piero's workshop 225 n. 31
fidejussores 194
Filelfo, Francesco 141
Filetico, Martino 147
Filippo Lippi, fra 43, 219
flags 8

florin xvii
Florence, *see also* Sansepolcro, government; captains:
  authority and location of Florentine captains in Sansepolcro 3, 103
  chapel of Sant'Egidio in hospital of Santa Maria Nuova 17–18
  grant to Sansepolcro of standard bearer of justice and conservators' residency in communal palace 103
  humanism in 18–19
  innovations in painting 18–20
  invention of perspective 18–20
  political control of Sansepolcro 2–3
Fontani, Niccolò 152
Francesco del Borgo (Francesco di Benedetto d'Antonio Cereo) 90
  charges of peculation 84
  commissions of copies of manuscripts of Greek mathematics 83, 188
  cousin once removed of Piero 83
  destination of his manuscripts 171, 188–9
  enthusiast for classical visual culture 83–6
  his humanist script 84, 227 n. 11
  importance in life of Piero 215
  manuscripts of Archimedes' *Opera* 85–6, 188–9
  manuscripts of Euclid 85, 171
  member of papal curia 83–6
  member of Piero cohort 6
  papal construction master and architect 83, 84
  sharing of knowledge of Greek manuscripts with Piero 83–4, 94, 189
Francesco di Giorgio Martini 145, 165
Francesco di Niccolò 133
Francesco di Pietropaolo Lotto 146
Francesco Laurana 149
Franciscans 4, 8, 53
  commission to Antonio d'Anghiari for polyptych for their high altar (Sansepolcro) 128
  sale of wooden altar frame for *Sant'Agostino* altarpiece 128
  Second-Order Clarians 121
  Third-Order women of Sant'Antonio, Perugia 120–7
Franciscans in Arezzo 44–5
  close relationship to Cross and Holy Land 44–5, 53–4
  and Bacci family 45
  choice of iconographic in their high altar chapel 53–4
Francis, Saint 44–5, 121
Fraterna 213
Frommel, Christoph 83, 85
Fucci, Giovanni 100

Gabriele di Stefano 198
Gamba, Enrico 88
Gasparre di Renzo di Carlo da Monterchi 101
Genari, Paolo 208
geometrical illustrations 86
geometrical perspective
  eye's relationship to painted image 18, 170
  invention of Brunelleschi 18–20, 170
  succeeded in depicting space as subject to geometrical laws 20
gesso 77
Gherardi, Cristofano (il Doceno) 6, 236 n. 7
Gherardi family and the Williamstown *Madonna with Child and Four Angels* 184–5, 236 n. 7
Giglio di Bartolo di Cristofano di Cresci 106
Gilio da Siena 81
Ginzburg, Carlo 225 n. 16, 232 n. 26
Giovanna, wife of Simone di Giovanni 128, 130
Giovanni di Piamonte 52, 61
Giovanni Onofrio Nardo 115, 161
Giovanni Santi 134–5, 146
Giovanpietro di Pertruto di Vico, *see* Corsecto Guelfi
Girolamo dei Griffoni da Pagliarimo 153, 155
Giusto di Giovanni 153
Giusto di Giovannozzo 36
Golden Legend (*Legenda Aurea*) 54, 59
Golden Section, *see* divine proportion; mean and extreme ratio
Grafton, Anthony 227 n. 9

grammar school of Sansepolcro
  salary of teacher xvii
  process of teaching Latin 5–6
Graziani Crossing 6, 30, 98, 152, 153, 194
Graziani family 12, 30, 194
  Anton Maria 5
  Benedetto di Baldino 99
  division of a building with the Della Francesca 98–9
  Nicolucio di Nicoloso 12
Greek study:
  Florentine school of Greek 18
  manuscripts of Greek authors 18
Greek geometry, *see also* Euclid; Archimedes:
  acquisition of knowledge of Greek geometry by Piero in Rome 79, 81, 82
  avoided use of numbers and diagrams 170
  basis of verbal concepts and magnitudes, not numerical quantities xxii, 81
  difficulty of comprehending and using Greek geometry 81
  Piero's combination of Greek verbal constructions with arithmetical representation 79, 82, 202, 216
  proofs based on magnitudes and similarities 170, 202
  role of Francesco del Borgo 83–6
  theoretical deductive procedure 81
  verbal arguments 170, 202
Gregory XII 31
guado, *see* woad
Guarino da Verona 23–4, 145
Guasparre di ser Giovanni di Matteo da Montevarchi 197
Guston, Philip xx

Heraclius 59–60
historical method xxi–xxii, 220 n. 1
humanism:
  civic and republican emphasis in Florence 18–19, 144, 217
  Petrarchian 83, 177, 217
  mathematical 217
  script 29, 42, 84–5, 187, 222 n. 24
Huxley, Aldus xx, 109

iconography 53
Inghirami, Alessandro d'Antonello 209
intromission theory of sight 174
irregular bodies, *see* Archimedean bodies
Israëls, Machtelt 74, 154, 227 n. 24
Iotta, wife of Sigismondo Malatesta 33, 34, 36, 40, 140
intarsia 24

Jacobus de Voragine 54, 225 n. 25
Jacopo da San Cassiano 85, 86, 88, 188
Jews in Sansepolcro 3
Joseph, Saint 207–8
Julian the hospitaler, Saint 106–7
Justus of Ghent 135, 144, 149, 165

Kemp, Martin xxiii

Laclotte, Michel 39
Latin culture:
  emphasis on knowledge of Latin 1, 82
  eschewed use of diagrams 170
  importance of university 1
  instruction in 5–6
  Piero's placement in uniting artisan and Latin culture 169
  use of written Latin and Greek texts 18
  verbal arguments 170
Lavin, Marilyn Aronberg xxiii, 51, 55, 62, 167, 206, 207, 208
lay religious culture 4, 65
Legenda Aurea, see *Golden Legend*; Jacobus de Voragine
Lendinara, Cristoforo Canozzi da 24
Lendinara, Lorenzo Canozza da 24
Leonardo da Vinci xx, 1, 94
Leon Battista Alberti, *see* Alberti, Leon Battista
Lightbown, Ronald xxiii, 62, 126
linear perspective (*see* geometric perspective)
lira of Cortona xvii
Londei, Enrico 232 n. 26
Longhi, Roberto 9, 46–7, 62, 111, 177, 223 n. 21
Lorentino d'Andrea d'Arezzo 61

Loreto 23
Lorini, Giovanni 108
Luca di Bartolomeo Pacioli (fra) 179, 186, 187
  conceptions of regular bodies and divine proportion 94, 218
  Piero's emphasis on proportion 217
  relationship with Piero 236 n. 9
  suggests Piero's presence in Ferrara 23, 24
Luca Manaria 156
Luca Signorelli, *see* Signorelli, Luca
Luciano Laurana 144

Malatesta, Carlo 31
Malatesta, Galeotto Roberto 31
Malatesta, Malatesta Novella (Domenico) 31, 37, 141
Malatesta, Roberto di Sigismondo 140
Malatesta, Sallustio di Sigismondo 140
Malatesta, Sigismondo di Pandolfo 29–43; *see also* Isotta; Rocca Malatestiana; Tempio Malatestiano:
  antagonism of Alfonso, King of Naples 33
  attracted by French Gothic and Roman cultures 32, 33
  capricious character 32
  chapels 36
  commissions to memorialize his image 33, 38, 41
  conflict with Federico da Montefeltro 140, 143
  construction of the Tempio and Rocca 32, 33, 38
  court of 29–43
  decisions by committee and Sigismondo 40
  imitation of court of the Este 32
  invested with title of *cavaliere* by the Holy Roman Emperor Sigismund 32
  library of 37
  marriage to Ginerva Este 32
  military commander 31, 32, 33, 140
  papal representative in Rimini 31, 32
  relationship with Leon Battista Alberti 33
  victory at Battle of Piombino 33
Malatesta Temple, *see* Tempio Malatestiano
Malatesta, Violante, wife of Malatesta Novella 141
Manetti, Giannozzo 195
Mantegna, Andrea 160
Marches 2, 31, 143
marriage negotiations 30
Martelli, Bartolomeo 104
Martin V 2, 31, 83, 143
Mary Mother of Christ 155
Masaccio 13, 14, 18–19, 61
Matteo di Giovanni 11, 11 (Illus.2), 12, 69, 146, 182
Matteo di ser Paolo da Anghiari 186, 195, 205, 208
Matteo Pasti 33, 40
Maxentius 57–8
Meiss, Millard 168
Melchiore di Piero da Citerna 36
Michael Foresius 85
Michelangelo Buonarotti xx, 112, 219
Michele d'Antonio Zanzani 210
Michele di Niccolò Dini da Firenze 20, 23
Modena 20, 23
Montebelli, Vico 88
Montedoleo, counts of:
  Caterina 210
  Piernofro di conte Giovanni 140
Montefeltro (de) family, *see also* Montefeltro (de), Federico:
  Antonio di Niccolò 140
  Battista Sforza 146–7, 166
  Giovanna, daughter of Federico and wife of Giovanni della Rovere 166, 168
  Guidantonio d'Antonio 136, 143
  Guidobaldo di Federico 88, 147, 187, 199, 201
  Niccolò d'Antonio 140
  Oddantonio 136, 140, 143, 166
  Violante di Niccolò d'Antonio 140–1
Montefeltro [de], Federico, 88, 142–6, 163–7
  accomodation with family of Niccolo d'Antonio 141
  as military commander 142, 143
  conflict with Sigismondo Malatesta 140, 143
  court in Urbino 142, 144, 199, 233 n. 8
  death 199

Montefeltro (de) family (*cont.*)
hypothesized participation in death of Guidantonio 136, 140, 143
knighthoods 163, 166
legacy tied to church 165–6, 167
letter to Florentine captain of Sansepolcro 146
library and purchase of manuscripts 142, 145, 171, 191
married life with Battista Sforza 147
Piero's appreciation of his patronage 201
Piero's gift of a manuscript of *De prospectiva pingendi* 187
political control of central Italy 142, 143
presence in Brera altarpiece 163, 166
support of artists and literary figures 144
title of Duke from Sixtus IV 166
wide intellectual interests 144, 145
Monterchi 101–2
Myrophore 117

Napolitani, Pier Daniele xxiii, 81, 189
Nardo di Gherardo 182
Nardo di Pippo 158, 209
Nardo di Renzo da Monterchi 224 n. 5
naturalism 23–4
Nelli, Ottaviano da Gubbio, *see* Ottaviano Nelli
Neri Tondoli 211
Nicola di maestro Antonio da Ancona 26–7
Madonna and Child 27
Saint Jerome in the Desert as copy of Piero's like-named panel painting 26–7
Niccolò di maestro Guasparre di Giovanni 209
Niccolò di Segna da Siena 9–10, 109, 110
Niccolò Niccoli 84
Niccolò Tognosi 10
Nicholas, IV 121
Nicholas V 47, 50, 52, 83, 85, 87, 188

On Literary Polish, see Decembrio, Angelo
Ottaviano Nelli da Gubbio:
design for a altarpiece for the Misericordia confraternity 67
possible apprentice master of Piero 7
projects in Sansepolcro 7, 8–9
Ottaviano Ubaldini della Carda 141, 145, 199

Pacioli, Luca, *see* Luca Pacioli
Palamidessi Giovanbattista 194, 195
Palamidessi, Michelangelo d'Antonio:
as witness for Della Francesca 99
member of Piero's cohort 6
possible source of Piero's knowledge of optics 15
presence with Piero 100, 194
Pantocrator 110, 230 n. 29
Paolo Gerardi 81
Paolucci, Antonio 42
Pappus 204
parentado 30, 35
paper production 89, 191
Pecham, John 174
Pedro Berruguete 165
perspective (*see* geometric perspective)
Perugia 2, 14, 120–7
Petrarch, Francesco 143, 146, 149–50, 177
Piccinino family 14
Piccinino, Niccolò 143
Pichi family 30, 90, 99
and the Misericordia altarpiece 52, 67–8, 68–9, 74, 75, 227 n. 31
Angelo di Nardo 196
Emilio 210
Francesco d'Andrea 90, 99, 152, 191
Luca di Guido 68–8
Meo 208
Nardo d'Angelo 128, 130
Niccolò di Guido's chapel in the Badia 196, 235 n. 3
Paolo marriage with Romana d'Antonio della Francesca 197, 210
Urbano di Meo di Nerio 67
Piero da Montepulciano 81, 90
Piero Trail xx
Pietro di Giovanni d'Ambrogio 21
Pieve di Santa Maria 100, 109
Pinelli, Antonio 52
Pisanello (Antonio di Puccio Pisano) 32, 41, 145
Pius II 32, 50, 71, 78, 87, 143, 225, n. 16

Plato 94, 218
Platonic bodies, *see* regular bodies
Pliny the Younger 2
Poggio Bracciolini 84
Polcri, Franco 72
Polidoro d'Angelo d'Antonello 211
Politiae Literariae, see Decembrio, Angelo

Raphael Sanzio xx, 47, 50, 87, 124
regular (Platonic) bodies 92–3, 94, 202, 203, 218
renunciation by young women of right to inherit 209–10
Renzo di Carlo da Monterchi 101
Rigi family:
  Bartolomea, daughter of Francesco di Gasparre 209–10
  Francesco 195
  Francesco di Gasparre 194
  Gasparre di Francesco 194, 196–7, 198, 209
  Nicolosio d'Andrea, 197
River Jordan 14, 26
Roberti (dei), Angelo d'Anechino di Pierpaolo 195
Roberto Nanni 71
Rocca Malatestiana 32, 33, 37, 38, 39, 40, 41, 43
Roeck, Bernd 232 n. 26
Rolin, Nicolas 138
Romagna 2–3, 31
Rome 2, 47
Ronchey, Sylvia 225 n. 16, 232 n. 26
Rossellino, Bernardo 84
Rule of Saint Clare 123

Salmi, Mario 73
Sansepolcro xvii; *see also* churches; confraternities; Sansepolcro government:
  geographical location 2
  importance in the life of Piero 214
  market for upper Tiber valley 2
  merchants 2, 96
  monies in xvii
  Piero's representation in paintings 16
  population 1
  town doctor xvii, 10
  trade with Florence 96
Sansepolcro, government:
  Christ's sepulcher as symbol of the town 108
  conservators 3, 20–1, 100, 107, 108, 158, 193, 194, 209
  council of sixty 3, 108
  council of the people (*Consiglio del Popolo*) 3, 21
  council of the twelve good men 3
  Florentine captains 3, 103, 104, 108, 146, 162
  innovation of standard bearer of justice and conservators' residence in communal palace 103, 108–9, 158
  integration into Florence's state and economy 96, 103
  New Residence 108, 158
  political participation 3
Santi, Giovanni (*see* Giovanni Santi)
Saracini, Maurizio 169
Sassetta (Giovanni di Stefano) 10, 22, 53, 128
Scipio "Africanus" 32
Servite friars (Servants of Mary) 4
Sforza, Francesco 32
Sforza, Battista, *see* Montefeltro (de) family
Sienese painters in Sansepolcro 7, 9–10
Sigismondo Malatesta (*see* Malatesta, Sigismondo)
Sigismund 32, 40, 41, 222 n. 5
Sigismundus 33, 34, 40, 41–2, 141, 222 n. 5
Signorelli, Luca 23, 115
Simone di Domenico d'Arezzo 7
Simone di Giovanni di Simone 128, 130
Simone Martini 113
Sinigallia 167
Sixtus IV 166, 168
Spinello Aretino 115
Stanze, see Vatican Palace
Surveyors, see *agrimensores*

Tartaglia, Gaspare Broglio 31, 34
Tempio Malatestiano 32, 33, 34, 36–7, 38, 40, 41, 43
terra verde xxii, 14, 185

Tiber river 207
Tino da Camaino 10
Toscanelli, Paolo 19
triumphs 149–50

Uffizi diptych, *see* Paintings in Piero della Francesca Index
Uguiccioni, Alexandro di Alexandro 211
Umbria 2
university culture, *see* Latin culture
Urbino 142–51

Valley of Walnuts 14
Valturio, Roberto 33, 37
Vasari, Giorgio 59, 159, 180, 236 n. 7
  apprenticeship of Piero xx–xxi, 7
  comments on Piero in Urbino 134, 135
  comments on Piero's paintings in Arezzo 115, 117–18
  estimate of Piero's age 5
  Piero as builder 156
  Piero's blindness 214
  Piero's knowledge of mathematics 6, 205
  Piero's paintings in Rome 47, 50, 52, 87
  Piero's presence in Loreto and Ferrara 23–4
Vatican Palace and its *Stanze* 47, 50
vernacular culture, *see* culture, artisan
vernacular language 187
Vespasiano da Bisticci 144, 145
Virgil 150
Vitelli, Vitellozo 211
Vitruvius 177, 201
Vittorino da Feltre 143
Van Eyck, Jan 138, 145
Volterra 147
Volto Santo 109–10

watermarks:
  multiplication of number with expansion of paper making 89
  use in dating manuscripts of Piero 89, 187–8, 189, 191
Weyden, Rogier van der 38–9
witnessing in contracts 12, 98
woad (*guado*) 2, 5, 96, 98, 100, 128, 153, 182
Woods-Marsden, Joanna 39, 149

Zoppo, *see* Simone di Domenico d'Arezzo